STRATEGY AND HUMAN RESOURCES
A General Managerial Perspective

CHARLES R. GREER

Neeley School of Business
Texas Christian University

D1365293

PRENTICE HALL   Englewood Cliffs, New Jersey 07632

Library of Congress Cataloging-in-Publication Data
Greer, Charles R.
    Strategy and human resources: a general managerial perspective /
Charles R. Greer.
        p.   cm.
    Includes bibliographical references and index.
    ISBN 0-13-192238-6
    1. Personnel management.   2. Strategic planning.   I. Title.
HF5549.G6924   1995   (.A3-Z)
658.3--dc20   94-39402
                                                                    CIP

Project Manager/Interior Designer: *Lorraine Landolfi*
Acquisitions Editor: *Natalie Anderson*
Managing Editor: *Fran Russello*
Production Coordinator: *Vincent Scelta*
Cover Designer: *Bruce Kenselaar*
Design Director: *Pat Wosczyk*
Copy Editor: *Nancy Marcello*
Editorial Assistant: *Nancy Proyect*
Production Assistant: *Renée Pelletier*

 © 1995 by Prentice-Hall, Inc.
A Simon & Schuster Company
Englewood Cliffs, New Jersey 07632

All rights reserved. No part of this book may be
reproduced, in any form or by any means,
without permission in writing from the publisher.

Printed in the United States of America

10 9 8 7 6 5 4 3 2 1

ISBN 0-13-192238-6

Prentice-Hall International (UK) Limited, *London*
Prentice-Hall of Australia Pty. Limited, *Sydney*
Prentice-Hall Canada Inc., *Toronto*
Prentice-Hall Hispanoamericana, S.A., *Mexico*
Prentice-Hall of India Private Limited, *New Delhi*
Prentice-Hall of Japan, Inc., *Tokyo*
Simon & Schuster Asia Pte. Ltd., *Singapore*
Editora Prentice-Hall do Brasil, Ltda., *Rio de Janeiro*

For Liz, Stacy, John, and Ardith

CONTENTS

EVALUATING STRATEGIC CONTRIBUTIONS OF TRADITIONAL AREAS 234

EVALUATING STRATEGIC CONTRIBUTIONS IN EMERGING AREAS 245

MACRO-LEVEL EVALUATION OF HUMAN RESOURCE EFFECTIVENESS 248

ACKNOWLEDGMENTS

I would like to express my appreciation to several people who provided assistance to this project in many ways. First of all, I owe a special thank you to my editor, Natalie Anderson of Prentice Hall, and her predecessor, Suzy Spivy. I am indebted to Aparna Cascella and Kathy Livingston for their invaluable research and editorial assistance. Their many hours in the library are greatly appreciated. Special thanks to my colleagues in human resources at Texas Christian University, Stu Youngblood and Larry Peters. Special thanks also to Chuck Williams, Texas Christian University, for his advice on general managerial issues. I have also been fortunate to work with other talented colleagues at TCU. Thanks to Dean Kirk Downey and the Neeley School for research support. A note of gratitude is owed also to David Lei, Southern Methodist University, and Vance Fried, Oklahoma State University, for sharing their insights on strategic management. Special thanks also to Joseph A. Pichler, CEO of the Kroger Company, for his mentorship during my academic training.

Several reviewers provided very helpful comments. These reviewers were Scott Snell, Pennsylvania State University; Marcus Hart Sandver, Ohio State University; Karen L. Neuman, Georgetown University; Douglas M. McCabe, Georgetown University; Brian Becker, SUNY Buffalo; James W. Walker, the Walker Group; Wayne Rockmore, East Tennessee State University, and Kenneth M. Jennings, University of North Florida. Special thanks to Richard D. Arvey, University of Minnesota, for his initial stimulus for the book, helpful suggestions, and encouraging feedback on earlier chapters. Any remaining weaknesses or faults are, of course, attributable to the author.

In addition, the research assistance of Nancy Erickson, Samantha Pendleton, Jennifer Sonnier, and Mike Hobbs is also acknowledged. Lisa Belser of the Banque Nationale De Paris also identified some helpful literature on international human resource management. Thanks also for the clerical assistance of Barbara Snell. Special thanks to Stacy Greer for compiling the author and subject indexes, Bernadette Szajna for assistance with graphics, and Lorraine Landolfi, my production editor.

Charles R. Greer

Fort Worth, Texas

PREFACE

This book deals with the interaction between strategy and human resources, as approached from a general managerial perspective. This approach has been adopted for its relevancy to managers in general, as opposed to human resource specialists only. Major features of the book include an investment orientation toward human resources and comprehensive discussions of the environment of human resources, strategy formulation, human resource planning, strategy implementation, and human resource evaluation. Extensive examples of applications of strategic human resource management in specific companies are provided throughout the book.

This book has been designed as a supplemental text in graduate courses for MBA students, students in specialized graduate programs focusing on human resource management, and other graduate students focusing on administration. As such, it is expected to be used with reading assignments involving articles or other supplemental texts. The book may also be suitable as a supplemental text in advanced undergraduate human resource management courses dealing with the strategic aspects of human resource management. In keeping with the general managerial perspective, discussions are presented from a practical point of view. The cases at the end of each chapter are designed to stimulate thought and discussion on important strategic issues.

The conceptual framework for this book, which is presented in Figure P-1, is comprised of a mission statement and eight components corresponding to individual chapters that draw from the principles of human capital theory, strategic management, strategic planning, environmental analysis, human resource planning, implementation, reward systems, and principles of evaluation. It also incorporates some sequential activities of rational/comprehensive strategic planning. The framework begins with an assumption that the company has a *mission* of obtaining an appropriate rate of return for shareholders while complying with the interests of the company's other stakeholders including employees and governmental agencies. Assuming such a mission, the framework of this book begins with development of an *investment perspective* for guiding managerial strategic decisions regarding human resources. The investment perspective is consistent with mission statements of economically rational organizations, and it provides a rational, financially justifiable basis for analyzing the value of alternative human resource strategies, policies, and practices.

Understanding and utilizing an investment perspective is required before human resource executives and managers can have an influential strategic role in the management of any organization. As will be discussed in Chapter 1, senior managers are accustomed to evaluating returns on investments in various endeavors, and human resource activities are increasingly being subjected to accountability standards for the resources devoted to them. Just as financial outlays for physical equipment are evaluated from an investment perspective, expenditures on human resource activities, such as training and development, should also be evaluated in terms of return on investment. Additionally, the investment perspective provides a valuable general managerial framework for evaluating programs, policies, and personnel activities in terms of their impact on enhancing and preserving the organization's investment in its human resources.

The second and third components of the conceptual framework are the *general environment* and *legal environment* of human resource management, respectively. An informed awareness of environmental trends and developments is required before managers can intelligently examine the potential opportunities and threats to which strategies must be directed. Because the environment of human resource management and the broader economic environment have changed so dramatically in the 1990s, a great deal of attention has been devoted to these developments in Chapter 2. In addition to these massive changes, the legal environment of human resource management continues to evolve and expand. As will be discussed in Chapter 3, in some respects the legal environment itself has become a source of uncertainty. Although human resource strategists in the past may not have incorporated the legal environment into their conceptual frameworks, further expansion of the law into areas of employer and employee relationships has made it a critical component to factor into strategies. For example, whether an employer chooses to manufacture in the United States or locate production facilities offshore may be highly dependent on trends in the U.S. legal environment.

Strategy formulation is the fourth component in the framework. The formulation of strategies for dealing with opportunities and threats in the environment is guided by the investment perspective of the first component in

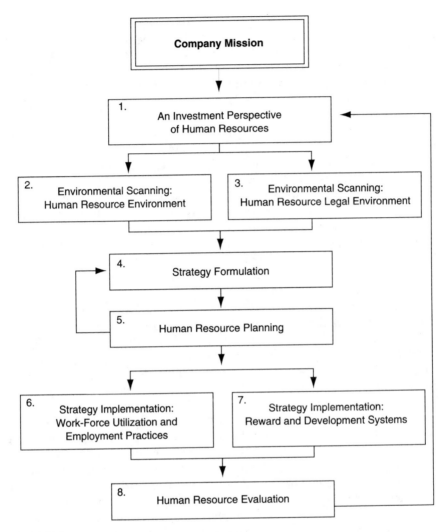

FIGURE P-1

the framework. Human resources and human resource management can play a major role in the organization's overall strategy, particularly where human resources are viewed as providing a major competitive advantage. As will be discussed in Chapter 4, some authors define *strategic human resource management* as the effective application of the organization's human resources to accomplish the organization's overall strategies. Such definitions have only an implementation perspective, while other authors see strategic human resource management as also being integrated with strategy formulation. The latter perspective will be employed in this book. *Human resource strategies* are narrower in focus than the domain of strategic human resource management. Human resource strategies define the manner in which the organization's practices, programs, policies, and activities will be aligned to obtain consistency with the organization's overall strategies. Such strategies play an implementation role and are valuable means of obtaining direction, consistency, and coherence in human resource efforts.

Human resource planning is the fifth component in the conceptual framework. Through such planning, which is discussed in Chapter 5, organizations prepare to match resources with the requirements needed for implementation of strategies. Human resource planning is positioned after strategy formulation although it could be expected to occur simultaneously with strategy or even precede strategy formulation where human resource planning identifies a competitive advantage that should play a dominant role in strategy formulation. However, in many organizations strategy formulation occurs first and then human resource planning is conducted either to determine the feasibility of the strategy or as a prelude to implementation of the strategy. The planning feedback loop to strategy formulation in Figure P-1 indicates the function's formulation roles of feasibility assessment and identification of competitive advantage.

The sixth and seventh components are involved with *strategy implementation*. These components are comprised of two sets of human resource strategy implementation activities. The first deals with efficient utilization of human resources, employee shortages, employee surpluses, and special challenges. Included in these general categories of implementation activities are cross-training, actions directed toward obtaining flexibility in work-force utilization, strategic recruiting, minority and female recruiting, flexible retirement, redeployment, early retirement, downsizing, layoffs, terminations, and special actions for dealing with dual-career couples and nepotism. These activities are discussed in Chapter 6. The second set, discussed in Chapter 7, is comprised of reward and development activities. Within the area of rewards, performance measurement and several strategically oriented compensation approaches are discussed, including skill-based pay, broad banding, variable compensation systems, executive compensation, and team-based pay. The discussion of development includes training programs, training methods, apprenticeships, and management development programs.

The eighth and final component is *human resource evaluation*. This component is comprised of general approaches to evaluation and specific applications to various human resource activities. As will be discussed in Chapter 8, in the past organizations did not place much emphasis on evaluation in human resources management. However, global competitiveness pressures have placed increased emphasis on the importance of justifying the use of resources. As a result, there should be much greater emphasis on evaluation in the human resources area in the future. As noted in Figure P-1, after evaluations are conducted, the results are fed back into the investment component in an iterative manner. The evaluation of human resource programs and activities then becomes an input in the next round of strategic decision making.

As the reader will note, numerous examples of human resource practices are provided throughout this book. These examples often involve companies that are exemplary in some aspect of strategic human resource management. Nonetheless, given the dynamic environment in which these companies currently operate, it is acknowledged that over time some of these companies may encounter difficulties. Hopefully, the reader will not discredit the principles for which the examples are offered because of difficulties in other aspects of a company's performance. In addition, in an attempt to provide a more comprehensive treatment of the issues addressed in this book, numerous endnotes were necessary to give credit to the many sources of the material. All endnotes cite the references employed and none are used for supplemental or explanatory purposes. Thus, the reader need not refer to the endnotes except in those cases where there is interest in the references.

1

AN INVESTMENT PERSPECTIVE OF HUMAN RESOURCES

As indicated in the preface, the conceptual framework for this book begins with an investment perspective for guiding managerial strategic decisions regarding human resources. Many human resource management practitioners and management scholars have long advocated that human resources should be viewed from an investment perspective. Nonetheless, current practices in some organizations indicate that employees are still viewed as variable costs of production while physical assets are treated as investments. When employees are viewed as variable costs, there is little recognition of the firm's contribution to their training or the costs of recruiting and training their replacements. Likewise, there is less incentive to provide training or make other investments in them. Lee Dyer has described the existing state of affairs as follows:

> I am constantly amazed at the contrast between the concern that strategists show for potential capital costs and the casual indifference they tend to display toward potential human resource costs (until, of course, the latter have gotten completely out of hand).[1]

A focus solely on investment in physical resources, as opposed to human resources, is short-sighted. Strategists have found that having superior production facilities or a superior product is usually not enough to sustain an advantage over competitors. Physical facilities can be duplicated, cloned, or reverse-engineered and no longer provide a sustainable advantage.[2] Strategists James Quinn, Thomas Doorley, and Penny Paquette have argued that "maintainable advantage usually derives from outstanding depth in selected human skills, logistics capabilities, knowledge bases, or other service strengths that competitors cannot reproduce. . . ."[3] Thus, their perspective recognizes the importance of having superior human resources. There is little doubt that organizations will need to invest heavily in their human resources in order to be competitive during the remainder of the 1990s and into the next century. Management scholar Edward Lawler has described these investment requirements as follows:

> To be competitive, organizations in many industries must have highly skilled, knowledgeable workers. They must also have a relatively stable labor force since employee turnover works directly against obtaining the kind of coordination and organizational learning that leads to fast response and high-quality products and services.[4]

According to Lawler, these investments will become increasingly important because of forecasted shifts in skill needs from manual to cerebral. As Charles Handy has stated, it has been forecasted that "70 percent of all jobs in Europe in the year 2000 would require cerebral skills rather than manual skills. In the USA, the figure is expected to be 80 percent. That would be a complete reversal of the world of work of some fifty years earlier."[5]

Contemporary management practices indicate that many leading companies have recognized the strategic importance of human resources and have adopted an investment perspective toward these resources. Further, there is greater awareness of the costs of treating employees as variable costs, which is beginning to change views of human resource practices.[6] There is also a growing recognition of the relationship between companies' overall strategies and their human resource practices. For example, companies pursuing strategies of innovation have the potential to be severely damaged by turnover because of reliance on individual expertise and unrecorded knowledge that has been quickly acquired. Accordingly, such companies tend to provide greater job security for some employees.[7] A final reason for beginning this book with an investment perspective is to reinforce the idea that for human resource management to play a meaningful role in the strategic management of organizations, it must be viewed as contributing to the bottom line. An investment perspective provides a valuable guide for adding value.

This chapter will begin with consideration of factors relevant to strategy-based human resource investment decisions. These factors include the organization's managerial values, risk and return trade-offs, the economic rationale for investment in training, the investment analysis approach of utility theory, and alternatives to human resource investments. Following the discussion of these factors, specific investments in strategy-related training and development will be considered. This will include investments in the future "employability" of employees, current practices in training investment, on-the-job training, management development, prevention of skill obsolescence, and reductions in career plateauing. In addition, there will be a discussion of alternative investments in human resources.

Investments in employment practices will also be discussed, beginning with the costs of layoffs, which became widespread in the late 1980s and 1990s. Then an examination of no-layoff policies, alternatives to layoffs, and employment guarantees will follow. There will also be a discussion of the relationship between work effort and job insecurity. Nontraditional investment approaches will also be examined. These include countercyclical hiring, investments in disabled employees, and investments in employee health.

HUMAN RESOURCE INVESTMENT CONSIDERATIONS

The first factor to be considered in the discussion of strategic human resource investment decisions will be the organization's management values.

Management Values

Fundamental values must be addressed in many human resource issues, particularly those involved in major strategic initiatives. When senior managers formulate and implement strategies, their values and philosophies are communicated to members of the organization through human resource policies and practices.[8] For example, senior managers who are committed to the preservation of the organization's human resources can manage the stress associated with major strategic events by dealing with rumors and providing accurate information, so that misinformation does not have such a debilitating impact on employees.[9] How employees are treated following significant strategic events, such as a merger or acquisition, is a reflection of these values and communicates whether the organization views employees from an investment perspective. Those adopting an investment perspective seek to enhance the value of their human capital or, at the very least, prevent its depreciation.

Risk and Return on Investment

Although there are a number of important benefits to investments in human resources, such investments contain an element of risk. Investing in human resources is inherently more risky than investing in physical capital because the employer does not own the resource. Employees are free to leave although contractual arrangements may limit their mobility. In order for investments in human resources to be attractive the returns must be great enough to overcome the risks. Further, for some investments, such as cash outlays to maintain no-layoff policies, the benefits are not easily quantified and there are meaningful costs. Decision makers have to be prepared to trade off current costs for long-term strategic benefits, such as a more flexible, committed work force and related positive aspects of the organizational culture to which such policies contribute.[10]

Economic Rationale for Investment in Training

Because human resource investments frequently involve training, it is instructive to consider the difference between specific and general training. Nobel Laureate economist Gary Becker has written extensively on this subject. His distinction between specific and general training in human capital theory provides guidance for understanding when employers will provide training. The decision whether to invest in training and development depends in part on whether the education imparts skills that are specific to the employing organization or are general and transferable to other employers. Employers generally invest in or pay part of the cost of *specific training* because employees cannot readily transfer such skills to other employers. After the completion of training, employers' investments are recouped by paying employees only part of the revenue derived from the workers' increased productivity (marginal product). Conversely, conventional *human capital theory* predicts that none of the cost of *general training* will be paid for by employers because employees can transfer skills developed at employers' expense to other employers. Accordingly, employers would rather hire an employee who has the requisite general skills. When employees having the requisite general skills cannot be hired, the employer must invest in general training without assurance that the unskilled employee will remain employed long enough after training for the employer to recoup the investment.[11]

In reality, employers probably invest in general training more than the basic specific and general training rationale would suggest. A recent study has found the following:

> ... under certain conditions [use of employment contracts and retention of employees based on productivity] the firm may share the costs of and returns on investment in general human capital and pursue no lay-off policy. General human capital will have the same implications as firm-specific capital.[12]

General training can also be obtained in on-the-job training as well as in formal programs. It can also occur unintentionally simply as a byproduct of the work situation as employees learn work skills that are applicable to other employers. Employers may make general training investments in employees by paying a wage during training which has been reduced by the training costs. The employer can still recoup investments in general training because employees incur costs of mobility, such as the costs of finding new jobs and relocating. If the costs of mobility are high enough (moving expenses, realtors' fees, psychological costs of moving children, etc.), the employer can pay a wage lower than the employee's new general skills would warrant at other places of employment. This investment can also be more attractive for the employer to the extent that lower wages are paid during the training period.[13]

Labor economists also argue that employers are more reluctant to lay off employees in which they have invested in specific training. (When employers pay part of the costs of general training, the firm will also be reluctant to lay off workers who have received this training.) Specific training can be obtained through formal programs. It can also be obtained through on-the-job experiences, as much of what employees learn on the job tends to be of a specific nature. Employees who receive specific training from an employer receive a lower wage after training than their productivity would warrant because no other employers have use for these specific skills.[14] Thus, it is likely that the employer will have invested more heavily in these employees and would not want to lose the investment.

To a certain extent the distinction between general and specific training is misleading. There are probably few skills that have no transferability to other employers. Likewise, probably few skills are completely general. Further, employers do not seem to make clear distinctions between general and specific training.[15] There are many considerations in layoff decisions in addition to the employer's investment such as equity, contractual obligations, and different business needs. Nonetheless, the concepts of specific and general training can provide insights into the conditions in which investments in human resources are more favorable.

Utility Theory

In considering investments in human resources in terms of hiring or development of current employees in order to pursue given strategies, there must be a method for evaluating the financial attractiveness of such investments. There must also be a method for "selling" the investment to senior management. These tasks may be accomplished by determining the returns for such investments through cost-benefit analytical approaches such as utility analysis. *Utility theory* attempts to determine the economic value of human resource programs, activities, and procedures. As such, utility theory might be used to determine the dollar value of a selection test that enables an employer to identify and hire managers for a specific job whose productivity is higher than those hired without the test. The calculations of utility might involve several variables. For example, validity of the selection test would be a critical variable, in that it provides an indication of the predictive ability of the test. Additionally, the increased productivity, its contribution to profitability, and the standard deviation of the contribution would be variables in the calculations. Finally, other variables might be included in the analysis, such as the cost of testing enough applicants to obtain a sufficient number having scores above the cutoff point.[16]

Another example of an application of utility theory is provided by Brian Becker and Mark Huselid's study in a national retailing company. Becker and Huselid's regression analysis approach explained return on sales for each store on the basis of the performance appraisals of the store supervisors. The model also controlled for differences in the supervisors' educational levels and their commitment to the company. Their study demonstrated that better estimates of the standard deviation of the performance appraisal variable could be obtained through a model based on the use of accounting data (return on sales) rather than the more commonly used subjective approaches. This study helps to enhance the legitimacy of utility theory for applications in real business environments.[17] An example of the application of utility analysis to a strategic selection problem is provided in Chapter 8.

Alternatives to Human Resource Investments

As indicated earlier, investments in human resources should support the organization's strategies. Unless there is the potential to build capabilities that provide an advantage over competition, cost considerations often lead to the rational decision to outsource through specialized service providers rather than invest in human resources. In general, *strategic outsourcing* is advocated where (1) world-class capabilities and a strategic advantage cannot be developed, (2) the resources devoted to services performed internally will be greater than those needed to outsource the service, and (3) excessive dependency on suppliers can be avoided. When an activity is performed internally at a higher cost, the misallocated resources will put the company at a disadvantage to its competitors.[18]

An interesting example of strategic outsourcing is provided by the approaches of Mastercard and Visa. Although the processing of transactions is a major activity in the credit-card business, Mastercard and Visa outsource this processing. Much of this processing is performed by American Express, which is very efficient in this activity. Instead of maintaining processing capabilities that do not provide a competitive advantage, Mastercard and Visa focus their efforts on areas of strength in retail networks, customer base, and marketing.[19]

INVESTMENTS IN TRAINING AND DEVELOPMENT

Specific investment approaches will be examined in this section, beginning with new approaches that result in enhanced employability of employees.

Investments in Employability

While the prevalence of employment security policies has dramatically declined, some companies are now investing in their human resources by providing developmental experiences, which make employees much more employable should the employment relationship end. These developmental investments might include the provision for growth opportunities, a learning environment, training, and retraining. Having a work force that is characterized by its employability is probably a necessary prerequisite for corporate survival. General Electric's experiences provide an example of the new employability approach. In the aftermath of General Electric's work-force reductions of 25 percent, there was a recognition by its CEO, Jack Welch, that the company would have to attract quality employees with desirable achievement opportunities instead of with job security policies.[20] Welch, widely regarded as one of the most visionary and effective CEOs, was strongly criticized for his actions as indicated in the following passage:

> Welch says that when he took over, the need for change was obvious, and he moved quickly. He was vilified as heartless in his zeal to reshape the corporation by eliminating jobs, earning himself the nickname "Neutron Jack." When Welch left a GE facility, the story went, the building was still standing but the people were gone.[21]

Interestingly, Welch has stated that strong managers like himself produce the only real job security in the current environment. His rationale is that such managers make the major structural changes necessary to increase their companies' competitiveness and ultimate survivability, often through the elimination of unneeded jobs. Conversely, he argues that weak managers who do not take such actions endanger the competitiveness of their companies, ultimately causing the loss of jobs.[22]

Because the types of experiences that result in future employability (e.g., valuable learning experiences and progressively more challenging assignments) are typically not the result of chance, but the product of intentional developmental programs, they involve resource allocations or monetary outlays and will be considered as investments in this discussion. Kanter's description of the employability concept is summarized in the following:

> If security no longer comes from being *employed*, then, it must come from being *employable*.
>   In a post-entrepreneurial era in which corporations need the flexibility to change and restructuring is a fact of life, the promise of very long-term employment security would be the wrong one to expect employers to make. But *employability security*—the knowledge that today's work will enhance the person's value in terms of future opportunities—that is a promise that can be made and kept. Employability security comes from the chance to accumulate human capital—skills and reputation—that can be invested in new opportunities as they arise.[23]

Current Practices in Training Investment

As indicated earlier, heavy investments in training will be necessary for future strategies and competitive advantage. Nonetheless, U.S. companies seem to lag behind the practices of companies in several other industrialized countries. For example, a study by the Congressional Office of Technology Assessment reported that "auto workers in Japan receive more than three times as much training each year as workers in American-owned assembly plants in the U.S."[24] U.S. workers not going on to college do not receive the training of their counterparts in other industrialized countries. In contrast, technical workers in other industrialized countries are often trained in well-developed *apprenticeship programs*. By the early 1980s, 59 percent of the German work force had been trained through apprenticeships. In Japan, new employees often receive months of training by their employers.[25]

Japanese companies are investing in human resources by training these workers.

There are some notable exceptions to the U.S. tendency to lag behind the Germans and the Japanese in employee training. One of the most progressive examples of investment in training technical and production workers is provided by Corning, Inc. Corning's experience demonstrates that a company can earn high returns by investing in human resources. In the mid-1980s, Corning faced a common dilemma of many U.S. companies in that its foreign competitors had acquired the same technology that had enabled Corning to be dominant in the past. Given its competitors' lower labor costs, it had to adopt a different approach unless it moved its production facilities overseas. Corning decided that to compete on a global basis it would need a world-class work force. It reopened a plant in Blacksburg, Virginia, in 1989 and staffed it with 150 production workers from a pool of 8,000 applicants. Although most of those hired had completed at least one year of college, Corning invested in extensive technical and interpersonal skills training. Training took up 25 percent of total working time during the plant's first year of operation. The plant's empowered workers take on duties previously performed by managers and use their broad range of skills in a team-based approach. An intensive emphasis on skills is maintained as workers must master three skill modules within two years in order to retain their jobs. In contrast to the narrow job definitions in many U.S. plants, the Corning plant has only four job classifications instead of the previous forty-seven. Because of the workers' broad skills, the plant can retool quickly. The result is that during the first eight months of operation, the plant made $2 million in profits in contrast to an expected $2.3 million start-up loss. Because of these successes, Corning is adopting the same approach in twenty-seven other factories.[26]

Other well-managed U.S. companies have invested heavily in training employees to work in teams. These companies include A. O. Smith, Boeing, Cummins, Ford, General Electric, IBM, Kodak, Motorola, Polaroid, Procter & Gamble, and Xerox.[27] Another example of a company that invests heavily in training is the Dana Corporation. Like Corning, the Dana Corporation has used training as a means of gaining an advantage vis-à-vis its competitors. In a recent year Dana invested $10 million in training 8,500 employees with the expressed purpose of enabling them to meet competitive needs.[28]

On-the-Job Training

On-the-job training is another way an employer may invest in human capital needed for strategic advantage. Such investments may be made by structuring a job so that employees learn while they work. For example, employees' skills may be increased by learning how to perform new tasks or operate new equipment. Employers may structure jobs so that these skills may be learned from other employees. They may also give employees time to learn new procedures or how to operate new equipment through self-instruction, such as by reading technical manuals. Employers may also permit lower productivity while workers lacking relevant skills learn them through interaction with skilled employees or through trial-and-error processes.

Gary Becker has noted that on-the-job training's impact on workers' productivity levels is frequently underrated.[29] Likewise, economist Lester Thurow argues that on-the-job training provides the bulk of skills used on the job while formal education serves a *signaling function* of communicating to employers the trainability of job applicants.[30] Economists calling attention to the importance of on-the-job training point out that a worker's productivity is determined by the capital intensity of the job; the type and extent of on-the-job training provided; the worker's ability to learn from the training, which is signaled by education; and how the jobs are structured, such as their promotion possibilities and responsibility level.[31] The contribution of on-the-job training to productivity has also been hypothesized to vary according to occupation as a result of differences in such factors as the rapidity of skill obsolescence and difficulty of job tasks. The contribution to worker productivity of on-the-job training has been verified in an empirical analysis of governmental investigative employees. In this analysis, on-the-job training was measured by the employees' years of job experience.[32]

Investments in Management Development

The continued development of managerial personnel is a critical strategic issue in most organizations and a particularly difficult challenge given the massive shifts in strategy. Before considering management development, it is useful to quickly review some evolving and forecasted trends in the managerial environment. It is clear that organizations are becoming less hierarchical and that many middle management positions have been eliminated. Larger numbers of workers are better educated and many are professionals. As a result, they expect to participate more in decision making. In the future more work is expected to be performed in task force or project teams, power will be shared, managerial status will be de-emphasized, and leadership responsibilities may be rotated.[33] Because of the participative aspect of these empowerment trends, many professionals and highly educated employees may have more exposure to managerial responsibilities and may develop related skills as a natural part of their work.

An important management development approach has been to rotate managers through successively more challenging assignments. Frequently these *job rotation programs* seek to provide a broad view of the organization and as a result may involve interdepartmental or *cross-functional assignments*. Use of job rotational programs is positively correlated with company size and is used most in transportation and communications and least in service industries.[34]

Advantages of job rotation include the development of generalists, avoidance of over-dependency on one supervisor, the challenge of new assignments, avoidance of dead-end career paths, cross-fertilization of ideas gained in other settings, increased interdepartmental cooperation as a result of the establishment of personal networking, and evaluation by different superiors in different settings. From a strategic perspective, a major advantage is that such programs develop a pool of managers exposed to an area of the business who can then provide management talent in the event of unexpected or sudden increase in the level of business in that area. Such rotational programs are also widely used for high potential or fast-track managerial personnel.[35]

Conversely, the disadvantages of such job rotational approaches include the institutionalization of short-term perspectives because of frequent changes in assignments as one is "rotated out," underdeveloped peer relationships, reduced loyalty to the organization if rotations are too frequent, expense when the rotation involves a geographic move, and personal impact on the employee and family.[36] Other disadvantages include productivity losses due to the learning time required after each new job assignment and the complications of rotations involving geographic transfers of dual-career families.

Aside from job rotational approaches, other methods of management development include sending high-level executives and less senior high-potential managers to executive development programs at prestigious universities. Shorter in-house training programs for less senior managerial personnel and more junior high-potential managers are quite common. Use of residential programs, such as those conducted at universities, has been found to be most likely in the financial industry and least likely in services.[37]

More systematic approaches toward in-house and off-site management development programs have been recommended by human resource practitioners and scholars. In some organizations such approaches are evident. From the author's personal observations of in-house programs for project managers in large banks and insurance companies, several companies are taking an investment perspective in systematic developmental approaches. Such programs involve high-level management in the analysis of the skills needed and in pilot tests of program content. They are conducted on a continuous basis, as opposed to one-shot training sessions. They also utilize customized cases and materials, involve participants in exercises in which skills are developed and practiced, provide exercises in which participants apply program content to real problems, and communicate either implicitly or explicitly that the managers are of critical importance to the organization.

Although these positive trends have been observed, a continuing problem exists. When organizations encounter economic downturns, management training programs are still an early casualty of budget cuts. Unfortunately, in many organizations management development is given a low priority and is viewed more as an avoidable cost rather than an investment. Where management development has to be "sold," it is important to build in several of the components just noted to include specification of the results expected and how they will be measured.[38] Given the expense of some programs such as executive MBA programs, it will be important to be able to determine the returns on the investment. Unfortunately, most cost-effectiveness studies of development programs have focused only on individuals and not on organizational impact or have used only subjective measures of organizational impact.[39]

Prevention of Skill Obsolescence

Technological change is often a cause of *skill obsolescence* in engineering, science, and the professions. Because of the rapidity of change, the knowledge half-lives in electrical engineering and computer science are five years and two and one-half years, respectively.[40] In addition, other professionals and managers run a risk of having their skills become obsolete because of changes in technology and methods. Technological change appears to affect individuals differently, as some grow and develop along with new technology while others fall behind.[41] Because technological obsolescence can limit an organization's strategic alternatives, obsolescence in this area can be devastating, and companies should have a strong incentive to invest in its prevention.

John Fossum, Richard Arvey, Carol Paradise, and Nancy Robbins have developed a model employing both expectancy theory and human capital theory to explain such differences in individuals' responses to changing technology. Given the critical strategic impact of technological change, such explanations should be of value to strategists. The model identifies motivation, along with individual, organizational, and external factors as determinants of whether individuals will develop the skills needed for new technology. Employees' expectations of their ability to acquire new skills and the perceived reward instrumentality of such skills help explain employees' motivation for skill acquisition. Such motivation is also related to the expected costs of investing in skill acquisition and the length of time for returns to be accrued. Nonetheless, the payback period can be misleading as several individual difference variables such as breadth of interests, education, aptitude, and personality also affect an individual's acquisition of new skills.[42]

A number of suggestions have been offered for the prevention of obsolescence. One suggestion is to provide challenge, particularly of a technical nature for technical specialists, in the early years of individuals' careers. Those who face such challenges are less likely to become obsolete in later career stages. Likewise, responsibility, authority, participation, and employee interaction also appear to be related to the prevention of obsolescence. Periodic reassignments requiring new learning also help to prevent obsolescence and facilitate development. It is important to guard against employees' becoming overspecialized. Although the organization may benefit in the short-term, excessive specialization may be exploitative and not be in the long-range best interests of either the individual or the organization. Organizations can explicitly encourage employees to stay abreast of developments in the field by incorporating knowledge acquisition activities and accomplishments in performance evaluation and reward systems. Organizations can also set goals for updating knowledge and reward such goal accomplishments. In addition to these suggestions, funding attendance at conferences and providing time to read professional literature and journals can help to prevent obsolescence.[43]

An example of one company's intensive efforts to prevent obsolescence is provided by Hewlett-Packard. The company's approach with its engineering work force has involved the establishment of cooperative programs with universities. In one year alone, 1,000 Hewlett-Packard employees were able to take courses at Stanford University while another 200 took courses at California State University, Chico.[44] Although Hewlett-Packard is involved at the leading edge of rapidly changing technology, it will be more important for other companies in lower-technology industries to make investments in their current employees. The magnitude of the future obsolescence problem becomes more apparent when it is considered that in the early 1980s over 2 million employees lost their jobs as a result of new technology.[45] As the rapid rate of technological change continues through the 1990s, the problem of obsolescence will need continued attention.

Reductions in Career Plateauing

Career plateaus occur when employees have occupied a job in an organization for some period of time, have mastered all aspects of the job, and have low prospects for promotion. Eliminating or reducing the incidence of plateaus is important because they have the potential to create resentment and a sense of futility, with a possible result of reduced productivity. Plateaus are a natural consequence of a lack of organizational growth or change. They also occur because of the pyramidal shape of organizations and organizational inflexibility. Other more employee-specific causes of plateaus are the personal choices of employees, the lack of career skills resulting from naive perceptions of organizational realities, and the lack of requisite skills for promotion.[46]

Employees may also lack appropriate skills because changes in the external environment and resultant shifts in strategies may not have been anticipated in a company's managerial development programs. In such instances the company may be forced to hire managerial talent from outside. Aside from the expense of external hiring there may be detrimental effects on morale. Further, those brought in may not have sufficient knowledge of the primary business to be effective.[47] A lesson to be derived from such situations is that investment in developmental programs is not sufficient for the avoidance of plateaus. Instead, alternative future strategic scenarios must be considered in the planning of developmental assignments in order to have promotable managers.

Another cause of plateaus is also related to developmental programs. Companies sometimes make inflexible decisions about which employees should continue in management development programs or those who should be placed on a fast track. Sometimes these decisions are based on performance during the early stages of an employee's career. Further, a decision may be made in the manner of a single elimination tournament in which one failure to be promoted or one unsuccessful performance may cause a manager to be taken out of the developmental program. Those left out of developmental programs or fast-track assignments are often relegated to dead-end career paths and become plateaued. In essence, the early identification of fast-trackers may become a self-fulfilling prophecy. Furthermore, perceptions of being plateaued tend to have the greatest detrimental impact on job satisfaction and company identification for employees who have less rather than more tenure on the job.[48]

Plateaus may also be avoided by more deliberate identification of *stars* (outstanding performers with high potential) and *solid citizens* (satisfactory or outstanding performers with less potential). More developmental assignments, challenges, and lateral moves for both categories can produce a pool of qualified managerial talent which should enable the organization to be more flexible and adaptive to strategic needs. Job rotation for plateaued employees can also reduce frustration and increase the chance for improved performance. The stress associated with career plateauing may also be reduced by managerial actions that provide recognition and appreciation in the absence of promotions, by job enrichment, and by mentoring assignments. Lateral transfers that provide growth opportunities may also be helpful in this regard.[49]

INVESTMENTS IN EMPLOYMENT PRACTICES

A number of specific employment practices also constitute human resource investments having strategic implications. Employment security policies were one such approach in the past as employers absorbed some costs when maintaining such policies. Prohibitions against layoffs and employment guarantees were adopted by several well-known, high-standards companies, beginning in the 1960s generally as a result of the personal values of the companies' top executives or a fortuitous strategic match with the company's rapid growth. By the mid-1990s it was clear that these policies were often untenable and layoffs became a daily feature of the business press. A description of the retreat from employment security practices is provided in Chapter 6.

Nonetheless, companies differ in the extent to which they have resorted to layoffs. Although some companies have a long history of avoiding layoffs in order to remain union free, there are other explanatory factors as well. Increasingly, companies find that they must operate in environments characterized by rapidly evolving technological change, compressed product life cycles, and heavy emphasis on quality. In many such environments, greater employment security helps provide the commitment, flexibility, and motivation required.[50]

Recognition of the Costs of Layoffs

Although there are many associated costs, layoffs are a fact of life in the United States and have been a recurring phenomenon linked with the business cycle. More recently widespread layoffs have also been caused by competitively driven structural changes in organizations. Nonetheless, the costs of layoffs are becoming better understood.[51] For example, a study of just under 100 surplus work-force situations revealed that it would have been more cost effective not to have laid off workers in 30 percent of the situations and to have laid off fewer workers in 20 percent.[52] Layoffs have been criticized on the grounds that they are sometimes inefficient, relative to other cost-reduction strategies. A major inefficiency or cost associated with layoffs is that a firm's layoff practices may make it less attractive as a potential employer. Consequently, the company may not compete well in the future for employees who are in short supply. As a result the employer may have to pay a premium to attract employees given their assessment of the risk of being laid off. A typical result of layoffs is that another 10 to 15 percent of an organization's work force will often quit after a layoff. The uncertainty of future employment often causes some of the better, more mobile employees to leave. Of course, these are the employees that the acquiring organization would like to keep. In addition to these costs, the expense of relocating employees and the losses of good employees to competitors may be collectively termed as transactions costs which have often not received sufficient attention from employers in the past.[53]

Further, the manner in which companies have determined which employees to lay off may have a detrimental impact. Because of their high salaries, professionals have frequently been victims of layoffs during downturns. An explanation may be that the technical professions are often prone to relatively rapid obsolescence.[54] A survey of midwestern manufacturing companies revealed that seniority was by far the most important criterion for layoffs. Seniority was identified as the major criterion in 95 percent of the unionized companies while a slightly smaller proportion of the nonunionized companies, 88 percent, chose seniority. These results may be interpreted as an indication that other factors were deemed less important than loyalty or fairness. Although the seniority considerations dominated such decisions, nonunion companies placed significantly more emphasis than unionized companies on performance considerations (75 percent and 55 percent, respectively). The breadth or transferability of employee skills was also a more important consideration in such decisions in smaller companies (fewer than 500 employees) versus larger companies (77 percent and 44 percent, respectively).[55]

The reliance on seniority indicates that companies are concerned about the fairness of layoff procedures since unfairness could have a detrimental impact on productivity and their competitiveness as well. Nonetheless, because the best employees are not necessarily the most senior, perceptions of unfairness may also arise with layoffs based on inverse seniority, to say nothing of the direct effects of retaining other than the best employees. Although most employers are concerned about the fairness of layoffs, there are examples of poorly administered layoffs. One involved a division of a major manufacturer that conducted layoffs because of decreasing demand for its product. While laying off employees, high-level executives were given bonuses if the company's stock surpassed a specified target level. Employees perceived that they were being laid off so that the executives would receive these bonuses. At one point employees became so opposed to the actions of the company that they drew up an elaborate chart of the company's daily stock price and derived a statistical equation which predicted a future decline of the stock. The chart was labeled "The [company] Limbo: How Low Can You Go???" There was a daily ritual at which declines in the stock price were greeted with enthusiasm.[56] Surely, when a company's layoff actions prompt employees to celebrate declines in its stock price because they think that its executives will not receive bonuses, productivity declines will result. Interestingly, in the time period following this incident the company's stock turned back up and soared to a remarkably high price, at which point the company sold the division.

Numerous other costs are also involved in layoffs, one major cost resulting from bumping practices. Because layoffs are typically conducted by inverse seniority, invariably where there is a union contract, employees with less seniority are "bumped" out of their jobs by more senior employees whose jobs have been targeted for elimination because of a lack of work. A chain reaction then occurs as more senior employees bump those less senior until, as in a game of musical chairs, the least senior is left without a job.[57] The width of the seniority unit that will govern bumping rights determines the impact of bumping. Narrower seniority units or definitions prevent a senior employee from displacing a junior employee in a job in which he or she is not qualified. With broader seniority units or definitions, senior employees can bump into new jobs for which they lack skills. As a result, training is needed for them to reach the proficiency levels of the junior employees who were bumped. Unions generally argue for broader seniority units on the basis of fairness while employers seek narrower definitions in order to minimize the dysfunctional aspects of bumping.[58]

A sense of the costs of bumping, in terms of productivity losses, may be gained by considering the situation of an employee bumping into a new semiskilled position. One study of bumping employees found them operating at 70 to 80 percent of normal productivity over thirteen-week learning curves. Associated costs also include rate reduction allowances sometimes paid to employees bumping into jobs that have lower pay and training costs for bumping employees who lack the skills to perform a job. In addition to bumping costs there are also termination, administrative, and intangible costs. Intangible costs sometimes involve declines in morale of the remaining work force and disruption of work group synergy.[59] These costs are presented in Table 1-1.

Avoiding Business Cycle–Based Layoffs

The advisability of laying off workers during economic downturns has been questioned by more companies and management scholars.[60] Although the *no-layoff policies* of such companies as Lincoln Electric are well-known, other examples from contemporary experience exist, such as Lockheed's loaning of engineers to Boeing. Employee loaning also occurred in Germany when a financially strapped shipbuilding company loaned sixty-eight skilled workers to Daimler-Benz for one year. Another example is provided by the Sony Corporation's refusal to lay off employees in its San Diego plant after a decline in sales. It paid off in increased employee commitment and increased performance in following years.[61] As Akio Morita, the chairman of Sony, has stated:

> American management treats workers as just a tool to make money. You know, when the economy is booming, they hire more workers, and [when] the recession comes, they lay off the workers. But, you know, recession is not caused by the workers.[62]

TABLE 1-1 COSTS OF LAYOFFS

COSTS RELATED TO "BUMPING" LESS SENIOR EMPLOYEES
- Reduced productivity during learning periods
- Costs of training employees assigned to other jobs
- Wage supplements for reassignments to jobs receiving lower compensation

COSTS RELATED TO THE TERMINATION OF EMPLOYEES
- Separation payments
- Higher rates for unemployment compensation
- Depletion of the firm's investments in training employees

ADMINISTRATIVE COSTS
- Human resource processing activities
- Clerical expenses
- Costs of conducting medical examinations of laid-off employees
- Increased supervisory obligations for managers of reassigned employees

INTANGIBLE COSTS
- Declines in morale of remaining employees
- Disruption of efficiencies in work processes
- Higher incidence of accidents
- Depletion of goodwill
- Irregular age distributions
- Voluntary turnover prompted by layoffs

Source: Adapted from Dan L. Ward, "Layoffs: What Does Flexibility Really Cost," in *Creating the Competitive Edge through Human Resource Applications,* eds. Richard J. Niehaus and Karl F. Price. New York: Plenum Press, 1988, pp. 169–191.

Another example comes from the Dutch company Vendex International. Its plans to lay off 18 percent of department store employees resulted in a replacement, instead, of the chief executive proposing the layoffs.[63] (In the United States Vendex has substantial interests in B. Dalton and Dillard's.)

Leading U.S. companies that have offered *employment guarantees* in the past have included Johnson Wax, Nucor Corporation, Worthington Industries, Hewlett-Packard, Hallmark, Federal Express, and Digital Equipment.[64] Hewlett-Packard has stated that a central concept in its culture and human resource philosophy is the sharing of responsibilities in economic upturns and downturns. In 1985 when orders at some of its manufacturing plants were lower than expected, employees were allowed to go on leave voluntarily without pay but with continued benefits and a guarantee of getting their jobs back after their return. After conditions deteriorated further, almost the entire non-sales work force was furloughed two days per month without pay. Senior management were not furloughed and continued to work full schedules but their pay was reduced by 10 percent. During the 1970s Hewlett-Packard also instituted a similar program whereby all employees shared in taking unpaid short furloughs, which allowed the company to avoid layoffs.[65]

Alternatives to Layoffs

In contrast to periods of permanent structural change, when a downturn is expected to be of relatively short duration alternatives to layoffs are often feasible. When companies avoid layoffs, they preserve their investments in employees' skills and are able to avoid the expense and delay of hiring and training new employees once recovery begins. When employees change employers, there is some loss of productivity because, if employed for more than a short time, they have acquired specific skills that do not apply to the new employer. Although layoffs are numerous, empirical evidence shows that firms attempt to avoid layoffs, thereby preserving their investments in human resources. A study of manufacturing firms found that they retain approximately 8 percent more labor during downturns than needed for production. Even after some excess labor is used in alternative assignments such as maintenance of equipment, painting, and training, approximately 4 percent is hoarded.[66] The assignments used for such excess labor are presented in Table 1-2 along with the proportion of companies making such assignments. As Table 1-2 indicates, these assignments involve various maintenance activities and training.

A number of alternatives have the potential to reduce layoffs in the short-term, although layoffs are better avoided through the use of long-term alternatives. Several basic short-term alternatives or tactics are presented in Table 1-3. Some deal with shutting off the inflow of personnel into the organization. When this is done, attrition can then help draw down excess employees. Unfortunately, during general downturns attrition usually does not have the desired impact because there must be high turnover for attrition to have an effect. When a downturn is sudden and severe and

TABLE 1-2   ASSIGNMENTS OF LABOR NOT NEEDED FOR REGULAR PRODUCTION DURING DOWNTURNS

ALTERNATIVE ASSIGNMENTS	PERCENT OF RESPONDING COMPANIES
No other work assigned	46
Maintenance of equipment	36
Overhaul of equipment	24
Painting	35
Cleaning	37
Reworking output	17
Training	18
Other	11

Source: Extracted from Jon A. Fay and James L. Medoff, "Labor and Output Over the Business Cycle: Some Direct Evidence," *American Economic Review*, 75, no. 4 (1985), 647. Reprinted with permission.

turnover is low, attrition may not work quickly enough to save labor costs.[67] Another set of these actions involves some form of redeployment of current employees or curtailment of subcontracts and reassignment of work from contractors to the company's own employees. A different set of actions involves sharing the economic loss through work sharing or incentives for early retirement. (The latter course of action can be quite expensive and is not always acknowledged.) Unsurprisingly, the survey of manufacturing companies noted earlier indicated that nonunion firms place greater importance than union firms on reductions in hours as an alternative to layoffs (69 percent and 37 percent, respectively).[68]

There are a few other short-term alternatives to layoffs, some of which involve pay cuts. Cuts may be accompanied in some instances by fewer days

TABLE 1-3   TECHNIQUES FOR AVOIDING LAYOFFS IN THE SHORT-RUN

ACTIONS TO BE TAKEN

Freeze hiring

Reduce wages

Centralize processing of exceptions to hiring freeze

Redeploy excess employees to jobs requiring little retraining

Retrieve work done by vendors, consultants, and contractors

Provide incentives for voluntary separation and early retirement

Shift work overloads from other sites to idle workers

Share available work with reduced hours (work sharing)

Encourage the exit of poor performers

Sources: Adapted from James F. Bolt, "Job Security: Its Time Has Come," *Harvard Business Review*, 61, no. 6 (1983), 115–123; Joseph T. McCune, Richard W. Beatty, and Raymond V. Montagno, "Downsizing: Practices in Manufacturing Firms," *Human Resource Management*, 27, no. 2 (1988), 145–161; and Thomas A. Kochan, John Paul MacDuffie, and Paul Osterman, "Employment Security at DEC: Sustaining Values Amid Environmental Change," *Human Resource Management*, 27, no. 2 (1988), 121–143.

worked or with commitments from management that it will make it up to employees when conditions improve. Unpaid leaves of absence are also alternatives. Those taking leaves are guaranteed the job at the end of the leave.[69]

Actions or tactics useful for avoiding layoffs in the long-term are presented in Table 1-4. One initial tactic is to conduct human resource planning with employment stability as a goal. As with the short-term tactics, several are related to the inflow of personnel into the organization. A lean staffing approach, staffing for the long-term, and focusing on nonspecialists where possible help to establish appropriate inflows. Greater flexibility in job assignment may be gained by providing employment guarantees in return for reductions in numbers of job classifications.[70] Another set of actions or tactics is related to maintenance of a productive work force through training or retraining, judicious termination of unproductive employees, and using human resource buffers to supplement understaffing.

The feasibility of *buffering* appears to be increasing. As will be discussed in Chapter 2, the range of jobs for which temporary or contract employees are used is expanding. For example, the services of accountants, computer technicians, engineers, and financial managers are increasingly being obtained on a temporary or contract basis.[71] Another example of *flexible employment arrangements* comes from the entertainment industry. The Walt Disney Company's Walt Disney World has three classifications of employees: (1) full-time in which employees work no fewer than four days and twenty hours per week, (2) casual regular in which weekly minimums of one day and maximums of less than four days apply except during peak periods when more days may be worked, and (3) casual temporary in which employees work during peak periods or as needed in non-peak periods.[72]

A tactic oriented more toward the long-term involves linking larger proportions of employee compensation to company performance, which has

TABLE 1-4   TECHNIQUES FOR AVOIDING LAYOFFS IN THE LONG-TERM

ACTIONS TO BE TAKEN

Direct human resource planning toward employment stability

Place emphasis on training and retraining

Maintain lean staffing even during periods of prosperity

Maintain stability with buffers (overtime, vendors, part-time workers)

Correct poor performance and terminate when warranted

Select new employees with the goal of long-term retention

Use probationary periods for new hires

Focus hiring toward nonspecialists where possible

Teach employees skills needed for next stage of product life cycle

Sources: Adapted from James F. Bolt, "Job Security: Its Time Has Come," *Harvard Business Review*, 61, no. 6 (1983), 115–123; and Joseph T. McCune, Richard W. Beatty, and Raymond V. Montagno, "Downsizing: Practices in Manufacturing Firms," *Human Resource Management*, 27, no. 2 (1988), 145–161.

the effect of reducing costs during downturns.[73] Of course employees would no longer be assured of an even income stream but the likelihood of being laid-off would decrease. As discussed in Chapter 7, such compensation appears more likely in the future. If profit sharing and variable pay become major parts of employees' compensation, there could be reduced layoffs.

Unfortunately, contemporary practice indicates that the most severe approaches for dealing with reductions in work forces appear to be the most common. Companies that have traditionally maintained no-layoff policies often have highly skilled employees in which the companies have training investments that need to be preserved. Some of these companies are also characterized by humanistic values. Beyond maintaining an investment perspective of human resources and humanistic values, the ability to effectively invoke less severe work-force reduction actions probably requires implementation routines and managerial experience with previous downturns.[74]

Employment Guarantees

Although the distinction between no-layoff policies and employment guarantees may be artificial, the latter, although a somewhat elastic concept, may take the concept a step further. *Employment guarantees* have been defined in the popular management literature as "oral agreements to move heaven and earth to avoid layoffs."[75] Employment guarantees are made feasible by many of the same actions as no-layoff policies. One of most important tactics is understaffing. Companies such as IBM, Motorola, and Control Data staff some of their operations with 70 to 85 percent of the number of permanent employees needed for production at normal demand levels. The difference in labor needed is usually made up with overtime, temporary employees, subcontracting, or employees contracted on a short-term basis. A second tactic is *flexibility in job assignment*, which is made possible by employees who can perform several tasks and the absence of restrictive work practices such as narrow task definitions. Such flexibility is also supported by retraining for those whose skills have become obsolete due to technological advances and redeployment of excess labor. An innovative tactic is to redeploy extra personnel into sales. A more common redeployment may be assignments to maintenance activities. A third tactic, *work sharing*, involves sharing the available work by reducing the number of hours for each employee. However, work sharing or job sharing may not be legal in some states.[76] (The topic of work-force flexibility is discussed in greater depth in Chapter 6.)

Numerous benefits to employment guarantees have been found, many of which should have a positive impact on strategy implementation. Most of these benefits are simply the obverse of how employees act when they are insecure about their jobs. Several benefits result when a work scarcity mentality is avoided. These include volunteering ideas for labor savings, working at an optimal pace, forgoing restrictive work practices, and performing tasks beyond the job description. Other benefits appear to be related to increased receptivity of employees to changes. These include accepting management-initiated changes, working overtime even when inconvenient, volunteering for job-broadening training, deployment flexibility, and increased loyalty. Additional benefits include increased retention, morale-related productivity gains, elimination of bumping costs, elimination of the need for early-retirement incentives, and reduced hiring and training costs during postrecessionary periods.[77]

The Work Effort and Job Security Relationship

Some companies have learned hard lessons that employees may not be willing to be sufficiently flexible in their work assignments when their employers have employment security policies.[78] Unfortunately, high-standards companies that provided such employment security in the past may have endangered their own adaptability and survival through these enlightened or progressive human resource practices. Not only have some employees failed to reciprocate by making personal adjustments needed for the welfare of the company, employees may become shielded from the realities of the marketplace and too complacent in today's era of intense competition. Interestingly, with an appropriate level of job insecurity, employees may work harder. A recent field study has found an inverted "U" shaped relationship between job insecurity and work effort. As presented in Figure 1-1, effort increases as insecurity escalates from low to moderate levels, but it declines with high levels of insecurity.[79] The implications for human resource investment policy are that there may be trade-offs between the benefits of employment security policies and the costs—to include the amount of effort that may be expected from employees. However, this relationship is obviously only an average tendency to which there are many exceptions.

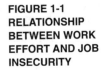

**FIGURE 1-1
RELATIONSHIP
BETWEEN WORK
EFFORT AND JOB
INSECURITY**

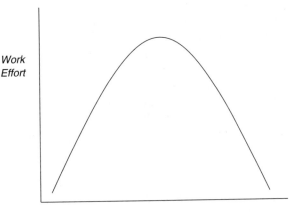

Work Effort

Job Insecurity

Source: Approximation of an inverted "U" relationship based on results reported in Joel Brockner, Steven Grover, Thomas F. Reed, and Rocki Lee Dewitt, "Layoffs, Job Insecurity, and Survivors' Work Effort: Evidence of an Inverted-U Relationship," *Academy of Management Journal,* 35, 2 (1992), 413–425.

NONTRADITIONAL INVESTMENT APPROACHES

Countercyclical Hiring

In addition to not laying off as many employees as technical production requirements might suggest, companies may pursue *countercyclical hiring* strategies of hiring a limited number of managers and professionals during economic downturns. In essence, companies would be stockpiling a limited number of high-quality key personnel for future use in pursuing strategies requiring certain personnel capabilities. As opposed to economic upturns when competitors are also attempting to obtain the same personnel, bargains in quality can be obtained during downturns. Several other benefits may result from countercyclical hiring. One benefit might be a more regular age distribution, which is lacking the spikes or troughs that occur with discontinuous hiring. As a result of dramatically increased health insurance costs, age distributions have become a concern to employers that have disproportion older work forces. Aside from the benefits of countercyclical hiring, there are obvious costs, such as hiring employees when they are not needed and equity issues with the current work force. There are also several implementation issues such as the ability to forecast future human resource demand accurately enough to pursue such a strategy.[80] Empirical studies of countercyclical hiring indicate that successful companies employ systematic approaches toward human resource management and are more likely to make investments in human capital by hiring during downturns.[81]

Investments in Disabled Employees

A nontraditional area of human resource investment involves providing support for programs that return disabled employees to the work force. Frequently, companies deal with employees who have become disabled by relying on the company's long-term disability insurance policy to provide economic support. Unfortunately, there is little emphasis on facilitating the employee's return to the job. In contrast, companies such as 3M, Burlington Northern, Control Data, and Eastman Kodak have developed programs that enable disabled workers to return to work.[82] According to 3M's rehabilitation program supervisor, "Returning an employee to work makes good economic sense. With today's electronic aids and devices, we can return almost any worker to most any job."[83]

Aside from the economic motivations for investing in disabled workers, the law provides additional incentives. As will be discussed in Chapter 3, the Americans with Disabilities Act of 1990 (ADA) requires employers to make reasonable accommodations for such workers. In addition to preserving the company's investment in the employee, there are obvious humanitarian benefits as well. Unfortunately, many companies are not aware of the support services that rehabilitation organizations provide or the devices that enable a disabled employee to perform the job again. Often relatively inexpensive devices or aids can allow a physically disabled employee to be a productive worker again. Such approaches include raising the height of desks in order to provide wheelchair access, providing curb ramps for wheelchairs, providing appropriate handrails, making simple changes in rest room facilities, lowering elevator controls, and removing structural barriers such as revolving doors. Simple changes in the job may also be made, such as allowing physically disabled workers to work shorter hours. Other inexpensive approaches include providing battery-powered scooters, computer attachments that enable the deaf to make telephone calls, and computerized speech-recognition aids. In order to facilitate the exchange of knowledge on how to accommodate disabled workers, companies such as AT&T, Du Pont, Hartford Insurance, IBM, and Sears are sharing with other companies the knowledge they have acquired in accommodating disabled workers.[84]

The return from investments in disabled workers can be quite attractive. One large Chicago bank changed the job of a transcriptionist so that only dictated work is typed. The employee, who is blind, types dictated work at up to ninety-six words per minute without errors.[85] The experiences of Pennsylvania Power and Light Company (PP&L) provide further endorsement of investing in disabled workers. PP&L found the quantity and quality of work performed by twelve part-time disabled workers to be equivalent to that of other employees in its cash receipts department. Further, to the extent that such programs can enable disabled workers to continue work, there may be some ability to limit insurance rates.[86]

Ironically, advances in medical technology may allow even more disabled people to join the work force. People who would not have survived a disease or injury in the past may now live but may be disabled. Further, with increasing life spans, there is greater likelihood that people will experience a disabling condition.[87] Disabled workers may become an even more attractive source of labor when there are labor shortages.

Investments in Employee Health

Another nontraditional investment approach involves improvement of employees' health. Such investments can increase employees' productivity. For example, in underdeveloped countries, increasing the quality of nutrition and providing basic medical care can increase the productivity of employees and would thus constitute investments in human resources. A company operating in Mexico as a "Maquiladora" recently found, after incidents of workers fainting on the job, that they were not getting enough to eat. As a result, the company now provides breakfast on the premises for all workers.[88] Interestingly, a similar case for investment in some special programs can be made in the United States and other developed countries.

Another such program has been directed at reduction or prohibition of smoking. The relationship between health problems and smoking is well-known. It has been estimated that 790,000 people died from health problems related to cigarette smoking between 1964 and 1987.[89] Further, absenteeism rates are approximately 50 percent higher for smokers and rates of early disability and mortality are approximately 300 percent higher. The combination of these and the secondary effects of smoking cost companies an extra $2,500 each year per smoker.[90] Because of these costs and the detrimental impact on productivity, some employers have adopted hard-line policies against smoking. Further, empirical evidence shows that policies prohibiting smoking on company premises have caused employees to quit smoking. Such a policy at the New England Telephone Company led to the following results: "Overall, 21 percent of the respondents who were smoking at the time they heard about the policy had quit smoking; 42 percent of quitters said they stopped smoking because of the policy."[91] This decline was statistically significant; however, the support program which accompanied the policy did not appear to produce differences in quitting behavior.[92] Nonetheless, another empirical study that employed an experimental design, with experimental and control groups drawn from two companies, found increased quitting behavior to be associated with training, financial incentives, and competition.[93]

There are several other examples of company actions in this area. Lockheed has made no smoking a condition for being hired in its Marietta, Georgia, plant.[94] Cardinal Industries, which has a similar requirement, pays for smoking cessation programs to help current employees who smoke. At Pullman Company PTC Aerospace, employees who smoke must pay an additional charge for health insurance that other employees do not have to pay. Litho Industries adopted a no-smoking policy for employees both on and off the job. Likewise, a number of fire and police departments have adopted comprehensive no-smoking policies. An Oklahoma City firefighter's 1984 discharge for smoking during off-duty time has been upheld by a federal appeals court.[95] The stressful nature of these emergency services and the prevalence of heart disease among firefighters probably explain the early adoptions of no-smoking policies in these organizations.

Less stringent policies have also been implemented. For example, to provide clean air and promote health, a Lockheed aircraft division in Fort Worth, Texas, prohibits current employees from smoking during working time. However, the company allows smoking during breaks in designated areas. Interestingly, the union representing the employees, the International Association of Machinists and Aerospace Workers, opposed the smoking ban.[96] The number of companies enforcing no-smoking policies has increased substantially according to surveys by the Bureau of National Affairs and the Administrative Management Society.[97] As resistance to no-smoking policies indicates, part of the investment component may be the expense of defending the policies in arbitration procedures or in court. Further, during the initial year after employees stop smoking, their levels of absenteeism and job tension increase while their job satisfaction declines. In addition, employers that give smokers breaks to leave the work area or the building may find that nonsmokers feel that they are treated unfairly unless they receive equal break time.[98]

Another investment in human resources is also related to health issues. Large numbers of companies have invested in fitness centers and physical conditioning programs. Many claim very positive returns for their investments. For example, Mutual Benefit Life Insurance found that after it provided a fitness center for its employees, the average number of workdays missed by the facility's users was 2.51 days and annual medical claims were $313. In contrast, nonusers averaged 4.25 missed work days and medical claims of $1,086. In addition to the fitness centers the company established an on-site health clinic. A return of two dollars for every dollar invested is claimed, without counting increased morale.[99] Claims of other fitness-related outcomes include better mental health, stress resistance, increased commitment, increased productivity, lower absenteeism, and lower turnover. Although the relationship between fitness and health benefits has been well established, other potential outcomes of fitness programs have not been adequately examined. More research is needed to determine the relationship between fitness programs and productivity, commitment, turnover, and absenteeism.[100]

Some organizations such as hospitals may need to make other nontraditional investments, such as in programs that reduce the incidence of employee burnout. These programs may involve support and close monitoring of the self-esteem of employees working in jobs having high potential for burnout. Because low self-esteem appears to be a cause of burnout, as well as a result, a downward spiral can occur without interventions to enhance burned-out employees' self-esteem.[101]

Finally, a more indirect health-related investment has been made by Sunbeam Oster Housewares, Inc. Sunbeam found that premature births were dramatically increasing its health-care costs. During a two-year period, six premature births cost its health-care program $1.2 million. As a result of finding that its employees were not well versed in prenatal care, Sunbeam established an on-site health clinic, required periodic checkups of pregnant employees, and made such employees attend an instructional program. The decline in health-care costs was dramatic. Average medical costs per birth declined from $27,000 in 1984 to $3,500 in 1989.[102] However, it is easy to visualize situations where such programs could be viewed as an undesired intrusion into the privacy of employees.

SUMMARY

This chapter has discussed the factors to be considered in making strategic human resource investment decisions and the specific investment approaches available to help accomplish the strategic objectives of organizations. Presentation of the investment considerations began with a discussion of managerial values, followed by an examination of the unique risk and return aspects of investments in human resources. Next, the economic rationale for investment in specific and general training was examined. Utility theory was also examined as a means for determining returns on investments in human resources. Alternatives to such investments in the form of strategic outsourcing were also discussed.

Specific human resource investments in training and development were then considered, beginning with investments in the future employability of employees. As noted, declines in the viability of employment guarantees and no-layoff policies have increased the importance of individual security through the notion of future employability. In order to have the world-class human resources needed to pursue strategic objectives, organizations must provide employees with skills and development they will need to be employable in the future. Training constitutes the bulk of investments in human resources. Nonetheless, the discussion of U.S. investments in training, relative to other leading industrial countries, indicated that the United States is lagging behind some of its competitors. On-the-job training was examined as an approach to investment in human resources. Management development programs were also examined from an investment perspective with specific attention to job rotational approaches. Other specific investment approaches such as the prevention of skill obsolescence and career plateauing were also discussed.

Investments in employment practices were also examined in relation to the accomplishment of strategic objectives. The costs of layoffs were discussed along with avoiding business cycle–based layoffs, alternatives to layoffs, and employment guarantees. There was also a discussion of the relationship between work effort and job insecurity. Additionally, nontraditional investment approaches were discussed, including countercyclical hiring, in which employers hire and stockpile high-quality candidates during economic downturns. Other nontraditional investments include programs that help disabled workers return to work and investments in employee health through programs such as those directed toward smoking cessation and employee fitness.

REFERENCES

1. Dyer, Lee, "Bringing Human Resources into the Strategy Formulation Process," *Human Resource Management*, 22, no. 3 (1983), 263.
2. Quinn, James B., Thomas L. Doorley, and Penny C. Paquette, "Beyond Products: Services-Based Strategy," *Harvard Business Review*, 90, no. 2 (1990), 58–67.
3. Ibid., p. 60.
4. Lawler, Edward E., III, *The Ultimate Advantage: Creating the High Involvement Organization*. San Francisco: Jossey-Bass, 1992, 21.
5. Handy, Charles, *The Age of Unreason*. Boston: Harvard Business School Press, 1989, 34.
6. Bolt, James F., "Job Security: Its Time Has Come," *Harvard Business Review*, 61, no. 6 (1983), 115–123; Peters, Tom, *Thriving on Chaos: Handbook for a Management Revolution*. New York: Harper & Row, 1987.
7. Jackson, Susan E., Randall S. Schuler, and J. Carlos Rivero, "Organizational Characteristics as Predictors of Personnel Practices," *Personnel Psychology*, 42, no. 4 (1989), 727–786.
8. Beer, Michael, Bert Spector, Paul R. Lawrence, D. Quinn Mills, and Richard Walton, *Managing Human Assets*. New York: Free Press, 1984.

9. Ivancevich, John M., David M. Schweiger, and Frank R. Power, "Strategies for Managing Human Resources During Mergers and Acquisitions," *Human Resource Planning,* 10, no. 1 (1987), 19–35.

10. Kochan, Thomas A., John Paul MacDuffie, and Paul Osterman, "Employment Security at DEC: Sustaining Values Amid Environmental Change," *Human Resource Management,* 27, no. 2 (1988), 121–143.

11. Chiang, Shin-Hwan, and Shih-Chen Chiang, "General Human Capital as a Shared Investment Under Asymmetric Information," *Canadian Journal of Economics,* 23, no. 1 (February 1990), 176–188; Becker, Gary, *Human Capital: A Theoretical and Empirical Analysis, with Special Reference to Education.* New York: National Bureau of Economic Research, 1964; Mitchell, Daniel J. B., *Human Resource Management: An Economic Approach.* Boston: PWS-Kent, 1989; Doeringer, Peter B., and Michael J. Piore, *Internal Labor Markets and Manpower Analysis.* Lexington, Mass.: Heath Lexington Books, 1971.

12. Chiang and Chiang, "General Human Capital as a Shared Investment Under Asymmetric Information," 176.

13. Chiang and Chiang, "General Human Capital as a Shared Investment Under Asymmetric Information."

14. Ibid.; Doeringer and Piore, *Internal Labor Markets and Manpower Analysis;* Mitchell, *Human Resource Management.*

15. Mitchell, *Human Resource Management.*

16. Boudreau, John W., "Utility Analysis," in *Human Resource Management: Evolving Roles and Responsibilities,* ed. Lee Dyer. Washington, D.C.: Bureau of National Affairs, 1988, 125–186; Cascio, Wayne F., *Costing Human Resources: The Financial Impact of Behavior in Organizations,* 3rd ed. Boston: PWS-Kent, 1991.

17. Becker, Brian E., and Mark A. Huselid. "Direct Estimates of SD, and the Implications for Utility Analysis," *Journal of Applied Psychology,* 77, no. 3 (1992), 227–233.

18. Quinn, Doorley, and Paquette, "Beyond Products."

19. Ibid.

20. Kanter, Rosabeth M., *When Giants Learn to Dance: Mastering the Challenge of Strategy, Management, and Careers in the 1990s.* New York: Simon & Schuster, 1989.

21. Swoboda, Frank, "Boundaryless Ambition at General Electric," *Washington Post—National Weekly Edition,* March 7–13, 1994, 21 (whole article on p. 21).

22. Ibid.

23. Kanter, *When Giants Learn to Dance,* pp. 321–322.

24. Hoerr, John, "Sharpening Minds for a Competitive Edge," *Business Week,* December 17, 1990, 78 (whole article on pp. 72–78).

25. Hoerr, "Sharpening Minds for a Competitive Edge."

26. Ibid.

27. Ibid.

28. Dana Corporation, *Annual Report,* 1987.

29. Becker, *Human Capital.*

30. Thurow, Lester C., *Education and Economic Equality,* 28, no. 3 (1972), 66–81.

31. Strober, Myra H., "Human Capital Theory: Implications for HR Managers," *Industrial Relations,* 29, no. 2 (1990), 214–239.

32. Maranto, Cheryl L., and Robert C. Rodgers, "Does Work Experience Increase Productivity? A Test of the On-the-Job Training Hypothesis," *Journal of Human Resources,* 19, no. 3 (1984), 341–357.

33. Schein, Edgar H., "Reassessing the 'Divine Rights' of Managers," *Sloan Management Review,* 30, no. 2 (1989), 63–68; Drucker, Peter F., "The Coming of the New Organization," *Harvard Business Review,* 66, no. 1 (1988), 45–53; Applegate, Lynda M., James I. Cash, Jr., and D. Quinn Mills, "Information Technology and Tomorrow's Manager," *Harvard Business Review,* 66, no. 6 (1988), 128–136; Semler, Ricardo, "Managing Without Managers," *Harvard Business Review,* 67, no. 5 (1989), 76–84; Schein, Edgar H., "International Human Resource Management: New Directions, Perpetual Issues, and Missing Themes," *Human Resource Management,* 25, no. 1 (1986), 169–176.

34. Saari, Lise M., Terry R. Johnson, Steven D. McLaughlin, and Denise M. Zimmerle, "A Survey of Management Training and Education Practices in U.S. Companies," *Personnel Psychology,* 41, no. 4 (1988), 731–743.

35. Greenlaw, Paul S., and John P. Kohl, *Personnel Management: Managing Human Resources.* New York: Harper & Row, 1986; Derr, C. Brooklyn, Candace Jones, and Edmund L. Toomey, "Managing High-Potential Employees: Current Practices in Thirty-three U.S. Corporations," *Human Resource Management,* 27, no. 3 (1988), 273–290.

36. Greenlaw and Kohl, *Personnel Management.*

37. Derr, Jones, and Toomey, "Managing High-Potential Employees"; Saari, Johnson, McLaughlin, and Zimmerle, "A Survey of Management Training and Education Practices in U.S. Companies."

38. Lawrie, John, "Selling Management Development to Managers," *Training and Development Journal*, 43, no. 2 (1989), 54–57.

39. Saari, Johnson, McLaughlin, and Zimmerle, "A Survey of Management Training and Education Practices in U.S. Companies"; Keys, Bernard, and Joseph Wolfe, "Management Education and Development: Current Issues and Emerging Trends," *Journal of Management*, 14, no. 2 (1988), 205–229.

40. Hewlett-Packard Corporation, *Hewlett-Packard Annual Report*, 1985.

41. Greenhaus, Jeffery H., *Career Management*. Chicago: Dryden Press, 1987; Wexley, Kenneth N., and Gary P. Latham, *Developing and Training Human Resources in Organizations*. Glenview, Ill.: Scott, Foresman, 1981.

42. Fossum, John A., Richard D. Arvey, Carol A. Paradise, and Nancy E. Robbins, "Modeling the Skills Obsolescence Process: A Psychological/Economic Integration," *Academy of Management Review*, 11, no. 2 (1986), 362–374.

43. Greenhaus, *Career Management*, Wexley and Latham, *Developing and Training Human Resources in Organizations*.

44. Hewlett-Packard Corporation, *Hewlett-Packard Annual Report*.

45. Ward, Dan L., "Layoffs: What Does Flexibility Really Cost?" in *Creating the Competitive Edge through Human Resource Applications*, eds. Richard J. Niehaus and Karl F. Price. New York: Plenum Press, 1988, 169–178.

46. Bowles, Valerie B., and Arthur R. Riles, Jr., "Work Place Challenges for Managers in the Twenty-First Century," in *Creating the Competitive Edge through Human Resource Applications*, eds. Niehaus and Price, 35–46; Gaertner, Karen N., "Managerial Careers and Organization-Wide Transformations," in *Creating the Competitive Edge through Human Resource Applications*, eds. Niehaus and Price, 85–95; Ference, Thomas P., James F. Stoner, and E. Kirby Warren, "Managing the Career Plateau," *Academy of Management Review*, 2, no. 4 (1977), 602–612.

47. Gaertner, "Managerial Careers and Organization-Wide Transformations."

48. Ibid., Choa, Georgia T., "Exploration of the Conceptualization and Measurement of Career Plateau: A Comparative Analysis," *Journal of Management*, 16, no. 1 (1990), 181–193.

49. Gaertner, "Managerial Careers and Organization-Wide Transformations"; Ference, Stoner, and Warren, "Managing the Career Plateau"; Elsass, Priscilla M., and David A. Ralston, "Individual Responses to the Stress of Career Plateauing," *Journal of Management*, 15, no. 1 (1989), 35–47.

50. Kochan, MacDuffie, and Osterman, "Employment Security at DEC."

51. Bolt, "Job Security: Its Time Has Come"; Peters, *Thriving on Chaos*.

52. Ward, "Layoffs: What Does Flexibility Really Cost?"

53. Greller, Martin M., and David M. Nee, *From Baby Boom to Baby Bust*. Reading, Mass.: Addison-Wesley, 1989; Perry, Lee T., "Least-Cost Alternatives to Layoffs in Declining Industries," *Organizational Dynamics*, 14, no. 4 (1986), 48–61; Beer, Michael, Bert Spector, Paul R. Lawrence, D. Quinn Mills, and Richard Walton, *Managing Human Assets*. New York: Free Press, 1984; McCune, Joseph T., Richard W. Beatty, and Raymond V. Montagno, "Downsizing: Practices in Manufacturing Firms," *Human Resource Management*, 27, no. 2 (1988), 145–161; Dyer, "Bringing Human Resources into the Strategy Formulation Process."

54. Raelin, Joseph A., "Job Security for Professionals," *Personnel*, 64, no. 7 (1987), 40–47; Hoffman, Eileen B., *Unionization of Professional Societies*. New York: Conference Board, 1976; Kaufman, H. G., *Career Development*. New York: AMACOM, 1974.

55. McCune, Beatty, and Montagno, "Downsizing: Practices in Manufacturing Firms."

56. Personal conversation between the author and an employee of the company, fall 1991.

57. Ward, "Layoffs: What Does Flexibility Really Cost?"

58. Rees, Albert, *The Economics of Trade Unions*, 3rd ed. Chicago: University of Chicago Press, 1989.

59. Ward, "Layoffs: What Does Flexibility Really Cost?" McCune, Beatty, and Montagno, "Downsizing: Practices in Manufacturing Firms."

60. Bolt, "Job Security: Its Time Has Come."

61. Mills, D. Quinn, *The New Competitors*. New York: John Wiley, 1985; Bolt, "Job Security: Its Time Has Come."

62. Hoerr, John, and Wendy Zellner, "A Japanese Import That's Not Selling," *Business Week*, February 26, 1990, 86 (whole article on pp. 86–87).

63. Wandycz, Katarzyna, "Dreesmann Family: Boardroom Fight," *Forbes*, July 24, 1989, 152.

64. Peters, *Thriving on Chaos*.

65. Hewlett-Packard Corporation, *Hewlett-Packard Annual Report.*
66. Fay, Jon A., and James L. Medoff, "Labor and Output Over the Business Cycle: Some Direct Evidence," *American Economic Review,* 75, no. 4 (1985), 638–655.
67. Bolt, "Job Security: Its Time Has Come"; Peters, *Thriving on Chaos;* Greenhalgh, Leonard, Anne T. Lawrence, and Robert I. Sutton, "Determinants of Work Force Reduction Strategies in Declining Organizations," *Academy of Management Review,* 13, no. 2 (1988), 241–254.
68. McCune, Beatty, and Montagno, "Downsizing: Practices in Manufacturing Firms."
69. Perry, "Least-Cost Alternatives to Layoffs in Declining Industries"; Bolt, "Job Security: Its Time Has Come."
70. Bolt, "Job Security: Its Time Has Come"; Peters, *Thriving on Chaos.*
71. Davidson, Margaret, "Temporary Financial Executives: Who Are They and Who Uses Them?" *Financial Executive,* 6, no. 2 (1990), 15–18; Mangum, Garth, Donald Mayall, and Kristin Nelson, "The Temporary Help Industry: A Response to the Dual Internal Labor Markets," *Industrial and Labor Relations Review,* 28, no. 4 (1985), 599–611.
72. *Welcome to Walt Disney World: A Cast Member's Handbook,* 1988.
73. Perry, "Least-Cost Alternatives to Layoffs in Declining Industries."
74. Greenhalgh, Lawrence, and Sutton, "Determinants of Work Force Reduction Strategies in Declining Organizations."
75. Peters, *Thriving on Chaos,* p. 417.
76. Peters, *Thriving on Chaos.*
77. Ibid.
78. Kochan, MacDuffie, and Osterman, "Employment Security at DEC."
79. Brockner, Joel, Steven Grover, Thomas F. Reed, and Rocki Lee Dewitt, "Layoffs, Job Insecurity, and Survivors' Work Effort: Evidence of an Inverted-U Relationship," *Academy of Management Journal,* 35, no. 2 (1992), 413–425.
80. Bright, William E. "How One Company Manages Its Human Resources," *Harvard Business Review,* 54, no. 1 (1976), 81–93; Greer, Charles R., "Countercyclical Hiring as a Staffing Strategy for Managerial and Professional Personnel: Some Considerations and Issues," *Academy of Management Review,* 9, no. 2 (1984), 324–330; Greer, Charles R., and Yvonne Stedham, "Countercyclical Hiring as a Staffing Strategy for Managerial and Professional Personnel: An Empirical Investigation," *Journal of Management,* 15, no. 3 (1989), 425–440.
81. Greer, Charles R. and Timothy C. Ireland, "Organizational and Financial Correlates of a 'Contrarian' Human Resource Investment Strategy," *Academy of Management Journal,* 35, 5 (1992), 959–984.
82. Bowe, Frank, "Intercompany Action to Adapt Jobs for the Handicapped," *Harvard Business Review,* 63, no. 1 (1985), 166–168.
83. Ibid., 166.
84. Bowe, "Intercompany Action to Adapt Jobs for the Handicapped"; Pati, Gobal C., and John I. Adkins, Jr., "Federal Officials Are Stepping Up Their Efforts to Enforce Affirmative Action Requirements," *Harvard Business Review,* 58, no. 1 (1980), 14–22.
85. Pati and Adkins, "Federal Officials Are Stepping Up Their Efforts to Enforce Affirmative Action Requirements."
86. Pati, Gobal C., and Glen Morrison, "Enabling the Disabled," *Harvard Business Review,* 60, no. 4 (1982), 152–168.
87. Ibid.
88. Personal observations reported by Professor Stuart Youngblood, Texas Christian University, January 1993.
89. Spitzer, Kirk, "New GD Policy Prohibits Smoking at Work Stations," *Fort Worth Star-Telegram,* July 29, 1989, business section, 1, 3.
90. Cascio, Wayne F., *Costing Human Resources: The Financial Impact of Behavior in Organizations,* 2nd ed. Boston: PWS-Kent, 1987.
91. Sorensen, Gloria, Nancy Rigotti, Amy Rosen, John Pinney, and Ray Prible, "Effects of a Worksite Nonsmoking Policy: Evidence for Increased Cessation," *American Journal of Public Health,* 81, no. 2 (1991), 202 (whole article on pp. 202–204).
92. Sorensen, Rigotti, Rosen, Pinney, and Prible, "Effects of a Worksite Nonsmoking Policy."
93. Jason, Leonard A., Shyamalanita Jayaraj, Caryn C. Blitz, Mark H. Michaels, and Lori E. Klett, "Incentives and Competition In a Workplace Smoking Cessation Intervention," *American Journal of Public Health,* 80, no. 2 (1990), 205–206.
94. ABC Radio News Broadcast, April 24, 1994.
95. Geyelin, Milo, "The Job Is Yours—Unless You Smoke," *The Wall Street Journal,* April 21, 1989, B1.

96. Spitzer, "New GD Policy Prohibits Smoking at Work Stations."
97. Geyelin, "The Job Is Yours—Unless You Smoke."
98. Manning, Michael R., Joyce S. Osland, and Asbjorn Osland, "Work-Related Consequences of Smoking Cessation," *Academy of Management Journal*, 32, no. 3 (1989), 606–621; Nobile, Robert J., "Putting Out Fires with a No-Smoking Policy," *Personnel*, 67, no. 3 (1990), 6–10.
99. Farrell, Christopher, Joseph Weber, and Michael Schroeder, "Why We Should Invest in Human Capital," *Business Week*, December 17, 1990, 88–90.
100. Falkenberg, Loren E., "Employee Fitness Programs: Their Impact on the Employee and the Organization," *Academy of Management Review*, 12, no. 3 (1987), 511–522.
101. Rosse, Joseph G., R. Wayne Boss, Alan E. Johnson, and Deborah F. Crown, "Conceptualizing the Role of Self-Esteem in the Burnout Process," *Group and Organization Studies*, 16, no. 4 (1991), 428–451.
102. Farrell, Weber, and Schroeder, "Why We Should Invest in Human Capital."

Case 1

MERGERS AND ACQUISITIONS

During the 1980s there was a frenzy of merger and acquisition activity in the United States. In one example alone, General Electric's acquisition of RCA, there was a reduction in employment of 160,000 workers.[1] Typically, the decision criteria for such actions were based on considerations such as the strategic fit of the merged organizations, financial criteria, and operational criteria. Mergers and acquisitions were often conducted without much regard for the human resource issues that would be faced when the organizations were joined.[2] As a result, several undesirable effects on the organizations' human resources commonly occurred. Irrespective of these effects, mergers and acquisitions have continued in the 1990s but not at the same pace. Layoffs often accompany mergers or acquisitions, particularly if the two organizations are from the same industry. (Such situations are sometimes called horizontal mergers.[3]) Additionally, morale and loyalty of employees may decline. This effect has been described as follows:

> During the first half of this decade [the 1980s] alone, mergers and corporate cutbacks have precipitated a net reduction of approximately 500,000 managerial and professional jobs, convincing organizational members that companies will not return their loyalty. As a result, those who remain in an organization may feel betrayed by their leaders, and there is often a drastic change in their work patterns.[4]

In additions to layoffs related to redundancies, top managers of acquiring firms may terminate some competent employees because they do not fit in with the new culture of the merged organization or because their loyalty to the new management may be suspect. As a result, it is sometimes necessary to hire new employees following a merger.[5] The desire for a good fit with the cultural objectives of the new organization and loyalty are understandable. However, the depletion of the stock of human resources deserves serious consideration, just as with physical resources. Unfortunately, the way that mergers and acquisitions have been carried out has often conveyed a lack of concern for human resources. A sense of this disregard is revealed in the following observation.

> . . . post combination integration strategies vary from such "love and marriage" tactics in truly collaborative mergers to much more hostile "rape and pillage" strategies in raids and financial takeovers. Yet, as a cursory scan of virtually any newspaper or popular business magazine readily reveals, the simple fact is that the latter are much more common than the former.[6]

Questions

1. Interview someone whose company went through a merger or acquisition during the 1980s or 1990s. What were their experiences? How were human resource management issues handled?

2. Given the lessons learned from the merger and acquisition experiences in the past, how do you think human resource issues will be handled in future mergers and acquisitions?

3. If human resources are a major source of competitive advantage and the key determinant of an organization's ability to pursue a given strategy, the human resource issues of mergers and acquisitions should be handled very carefully. Discuss these issues and the relative priority they should receive.

4. Why were the human resource aspects of mergers and acquisitions handled as they were in the past?

5. Hewlett-Packard has stated its objective toward human resources as follows:

> Objective: To help HP people share in the company's success which they make possible; to provide job security based on their performance; to insure them a safe pleasant work environment; to recognize their individual achievements; and to help them gain a sense of satisfaction and accomplishment from their work.[7]

Why is Hewlett-Packard's approach toward human resources so different from those of other companies described in this case?

REFERENCES

1. McCune, Joseph A., Richard W. Beatty, and Raymond V. Montagno, "Downsizing: Practices in Manufacturing Firms," *Human Resource Management*, 27, no. 2 (1988), 145–161.

2. Buono, Anthony F., and James L. Bowditch, *The Human Side of Mergers and Acquisitions: Managing Collisions Between People, Cultures, and Organizations.* San Francisco: Jossey-Bass, 1989.

3. Greller, Martin M., and David M. Nee, *From Baby Boom to Baby Bust.* Reading, Mass.: Addison-Wesley, 1989.

4. Buono and Bowditch, *The Human Side of Mergers and Acquisitions,* 6–7.

5. Buono and Bowditch, *The Human Side of Mergers and Acquisitions.*

6. Ibid., p. 263.

7. Hewlett-Packard Corporation, *Hewlett-Packard Annual Report,* 1985, 16.

2

THE HUMAN RESOURCE ENVIRONMENT

As indicated in the conceptual framework, following the development of an investment perspective for making strategic decisions concerning human resources, managers need to scan the environment before formulating strategy. This chapter examines the numerous factors making up the environment of human resources as well as emerging trends. Because of its complexity and importance, the legal environment of human resources is covered separately in Chapter 3.

Unarguably, the human resource environment is currently more turbulent than in any other period since World War II. During the first half of the 1990s alone, many developments at home and abroad had massive impacts on human resources. Eastern European countries were freed from occupation by the Soviet Union, the Soviet Union broke up into independent but unstable nations, civil wars broke out, and in less than one year East and West Germany were reunited. Almost overnight, previously Communist Eastern European countries became markets for Western goods, suppliers of labor, and business competitors. Iraq invaded oil-rich Kuwait and quickly suffered a stunning defeat by allied forces, but the Allies' victory seemed illusory in an increasingly less certain world. In the economic sphere massive changes resulted from demilitarization, structural changes, and increased global trade. The European Community became a reality and the United States, Canada, and Mexico ratified the North American Free Trade Agreement (NAFTA). Almost inconceivably, icons of American business such as General Motors and IBM struggled to reorganize in order to make their products viable against global competitors and changing markets.[1]

Developments such as these affect business and human resources. It seems clear that the economic turbulence that characterized the 1980s will continue through the remainder of the 1990s. A dynamic political environment seems likely as well. During such times of rapid change, the difficult processes of formulating viable competitive strategies and planning for their implementation become even more difficult as well as more important. Only some of the developments that occurred in the first half of the 1990s could have been forecasted. Nonetheless, those organizations that scanned the environment, developed strategies, and planned alternatives for dealing with changing conditions probably fared better than those that did not.

This chapter will identify issues and trends relevant to strategy and human resources by following an environmental scanning framework. This framework is comprised of the following categories: technology and organizational structure, worker values and attitudinal trends, managerial trends, demographic trends, trends in the utilization of human resources, international developments, and other developments. These trends and developments will be discussed in the following sections.

TECHNOLOGY AND ORGANIZATIONAL STRUCTURE

Impact of Technology

Technology, particularly information technology, is having a major impact on the structure of organizations and on the nature of managerial work. Computerized information systems have eliminated the need for many middle management positions. Since much of middle management involves dissemination of information and coordination of activities, many of its functions can be performed by computers. With this removal of a level of the organizational hierarchy, a valuable training ground for top executives is being eliminated. Further, the context in which much work is currently being performed is expected to change. The era of the "smart machine" and the skilled professionals who operate such machines will probably produce conditions in which there is less need for supervision or else a very different type of supervision. Human resource strategists will need to consider changes in the nature of managerial work which will result from the accumulation of knowledge power in nonmanagerial, technical positions.[2]

Managers who can be effective in such environments will require new skills. Not only will the number of managerial positions change but also the nature of management will change in many settings as well because of other developments. Thus in information-based, lean, and flat organizations, alternative job assignments and opportunities will be needed for the development of tomorrow's high-level managers.[3]

Although the need for middle managers and low-skilled employees has been lessened by information technology, it is useful to reflect on these developments before concluding that the jobs of human beings are being eliminated. Sar Levitan has put the effects of these developments in perspective.

> There is nothing new about the prediction that labor will become less important as new technology replaces human labor with machines—this prediction has been heard repeatedly since the beginning of the industrial age. It can be asserted with some confidence, however, that this forecast is no more true today than it was a century ago. On the contrary, the overall employment-to-population ratio is now at a historical high. . . . Even if the 15,000 robots in operation today increased twentyfold in the next decade, their work will be confined primarily to repetitive and hazardous work now being done by humans and will replace only a tiny fraction of the estimated 131 million people in the labor force by 1997. For every "working" robot, there will still be more than 400 people in the labor force.[4]

Even if the total number of jobs is not reduced, an impact of increasing technology is that skill and managerial educational requirements tend to increase. Although managers in advanced technological environments cannot have detailed knowledge of all aspects of the technology their subordinates work with, they must have a conceptual understanding in order to provide effective support and direction.[5]

Another impact of technology is that manufacturing is moving toward much shorter developmental cycles. New product development approaches based on concurrent or parallel engineering avoid the delays of sequential developmental processes. In parallel processes, engineering, design, purchasing, marketing, software, hardware, field support, and manufacturing specialists work together, beginning with the earliest product development phases.[6] The availability of highly trained specialists who have the skills to work effectively in nontraditional environments cannot be taken for granted. Training programs and developmental assignments must be planned to assure the availability of such workers.

New Organizational Structures

Not only is the nature of work and management expected to change, but organizations will change as a result of advances in information technology as well. It is likely that the distinctions between management and labor will become blurred. Workers will become increasingly responsible to act on matters which they become aware of through computerized information systems. Further, there will be a shift from individual to joint accountability because all group members will have much of the same information for decisions. Because of the knowledge power of skilled workers who will operate the technology of the future, the structure of many of today's organizations will be poorly suited for the future. Regardless of the exact form of future organizations, they will probably be much less hierarchical. More work is also expected to be performed in task force teams and project-oriented work groups. Temporary organizations such as task forces will require different managerial skills. Likewise, there is evidence that organizations may be more flexible, porous, and adaptive. Their organizational structures may become less pyramidal and more like a set of concentric circles.[7]

Changes entailing more real participation, de-emphasis of managerial status, new forms of superior–subordinate relations, and rotating leadership roles will require different managerial skills than exist today. Power is envisioned to shift from one part of the organization to another as tasks demand.[8] Most companies cannot take for granted the emergence of managers with the skills to operate in such environments. As a result, their numbers and skill requirements will have to be anticipated and developmental experiences planned so that the organization will have an adequate number on hand when the need emerges.

There are other views on the structure of future organizations. Aside from the structural changes noted, one view is that there will be three basic structural forms, not counting hybrids: (1) *bureaucracy*, (2) *unbundled corporations*, and (3) *respondent corporations*. Because unbundled corporations are seen as having the ability to adapt to rapidly changing conditions, which should characterize the future, they may become the dominant organizational form and will be discussed in this section, along with respondent corporations, as trends for the future.[9] Because most readers are familiar with bureaucracies, such as large governmental agencies, which emphasize rule-oriented and standardized approaches to the performance of routine tasks in relatively stable environments, they will not be addressed in this section.

Essentially, *unbundled corporations* or organizations employ a portfolio or conglomerate approach toward their peripheral business units. As a result, units are retained or divested according to profitability and risk criteria. An example of an unbundled corporation is Johnson & Johnson, which had 166 autonomous units in 1992. Johnson & Johnson has had over 100 consecutive years of profitability and has achieved exceptional growth even during recent years.[10] An indication of its willingness to divest units is provided by the following: "Of twenty-one units identified as 'principle domestic operations' in J&J's 1982 annual report, a third have been sold or shut."[11] Other companies are pursuing similar strategies. Charles Snow, Raymond Miles, and Henry Coleman use the term *network organizations* to describe organizations that are very similar to unbundled corporations. They point out that one of the driving forces for the evolution or creation of such organizations is the need to outsource activities that other companies, consultants, or joint venture partners can perform better or more quickly. As with the Johnson & Johnson example, network organizations divest assets that fail to provide acceptable returns on investment.[12]

In network or unbundled organizations, many of the traditional support services of bureaucracies are performed by consultants and vendors. For example, some traditional human resource management functions such as training are performed by vendors, along with some compensation and payroll functions. An advantage results from the potential to redeploy resources rapidly to more profitable alternatives. Further, developing managers have more opportunities to exercise general managerial skills in running relatively autonomous business units that function as profit centers. For a small group of fortunate employees who form the core unit of the unbundled corporation, there is commitment from the corporation. These units, which may be quite small, are comprised of high-impact employees who coordinate the work of vendors, manage change, and manage the portfolio of business units.[13]

Of course, while the jobs of the core of permanent employees are protected, there is a low commitment to the employees of the peripheral units. Essentially, the employment security of the core employees comes at the expense of the peripheral's employees. Because of the social costs to the communities absorbing such employees, there may be potential for additional legislation in the future. An example of existing legislation of this nature is the Worker Adjustment and Retraining Notification Act (WARN), which requires 60 days' advance notice of plant closures and large-scale layoffs, except where conditions causing such closures or layoffs cannot be predicted. Additionally, other implications for human resource strategy are that some of the benefits of using temporary workers may be offset by the reduced control and inefficiencies of dealing with "employees" through a vendor–supplier relationship. Further, when scarce labor is involved, the wage savings of unbundling may be wiped out by the increased costs of components purchased from vendors who must employ such labor.[14]

The third basic structural form, the *respondent corporation*, is essentially an entrepreneurial corporation which exists by filling niches to supply customized services to unbundled corporations and bureaucracies. In such corporations, decision making is quick and likely retained at the level of the central entrepreneurial figure. Unfortunately, these corporations are risky and have high failure rates. The positive trade-offs, from the employee's perspective, are that although there is greater risk and less individual development from participative decision making, there should be opportunities to develop as a generalist and acquire new skills.[15]

Stimulus for Small Business

Some of employment accounted for by small businesses may be related to the formation of respondent corporations because employment in the largest U.S. corporations has declined. Between 1970 and 1986 the proportion of U.S. employment accounted for by *Fortune* 500 companies declined from 18.9 to 12.2 percent.[16] A recent study by Donald Hicks of job losses and creations in the Dallas metropolitan area found that virtually all job losses from a regional recession were offset by new jobs three years later. Interestingly, 61 percent of these new jobs came from new businesses while 25 percent came from existing small companies.[17] Some of the human resource knowledge base developed for large corporations may not be directly applicable to quickly responding, lean respondent corporations and smaller businesses. Nonetheless, recent literature describes small business applications of such managerial innovations as total quality management and team building. Further, there has been a tendency for some innovative smaller companies to decentralize the human resource management function by distributing greater personnel responsibilities to line managers.[18] A future challenge for the managers of these organizations will be to develop or adapt existing human resource practices for these settings. Interestingly, some human resource executives who lost their jobs as a result of corporate downsizing now operate successful consulting firms that supply human resource services to smaller businesses.

WORKER VALUES AND ATTITUDINAL TRENDS

Before examining worker attitudes and values, it is important to note that attributing fewer work-oriented values to a younger generation has been a longstanding tradition. As a result, popular views on the work values of younger employees may be biased. Seymour Lipset has observed the following:

> Beliefs about the work ethic vary over time and place. There is, however, a general inclination for older people to believe that things were better—or at least more moral, more decent—when they were young.[19]

Several arguments can be used to support the contention that the work ethic in the United States is still strong and that it has remained relatively stable. One argument is that employees have worked the same number of hours per week for over forty-five years and that when commuting is included, they are spending more time in work-related activities. Workers are involved in more hours of work-related activity each week (including commuting time) and are spending less time in leisure. Another argument is that the overwhelming majority of U.S. workers enjoy their jobs, and as a result, work appeals to them. A final argument is that U.S. workers are second only to the Japanese in the proportion who keep working after they reach sixty-five years of age. The meager retirement benefits for Japanese workers may explain their tendency to remain employed.[20]

Lipset's warning and arguments notwithstanding, there have been some shifts in work values of importance to strategic management. Among the most important of these are values and attitudes of employees toward their employers. As discussed in the previous section, unbundled organizations typically display low loyalty to the employees of their peripheral units. This lack of loyalty seems to be reflected in the attitudes of the younger cohorts of today's employees as well. As Terence Pare observed in 1989, "This year's college grads aren't into permanence. They show no loyalty toward their corporate employers and expect none in return. It may be a perfect match."[21] Pollsters Daniel Yankelovich and Bernard Lefkowitz's prescient observations from more than a decade ago noted declining loyalty to employers.[22] Ample evidence exists that levels of loyalty have probably declined on both sides, along with shifts in some other fundamental work-related values. However, decreased loyalty is probably not a unique characteristic of younger workers. In a survey, 57 percent of the respondents indicated that they were "less loyal to their employers than they were five years ago."[23] Reasons for declining loyalty include executives' receipt of large bonuses during cutbacks and perceived lack of concern on the part of management for the welfare of employees. Indeed, there has been a growth of cynicism in the work force, probably resulting from such factors as excessive focus on the bottom line to the exclusion of other values and lofty executive salaries.[24]

An understanding of trends in other work values, particularly those of younger workers, is critical to understanding the future human resources environment. One study of work values analyzed data collected from a survey of high school students and young, newly hired male smelter workers and female telephone operators. The study found that high school students tended to place greater emphasis on extrinsic values than the recently hired employees. Conversely, the recently hired employees placed greater value on the intrinsic aspects of work. These employees had strong work values of wanting to take pride in their work, being involved in their jobs, and performing meaningful work. The initial work experience of young employees, even in relatively low-level jobs, apparently has the potential to shift their work value foci from extrinsic to intrinsic work aspects. Interestingly, only after lengthy socialization in the work environment do work values change from intrinsic to extrinsic.[25] The implications of these findings are that blaming young entrants to the labor market for an emphasis on extrinsically oriented work values may be counterproductive since the real cause for such values may be companies' mismanagement of the socialization process of young workers.

Further, a recent study indicates that younger U.S. workers are not more materialistic than workers from other countries. This comprehensive study compared work values of subjects from the United States, Germany, Holland, Israel, Korea, Taiwan, China, and Hungary. The U.S. sample was drawn from undergraduate and graduate business students mostly between the ages of twenty-one and thirty-nine, of which over 90 percent were employed in full-time jobs from a broad range of occupations. The responses of the subjects who were asked to rank twenty-four work values revealed the following: (1) U.S. subjects ranked pay fifteenth, which was about the same for most other countries. (2) Having an interesting job was the most important value for U.S. students, as well as for subjects from Germany and Holland. Job interest was also ranked as one of the top three work values by subjects from Israel, Korea, and Taiwan. Subjects from Hungary and China viewed job interest less importantly, ranking it at seventh and eighth place, respectively. (3) The second-ranking work value for the U.S. subjects was achievement, which was also ranked first or second by subjects from all countries except Germany. Surprisingly, German subjects—who were small business managers and employees, or business students—ranked achievement in ninth place. (4) When compared to German subjects, U.S. subjects placed much higher value on advancement and responsibility, while German subjects placed much higher emphasis on benefits, security, and supervision. (5) A final difference of interest is that while U.S. subjects— along with subjects from Germany, Holland, Israel, and Taiwan—placed contribution to society in last or next to last place, subjects from China ranked it much higher, fourth place, apparently as a result of their collective culture.[26]

The implications for strategic management of these results are that U.S. workers are interested in the types of jobs they perform and that they still have desirable work values. Younger workers who currently account for a major portion of the work force and who will dominate it during the rest of the decade and beyond, feel entitled to meaningfulness and involvement. They want interesting work, to participate in decisions affecting them, autonomy, and opportunities to grow. Pay will remain important, but workers will probably not be as focused on pay as in the past.[27] These findings are consistent with the description of changing work values conveyed in the following quotation, "After a decade of excessive consumerism and blind ambition, American workers between the ages of 25 and 49 are beginning to emphasize public service and family life as measures of success. . . ."[28] The trend toward greater interest in aspects of job satisfaction, such as autonomy and interesting work, is even reflected in the significant impact such factors have on workers' intentions to vote for unionization. Recent research has also demonstrated the significance of values as determinants of job choice decisions.[29]

The values of older workers may also be important to strategic management. If labor shortages develop, older workers will have to be persuaded to stay on the job or be drawn back into the labor force. One critical element to their return may be job satisfaction. Unfortunately, there is evidence of continuing bias against older workers in various aspects of the work relationship.[30] Although empirical evidence of a positive relationship between job satisfaction and age exists, the relationship is curvilinear and reflects a decline in job satisfaction among older workers, as a result of such factors as lost influence and unmet expectations.[31] Since downsizing organizations have also been targeting older, higher-paid workers for voluntary early retirement programs as a means of cutting costs, older workers may also feel unappreciated. In planning for the environmental challenges of the future, strategic managers may need to develop approaches to prevent the decline of job satisfaction of older workers.

MANAGERIAL TRENDS

Several managerial trends are having an impact on human resources. Those discussed in this section include management of diversity, work teams, total quality management, integrated manufacturing, reengineering, management of professionals, and managing in the aftermath of mergers and acquisitions.

Management of Diversity

Because of the increased heterogeneity of the work force, which will be discussed later in this chapter, managers must be prepared to deal with the challenges associated with such demographic changes. Effective *management of diversity* can increase an organization's productivity through several avenues, one of which is increased problem-solving ability. Such productivity may result from increases in creativity that have been hypothesized to be related to heterogeneity. For example, bilingualism and biculturalism have been found to be related to divergent thinking, which in turn has been hypothesized to be associated with creativity. Recently it has been demonstrated that ethnic heterogeneity in small groups is associated with increased quality of ideas generated for solving problems. Increased heterogeneity may also bring another benefit—the prevention of the "groupthink" phenomenon which occurs only in cohesive groups. However, whether these benefits will be obtained is dependent on how well diversity is managed. Such factors as the amount of diversity, communications, ease of discussing differences, cultural awareness training, and awareness of background information on group members affect the quality of idea generation.[32]

Through such contributions, the management of diversity may enable companies to gain competitive advantages. In addition to diversity-related creativity and problem-solving advantages, companies may also be able to tap gender and racially diverse markets better with a more diverse work force. They may also obtain better acceptance from these markets as a result of a good public image based on diversity. As an example, the Avon Corporation has had success with this strategy. Companies having good records in managing diversity may also be able to attract better employees. Organizations that do a good job of managing diversity also tend to be more flexible because they have broadened their policies, are more open-minded, have less standardized operating methods, and have developed skills in dealing with resistance to change.[33]

Although prejudice still exists, there is evidence that progress has been made. For minorities and females, obtaining jobs with companies is no longer the problem that it was in the past. Instead, any apprehension about minorities and females is more likely to be based on perceptions of their qualifications. These perceptions are affected by the fact that, on average, minorities and females have less training and education.[34] As Roosevelt Thomas has stated: "Companies are worried about productivity and well aware that minorities and women represent a disproportionate share of the undertrained and undereducated."[35] To the extent that companies generalize from classes to individuals and make unfounded attributions, they underestimate the value and contribution that minorities and females can make. Unsurprisingly, the careers of minorities and females tend to plateau earlier than those of male non-minorities.

Nonetheless, a recent longitudinal study of scientific and engineering managerial personnel found favorable treatment of blacks and women. Most such studies are cross-sectional and cannot reflect trends which indicate whether minorities and women are closing the gap on whites and men as a result of egalitarian promotion practices. With cross-sectional studies, lower proportions of blacks and women in managerial jobs may be indicative of the effects of only past discrimination.[36] The promotional situations of blacks and women were described in the longitudinal study as follows:

> . . . in general, black workers enjoyed better promotion opportunities than equally situated white workers in both sectors [private and public]. Better promotion opportunities for blacks were also consistently found in separate analyses conducted for men and women . . . despite the fact that blacks enjoyed higher promotion opportunities than whites in both sectors, these opportunities were better in the public sector. However, workers' gender was significant in the private sector only where women enjoyed better promotion opportunities than equally qualified and situated men.[37]

One caveat on the implications of the diversity literature seems warranted. Some of the empirical literature recommends that researchers should seek to determine the optimal level of heterogeneity since there is a curvilinear relationship between heterogeneity and performance.[38] An example of such a recommendation is the following: "Groups should pay careful attention to how much they increase diversity . . . too much diversity can lead to communication problems and unavoidable conflict."[39] Unfortunately, if one had knowledge of an optimal level of heterogeneity, the application of such information to increase performance might lead to specific consideration of race, ethnicity, or gender in making work assignments, which would appear to violate civil rights legislation.

Work Teams

Work teams have been of increasing interest to managers in a number of leading companies, such as Procter & Gamble, Eli Lilly, and Motorola. These companies have developed substantial expertise in the utilization of teams.[40] John R. Katzenback and Douglas K. Smith define *work teams* as "a small number of people with complementary skills who are committed to a common purpose, performance goals, and approach for which they hold themselves mutually accountable."[41] A number of benefits have been attributed to the use of work teams as an organizational form. These include improved decision making, improved performance, improved quality, and increased flexibility afforded by the ease with which they can be created and disbanded.

The use of teams may also lead to reduced labor costs, lower employee turnover, greater service efficiency, facilitation of change resulting from reduced individual threat, and shorter product development cycles. Empirical analysis of the long-term performance of work teams involved in business simulations has provided some evidence of their effectiveness.[42]

In spite of the advantages, there are also disadvantages with the use of work teams as they are sometimes subject to the dysfunctional groupthink phenomenon and norms of production restriction. Further, as researchers Eric Sundstrom, Kenneth P. De Meuse, and David Futrell have pointed out, the literature on work teams provides mixed evidence on their effectiveness and identifies a large number of factors that potentially influence work team effectiveness. These include developmental aspects, the boundaries of the teams, and the organizational context.[43] Although work team effectiveness is a complex subject, effective work teams have some common characteristics, which include relatively small size, dedication to a common purpose, commitment to common performance standards, willingness to be collectively accountable, equitable and effective work and role assignment procedures within the team, and whether team members have complementary skills. Effective work teams also require compensation approaches that reward teamwork, such as gain sharing or team bonuses.[44]

Aside from their complexity and the potential disadvantages of teams, there is great interest in their potential contributions. For example, in design and production situations, *cross-functional work teams* have been found to be effective in reducing the time required from initial product design to eventual production through simultaneous engineering. Such teams, which typically include both design and production engineering personnel, as well as program managers, who mediate differences, are ideally housed in the same room. Another benefit derived from these teams is the broadening experience that takes place within the teams across the engineering specialties.[45]

An example of the use of work teams having a great deal of autonomy is provided by the experiences of Steelcase, Inc., which introduced work teams into its new Context plant. The plant's hourly employees are organized into some forty-seven work teams, several of which are cross-functional in nature. In addition to normal production work, these teams perform many activities that normally would have been managerial responsibilities, such as scheduling production, scheduling vacations, ordering materials, and purchasing new equipment. Performance evaluation and compensation reviews are still the responsibility of managerial personnel.[46]

Steelcase has derived a number of important benefits from its work groups. One is that the teams, which include machine operators, tend to make better machinery purchasing decisions than managers. Another benefit is that there are savings in labor costs as the proportion of indirect labor costs is lower than other plants in the industry. For example, there is no need for the position of assistant foreman. An additional benefit is that the Context plant has experienced an annual turnover rate lower than one percent. Further, communication has been facilitated as a result of the use of work teams. Finally, Steelcase has found that its workers have not become complacent because of the sense of ownership produced by the teams.[47]

Total Quality Management

Another managerial trend of importance to management strategists is *total quality management* (TQM). TQM, pioneered by W. Edwards Deming, is a broad-based, systematic approach for achieving high levels of quality. Many leading companies—such as Motorola, Cadillac, and Xerox—whose strategies require them to survive against the pressures of world-class competition, have implemented TQM. In a strategic context, TQM is probably most accurately categorized as a tactic for carrying out strategies requiring high levels of product or service quality. Essentially, TQM pulls together a number of well-known managerial principles into a coherent and systematic framework. Through the systematic interaction of these principles, TQM has the potential to lead to increased quality. TQM principles emphasize the following: (1) articulation of a strategic vision, (2) objective and accurate measurements, (3) benchmarking, (4) widespread employee empowerment and team building, (5) striving for continuous improvement, (6) emphasis on a systems view of quality which conceptualizes quality-related activities as being highly interdependent, (7) leadership committed to quality, and (8) great emphasis on customer satisfaction.[48]

Interestingly, TQM programs have the potential to increase the importance of the human resource management function. Human resource management plays a major role in providing more systematic training, facilitating changes that empower employees, instituting team-based reward systems, and communicating to workers their role in quality.[49] David Bowen and Edward Lawler have described the relationship between TQM and human resource management as follows:

> The importance of the HR side of the quality equation provides HR departments with a golden opportunity. Quality can be the "business issue" that truly brings senior managers and HR execs together to move from *just* HRM to *strategic* HRM. A major role in the quality improvement effort puts HR in a position to contribute directly and visibly to the bottom line, to add value to the company's products and services in the same way that other functions, such as sales, accounting, and production, add value.[50]

Before the human resource function can make full contributions to TQM efforts, high quality must be assured within the function itself. Unfortunately, measurement of the function's contributions is often difficult because of their indirect effects. Nonetheless, as discussed in Chapter 8, valid measures of human resource effectiveness can be developed. One means by which this might be accomplished is through external benchmarking. *Benchmarking*, which is discussed in more depth in Chapter 8, provides a useful means of both evaluating the quality of human resource programs, activities, and impact as well as a means of identifying areas in which resources should be concentrated. The following quotation by David Ulrich, Wayne Brockbank, and Arthur Yeung describes this practice.

> Benchmarking HR practices provide the means of focusing attention on highest value-added HR activities—those practices which are more likely to be practiced by successful companies. Rather than fall into the trap of trying to do everything well and please everyone with insufficient resources—which results in no one being satisfied—HR professionals could use benchmarking to focus limited resources on critical activities.[51]

Evaluation of the human resource function can also be accomplished by asking other managers in the organization to evaluate the quality of services provided by the human resource management function.[52] One guide for evaluation is to place greater emphasis on measuring the most critical human resource management attributes, with secondary emphasis on the precision with which these attributes can be measured. This point is evident in the following statement by Curt Reiman, director of the Baldrige Award for the U.S. Department of Commerce: "A company doesn't earn money making measurements. The trick is to avoid great measurements of irrelevant things. You may have to live with approximate measurements of exactly the right things."[53] Along this same line, proponents of TQM also advocate the use of Pareto analysis.[54] The basis of Pareto analysis is that a small number of factors has a disproportionately large impact on outcomes, such as quality. Therefore, by correcting a few critical problems, disproportionate improvements in quality can be obtained.

From a human resource management perspective, one of the important impacts of TQM is its great emphasis on training. TQM maintains that errors and mistakes, which detract from the quality of companies' products and services, are a predictable result of untrained workers and therefore training must be provided. Consistent with the emphasis on measurement, training is evaluated with the use of control groups and experimental designs in some companies using TQM.[55]

In contrast to training, TQM is sharply at odds with conventional human resource practice in the area of performance evaluation. According to Deming, traditional performance evaluation systems are flawed because they are directed toward the individual, instead of the team. Such systems also focus on assigning blame for past mistakes instead of pointing out direction for the future and may even detract from teamwork. Deming has also argued that faulty systems and procedures are usually the cause of quality problems, not the performance of individual employees. TQM proponents maintain that compensation should be directed toward teams instead of individuals. In addition to disagreement over performance evaluation, there is also controversy among TQM proponents over the appropriateness of team-based pay. Even some companies that have won the Baldrige Award for quality have not extended TQM into the areas of performance evaluation or compensation. Instead, companies implementing TQM have focused on problem areas that detract from quality, are relatively easy to fix, and do not involve much risk. For example, many companies focus their TQM efforts on improving training and communications. Fewer companies have shifted from more traditional compensation systems to team-based pay, abandoned their performance evaluation systems, or instituted self-managed teams. Motorola and Cadillac are exceptions in that they have instituted such teams.[56]

As with any managerial innovation, TQM is not without problems. One criticism is that TQM efforts can lead to goal displacement, in which TQM becomes an end instead of a means. In such cases attention is diverted from productive activities to gaining approvals from committees, filling out forms, and other bureaucratic procedures. The well-publicized difficulties encountered by Florida Power & Light and the Wallace Company after they won the Baldrige Award for quality provide wonderfully ironic examples of this problem. Additionally, although not the fault of TQM, during economic difficulties some companies have reduced the level of employee empowerment. Executives in these companies have blamed employee empowerment for slower decision making. However, this appears to be a shortsighted criticism since the critical decision implementation process is facilitated by employee empowerment. Nonetheless, even in Japan there has been second-guessing of employee empowerment and consensus decision approaches because of their slowness. As a result, some leading Japanese companies have turned to more top-down–oriented chief executive officers.[57] Another problem is incompatibility of some basic TQM concepts and downsizing strategies. As Bernado De Sousa from Ciba-Geigy Ltd. has stated,

> Because the aim of TQM is to add value to all stakeholders in every activity, it must of necessity make a company more efficient. . . . Increased productivity implies producing more with the same resources or, in a saturated market, producing the same amounts with fewer resources. In the latter case, which is the rule rather than the exception in the industrialized nations today, downsizing is the inevitable consequence.[58]

Although De Sousa claims that layoffs can be avoided, presumably by attrition, worker insecurity resulting from downsizing or layoffs would seem to undermine the TQM philosophy.

Integrated Manufacturing

Integrated manufacturing systems provide a new approach for streamlined manufacturing. Such systems are commonly comprised of *advanced manufacturing technology* (AMT), TQM, and *just-in-time* (JIT) inventory control methods. AMT is a manufacturing approach based on highly computerized technologies such as computer-aided manufacturing (CAM). Just-in-time inventory control is a method for delivering manufacturing components to the production line at the shortest practical time before they are needed. When these technologies and managerial systems are combined, integrated manufacturing systems have the potential to provide greater dissemination of information, remove barriers associated with functional specialization, promote collaboration to solve quality problems, and develop congruence between goals of cost, quality, and desired production lead times.[59]

These systems require knowledge workers whose levels of technical and problem-solving skills are advanced beyond those needed for earlier forms of manufacturing and have major implications for human resource management. Scott Snell and James Dean conducted an empirical analysis of the types of human resource practices associated with various components of integrated manufacturing systems. In companies where there is greater emphasis on AMT and TQM, there is more selectivity in hiring, more comprehensive training, greater developmental use of performance appraisal, and greater emphasis on external pay equity. These results are consistent with companies' motivations to hire and maintain high-quality work forces and to preserve their investments in human resources. An interesting strategic question remains as Snell and Dean were unable to determine whether companies invest in superior human resources in order to implement integrated manufacturing systems or whether such systems are implemented because companies already have superior human resources.[60]

Reengineering

Reengineering, which is also called process innovation, core process redesign, or business process reengineering, has been practiced since the late 1980s, often by companies facing intense competitive pressures. Essentially, reengineering is directed at achieving large cost savings by eliminating unneeded activities and consolidating work. It also sometimes redirects work across traditional departmental boundaries in order to accomplish work more quickly in cross-functional teams. Accordingly, reporting relationships are sometimes changed along with reward structures. The type of service desired by customers is the key to the process.[61]

An example of reengineering is provided by its application at Texas Instruments where the driving force was the desire to reduce the time required for making customized semiconductor chips for a customer. In another example the driving force was increased competition. In this case, GTE revamped its customer service process when it found that customers wanted to call only one number for repair service, to obtain answers to billing questions, or to obtain additional services. Prior to reengineering, customers having service problems called repair clerks who then recorded the information and then forwarded it to repair personnel. These activities were subsequently combined into one job performed by employees called front-end technicians who now also operate testing and switching equipment relocated from repair personnel. As a result, the front-end technicians solve 30 percent of all service calls and a smaller percentage of calls must be passed on to other repair personnel.[62] Another example involves a bank. In order to reduce its operating costs the Banca di America e di Italia (BAI) reengineered its retail banking operations with the goal of becoming a paperless bank. After reengineering activities involved in depositing checks, the number declined from sixty-four to twenty-five. As a result of these and other changes, employees in each branch declined from seven to nine prior to reengineering to three or four afterward. With these labor savings the bank was able to open fifty new branches with its existing work force.[63]

Often reengineering requires cross-functional coordination and the crossing of organizational boundaries. Because it may disrupt existing power relationships and eliminate organizational jobs, it has high potential for conflict. Because the process often fails to obtain desired improvements and it has high potential for destructive consequences, organizations should not engage in reengineering unless they perceive a serious need. Furthermore, reengineering typically does not achieve the level of improvement desired. The conventional wisdom is that the organization's strategy should provide direction to the process by indicating the major business activities that should be reengineered. Activities unnecessary to these business needs are potential targets for elimination. As with any intervention of this nature, the organization's culture will have a major impact on its success. In many contemporary organizational cultures, the broad direction for reengineering should come from top management, while the specifics of reengineering should be the responsibility of those who perform work. In addition to the requirement for extensive time commitment from the chief executive, successful reengineering is more likely to take place where it is applied to a broad range of activities, where work redesign is accompanied by training programs, and where there is extensive communication with employees.[64]

As a closing note on reengineering, it should be noted that some high-level executives are not convinced of the ultimate value of reengineering. They have observed the elimination of jobs and such a massive increase in the workload of the remaining employees that they have serious concerns about the long-range, detrimental human impact of such programs. Because of such reactions, the use of reengineering may diminish somewhat in the future.

Management of Professionals

Because of their nature, professionals require a different form of management and provide a challenge for human resource management. Important characteristics of professionals are that they often have low organizational loyalty, require substantial autonomy, follow an external code of ethics established by their profession, adhere to standards of the profession, and have a high need for intellectual and technical challenges.[65] The availability of managers who can manage the work of professionals cannot be taken for granted. The difficulties are well-known and there has been a longstanding controversy over whether such managers should be members of the relevant profession themselves or laypersons. The problems of failing to plan for the development of managers who can be effective in such settings are apparent. As Mary Anne Von Glinow has stated:

> Maximizing a professional's productivity has led to the adoption or development of new methods of work organization that limit hierarchical levels of supervision, link pay and other rewards to performance, ease the tensions between the competing cultures of professionals and other employees, and give professionals greater participation in the decisions that affect their lives. . . . These managerial challenges and their solutions are crucial to the success and long-term survival of every high tech firm. The changes . . . require different and sometimes counterintuitive management skills and practices.[66]

A human resource problem for the future will be to develop career paths for professionals. To move up in an organization, professionals have traditionally had to pursue an administrative track. Since they are often unprepared for management or administrative careers, they may not find such work satisfying. As a result, dual-career ladders are sometimes provided, one in management and the other within the professional work.[67] Planning for career progressions for professionals will require greater attention to the development of alternative tracks that will both satisfy the needs of professionals and their employing organizations. A remarkable example of turnover problems among professionals is provided by large public accounting firms. A recent study of one such firm found that retention rates, after sixty months with the firm, ranged from 6 to 29 percent.[68] A challenge for the future will be to develop career tracks for professionals which will enhance organizational loyalty.

Managing in the Aftermath of Mergers and Acquisitions

Although the level of merger and acquisition activity has lessened, mergers and acquisitions are a permanent feature of the economy. Whether a merger or acquisition is successful depends on more than financial considerations. Success often depends on how well the two organizations' human resources are integrated. As a result, the degree to which human resource aspects of mergers and acquisitions are planned can be critical.[69] As Bruckman and Peters have stated:

> The amount of time and energy needed to successfully merge two sophisticated organizations, however, is more likely to resemble the planning and execution of the invasion of Normandy, accompanied by the resultant clash of cultures from many elements attempting to work together toward one end.[70]

There is much evidence of the failure to work through human resource issues even when an organization is acquired for its human resources. An example of such a failure is the Shearson–E. F. Hutton merger in which the brokers that made E. F. Hutton attractive to Shearson left for a competitor soon after the merger. As Greller and Nee stated, "The 'disaster' resulted from Shearson's discounting the human resource requirements of the transaction."[71] It has been argued that planning for the contingencies of a merger is critical because human resources will pay the price. If a company is successful in fending off a takeover, personnel layoffs are generally required to pay the costs of the defensive actions. Conversely, if the company loses in the takeover battle, there may be redundant employees and the new entity will have to resort to layoffs.[72]

DEMOGRAPHIC TRENDS

Many of the demographic trends over the next decade are relatively well-known. James Walker's human resource planning book in 1980 was one of the first to call attention to the implications of the dramatic demographic changes. More recently, implications of the massive changes in demography have been more fully described. Major changes include an aging work force, the baby boomer age bulge, the baby bust labor shortage, increased racial diversity, greater feminization of the work force, and dual-career couples. These developments, particularly the variations in growth across different age cohorts, will have major implications for the career potential of individual workers. Planning will be necessary to avoid age bulges, age gaps, and surpluses in job categories or job families.[73]

An Aging Work Force

An indication of aging trends is that the average age of workers will increase from thirty-two in 1989 to forty by the year 2000. Further, life expectancy has increased substantially, from sixty-three in 1940 to seventy-five in 1990.[74] Some of the implications of aging are that the work force will be more experienced, stable, and reliable. As a result, it should be more productive. On the other hand, an older work force may lead to less flexibility as older workers may not adapt as quickly to a dynamic economy. Greater costs will also result from greater pension contributions, which are likely to be associated with an aging work force.[75] One implication of this trend is that as the work force ages there should be correspondingly greater health-care costs. Huge increases had already occurred in the late 1980s as health-care costs rose an average 29 percent in manufacturing companies between 1988 and 1989.[76] Companies' age distributions have already begun to affect their production costs and ability to compete. Interestingly, during the postwar period in which Japan's remarkable economic growth occurred, it had a relatively smaller proportion of retired people to support than other industrial countries.[77]

The Boomer Age Bulge

Projections of the labor force through the year 2000 reveal vast differences in the size of age cohorts. As Table 2-1 indicates, the 25 to 34 age cohort is expected to decline 11.5 percent from 1990 levels and the 45 to 54 cohort will increase by 50.4 percent. The implications of these projections are dramatic.

There will be a shortage of workers 25 to 34 while the career opportunities in management for workers in the 35 to 44 age cohort may be constrained by the abundance of more experienced members of the 45 to 54 age cohort.[78]

The effects of information technology were identified earlier as contributors to declining middle management opportunities that were first signaled during the 1981–1982 recession. With the large cohort of educated workers and reduced middle-management opportunities, there will be fierce competition for such positions in the future. Correspondingly there will be plateaued employees whose motivation may decline. Career alternatives such as horizontal career paths, greater job responsibilities, enhanced decision-making opportunities, task force assignments, and redesigned jobs affording enhanced skill development may be needed for such employees.[79]

The importance of demographic changes in the labor force and population, and the impact of irregular age distributions may be seen in the experiences of ARCO. ARCO was forced to reduce the size of its work force during two years in the mid-1980s. Reductions were achieved through the use of voluntary early retirement packages as well as involuntary terminations. As a result, the average age level of ARCO's employees declined from forty-two to thirty-eight. After layoffs and restructuring, many younger employees were promoted but there were fewer promotional opportunities in general. ARCO then found itself in a situation that many companies will face in the future. It found that perceptions of careers had to be changed from rapid advancement to lateral moves and experience broadening assignments.[80]

The Baby Bust Labor Shortage

At present there is skepticism about the accuracy of projections of labor shortages for the 1990s. Nonetheless, entry-level shortages have been predicted to occur by 2000 along with simultaneous gluts in the 25 to 44 age cohort. If shortages of younger workers occur, older individuals and immigrants will be looked to as sources of labor. Employers may hire retired workers to fill entry-level jobs and create more varied work schedules to accommodate their needs.[81] Although older workers generally are not inter-

TABLE 2-1   CIVILIAN LABOR FORCE

AGE CATEGORY	1990	2000*	PERCENTAGE CHANGE
25 to 34	35,803,000	31,677,000	−11.5
35 to 44	31,844,000	38,772,000	+21.8
45 to 54	20,493,000	30,818,000	+50.4
55 to 64	11,860,000	13,936,000	+17.5

*Projections based on moderate growth assumptions.

Source: Labor force and labor force projections aggregated from data obtained from Howard N. Fullerton, Jr. "Evaluation of Labor Force Projections to 1990," *Monthly Labor Review*, Vol. 115, No. 8, 1992, p. 5; Howard N. Fullerton, Jr. "New Labor Force Projections, Spanning 1988 to 2000," *Monthly Labor Review*, Vol. 112, No. 11, 1989, p. 8.

ested in full-time work, they appear to be interested in "fill-in" work of a part-time nature if the jobs provide flexibility and are close to home. The Senior Employment Service in New York and Operation Able in Chicago provide examples of successful employment of older workers. Companies such as Cigna, Digital Equipment, Grumman, and Hewlett-Packard are already using innovative approaches in staffing with older workers, frequently hiring their own retirees. The Days Inns hotel chain has staffed 25 percent of its reservation work force with older workers.[82]

Interestingly, the reserve of female workers that provided needed labor in the past has been depleted by their current involvement in the labor force. Liberalized policies which would allow greater immigration of skilled workers are also being viewed as a remedy for shortages of labor. Contrary to common beliefs, the long-run economic benefits of anticipated levels of immigration are expected to outweigh the short-run costs. Experiences such as those of Los Angeles in the 1970s, in which a million people immigrated into the area, reveal a positive economic impact.[83] Also of interest, the greatest immigration level since 1914 occurred in 1992 when 846,000 immigrants entered the United States.[84]

From a different perspective, if the predicted labor shortages materialize, they will occur simultaneously with a surplus of unqualified workers. Many unqualified workers will be disadvantaged minorities whose educations have not matched their more affluent non-minority co-workers.[85] Unless conditions change, the economic future does not bode well for disadvantaged minorities. With current patterns of population concentration, 40 percent of U.S. blacks live in 11 cities. Of these cities only Atlanta and Los Angeles are located in high-growth areas.[86]

Unfortunately for unqualified workers, U.S. employers will need entry-level workers whose skills are on par with global standards. As Peter Morrison has stated, "When today's first-graders reach adulthood they will compete within a global labor market and will need intellectual skills and levels of education and literacy never demanded of their predecessors."[87] Stated differently, "Jobs that are currently in the middle of the skill distribution will be the least-skilled occupations of the future, and there will be very few net new jobs for the unskilled."[88]

Increased Racial Diversity

The work force will become much more diverse during the remainder of the 1990s. Nonwhites will have contributed 29 percent of the entrants to the work force during the 15-year period leading up to the year 2000. By the year 2000, over 15 percent of the work force will be comprised of nonwhites.[89] As noted earlier in this chapter's discussion of the management of diversity, organizations will need to plan to take advantage of the diversity these workers bring instead of forcing conformity. Likewise, organizations will need to be proactive in helping to create a work environment in which the creativity and innovativeness of diversity will flourish.[90]

Greater Feminization of the Work Force

Females have constituted a growing portion of the work force for several decades. This growth should result in a work force which is 47 percent female by the year 2000.[91] The increased entry of women in different occupational categories has produced some interesting results. Women have fared well as information workers, making up almost one third of the number of computer scientists. Women appear to advance most rapidly in cutting-edge industries because the "old rules" do not appear to apply. As an example of their success in these industries, women constitute 30 percent of the managers and 40 percent of the professionals at Apple Computer. Outside of the information worker category, women have made some tremendous strides as well. Women now constitute 49.6 percent of accountants. They also comprise over 32 percent of medical school and 40 percent of law school graduating classes.[92]

The large number of baby boom women in the labor force who are having babies has necessitated the implementation of work scheduling approaches that will allow them to avoid long service interruptions. Approaches include part-time schedules, flextime, flexi-scheduling, and allowing employees to work part of the time at home. Experiences with the latter for managerial and professional personnel have been reported at both General Motors and Citibank.[93]

Dual-Career Couples

An issue related to increased feminization of the work force is the number of dual-career families. In the late 1980s, 67 percent of couples had two wage earners, a 15 percent increase from the previous decade. In order to accommodate such families, employers will need to offer support services such as "sick child" care programs and day care. As a result, there may be reductions in absenteeism, lower turnover, recruiting advantages, and a positive impact on productivity.[94] In order to help such dual-career couples as well as single parents, several new forms of support are currently being provided by companies. For example, referral services for child care are provided by one of the large public accounting firms and IBM. Other companies have set up child-care facilities on company premises. Campbell Soup Company has had success with such a program while Corning Glass and Merck & Company have encountered high costs and resentment from employees who do not need the services. Another service that might be offered by some companies in the future is counseling for the spouse who gives up a job for the other's transfer.[95]

TRENDS IN THE UTILIZATION OF HUMAN RESOURCES

Relocation of Work

Workers are relocating in the United States in patterns that are very different from past migration flows. Telecommunications, fax machines, personal computers, and express mail make up a set of forces that have allowed information workers to migrate from cities to rural areas and small towns. This migration has created what futurists Naisbitt and Aburdene call the *electronic heartland.* These workers have been attracted to the heartland because of less crime, a lower cost of living, and quality of life benefits. Workers who are making this relocation include owners of home-based businesses, writers, artists, stock traders, composers, software developers, and engineers.[96]

Another off-site variation is simply for work to be performed at home. Such work, often termed *telecommuting* or *telecommunicating,* does not necessarily involve geographic relocation. Such work has been predicted to expand in the future. Telecommuting is expected to bring several individual benefits including the avoidance of commuting as well as at-home child care, ease of working for multiple employers, access to jobs by disabled workers, and life style advantages. Organizational benefits include recruiting advantages, lower costs in using part-time workers, increased ability to use skilled professionals on an ad hoc basis, and reduced likelihood of unionization. Nonetheless, potential problems with such arrangements include control difficulties, career limitations related to lack of visibility, social isolation, and reduced loyalties to both employer and employee.[97]

Companies are also relocating their operations. In information systems and data processing, companies are relocating their facilities to areas where there are favorable costs. For example, a New York money center bank relocated its data processing operations to a nearby state where real estate and the cost of living are lower. Information is transmitted electronically back and forth with no delay in information system responsiveness while achieving substantial cost savings.

It is increasingly common for automobile rental companies and hotels to locate their reservations operations in areas of the country where there are wage advantages. For example, Hertz has its reservations and accounting operations in Oklahoma City. Thrifty and Avis both have reservations operations in Tulsa, and Budget's reservations operations are in Carrolton, Texas. Reservations operations for Hyatt Hotels are located in Omaha, Nebraska. These geographic areas offer wage advantages over many areas in the United States and location is irrelevant to the nature of the work performed.

Recently, manufacturing companies have been relocating out of California because of the high costs of land and labor and the regulatory environment. For example, California-based Applied Materials built a new $100-million facility in Texas because of such factors. Other examples include Weiser Lock, which closed a plant in California and moved it to Tucson where labor and cost of living are substantially lower. Similarly, Atlas Pacific Engineering relocated from northern California to Pueblo, Colorado, for lower labor and land costs. Within the next ten to twenty years, Hughes Aircraft plans to relocate much of its manufacturing operations out of the state of California.[98] Companies from services industries are also relocating. For example, the Bank of America relocated its credit-card unit from Pasadena to Phoenix.[99] Additionally, the expense of operating in such high-cost areas as New York City has prompted some large companies to move their headquarters to less expensive areas. For example, W. R. Grace announced its intentions to move its headquarters to Florida while J. C. Penney and Mobil had already moved their headquarters from New York to the Dallas/Fort Worth area.[100]

Growing Use of Temporary and Contingent Workers

Another important human resource issue is the increasing use of *temporary* or *contingent workers*. Temporary employees are often used to provide a buffer of protection for the jobs of the core of permanent employees. Further, the use of such workers is increasing and there is likely to be additional unbundling in the future. In contrast to core employees, contingent workers have short-term affiliations with employers. Examples include *temporaries, subcontracted workers, part-time workers, consultants, life-of-the-project workers, and leased employees.* Companies are also using more "leased" employees who are "rented" from a temporary help agency on a long-term basis. Unsurprisingly, unions typically resist the use of temporary workers.[101]

Although there is growing use of higher-skilled temporary employees, the largest category of temporaries is still administrative support or clerical work. The second largest category is industrial help workers such as laborers, equipment cleaners, helpers, and handlers. Since demand for such industrial workers is cyclical and seasonal, the advantages to the employer are obvious.[102] Bureau of Labor Statistics projections also indicate growth in the business services area to 8.3 million jobs by 2000.[103] The largest category in this sector is personnel supply. Temporary workers are even being used in the health-care industry as registered nurses, practical nurses, and X-ray technicians.[104]

As indicated, the nature of temporary jobs is changing as there is a shift toward the higher-skill levels. Types of workers utilized as temporaries have expanded to include accountants, computer specialists, engineering personnel, financial executives, and technical writers. In information systems, temporary management services are being used for project management, installation of new systems, or during transitional periods. Temporary management personnel and executives are sometimes early retirees from major computer companies or managers who have lost their jobs as a result of restructuring.[105]

Factors Prompting Use of Temporary or Contingent Employees

A number of factors encourage the use of temporary or contingent employees. One is the uncertainty in economic outlook faced by employers. In recent years employers have become more reluctant to hire permanent employees and have increased their use of contingent employees. Since the 1990s also appear to be turbulent, such use of temporaries can be expected to continue as well. Another factor is fluctuating workloads.[106] An example of adaptation to such fluctuations is provided by a rural area client of Atlanta-based Norrell Corporation. The client organization has only 50 employees while Norrell supplies it with 450 temporaries. Because the client organization needs the bulk of its employees for only a seven-month cycle, it uses temporaries. Previously, the organization had 400 full-time employees and was overstaffed part of the time and understaffed the rest of the time.[107] Companies can also avoid paying overtime by using temporaries during peak demand periods. Growing and declining companies have been found to use more temporary employees. The use of temporaries who can be dismissed on short notice allows these companies to protect the core of permanent employees.[108]

Other factors prompting the use of contingent workers include avoidance of recruiting, hiring, and training expenses for workers to be used only a short time and avoidance of severance costs. Use of temporaries has also been prompted by the perverse effects of legislation, such as the Worker Adjustment and Retraining Notification Act's requirement of advance notice of plant closures, which was designed to protect employees who work full-time. Other advantages for employers in the use of such workers include flexibility, potential savings in labor costs, and acquiring labor needed during hiring freezes.[109]

Employee leasing is different than the use of temporary workers as there is no implication that employees will be other than full-time, long-term employees. Often, when an employer makes the decision to lease employees, his or her employees then become employees of a leasing firm. The leasing firm then supplies these same employees to the original employer. As with the use of temporaries, there are also some advantages with employee leasing. One primary reason for leasing is that small employers can obtain more economical health insurance by virtue of the leasing company's larger numbers of employees and inclusion under pooled rates. Another motivating factor is that all payroll and administrative services are performed by the leasing company, leaving the management of the small company free to focus on other aspects of the business.[110]

In addition to benefits for employers, there are some benefits for temporary or contingent workers. These include the flexibility to match life style and family obligations with work, and the ease of finding a job. For women, who constitute approximately two thirds of the temporary work force, the benefits also include exposure in the job market, opportunities to obtain work experience and work skills, and the opportunity to sample employment situations. Opportunities to reacquire work skills and confidence may have appeal for women who have withdrawn from the labor force for substantial lengths of time. Youthful workers may also be attracted by temporary work as opportunities to gain work experience.[111]

Factors Limiting Use of Temporary or Contingent Employees

Although there are several advantages for employers in using temporary employees, there are also disadvantages. One disadvantage is the increased likelihood of missing affirmative action goals. Employers may not obtain desired numbers of female and minority employees in their permanent work force if they curtail hiring and rely extensively on temporary workers. Another disadvantage is the need to train such workers. With temporary executives, disadvantages may include inordinate emphasis on short-term financial performance and absence of company loyalty. Disadvantages for temporary employees include lower opportunities to receive health insurance and retirement benefits, lower pay, and fewer training and educational opportunities. However, temporaries frequently have benefit coverage from spouses' employment.[112]

There are other disadvantages with the use of leased employees. One is that some of the advantages of small size, such as exclusion from coverage by various federal laws based on size limits, are lost because of the leasing company's larger size. The use of a leasing company also may not eliminate liability, as there may be a shared employment relationship. Another disadvantage is that a number of leasing companies have failed, leaving the employers using leased employees liable for workers' compensation.[113]

INTERNATIONAL DEVELOPMENTS

Global Competition

Companies competing on a global basis will need to use world-class labor to obtain the quality needed for some product markets. For example, the Dana Corporation uses its training programs to develop employees who can produce at the level of world competitive standards. One of Dana's accomplishments has been to develop some of its U.S. workers into world-class machinists.[114] One large food manufacturer has specialized information services performed on the basis of world-class expertise; programming is done in Mexico while routing work is done in England.

Moving foreign nationals across international boundaries is another approach for highly skilled individuals. However, the use of U.S. expatriate workers in overseas holdings may be declining. In some U.S. companies with large overseas holdings, the number of U.S. expatriate workers is relatively small. For example, during one year Honeywell had 27,159 employees overseas but only approximately 200 were U.S. citizens.[115] Instead, there may be a growing tendency to bring foreign nationals to the United States for a few years' training in the parent company with the intention of having them take on managerial or professional responsibilities in their home countries. The legal restrictions involved in these actions may be critical. Some large organizations have human resource management specialists who have developed expertise in working through the legalities for such moves.

Global Sourcing of Labor

Innovative uses of labor on a global basis are evident. One example is a large U.S. insurance company in which claims are processed in a low-wage European country. The combination of a common language, an educated labor force, a shortage of jobs, and relatively low wages makes this option attractive. As operations have been set up, claims data are sent from the United States using overnight air mail and electronic transmission. An interesting benefit of this relationship is that, in addition to the low cost of labor, there is a time differential advantage as work delivered overnight can be worked on several hours prior to the normal starting time of 8:00 A.M. on the East Coast. Additionally, U.S. companies sometimes have data entry performed offshore in order to take advantage of wage differentials. In some instances, data entry is even performed by clerical workers who do not even speak English. For example, American Airlines has data entry performed in mainland China and Barbados.[116]

Several Asian countries such as Korea, Singapore, Taiwan, Malaysia, and Indonesia are major U.S. trading and outsourcing partners. Nonetheless, the dramatic changes in Eastern Europe also have implications for labor supplies. The workers in the former East Germany are especially intriguing. Although the eastern part of Germany has low productivity, the prospects for rapid productivity growth are good because the labor force is literate, competent, and mechanically adept. Further, there is still a strong work ethic even after the effects of 45 years of communism. As a result, the transition of these German workers to modern production environments should be rapid. This expected transition to high productivity is in stark contrast to expectations of the labor force in many U.S. cities where illiteracy among workers is high.[117] Although the former East German work force may be more skilled than those of some Eastern European countries, the labor forces of these countries are attractive in many respects and are now accessible to Western companies.

North American Free Trade Agreement

In 1993 the U.S. Congress ratified the North American Free Trade Agreement.[118] The agreement with Canada and Mexico phases out tariffs on goods produced in these countries and the United States. For example, tariffs on automobiles will be eliminated as follows:

> Mexican tariffs, which average 10% on imports from the U.S. and 20% on automobiles (against the U.S. average of 3% on imports from Mexico) would be eliminated, some immediately and others over a period of 10 years, and Mexican non-tariff barriers would also be removed.[119]

Fears of job losses prompted organized labor to oppose the act, and one AFL-CIO economist argued that as many as 500,000 jobs would be lost.[120] A number of manufacturers in such industries as auto parts, glass, and furniture also voiced opposition to the act.[121] Nonetheless, the act was passed and greater trade was probably inevitable even if its critics had prevailed. Former President Carlos Salinas of Mexico described this inevitability in the following statement:

> The economic relationship between Mexico and the U.S. is already so strong that the agreement would [simply] recognize that reality. With Japan and Asian-Pacific countries making their own region, the only way to compete with them is by getting together. It's a matter of [economic] viability in the medium and long run. It will happen sooner or later. If it's later, the better for our competitors.[122]

In contrast to the arguments of the opponents of the act, there were a number of very strong arguments for it. One was that in recent years, the third largest and most rapidly expanding market for U.S. goods had been Mexico. Another was that shared production arrangements with Mexico provide the United States with a viable manufacturing strategy for global competition. Finally, the act would help solidify the beneficial changes brought about by the Salinas administration and provide a pattern to be used in developing increased trade with other Latin American countries.[123]

European Community

Business leaders are watching with interest the formulation of the rules by which commerce will be conducted across the borders of the countries of the European Community. Access to this huge market has major human resource implications for many U.S. companies that have supplied goods to these countries in the past. Trade-inhibiting physical barriers between countries were eliminated on January 31, 1992, and there had also been progress in the harmonization of technical barriers. The relaxed rules under which European Community companies now operate have produced efficiencies in shipping goods across borders which have implications for U.S. companies that must compete.[124]

OTHER DEVELOPMENTS

Acquired Immune Deficiency Syndrome

In addition to increasing costs associated with an aging population, the spread of the acquired immune deficiency syndrome (AIDS) has increased employers' health-care costs. The costs of treating AIDS has ranged from $40,000 to $90,000 per case. As early as 1987, one third of companies responding to a survey by the American Society for Personnel Administration reported having employees with AIDS. Pacific Bell found that AIDS was the leading cause of death among its active employees.[125]

Aside from the obvious impact on health-care costs, AIDS also has a potentially detrimental impact on the productivity of the work force. As skilled employees become unable to work, the organization loses their skills.

Although more difficult to quantify, the illness and death of co-workers undoubtedly has a negative effect on the work group. Employer attempts to deal with AIDS have evolved and are perhaps best exemplified by Pacific Bell's response. Pacific Bell's humane treatment of employees with AIDS has allowed it to avoid dysfunctional reactions by other employees, who out of fear and ignorance may respond in such ways as refusing to work in contact with employees having AIDS. Additionally, the company has been able to reduce the health-care costs for employees having AIDS by developing programs where more personal care is given in non-hospital settings such as hospices or at home. Several companies such as Chemical Bank, Johnson & Johnson, IBM, Time, Inc., and Warner-Lambert have policies that ensure fair treatment of afflicted workers.[126]

These compassionate approaches may reduce dysfunctional organizational side effects of AIDS in the work force. Until the spread of AIDS is curbed and a cure developed, larger numbers of workers will become ill in the future. To the extent that medical technology and educational programs are unable to check the spread of AIDS, companies will need to plan for the loss of greater numbers of prime working age employees. In the worst case, companies may have to plan for larger training and development programs to insure the availability of critical employees. On a related issue, health-care organizations need to manage the impact of providing care for AIDS patients because it takes a psychological toll on their medical staffs. A recent empirical study has demonstrated that organizational support systems can ameliorate the negative consequences.[127]

Substance Abuse

An indication of the magnitude of the substance abuse problem is provided by the recent experience of General Motors. In one year, more than 14,000 of GM's employees received help from the company's employee assistance program (EAP). Of the employees treated by the program, 49 percent had a drug-related problem while 53 percent had an alcohol problem.[128] The implications for human resource management are that substance abusers have absenteeism rates that are four to eight times higher than those of other employees. On the other hand, some substance abuse programs such as those of the Southern Pacific Railroad and the U.S. Navy have reported dramatic results in reducing substance abuse in the work force.[129]

SUMMARY

This chapter has provided an overview of several trends and developments that are likely to affect human resources during the remainder of the 1990s and into the 2000s. Information technology's impact on jobs and skill level requirements were considered along with its impact on organizational structure. As a result of information technology, organizations are becoming less hierarchical and more adaptive. Some are even rotating leadership responsibilities among team members based on the stage of product development cycles. The emergence of unbundled or network organizations was also discussed. Such organizations, which take contingent views toward organizational units and their workers, are becoming commonplace. The examination of worker values and attitudes revealed that employees are becoming less loyal toward their employers, more concerned with having interesting jobs which allow them to grow, and more inclined to feel that they are entitled to participate in decisions affecting them.

Several important managerial trends were examined including the need to manage an increasingly diverse work force and harness its capacity for creativity. The management of work teams was discussed along with the continued emphasis on TQM, which requires a number of changes in the human resource function, including a stronger service orientation. The implications of several other managerial trends were also discussed including integrated manufacturing, process reengineering, managing an increasing number of professionals, and helping the organization prepare for and deal with the aftermath of mergers and acquisitions.

Several other trends were also examined including demographic trends such as age bulges and gaps that have resulted from the baby boom and the baby bust. Age bulges will require innovative measures to provide meaningful career advancement for employees whose career routes are blocked by the glut of other candidates. The implications of the increasing number of females in the work force and the growing number of dual-career families were also discussed.

Trends in the utilization of human resources were also examined including the increasing use of temporary or contingent workers, which has expanded to professionals. Implications of the migration of information workers to rural areas and small towns for cost of living and quality of life reasons were also discussed along with the relocation of companies seeking to take advantage of low costs in midwestern, southwestern, and mountain states. The increased internationalization of business and global sourcing of labor were also examined, and it was concluded that human resource strategy must adopt an expanded international perspective. Finally, the human resource implications of AIDS and drug and alcohol abuse were examined.

REFERENCES

1. Verity, John W., and Stephanie A. Forest, "Does IBM Get It Now?" *Business Week*, December 28, 1992, pp. 32–33; Kerwin, Kathleen, and David Woodruff, "Is Detroit Pulling Up to Pass?" *Business Week*, January 11, 1993, p. 63.
2. Drucker, Peter F., "The Coming of the New Organization," *Harvard Business Review*, 66, no. 1 (1988), 45–53; Schein, Edgar H., "Reassessing the 'Divine Rights' of Managers," *Sloan Management Review*, 30, no. 2 (1989), 63–68; Schein, Edgar H, "Increasing Organizational Effectiveness through Better Human Resource Planning and Development," *Sloan Management Review*, 19, no. 1 (1977), 1–20.
3. Drucker, "The Coming of the New Organization."
4. Levitan, Sar, "Beyond 'Trendy' Forecasts: The Next 10 Years for Work," *The Futurist*, 21, no. 6 (1987), 29.

5. Greller, Martin M., and David M. Nee, "Baby Boom and Baby Bust: Corporate Response to the Demographic Challenge of 1990–2010," in *Creating Competitive Edge through Human Resource Applications*, eds. Richard J. Niehaus and Karl F. Price. New York: Plenum Press, 1988, 17–34; Schein, "Increasing Organizational Effectiveness through Better Human Resource Planning and Development."

6. Bussey, J., "Speeding Up: Manufacturers Strive to Slice Time Needed to Develop Products," *The Wall Street Journal*, February 23, 1988, pp. 1, 13; Port, Otis, Zachary Schiller, and Resa W. King, "A Smarter Way to Manufacture," *Business Week*, April 30, 1990, pp. 110–117.

7. Schein, "Reassessing the 'Divine Rights' of Managers"; Schein, Edgar H., "International Human Resource Management: New Directions, Perpetual Issues, and Missing Themes," *Human Resource Management*, 25, no. 1 (1986), 169–176; Applegate, Lynda M., James I. Cash, Jr., and D. Quinn Mills, "Information Technology and Tomorrow's Manager," *Harvard Business Review*, 66, no. 6 (1988), 128–136; Drucker, "The Coming of the New Organization"; Peters, Tom, "Restoring American Competitiveness: Looking for New Models of Organizations," *Academy of Management Executive*, 2, no. 2 (1988), 103–109; Semler, Ricardo, "Managing Without Managers," *Harvard Business Review*, 67, no. 5 (1989), 76–84.

8. Schein, "International Human Resource Management."

9. Greller, Martin M., and David M. Nee, *From Baby Boom to Baby Bust*. Reading, Mass.: Addison-Wesley, 1989.

10. Tanouye, Elyse, "Johnson & Johnson Stays Fit by Shuffling Its Mix of Businesses," *The Wall Street Journal*, December 22, 1992, pp. A1, A4; Greller and Nee, *From Baby Boom to Baby Bust*.

11. Tanouye, "Johnson & Johnson Stays Fit by Shuffling Its Mix of Businesses," A1.

12. Snow, Charles C., Raymond E. Miles, and Henry J. Coleman, Jr., "Managing 21st Century Network Organizations," *Organizational Dynamics*, 20, no. 3 (1992), 5–20.

13. Greller and Nee, *From Baby Boom to Baby Bust*.

14. Ibid.; Greller and Nee, "Baby Boom and Baby Bust: Corporate Response to the Demographic Challenge of 1990–2010"; Rothstein, Mark A., Andria S. Knapp, and Lance Liebman, *Cases and Materials on Employment Law*, 2nd ed. Westbury, N.Y.: Foundation Press, 1991; Colosi, Marco L., "WARN: Hazardous to HR Health?" *Personnel*, 66, no. 4 (1989), 59–67.

15. Greller and Nee, *From Baby Boom to Baby Bust*.

16. Belous, Richard S., "How Human Resource Systems Adjust to the Shift Toward Contingent Workers," *Monthly Labor Review*, 112, no. 3 (1989), 7–12.

17. Neumeier, Shalley, "Economic Intelligence: How Jobs Die—and Are Born," *Fortune*, July 26, 1993, 26.

18. Schuler, Randall S., and Drew L. Harris, "Deming Quality Improvement: Implications for Human Resource Management as Illustrated in a Small Company," *Human Resource Planning*, 14, no. 3 (1991), 191–207; Darling, John R., "Team Building in the Small Business Firm," *Journal of Small Business Management*, 28, no. 3 (1990), 86–91; Forward, Gordon E., "Wide-open Management at Chaparral Steel," *Harvard Business Review*, 64, no. 3 (1986), 96–102; Rogers, T. J., "No Excuses Management," *Harvard Management Review*, 68, no. 4 (1990), 84–98; Semler, Ricardo, "Managing Without Managers."

19. Lipset, Seymour M., "The Work Ethic—Then and Now," *The Public Interest*, 98, (Winter 1990), 61.

20. Lipset, "The Work Ethic—Then and Now"; Harris, T. George, and Robert J. Trotter, "Work Smarter, Not Harder," *Psychology Today*, 23, no. 2 (1989), 33; Skrzycki, Cindy, "Poll Finds Less Worker Emphasis on Materialism," *Washington Post*, January 10, 1989, C1, C4.

21. Pare, Terence P., "The Uncommitted Class of 1989," *Fortune*, 119 (June 5, 1989), 199.

22. Yankelovich, Daniel, and Bernard Lefkowitz, "Work and American Expectations," *National Forum: Phi Kappa Phi Journal*, 62, no. 2 (1982), 3–5.

23. Braham, James, "Dying Loyalty: Companies, Employees Both Less Faithful," *Industry Week*, June 1, 1987, 16 (whole article on pp. 16–17).

24. Braham, "Dying Loyalty: Companies, Employees Both Less Faithful"; "Complain, Complain, Complain: Worker Cynicism on the Rise," *Management Review*, 76, no. 6 (1987), 10–11; Kanter, Donald L., and Philip H. Mirvis, "Cynicism: The New American Malaise," *Business and Society Review*, 77, no. 2 (1991), 57–61.

25. Pinfield, Lawrence T., "A Comparison of Pre- and Postemployment Work Values," *Journal of Management*, 10, no. 3 (1984), 363–370.

26. Elizur, Dov, Ingwer Borg, Raymond Hunt, and Istvan M. Beck, "The Structure of Work Values: A Cross Cultural Comparison," *Journal of Organizational Behavior*, 12 (1991), 21–38.

27. Offermann, Lynn R., and Marilyn K. Gowing, "Organizations of the Future: Changes and Challenges," *American Psychologist*, 45, no. 2 (1990), 95–108; Yankelovich and Lefkowitz, "Work and American Expectations."

28. Skrzycki, "Poll Finds Less Worker Emphasis on Materialism," p. C1.
29. Jarley, Paul, and Jack Fiorito, "Unionism and Changing Employee Views Toward Work," *Journal of Labor Research,* 12, no. 3 (1991), 223–229; Judge, Timothy A., and Robert D. Bretz, Jr., "Effects of Work Values on Job Choice Decisions," *Journal of Applied Psychology,* 77, no. 3 (1992), 261–271.
30. Offermann and Gowing, "Organizations of the Future."
31. Wagel, William H., "On the Horizon: HR in the 1990s," *Personnel,* 67, no. 1 (1990), 11–16; Luthans, Fred, and Linda Thomas, "The Relationship Between Age and Job Satisfaction: Curvilinear Results from an Empirical Study," *Personnel Review,* 18, no. 1 (1989), 23–26.
32. McLeod, Poppy L., and Sharon Alisa Lobel, "The Effects of Ethnic Diversity on Idea Generation in Small Groups," *Academy of Management Best Papers Proceedings,* 1992, 227–231; Cox, Taylor H., and Stacy Blake, "Managing Cultural Diversity: Implications for Organizational Competitiveness," *Academy of Management Executive,* 5, no. 3 (1991), 45–56.
33. Cox and Blake, "Managing Cultural Diversity."
34. Thomas, R. Roosevelt, "From Affirmative Action to Affirming Diversity," *Harvard Business Review,* 68, no. 2 (1990), 107–117.
35. Thomas, "From Affirmative Action to Affirming Diversity," 108.
36. Shenhav, Yehouda, "Entrance of Blacks and Women into Managerial Positions in Scientific and Engineering Occupations: A Longitudinal Analysis," *Academy of Management Journal,* 35, no. 4 (1992), 889–901.
37. Shenhav, "Entrance of Blacks and Women into Managerial Positions in Scientific and Engineering Occupations," 896.
38. McLeod and Lobel, "The Effects of Ethnic Diversity on Idea Generation in Small Groups."
39. Ibid., 229.
40. Katzenbach, Jon R., and Douglas K. Smith, "Why Teams Matter," *The McKinsey Quarterly,* 3 (1992), 3–27.
41. Katzenbach and Smith, "Why Teams Matter," 5.
42. Bergstrom, Robin P., "The Team's the Thing," *Production,* 104, no. 5 (1992), 46–51; Dean, James W., Jr., and Gerald I. Susman, "Organizing for Manufacturable Design," *Harvard Business Review,* 67, no. 1 (1989), 28–32; Sundstrom, Eric, Kenneth P. De Meuse, and David Futrell, "Work Teams: Applications and Effectiveness," *American Psychologist,* 45, no. 2 (1990), 120–133; Katzenbach and Smith, "Why Teams Matter"; Jackson, Susan E., and Eden B. Alvarez, "Working Through Diversity as a Strategic Imperative," in *Diversity in the Workplace: Human Resources Initiatives,* eds. Susan E. Jackson and Associates. New York: Guilford Press, 1993, 13–29; Wolfe, Joseph, Donald D. Bowen, and C. Richard Roberts, "Team-Building Effects on Company Performance," *Simulation and Games,* 20, no. 4 (1989), 388–408.
43. Sundstrom, De Meuse, and Futrell, "Work Teams."
44. Katzenbach and Smith, "Why Teams Matter"; Sisco, Rebecca, "Put Your Money Where Your Teams Are," *Training,* 29, no. 7 (1992), 41–45.
45. Dean and Susman, "Organizing for Manufacturable Design."
46. Bergstrom, "The Team's the Thing."
47. Ibid.
48. Hart, Christopher, and Leonard Schlesinger, "Total Quality Management and the Human Resource Professional: Applying the Baldrige Framework to Human Resources," *Human Resource Management,* 30, no. 4 (1991), 433–454; Barrier, Michael, "Small Firms Put Quality First," *Nation's Business,* May 1992, pp. 22–32; Blackburn, Richard, and Benson Rosen, "Total Quality and Human Resource Management: Lessons Learned from Baldrige Award–Winning Companies," *Academy of Management Executive,* 7, no. 3 (1993), 49–66; Bowen, David E., and Edward E. Lawler, III, "Total Quality-Oriented Human Resources Management," *Organizational Dynamics,* 20, no. 4 (1992), 29–41.
49. Blackburn and Rosen, "Total Quality and Human Resources Management"; Hart and Schlesinger, "Total Quality Management and the Human Resource Professional."
50. Bowen and Lawler, "Total Quality-Oriented Human Resources Management," 31.
51. Ulrich, Dave, Wayne Brockbank, and Arthur Yeung, "Beyond Belief: A Benchmark for Human Resources," *Human Resources Management,* 28, no. 3 (1989), 312.
52. Bowen and Lawler, "Total Quality-Oriented Human Resources Management."
53. Barrier, "Small Firms Put Quality First," 25.
54. Bowen and Lawler, "Total Quality-Oriented Human Resources Management."
55. Blackburn and Rosen, "Total Quality and Human Resources Management."
56. Bowen and Lawler, "Total Quality-Oriented Human Resources Management"; Duncan, Jack, and Joseph G. Van Matre, "The Gospel According to Deming: Is It Really New?" *Business Horizons,* 33, no. 4 (1990), 33–39; Barrier, "Small Firms Put Quality First"; Blackburn and Rosen, "Total Quality and Human Resource Management."

57. Harari, Oren, "Ten Reasons Why TQM Doesn't Work," *Management Review*, 82, no. 1 (1993), 33–38; Blackburn and Rosen, "Total Quality and Human Resource Management"; Harari, Oren, "The Eleventh Reason Why TQM Doesn't Work," *Management Review*, 82, no. 5 (1993), 34–37; Niven, Daniel, "When Times Get Tough, What Happens to TQM," *Harvard Business Review*, 71, no. 3 (1993), 20–34; Schlesinger, Jacob M., Michael Williams, and Craig Forman, "Japan Inc., Wracked by Recession, Takes Stock of Its Methods," *The Wall Street Journal*, September 19, 1993, A1–A4.

58. Niven, "When Times Get Tough, What Happens to TQM," 32.

59. Snell, Scott A., and James W. Dean, Jr., "Integrated Manufacturing and Human Resource Management: A Human Capital Perspective," *Academy of Management Journal*, 35, no. 3 (1992), 467–504.

60. Ibid.

61. Stewart, Thomas A., "Reengineering: The New Management Tool," *Fortune*, August 23, 1993, 41–48; Moad, Jeff, "Does Reengineering Really Work?" *Datamation*, August 1, 1993, 22–28.

62. Stewart, "Reengineering: The New Management Tool," 41–48; Moad, "Does Reengineering Really Work?"

63. Hall, Gene, Jim Rosenthal, and Judy Wade, "How to Make Reengineering Really Work," *Harvard Business Review*, 71, no. 6 (1993), 119–131.

64. Stewart, "Reengineering: The New Management Tool"; Moad, "Does Reengineering Really Work?" Hall, Rosenthal, and Wade, "How to Make Reengineering Really Work."

65. Von Glinow, Mary Anne, *The New Professionals: Managing Today's High-Tech Employees*. Cambridge Mass.: Ballinger, 1988.

66. Von Glinow, *The New Professionals*, 27.

67. Von Glinow, *The New Professionals*.

68. Barkman, Arnold I., John E. Sheridan, and Lawrence H. Peters, "Survival Models of Professional Staff Retention in Public Accounting Firms," *Journal of Managerial Issues*, 4, no. 3 (1992), 339–353.

69. Bruckman, John C., and Scott C. Peters, "Mergers and Acquisitions: The Human Equation," *Employment Relations Today*, 14, no. 1 (1987), 55–63.

70. Bruckman and Peters, "Mergers and Acquisitions," 57.

71. Greller and Nee, *From Baby Boom to Baby Bust*, 47.

72. Bruckman and Peters, "Mergers and Acquisitions."

73. Walker, James W., *Human Resource Planning*. New York: McGraw-Hill, 1980; Greller and Nee, "Baby Boom and Baby Bust: Corporate Response to the Demographic Challenge of 1990–2010"; Greller and Nee, *From Baby Boom to Baby Bust*; Johnston, William B., and Arnold H. Packer, *Workforce 2000: Work and Workers for the Twenty-first Century*. Indianapolis: Hudson Institute, 1987.

74. American Association of Retired Persons, *The Aging Work Force: Managing an Aging Work Force*. Washington, D.C.: American Association of Retired Persons, 1990.

75. Johnston and Packer, *Workforce 2000*.

76. Jasinowski, Jerry, and Sharon Canner, *Meeting the Health Care Crisis*. Washington, D.C.: National Association of Manufacturers, 1989.

77. Rutledge, John, and Deborah Allen, *Rust to Riches*. New York: Harper & Row, 1989.

78. Fullerton, Howard W., "Evaluation of Labor Force Projections to 1990," *Monthly Labor Review*, 115, no. 8 (1992), 3–14; Howard W. Fullerton, "New Labor Force Projections, Spanning 1988 to 2000," *Monthly Labor Review*, 112, no. 11 (1989), 3–12.

79. Bowles, Valerie B., and Arthur R. Riles, Jr., "Work Place Challenges for Managers in the Twenty-first Century," in *Creating the Competitive Edge through Human Resource Applications*, eds. Richard J. Niehaus and Karl F. Price. New York: Plenum Press, 1988, 35–46.

80. ARCO, *ARCO Annual Report*, 1986.

81. Greller and Nee, "Baby Boom and Baby Bust: Corporate Response to the Demographic Challenge of 1990–2010"; American Association of Retired Persons, *The Aging Work Force*; Machan, Dyan, "Cultivating the Gray," *Forbes*, September 14, 1989, 127–128; Morrison, Peter A., "Applied Demography: Its Growing Scope and Future Direction," *The Futurist*, 24, no. 2 (1990), 9–15.

82. Machan, Dyan, "Cultivating the Gray."

83. Greller and Nee, "Baby Boom and Baby Bust: Corporate Response to the Demographic Challenge of 1990–2010"; Murray, Alan, "Bush Sees Labor Shortage, Looks Abroad," *The Wall Street Journal*, February 7, 1990; Johnston and Packer, *Workforce 2000*.

84. Usdansky, Margaret L., "256,561,239 Live in the USA," *USA Today*, December 31, 1992, 1A.

85. Morrison, "Applied Demography."

86. Johnston and Packer, *Workforce 2000*.

87. Morrison, "Applied Demography," 11.

88. Johnston and Packer, *Workforce 2000*, 100.

89. Johnston and Packer, *Workforce 2000*.

90. Jackson, Susan E., and Randall S. Schuler, "Human Resource Planning: Challenges for Industrial/Organizational Psychologists," *American Psychologist*, 45, no. 2 (1990), 223–239.

91. Johnston and Packer, *Workforce 2000*.

92. Naisbitt, John, and Patricia Aburdene, *Megatrends 2000: Ten New Directions for the 1990s*. New York: William Morrow, 1990.

93. Schrenk, Lorenz P., "Environmental Scanning," in *Human Resource Management: Evolving Roles and Responsibilities*, ed. Lee Dyer. Washington, D.C.: Bureau of National Affairs, 1988, 1-88 to 1-124; Kovach, Kenneth A., and John A. Pearce II, "HR Strategic Mandates for the 1990s," *Personnel*, 67, no. 4 (1990), 50–55; Redwood, Anthony, "Human Resources Management in the 1990s," *Business Horizons*, 33, no. 1 (1990), 74–80; Stautberg, Susan S., "Status Report: The Corporation and Trends in Family Issues," *Human Resource Management*, 26, no. 2 (1987), 277–290.

94. Morrison, "Applied Demography."

95. Stautberg, "Status Report."

96. Naisbitt and Aburdene, *Megatrends 2000*.

97. Metzger, Robert O., and Mary Ann Von Glinow, "Off-Site Workers: At Home and Abroad," *California Management Review*, 30, no. 3 (1988), 101–109.

98. Stern, Richard L., and John H. Taylor, "Is the Golden State Losing It?" *Forbes*, 146, no. 10 (October 1990), 86–90.

99. Kerwin, Kathleen, and Ronald Grover, "California Steamin': Business Makes Tracks from L.A.," *Business Week*, May 13, 1991, 44–45.

100. Barsky, Neil, "Grace Will Move Most of Its Staff Out of New York," *The Wall Street Journal*, January 9, 1991, B1.

101. Barrier, Michael, "Temporary Assignment," *Nation's Business*, 77, no. 10 (October 1989), 34–36; Mangum, Garth, Donald Mayall, and Kristin Nelson, "The Temporary Help Industry: A Response to the Dual Internal Labor Markets," *Industrial and Labor Relations Review*, 28, no. 4 (1985), 599–611; Belous, Richard S., "How Human Resource Systems Adjust to the Shift Toward Contingent Workers," *Monthly Labor Review*, 112, no. 3 (1989), 7–12; Moberly, Robert B., "Temporary, Part-Time, and Other Atypical Employment Relationships in the United States," *Labor Law Journal*, 38, no. 11 (1987), 689–696.

102. Howe, Wayne J., "Temporary Help Workers: Who They Are, What Jobs They Hold," *Monthly Labor Review*, 109, no. 11 (1986), 45–47.

103. Personick, Valerie A., "Industry Output and Employment: A Slower Trend for the Nineties," *Monthly Labor Review*, 111, no. 11 (1989), 25–41.

104. Barrier, "Temporary Assignments"; Mangum, Mayall, and Nelson, "The Temporary Help Industry."

105. Personick, "Industry Output and Employment"; Davidson, Margaret, "Temporary Financial Executives: Who Are They and Who Uses Them?" *Financial Executive*, 6, no. 2 (1990), 15–18; Ludlum, David A., "Now It's Temporary Managers," *Computerworld*, September 5, 1988, 92; Mangum, Mayall, and Nelson, "The Temporary Help Industry."

106. Mitchell, Daniel J. B., and Mahmood A. Zaidi, "Macroeconomic Conditions and HRM-IR Practice," *Industrial Relations*, 29, no. 2 (1990), 164–188; Barrier, "Temporary Assignment." Howe, "Temporary Help Workers"; Moberly, "Temporary, Part-Time, and Other Atypical Employment Relationships in the United States."

107. Barrier, "Temporary Assignment."

108. Darrow, Terri L., "Temporary Expertise Develops into a Permanent Solution," *Management Review*, 78, no. 11 (1989), 50–52; Mangum, Mayall, and Nelson, "The Temporary Help Industry."

109. Howe, "Temporary Help Workers"; Barrier, "Temporary Assignment"; Rothstein, Knapp, and Liebman, *Cases and Materials on Employment Law;* Colosi, "WARN: Hazardous to HR Health?" Barrier, "Temporary Assignment"; Darrow, "Temporary Expertise Develops into a Permanent Solution."

110. Resnick, Rosalind, "Leasing Workers," *Nation's Business*, 80, 11 (1992), 20–28.

111. Belous, "How Human Resource Systems Adjust to the Shift Toward Contingent Workers"; Mangum, Mayall, and Nelson, "The Temporary Help Industry"; Howe, "Temporary Help Workers."

112. Belous, "How Human Resource Systems Adjust to the Shift Toward Contingent Workers"; Davidson, "Temporary Financial Executives"; Darrow, "Temporary Expertise Develops into a Permanent Solution"; Moberly, "Temporary, Part-Time, and Other Atypical Employment Relationships in the United States."

113. Resnick, "Leasing Workers."

114. Dana Corporation, *Annual Report*, 1987.

115. Honeywell Corporation, *Annual Report*, 1985.

116. Metzger and Von Glinow, "Off-Site Workers: At Home and Abroad."

117. Flint, Jerry, "Letter from Germany," *Forbes*, October 29, 1990, 72–76.
118. Davis, Bob, and Jackie Calmes, "House Approves NAFTA, Providing President with Crucial Victory," *The Wall Street Journal*, November 18, 1993, A1–A14.
119. Concerning Cars, Inc., "5:2 Export Odds Against U.S. with #3 Trading Partner Will Disappear," *Concerning Cars and Trucks: Information in the Public Interest*, 6, no. 6 (1993), 2.
120. Friedman, Sheldon, "Why a Bad NAFTA Is Worse Than No NAFTA," *Labor Law Journal*, 43, no. 8 (1992), 535–39.
121. Magnusson, Paul, "How Many Broom-Makers Does It Take to Kill a Trade Pact?" *Business Week*, July 20, 1992, 29–30.
122. Salinas, Carlos, "We Had to React Quickly: An Interview with President Carlos Salinas," *Forbes*, August 17, 1992, 66.
123. Masur, Sandra, "The North American Free Trade Agreement: Why It's in the Interest of U.S. Business," *Columbia Journal of World Business*, 26, no. 2 (1991), 99–103.
124. Cerruti, James L., and Joseph Holtzman, "Business Strategy in the New European Landscape," *Journal of Business Strategy*, 10, no. 6 (1990), 18–23; Goette, Eckart E., "Europe 1992: Update for Business Planners," *Journal of Business Strategy*, 10, no. 2 (1990), 10–13; Devinney, Timothy M., and William C. Hightower, *European Markets After 1992*. Lexington, Mass.: Lexington Books, 1991; Oster, Patrick, Bill Javetski, and Gail E. Schares, "It's 1993—and Europe Can Pop a Few Corks After All," *Business Week*, January 11, 1993, 48.
125. Kirp, David L., "Uncommon Decency: Pacific Bell Responds to AIDS," *Harvard Business Review*, 67, no. 3 (1989), 140–151.
126. Ibid.
127. George, Jennifer M., Thomas F. Reed, Karen A. Ballard, Jessie Conlin, and Jane Fielding, "Contact with AIDS Patients as a Source of Work-Related Distress: Effects of Organizational and Social Support," *Academy of Management Journal*, 36, no. 1 (1993), 157–171.
128. General Motors Corporation, *Public Interest Report 1989*. Detroit: General Motors Corporation, 1989.
129. Giles, Albert L., and Gregory R. Post, "Comprehensive Screening Ensures Drug Test Accuracy," *Risk Management*, 36, no. 9 (1989), 28–31.

Case 2

RESURGENCE OF U.S. MANUFACTURING

According to economists John Rutledge and Deborah Allen, the future may bring a resurgence of U.S. manufacturing. This may be stimulated by increased investment during the remainder of the 1990s in the capital base of machinery and tools by which products are manufactured. At present, many U.S. manufacturers are using outdated tools and machines, compared with those of global competitors. As a result, some U.S. products are still not competitive in price or quality.

Factors expected to drive the resurgence of manufacturing include a relatively low rate of inflation, the Tax Reform Act of 1986, and the demographic influences associated with the baby boom. U.S. manufacturing investment stagnated during the 1970s because of high rates of inflation, which reached 14 percent at the end of the 1970s. High inflation caused investors to purchase tangible assets, such as hotels and office buildings, as inflation hedges. Since stocks and bonds do not provide this same hedge, they became less attractive investments and funding for the plant and equipment needed for production of goods became more difficult to obtain. The attack on inflation during the 1980s and tax reform in 1986 made tangible assets less attractive as inflation hedges and tax shields. Stocks and bonds then became relatively more attractive.[1]

A major influence on manufacturing during the remainder of the 1990s appears to be the aging of the baby boomers. As the baby boomers reach their mid-forties, according to life-cycle theories, they should start to save more. The savings of this huge age cohort are expected to serve as a major stimulus to funding the new plant and equipment which may make U.S. manufacturing competitive again in world markets. Rutledge and Allen predicted that "by 1995, the savings rate should be back to 6 percent and 10 percent by 2000, with most of the gain caused by the aging of the Baby Boomers."[2]

Rutledge and Allen's predictions appear to have been on track as exports of manufactured goods rose from $168 billion in 1985 to $370 billion in 1992.[3] Additionally, employment in manufacturing has been fairly stable in recent years while manufacturing productivity has increased by an average of just under 3 percent per year and inflation-adjusted manufacturing pay levels have remained constant. With increased productivity, fewer workers are needed to manufacture the same amount of goods. Thus, the health of the industry is not necessarily indicated by whether there is a growing or declining level of employment. Within the rapidly growing services industry, vendors supplying services such as computer systems support, account for manufacturing competitiveness as well as employment.[4]

Although manufacturing jobs are expected to drop slightly to 19.1 million by 2000, this is higher than the 18.4 million jobs in 1983. Of more importance for strategy and human resource management is the changing distribution of jobs within manufacturing. Although only 316,000 total jobs are expected to be lost in manufacturing by the year 2000, the lower-skilled jobs will have relatively large losses as operators, fabricators, and laborers should lose approximately 714,000 jobs. Fortunately, the growth in technical, professional and managerial jobs will partially offset the job losses in the lower-skilled areas.[5]

Questions

1. Based on the information you know about current economic and business conditions, what are the greatest threats to Rutledge and Allen's predictions of a resurgence of manufacturing in the United States?
2. Even if there is a resurgence in U.S. manufacturing, how might the skills of employees and work organizations of future manufacturing environments differ from those of the past?
3. How would you expect the managerial trends discussed in Chapter 2 to affect human resource practices and policies in future manufacturing industries?
4. Describe how the human resource and managerial environment of a manufacturing firm in the mid-1990s differs from the same environment in the 1960s. (You may need to do some reading or interview someone who can provide a historical perspective.) Try to explain these differences with respect to the effects of technology, organizational structure, worker values, managerial trends, demographic trends, and trends in the utilization of human resources.

5. Explain how the North American Free Trade Agreement may affect manufacturing in the United States by the year 2000.

REFERENCES

1. Rutledge, John, and Deborah Allen, *Rust to Riches*. New York: Harper & Row, 1989.
2. Ibid., 74–75.
3. Flint, Jerry, "The Myth of U.S. Manufacturing's Decline," *Forbes*, January 18, 1993, 40–42.
4. Masur, Sandra, "The North American Free Trade Agreement: Why It's in the Interest of U.S. Business," *Columbia Journal of World Business*, 26, no. 2 (1991) 99–103; Flint, "The Myth of U.S. Manufacturing's Decline."
5. Personick, Valerie A., "Industry Output and Employment: A Slower Trend for the Nineties," *Monthly Labor Review*, 111, no. 11 (1989), 25–41.

3

THE HUMAN RESOURCE LEGAL ENVIRONMENT

The third component of the conceptual framework for this book is the legal environment of human resources. Because of its increasing coverage and complexity, the legal environment has more strategic importance than ever before. All managers making input into strategic decisions, not just those involved in human resources, must be familiar with the laws that regulate employer conduct in dealing with employees. Because the coverage of such laws and regulations has become so pervasive they must be considered as input in overall strategy formulation and have probably increased the involvement of human resource management in the process. There is also growing recognition of the strategic importance of having good human resource management programs in order to limit the financial outlays of litigation initiated by disgruntled employees and job applicants. Further, as the following quotation by Francine Hall and Elizabeth Hall indicates, practices insuring legal compliance can sometimes provide a source of strategic advantage.[1]

> While few firms have missions that are inconsistent with the ADA [Americans With Disabilities Act of 1990], many have yet to seize the opportunity to link compliance with purpose. . . . There are many examples of how select

Author's Note: In preparing this chapter the author drew on a large number of articles and books. A few sources were particularly helpful and were cited several times. These sources, which would be excellent reference books for practitioners, are Robert Jacobs and Cora Koch's *Legal Compliance Guide to Personnel Management,* David Twomey's *Equal Employment Opportunity Law,* Patrick Cibon's and James Castagnera's *Labor and Employment Law,* Commerce Clearing House's *Labor Law Course,* and Mark Rothstein, Andria Knapp, and Lance Liebman's *Cases and Materials on Employment Law.*

companies have tied their human resource initiatives to their strategic advantage. Johnson and Johnson, Stride-Rite, and others have become examples of the "family friendly" movement. McDonald's has been a forerunner by embracing the ADA and modeling the employment of learning-disabled young adults. Most families (the target market for McDonald's) can identify with the need to give a child a chance.[2]

Importance to Strategy

The importance of the human resource legal environment can be demonstrated with a few examples. For instance, in order to respond more quickly to the needs of its customers, a company might consider a decentralization strategy in which traditional functional responsibilities are reassigned to line units. The human resource function might be decentralized by reassigning corporate-level human resource responsibilities such as recruitment and staffing to the line units. However, with passage of the Americans with Disabilities Act of 1990, the company may wish to avoid increased liability from violations of disabled applicants' rights which might be more likely when line managers have sole responsibility for recruitment and staffing. The legal environment might cause the company to modify its approach to decentralization.

Similarly, the advance notification requirements of the Worker Adjustment and Retraining Notification Act, which are covered in the Chapter 6 discussion of strategy implementation, may affect the timing of a company's strategic decision to withdraw from a line of business. More strategic implications of the legal environment, specifically those involving economy and managerial flexibility, will be discussed at the end of the chapter after coverage of the various federal laws. The greatest emphasis in this chapter will be the federal regulatory environment, although some areas of state law will also be covered. Areas of the legal environment to be discussed include equal employment opportunity, compensation, employee relations, and labor relations and collective bargaining.

EQUAL EMPLOYMENT OPPORTUNITY

Continued emphasis on equal employment opportunity and affirmative action appears to be a reality for the foreseeable future and is an issue of importance for strategic management. The following section will provide a review of equal employment opportunity legislation, beginning with civil rights legislation.

Civil Rights Legislation

Title VII of the Civil Rights Act of 1964 provides the basic requirements for equal employment opportunity. As amended by the Equal Employment Opportunity Act of 1972, Title VII prohibits the following discriminatory practices:

> It shall be an unlawful employment practice for an employer—(1) to fail or
> refuse to hire or to discharge any individual, or otherwise to discriminate
> against any individual with respect to his compensation, terms, conditions, or
> privileges of employment, because of such individual's race, color, religion,
> sex, or national origin; or (2) to limit, segregate, or classify his employees or
> applicants for employment in any way which would deprive or tend to
> deprive any individual of employment opportunities or otherwise adversely
> affect his status as an employee, because of such individual's race, color, reli-
> gion, sex, or national origin.[3]

In addition to employers having at least 15 employees, the act also
applies to employment agencies and labor organizations. In addition to
specifying these unlawful practices, the Civil Rights Act of 1964 established
the Equal Employment Opportunity Commission (EEOC) to administer and
enforce the legislation.[4] In 1972 the Equal Employment Opportunity Act
expanded the EEOC's enforcement powers by allowing it to go to court to
bring charges of discrimination.[5]

This legislation prohibits two forms of discrimination. The first form is
called *disparate treatment*. With this type of discrimination, the employer
intentionally discriminates against individuals on the basis of one of the prohibited criteria, such as by not hiring them because of their race. The legislation also prohibits employment practices having an indirect but *adverse
impact* on protected groups, which is called *disparate impact* discrimination.
In contrast to the other form, a discriminatory intent is not required to establish that discrimination has occurred. The term *adverse impact* is frequently
used synonymously with the term *disparate impact*.[6]

An example of disparate impact discrimination would be where an
employer uses an invalid selection test, having no ability to predict successful job performance. In addition to the test's lack of validity, it rejects a disproportionate number of applicants from protected groups. Because of the
test's adverse impact and lack of validity, this would constitute a form of disparate impact discrimination. This interpretation of Title VII was established
in the landmark U.S. Supreme Court decision, *Griggs v. Duke Power Co.*,
which prohibited the use of selection tests having an adverse impact but no
relationship to job performance.[7] Specifically, the court stated the following:

> The Act proscribes not only overt discrimination but also practices that are
> fair in form, but discriminatory in operation. The touchstone is business
> necessity. If an employment practice which operates to exclude Negroes can-
> not be shown to be related to job performance, the practice is prohibited.[8]

On the other hand, if such a test is valid or job-related, which means
that it predicts applicants' performance on the job, it can be used. This is true
even if it has an adverse impact by rejecting a disproportionate number of
applicants from protected groups. However, as a result of provisions of the
Civil Rights Act of 1991, if a plaintiff can demonstrate that the employer is
unwilling to use an alternate selection procedure having less adverse impact,

the employer's use of the test may constitute a violation of the law. Additionally, although tests appear to trigger more concerns over disparate impact, the need to establish validity also extends to other selection procedures, such as the use of educational criteria for selection purposes, since they may also have a disparate impact.[9]

In addition to validity-based exceptions to prohibitions against the use of procedures having a disparate impact, there are other exceptions. Employers can use selection criteria having a disparate impact by demonstrating a *business necessity*. For example, a public transportation agency's decision not to hire methadone users was upheld, even for jobs in which safety was not an issue.[10] *Bona fide occupational qualifications* (BFOQ) may also provide highly restricted exceptions to prohibitions against disparate treatment. As an example, actors and models can be selected on the basis of their gender. Further, although race BFOQ's are prohibited, in some narrowly defined instances, applicants have been selected on the basis of race. These have been justified for reasons of business necessity and have involved actors and police undercover roles. As a result of the Civil Rights Act of 1991, the status of this special exemption is now in question.[11]

In order to enforce the law, the EEOC, along with other enforcement agencies, adopted the *Uniform Guidelines on Employee Selection Procedures*, which cover such issues as the validation of selection procedures.[12] These guidelines essentially call for sound psychometric procedures that employers should follow in the absence of legislation. Any doubts about the employer's obligation to follow the guidelines were resolved in 1975 in a second landmark U.S. Supreme Court decision involving *Albemarle Paper Co. v. Moody*.[13] In this case the employer had not conducted a suitable job analysis and its test validation was deficient.[14] In this ruling, the Supreme Court made it clear that employers should follow the guidelines. The Court's emphasis on job analysis in this decision points out the underlying importance of job analysis to test validation, performance evaluation, and job evaluation.

One of the technical details explained in the guidelines is the definition of *adverse impact*. Specifically, the guidelines define *adverse impact* as the following:

> A selection rate for any race, sex, or ethnic group which is less than four-fifths ($^4/_5$) (or eighty percent) of the rate for the group with the highest rate will generally be regarded by the Federal enforcement agencies as evidence of adverse impact.[15]

There are problems with such definitions of *adverse impact* since ratios computed on the basis of small numbers of employees can cause unstable results. In such cases, statistical significance tests would be more appropriate. Interestingly, it appears that courts are able to deal with these limitations. As Richard Arvey and Robert H. Faley have observed, "Courts, judges, and lawyers are now demonstrating considerable statistical sophistication in employment discrimination cases."[16]

As a result of congressional disappointment with a number of U.S. Supreme Court decisions in 1989, which were felt to decrease the impact of existing civil rights legislation, the Civil Rights Act of 1991 was passed and signed by President Bush. Several provisions of the act represent significant changes in the regulatory environment. Disparate impact is now part of the statute along with a burden of proof procedure that requires stronger employer justification of selection practices. The consequences of these changes are that employers have greater motivation to perform competent job analysis, specify important dimensions of job performance, and validate selection procedures.[17] Because there are several common approaches to job analysis, guides to their strengths and weaknesses, such as one prepared by Hubert Feild and Robert Gatewood, may be helpful in this regard.[18]

Some observers have predicted that employers may resort to hiring by quota in order to eliminate any disparate impact on protected groups. There have been anecdotal reports of quota-based overt reverse discrimination in retention decisions where companies have been acquired by other companies.[19] In any event, "bottom line" defenses, at which such efforts may be directed, are questionable. The inadequacy of such defenses has been pointed out in the Supreme Court's *Connecticut v. Teal* decision.[20]

The Civil Rights Act of 1991 also prevents the *race-norming* of test scores. An example of such a practice could involve test cutoff scores. With this example of race-norming, members of a protected group are hired if their scores are above the eightieth percentile of scores from applicants in the protected group. Applicants from unprotected groups would be hired if their scores are above the eightieth percentile of scores obtained by unprotected group members. Such a practice is likely to expose employers to reverse discrimination liabilities. Other important components of the Civil Rights Act of 1991 are the provision for punitive, as well as compensatory, damages for intentional discrimination; employers' defenses in so-called mixed-motive discrimination cases in which selection decisions have drawn on both legal and illegal criteria; and the timing of charges against discriminatory seniority systems.[21] The Civil Rights Act of 1991 also has strategic implications for U.S.-based multinational corporations having U.S. employees in their foreign operations. As a result of the 1991 amendment, the Civil Rights Act now applies extra-territorially to these employees.[22]

In addition to this legislation, employers doing business with the federal government must comply with the equal employment opportunity requirements specified in Executive Order 11246, its amendments, and Executive Order 11141. These orders prohibit employment discrimination based on race, color, religion, sex, or national origin. Smaller employers having contracts of at least $10,000 are prohibited from discriminating while employers having at least 50 employees and federal contracts of at least $50,000 or more must file written *affirmative action plans*. These plans must be filed with the Office of Federal Contract Compliance Programs (OFCCP), which enforces the executive orders. As a part of the preparation of an affirmative action plan, the employer must conduct a *utilization analysis* of members of protected groups within the company, at both entry-level and higher-level positions. These utilization levels must then be compared with an *availability analysis* of minorities and females in the company's relevant labor markets. Where minorities and females are under-represented according to the utilization analysis, the employer must negotiate acceptable goals and timetables with the OFCCP. Aside from the affirmative action plan requirements of the OFCCP, courts may require employers that are found guilty of egregious Title VII violations to pursue affirmative action plans.[23]

Unfortunately, although the Civil Rights Act was passed over three decades ago and progress has been made, justification for the continuance of affirmation action programs is apparent. Behaviors even at the highest levels of government provide evidence of the need for protection against discrimination and advancement of minorities and women. An example of such need is provided by the U.S. Senate's confirmation hearings in 1993 of Zoe Baird, the Clinton administration's first nominee for the U.S. attorney general position. The ill-fated hearings provided the following exchange: "Senator Joseph Biden asked Ms. Baird to state how many hours she was away from her child. Would he have asked that of any male nominee?"[24] Ironically another legal issue, Ms. Baird's employment of an illegal alien in a domestic role, eventually ruined her and another nominee's chances for confirmation.

Age Discrimination

Discrimination against employees and job applicants of age forty or over is prohibited by the Age Discrimination in Employment Act (ADEA), which covers private sector employers having at least twenty employees. The act also covers governmental employers at the state and local level. Since passage of the ADEA in 1967, it has been amended in 1978 and 1986. The original legislation protected individuals of ages forty to sixty-five while the 1978 amendments increased the upper limit of the protected age category to seventy. In 1986 the ADEA was amended to eliminate the upper limit of the protected age category, making it illegal to discriminate against anyone forty years of age or older. Exceptions to these prohibitions include executives, who can be required to retire at age sixty-five; firefighters and police officers; and elected governmental officials and policy-level appointees. In addition to ethical motivations for complying with the provisions of ADEA, another reason for compliance is that the financial costs for violating the act can be severe. For willful violations of the act, employers may be liable for double the amount of actual damages.[25]

In order to cope with the removal of upper age limits in the legislation, employers are advised to adopt objective performance standards, preferably in writing. By using such standards as a basis for treatment of all employees, regardless of age, any decrease in performance can be documented and properly attributed to legitimate aspects of performance rather than age.

Another suggestion is to ensure that periodic performance evaluations are conducted for all employees, including those age forty and older. A further suggestion is to train employees' supervisors and managers not to use age in making employment decisions. As discussed later, in this era of downsizing, managers need to exercise care in administering voluntary early retirement programs so as to not violate ADEA. Finally, managers should attempt to maintain high levels of job satisfaction and self-esteem among older employees. Declines in such attitudes have been found to be associated with perceptions of age discrimination.[26]

In addition to the amendments to ADEA already noted, the act was amended again in 1990 by the Older Workers Benefit Protection Act. This act prevents employers from providing lower levels of benefits to older workers unless it can be demonstrated that the provision of equal benefits for older workers is more costly. The act also addresses the coercive circumstances in which older workers sometimes waive their rights to pursue age discrimination claims. Along with company downsizing strategies, there has been an increase in the number of companies using such waivers to reduce the number of older employees in their work forces. This procedure commonly involves offering early retirement settlements to older workers in return for waivers of such employees' rights to pursue age discrimination claims under ADEA.[27] Unfortunately, the conditions under which these waivers are obtained may be described as follows: "The employee in such an instance is usually given two options: sign the waiver and receive the benefits or suffer a dismissal due to the elimination of the job through what is commonly called 'company reorganization efforts.'"[28] As a result of this amendment to ADEA, specific procedures are required for the legitimate use of such waivers in downsizing strategies. The amendment requires that the wording must be understood by an average employee and that waived rights must be specified. Also, postagreement rights cannot be waived, and consideration beyond the employee's current pension and compensation entitlements must be provided. Employees must also be provided with written advice to obtain assistance from an attorney. Additionally, the employee is permitted to revoke the waiver within a seven-day period, and a time period of twenty-one days is provided for employees' consideration of the offer. A consideration period of forty-five days and other conditions apply when exit incentives are involved.[29]

Sexual Harassment

Charges of sexual harassment are occurring with increasing frequency in both private sector companies as well as in governmental organizations. Clearly, the U.S. Senate confirmation hearings of Clarence Thomas highlighted the emotionally charged nature of the issue. Even a popular novel, *Disclosure* by Michael Crichton, describes the difficulty of discerning the truth in such matters.[30] In the state of Colorado alone, there has been a 33 percent annual escalation in harassment suits brought by women during recent years. Further, at the national level there were 7,496 such accusations resulting in lawsuits in one year. Interestingly, males filed 9.5 percent of these accusations.[31] The Navy's embarrassing Tailhook scandal points out how resistant some organizations have been to this form of sex or gender discrimination.[32] Even the FBI has not been immune from such problems, as there have been allegations about the sexual harassment of female agents.[33] Although discrimination according to sex was first prohibited by Title VII of the Civil Rights Act of 1964, courts did not begin to treat sexual harassment as a violation of the act until the late 1970s, followed shortly by its codification in 1980 in the Equal Employment Opportunity Commission's *Guidelines on Discrimination Because of Sex.*[34] Sexual harassment is specified in the EEOC guidelines as follows:

> Unwelcome sexual advances, requests for sexual favors, and other verbal or physical conduct of a sexual nature constitute sexual harassment when (1) submission to such conduct is made either explicitly or implicitly a term or condition of an individual's employment, (2) submission to or rejection of such conduct by an individual is used as a basis for employment decisions affecting such individual, or (3) such conduct has the purpose or effect of unreasonably interfering with an individual's work performance or creating an intimidating, hostile, or offensive working environment.[35]

In the 1986 *Meritor Savings Bank v. Vinson* decision, the U.S. Supreme Court agreed that sexual harassment constitutes gender discrimination, which is prohibited by Title VII.[36] An important component of the EEOC's specification of sexual harassment is that it places emphasis on the "unwelcome" nature of sexual advances, not simply whether such advances are voluntary. The first two specifications of sexual harassment, also called sexual blackmail or *quid pro quo* actions, require little explanation. However, the definition of an "intimidating, hostile, or offensive working environment" needs further explanation. Aside from physical contact, such as touching and pinching, lesser actions such as using sexually vulgar language, telling dirty jokes, and placing sexually demeaning pictures on walls and lockers have been found to contribute to such environments. One of the critical determinants of such an environment is whether a *reasonable* person would have been offended, although the term is subject to varying interpretations. In order to reduce the likelihood of charges of sexual harassment, companies need to educate their employees of both genders that actions as seemingly harmless as telling an off-color joke can be viewed as contributing to a hostile or offensive environment. Employees have to be aware that their actions may be offensive to others and have to modify their behavior or else face disciplinary action.[37]

Unfortunately, a cause of sexual harassment is that many men do not perceive such behaviors to be offensive while many women do.[38] This could be a costly difference in perceptions because sexual remarks were the basis for approximately 50 percent of the sexual harassment claims examined in a recent study.[39] Interestingly, hostile environment cases have accounted for the bulk of sexual harassment, as one study found 75 percent due solely to a hostile environment and another 19 percent resulting from a combination of hostile environment and quid pro quo harassment.[40]

Even with the best training program, there is always a strong likelihood that someone will behave in a manner offensive to another employee. The literature points out that if the behavior constitutes an isolated event and not a pattern (and presumably not too extreme), the employer may not incur liability. The likelihood of liability may also be reduced if the employer quickly repudiates the behavior and takes disciplinary action against the harasser. Needless to say, before taking disciplinary action, the employer must make sure that the accused has an opportunity to present his or her side of the incident and that the other elements of due process have been preserved. Of course, due to the sensitive nature of sexual harassment, it is essential to handle such matters with confidentiality.[41]

Employers should take several precautions against sexual harassment. Some of these actions may also be helpful for reducing employer liability in the event that sexual harassment charges are filed. Specifically, the employer should do the following: (1) Institute a policy prohibiting sexual harassment. Nonetheless, employers should realize that such policies are not, by themselves, adequate shields against liability. (2) Communicate the policy to all employees. (3) Train employees as to behaviors that will likely be viewed as sexual harassment. (4) Implement a complaint procedure for reporting allegations of sexual harassment. This procedure should bypass the employee's immediate supervisor because the harasser often occupies this position. (5) Investigate, in a timely manner, all claims of sexual harassment. (6) Repudiate the behavior after verifying the truthfulness of the allegation. (7) Take timely and appropriate disciplinary action against the harasser. (8) Set a consistent pattern of appropriate disciplinary action over time.[42] (9) Insure that there is no retaliation against an employee making a complaint. Unfortunately, retaliation—which is also a violation of Title VII—has been a common problem for women making such complaints.[43] The fact that supervisors are usually the harassers compounds the problem. One study has found them to be the harassers in approximately 79 percent of the cases.[44]

Aside from these suggestions derived from court decisions and practitioner advice, a recent empirical analysis of federal sexual harassment cases provides additional guidance. Specifically, the study found that complainants were more likely to prevail in instances of severe harassment where they had witnesses or documentation, where they informed the employer of the problem before initiating litigation, and where the employer failed to act.[45] Another earlier study by the same researchers analyzed charges of sexual harassment filed with a state human rights agency. As in the more recent study, complainants were more successful when the sexual harassment was severe, there were witnesses, and the employee informed management of the problem prior to pursuing the issue through outside agencies.[46]

Another problem area for employers was identified in the *Meritor Savings Bank v. Vinson* decision. According to this decision, liabilities can be incurred without the employer's knowledge that sexual harassment is occurring, as long as the employer should have known.[47] In addition to being responsible for the actions of their supervisory and managerial personnel, employers are also liable for the actions of co-workers. Furthermore, employers may even be liable for the actions of customers. In the latter circumstance, as demonstrated in the *EEOC v. Sage Realty Corp.* decision, the employer may incur sexual harassment liabilities for such actions as requiring employees to wear proactive attire.[48]

Unfortunately, the legal protections against the serious problems of sexual harassment also have the potential to cause other harm. The following account of a female consultant's experience is illustrative of the problem. While conducting a seminar for a group of accountants, the consultant was emphasizing a point about the positive value of physical touch in a business context. This incident occurred while the consultant briefly took on the role of a manager who was temporarily turning over authority to a subordinate manager. To emphasize her point, she selected a member of the group, placed her hand on the man's shoulder, and made a statement to the effect that she was placing him in command during her absence. The positive impact of physical touch was quickly conveyed to the audience. Then, in an attempt to demonstrate inappropriate office behavior and add a point of humor, the consultant touched the bare knee of a male participant wearing Bermuda shorts. The incident and consequences are described in the following account:

> Saying, "Of course how and where you touch is very important," I touched the man's bare knee. As I walked away, I heard him say, "I'm a happily married man." I smiled in acknowledgment, assuming he was just making a follow-up remark to generate a little more audience laughter. . . . Two days later, I received . . . a letter of complaint from the man in the audience. He complained that he and his wife (who had not attended the seminar) felt sexually harassed and were calling for my resignation. . . . Since there were 50-some witnesses (other audience members) who could speak about the situation, I was ultimately cleared of any wrongdoing. But the male accuser wouldn't leave it alone. . . . Before it was over, I was fired from my seminar contract of seven years. . . .[49]

Thus, some allegations of sexual harassment will be false and have the potential to damage innocent individuals unless managers exercise appropriate diligence in ascertaining the truth. Further, the employer should take care to preserve the rights and reputation of the accused. Taking premature disciplinary action against an innocent accused employee only compounds the problem.

Aside from the prohibited behavior involved in sexual harassment, office romances are common relationships among consenting adults. Such relationships will probably increase in the future as workplaces become even more balanced in their proportions of male and female employees. Such romances are usually not job-related and therefore none of the employer's business. Nonetheless, when a supervisory relationship is involved, or the romance involves two high-level managerial equals, such relationships can create morale problems, conflicts of interests, and biases in power alliances.[50] Of course, problems of sexual harassment are more likely to arise with supervisory relationships. The probability of such romances evolving into claims of sexual harassment are increased by the fact that in the bulk of such relationships (74 percent), the male is higher in the organization's hierarchy than the female. In more than 25 percent of these romances, the male is her supervisor.[51] In closing this discussion of sexual harassment, some of the best overall guidance to pass on to supervisory personnel may be that offered by a seasoned manager with whom the author has worked. That advice is the following: "Remember that today's willing participant in an office romance is tomorrow's litigant."

Pregnancy Discrimination

As indicated in Chapter 2, by the year 2000, 47 percent of the work force will be comprised of women.[52] These women are expected to have 2.3 million babies in the year 2000. As a result of the increasing number of employees who will be having babies, it is important that employers and management strategists understand these female employees' legal protections. The primary legislation in this area is the Pregnancy Discrimination Act, passed in 1978 as an amendment to Title VII. The act applies to employers having at least fifteen employees and provides several protections. Employers are not allowed to reject job applicants or refuse to promote employees for reasons of pregnancy, demote or otherwise penalize pregnant workers, nor terminate employees based on pregnancy. Further, when employers provide health insurance, medical leave, post-leave reinstatement, and disability benefits, they cannot deny such benefits when pregnancy is the medical condition. Another provision of the act is that employers cannot require pregnant employees to take leave at a date determined by the employer. A number of states have similar legislation.[53]

Empirical research has found that the most prevalent form of discrimination specifically directed against pregnancy occurs when employers do not reinstate female employees after they return from medical leave for childbirth. Employers are significantly more likely to fill the jobs of women on leave for childbirth than for employees on leave for other medical reasons.[54] As will be addressed later, the Family and Medical Leave Act of 1993 provides such protections and should eliminate these problems, except for employees working for employers too small to be covered by the act.[55]

Disability Discrimination

The Americans with Disabilities Act of 1990 (ADA) went into effect in 1992 and covered employers of twenty-five or more employees in both the private and public sectors. Employers having fifteen or more workers were also covered in 1994. ADA goes beyond the Rehabilitation Act of 1973, setting broad prohibitions against discrimination in the employment of disabled workers. It also requires *reasonable accommodation* of such individuals in the workplace and has very broad implications for employers. The Equal Employment Opportunity Commission (EEOC) administers the act and has issued regulations and guidance for compliance with it.[56] Key provisions of Title I of the act specify the following:

> Section 102. (a) GENERAL RULE. No covered entity shall discriminate against a qualified individual with a disability because of the disability of such individual in regard to job application procedures, the hiring, advancement, or discharge of employees, employee compensation, job training, and other terms, conditions, and privileges of employment.
> Section 102. (b) CONSTRUCTION. As used in subsection (a), the term "discriminate" includes . . . (5) (A) not making reasonable accommodations to the known physical or mental limitations of an otherwise qualified individual with a disability who is an applicant or employee, unless such covered entity can demonstrate that the accommodation would impose an undue hardship on the operation of the business of such covered entity. . . .

The act protects three types of disabilities: (1) workers who currently have disabilities, (2) workers who formerly had disabilities, and (3) workers who are perceived by others to have disabilities. If qualified individuals with a disability can perform the essential functions of the job, the employer cannot discriminate against them. Further, if these otherwise qualified individuals can perform the essential functions only after reasonable accommodation, the employer is required to make such accommodation, unless it would pose an undue hardship. Although accommodations are not required where there is undue hardship, a great deal of uncertainty exists about this provision. Factors such as the costs of accommodation, the number of employees in the facility, the employer's financial resources, administrative factors, and the impact on production processes are considered in determining undue hardship. However, large employers will probably find that only extreme accommodations will meet the definition of undue hardships. Thus, the undue hardship provision is not expected to provide a very useful defense for large employers.[57]

Going back to the types of disabilities, the second classification of disabilities pertains to diseases, such as cancer, heart disease, or mental illness, from which the worker has recovered. This prevents the employer from discriminating against such workers because of concerns about recurrence of the illness. The third classification prevents employers from discriminating against workers affected by such conditions as the HIV virus. Although ADA does not define HIV or AIDS as disabilities, several court decisions have found them to be disabilities. Additionally, in proposed EEOC regulations, HIV and AIDS have been mentioned as disabling impairments. Current drug users are not protected by ADA. However, former users no longer using illegal drugs, who have finished rehabilitation programs or are currently completing such programs, are protected.[58]

Other forms of equal employment opportunity legislation generate little litigation as to who is protected. This is because they pertain to relatively unambiguous characteristics such as gender, age, and race. On the other hand, the determination of who is a *qualified individual with a disability* (QUID) is a likely subject for litigation. Additionally, there are complications in determining whether an applicant fits the QUID definition because of differences across jobs in their essential functions. Due to the necessity of making individualized assessments of each employee's ability to perform essential job functions and the ambiguity involved in making reasonable accommodations, employers are advised to appoint ADA review officers who can provide expertise and facilitate compliance.[59]

One interesting feature of the law is that it prevents employers from using selection procedures that reject applicants because of their disabilities rather than their ability to do the work. For example, giving a blind applicant a paper and pencil test would eliminate him or her from further consideration although the person could possibly perform the major activities of the actual job. In this regard, work samples tests may be used more frequently in the future because of their direct assessment of such abilities.[60]

The types of accommodations required by ADA not only include modification of facilities and adaptation of machines but also extend to making changes in jobs and adapting work schedules. Interestingly, the current movement toward work teams may help since disabilities could be offset by other members' abilities within the teams. However, it is unknown whether this extent of accommodation will be required under ADA. Fortunately, many jobs can be performed by disabled workers after relatively low-cost accommodations. It has been reported that one half of these accommodations can be done for $50 or less and two thirds for under $500. In preparing for compliance with ADA, employers must conduct adequate job analysis in order to identify the essential elements of their jobs. These functions are then included in written job descriptions against which applicants' abilities to perform the jobs are measured. To be used as a defense against charges of discrimination, employers must have these job descriptions, containing the essential functions in written form, prior to the initiation of recruiting efforts.[61]

Another ADA selection rule is that employers cannot inquire about job applicants' disabilities. Instead, they must direct their efforts toward assessment of whether applicants can perform the essential functions of jobs. A positive aspect in this area is that increasing education may prove to be effective in helping to eradicate discrimination against the disabled because such discrimination generally results from ignorance, not hostility. A practical bit of advice for selection decisions is to place the most emphasis on other relevant qualifications to perform the job, as opposed to the disability.[62]

An interesting dilemma in making reasonable accommodations is that ADA requires employers to keep information on disabilities confidential except for managerial personnel who are directing work accommodations. First aid personnel and governmental compliance officials can also be told of the disability. Unfortunately, under some conditions, when co-workers are unaware of the disability, accommodation may be perceived as favoritism. For example, accommodation for Crohn's disease may involve allowing the affected employee to take rest room breaks when needed, in contrast to restrictions for other employees. Obviously, if the employee voluntarily tells co-workers of the condition, associated problems can be avoided. However, employers cannot force or coerce employees to inform co-workers of their disabilities. For the employer's protection, it is advisable to obtain a signed statement from the disabled employee that he or she is aware of confidentiality rights but is voluntarily informing co-workers of the disability. Periodic educational programs to inform employees about ADA and its dual obligations of reasonable accommodation and confidentiality may help head off perceptions of favoritism.[63]

Under ADA, any medical examinations or inquiries must occur only after applicants are given a conditional or tentative job offer. The medical exam must be a regular component of the preemployment procedures for the job in question, and any medical conditions used to reject applicants must meet the job-relatedness standard. Under ADA, tests for illegal drug use are not defined as medical examinations. To control health insurance costs that may increase as a result of ignoring unrelated disabilities in the selection process, employers may wish to adopt wider exclusions of preexisting conditions. It should be remembered that while ADA protects disabled job applicants from discrimination, it also protects current employees. This is critical because the majority of disabilities arise among employees who are already on the job. Frequently these disabilities are a result of the aging process and the associated incidence of such diseases as diabetes and cancer.[64]

Religious Discrimination

As indicated earlier, Title VII prevents discrimination on the basis of religion. In order to avoid such discrimination, employers must be prepared to take reasonable actions to accommodate employees' requests. For example, as established in the Supreme Court's decision in *Ansonia Board of Education v. Philbrook,* if an employee makes a request to take days off from work for religious observance, the employer must attempt a *reasonable accommodation.* In the Ansonia case, the employer's offer of unpaid leave was a reasonable accommodation. In situations where the employer cannot make such accommodation, it need not do so if it would incur undue hardship. Additionally, the employer is not required to select from alternative methods of accommodation suggested by the employee.[65]

In the Supreme Court's decision in *Trans World Airlines, Inc. v. Hardison,* an employee wanted to take off Saturdays for religious observance. Before obtaining a transfer, the employee had been able to take off Saturdays because he had sufficient seniority to do so. After the transfer, he had insufficient seniority to do so. The company then asked the union to allow the employee to switch assignments but it refused to violate its seniority-based assignment contract provisions. The employee then requested that the employer allow him to work four-day weeks, by filling in with another employee, which the employer refused because of a detrimental impact on other work functions and the premium pay required. The Court ruled that because TWA would have incurred undue hardships with all alternatives, it was not required to make such accommodations. It also ruled that the employer is not required to make changes in work assignments of other employees if seniority-based contractual rights would be violated. Where special dress or grooming are involved in religious beliefs, employers can limit these practices when they pose safety risks or cannot be tolerated due to a business necessity, such as where facial hair is prohibited by sanitation rules in restaurants.[66]

Employers may reduce the likelihood of religious discrimination problems by adopting seniority systems for assignment of work on weekends. They can also minimize such problems by permitting employees to obtain days off for religious observance through trades with other employees. Other preventative measures include adopting and enforcing a policy against religious harassment and providing a procedure for the filing of grievances on religious discrimination. Employers should maintain detailed documentation on employee requests and reasons why they could not be granted.[67]

There are some circumstances in which employers are able to take religion into consideration because it is a bona fide occupational qualification, such as when hiring for a church-affiliated religious school. Additionally, under Title VII, religious institutions are provided some latitude for religion-based employment discrimination that other organizations are not allowed. Interestingly, religious discrimination is usually not a problem with the generally recognized religions. Instead, problems often arise from obscure religions or individuals' definitions of religions.[68] Teresa Brady provides a glimpse into the bizarre issues that can be encountered in this area:

> Brown alleged that he was the victim of religious discrimination when he was fired due to his personal, religious belief that "Kozy Kitten People/Cat Food" was contributing significantly to his state of well-being and therefore to his overall work performance by increasing his energy. Brown failed to establish a religious belief that is generally accepted in society as a religion.[69]

Sexual Orientation

Although there is no federal law prohibiting employment discrimination on the basis of sexual orientation, several states have adopted such legislation. Between 1989 and June 1993, seven states had passed such laws: California, Connecticut, Hawaii, Massachusetts, Minnesota, New Jersey, and Vermont. In addition to states, cities and local governments have passed similar laws. Of the fifty most heavily populated U.S. cities, thirty-one had passed such laws by June 1993. Where such laws have been passed, religious organizations have usually been exempted from coverage. Thus, there had been a trend toward prohibition of discrimination in employment on the basis of sexual orientation by the time that the Clinton administration attempted to accomplish the same effect in the U.S. military. The federal courts have ruled that the Title VII protections against hostile environment sexual harassment do not apply to gays because the law protects against only gender-based discrimination, not sexual orientation.[70]

COMPENSATION

U.S. employers must be concerned about a number of regulations affecting wages and benefits. These regulations, along with work-force skills and their supply in the labor force, affect the employer's cost of doing business in the United States and, therefore, may impact an employer's plant location strategies. Labor costs were a major issue in the debate over the proposed North American Free Trade Agreement.

Wages and Benefits

Federal legislation in this area includes the Fair Labor Standards Act (FLSA) first passed in 1938, which as amended sets minimum wages and governs the employment of underage workers. This legislation has numerous special provisions for specific industry and employee classifications. Under the FLSA, exempt employees do not have to be paid overtime wages for work over forty hours per week. *Exempt employees* are executives, professionals, and outside salespersons. Those employers covered by the FSLA must also comply with the Equal Pay Act of 1963, which mandates that men and women must be paid equal amounts of pay for equal work. Legitimate exceptions to this requirement are those pay differences resulting from variations in seniority, merit, production quality, and production quantity.[71]

Another law is the Employee Retirement Income Security Act of 1974 (ERISA), which governs the funding and administration of pension plans. ERISA is a very complex law mandating actuarially determined funding levels for defined benefit pension plans. *Defined benefit plans* are those that promise a benefit at the time of retirement. A defined benefit example would be promising 2 percent of one's highest pay for every year worked for the company as an annual pension. In addition to administration and funding requirements, the legislation established the Pension Benefits Guaranty Corporation which insures pension benefits, much like the Federal Deposit Insurance Corporation.[72]

Both federal and state laws are involved in unemployment compensation. At the federal level, the Unemployment Tax Act specifies compliance standards for federal funding to the states for unemployment claims. Also at the federal level, the Social Security Act controls the funding aspects of the system. Employers having a payroll of at least $1,500 each quarter and one or more employees for one or more days in any of twenty weeks per year are required to pay unemployment taxes. However, there is an extensive list of exceptions. The states specify different requirements for eligibility although federal regulations set minimum standards. Employers' unemployment compensation tax rates are determined by the number of claims filed by their former employees. Because unemployment claims can also be an avenue for wrongful discharge or discrimination-based litigation, employers should carefully monitor any claims and contest those where appropriate.[73]

Several other laws also affect compensation, which cannot be covered in depth in this discussion because of space limitations. These include workers' compensation laws that provide benefits for disabled workers at the state level. Because workers' compensation legislation and systems vary across the states, differentials in system efficiencies and administrative costs impact the attractiveness of states as potential business sites. In the past, such systems have been notoriously inefficient and subject to abuse. Additionally, other federal laws affecting compensation include two Depression era laws—the Davis Bacon Act of 1931, which sets minimum (prevailing) wage standards for construction contractors doing business with the federal government, and the Walsh-Healy Public Contracts Act of 1936, which sets minimum (prevailing) wage standards for employers having contracts with the federal government. Additionally, the federal Portal-to-Portal Act of 1947 specifies the work-related activities for which employers are required to pay.[74]

Health-Care Benefits

As of late 1994, federal health-care reform legislation was still being debated. However, a major development in health-care benefits had already occurred by 1992. A ruling of the Financial Accounting Standards Board (FASB) in the form of statement #106 had major strategic implications for employers who promised health-care benefits for their retirees. This change in tax regulations required employers to deduct the liabilities of promises to employees for postretirement benefits from their annual earnings reports.[75] FASB #106 does not pertain to pensions but has major implications on the funding of health-care benefits for retirees. FASB #106 rule alone caused Ford to recognize a $7.5 billion liability while Exxon's and American Airlines' (AMR) liabilities were $800 million and $600 million, respectively.[76]

One predicted result of this standard is that companies may withdraw from benefit programs and simply provide funds to employees to purchase their own benefits. The manager of accounting policy and controls at the Xerox Corporation predicted that the benefits of future retirees may be comparatively smaller than those of currently vested retirees.[77] This is evident in Texas Instruments' approach: "By 1998, the company won't pay any premiums [health insurance] for employees who retire with less than 15 years' service . . . —and only a portion for workers with up to 30 years at TI."[78] Similarly, Unisys announced that it would stop paying for future retirees' health insurance, thereby eliminating costs of $100 million per year.[79]

Family and Medical Leave

One area of recent legislation is particularly relevant to increasing feminization of the work force. With some 80 percent of American female workers of child-bearing age, maternity leaves and guarantees of job availability upon return are important. Although the U.S. legislative requirements lagged behind those of many European countries, even before passage of the Family and Medical Leave Act of 1993 (FMLA) several high-standards U.S. companies provided such leaves. For example, Time, Inc. and AT&T allowed liberal unpaid leave periods for parents after childbirth or adoption.[80] Companies allowing employees to take lengthy unpaid parental or family care leaves included Johnson & Johnson, Aetna Life and Casualty, Allstate Insurance, Arthur Andersen, Atlantic Richfield, Champion International, Corning, Inc., Du Pont, Gannett, Hallmark Cards, John Hancock Mutual Life, Levi Strauss, Merck, Pacific Gas & Electric, Polaroid, Procter & Gamble, Travelers, U.S. Sprint, and Wells Fargo Bank.[81]

Even prior to passage of the FMLA, a state law in California required employers to provide unpaid maternity leave.[82] The obvious implications of such legislation are that companies will need to plan for temporary vacancies created by employees on maternity leave. Although support programs such as child care and maternity leave carry an economic cost, some observers argued that they are necessary to preserve workers' effectiveness.

> A good support system is the single most important aid if a woman is to remain an effective employee. As we . . . approach the year 2000, there are going to be even more single women in the workforce who will require corporations to meet the needs of their dual agenda—career progress and family harmony. In addition, the number of two-paycheck families will continue to rise, with the concomitant problems of division of responsibilities as each partner struggles with the demands of work and family.[83]

With the passage of FMLA in 1993, the leave components of such support systems became mandated by law. Specifically, the act requires that employers provide unpaid leave to employees making such requests for the following reasons: (1) to provide care for newly born children, for newly placed adopted children, and for foster care; (2) to provide care for seriously ill spouses, children, or parents; or (3) the employee has his or her own serious health problems that prevent job performance. When such requests are foreseeable, employees must make them thirty days in advance of the desired leave. Employers are also entitled to medical certifications of the existence of serious health conditions if they so request. Once employees go on such leaves, employers are required to continue health-care coverage, and when employees return they are entitled to equivalent jobs, pay, and benefits. An exception to this provision is that for the employer's highest-paid employees (top 10 percent), the employer does not have to hold the position until the employee returns under conditions where substantial economic damage can be demonstrated.[84]

The leave requirement is limited to a maximum of twelve weeks per twelve-month period. Such leave may also be of an intermittent nature when it is for illness of the employee or his or her family members. With regard to coverage, the FMLA applies to employers having 50 or more employees within a 75-mile area and provides rights to employees who have worked at least one year for the employer and have worked 1,250 or more hours in the past 12 months. Under the provisions of FMLA, the definition of children also includes mentally or physically disabled individuals of age eighteen or more who must have others care for them.[85] Additionally, the act "allows employers to require employees to use up available vacation, personal, or sick leave time before the unpaid leave begins."[86]

EMPLOYEE RELATIONS

Legal influences in the area of employee relations include the evolving area of negligent hiring, the employment of immigrants, employment at will, drug testing, and safety.

Negligent Hiring

Negligent hiring has become an increasingly attractive area for litigation as employers are being found liable for acts of violence committed by their employees. Such liability has typically been incurred in situations where the employee had access to customers in isolated circumstances or had easy access to their property. For example, an apartment complex owner hired a resident manager who subsequently raped a tenant in her apartment. The employee turned out to have had a history of violence. Although the employer was unaware of the employee's violent background, the tenant sued and the employer was found liable for negligent hiring. In some circumstances the employer's liability may even extend beyond actions occurring during the course of business.[87] A similar incident occurred when a convenience store chain hired a clerk who had previously been imprisoned for murder. Because of the isolated nature of the work, customers and other employees were vulnerable to the employee's violent nature. In this case the employee murdered a store co-worker, and the employer was found to be negligent for failing to check on the employee's background. As a result the employer agreed to settle the case by paying the deceased employee's family $4.95 million.[88]

Unfortunately, such situations constitute a "Catch-22" for employers because of privacy protections, defamation suits that make it increasingly difficult to obtain meaningful information on job applicants from previous employers, and the difficulty of obtaining information on the criminal records of applicants. The difficulty of checking for violent criminal backgrounds is indicated by the fact that some states, such as North Carolina and Massachusetts, have prohibited private sector employers from obtaining such information. Furthermore, employers cannot use arrest information in making employment decisions and may not be able to use convictions unless they are job-related.[89]

Although negligent hiring situations pose substantial difficulties for employers, past court rulings provide some guidance for action. For example, for negligence to occur, the actions of the employer must have been unreasonable. It is also critical that the employer must have known, or should have known, about the vicious or violent nature of the employee. Further, greater precautions and a more intensive background investigation are in order when the employee will have close and unsupervised contact with customers or other employees. Examples of jobs falling within this category might be maintenance workers having special access, as noted earlier; bus drivers; and child-care workers. In addition to exercising greater care where customers and fellow employees may be more vulnerable, the employer should investigate gaps in an applicant's employment record. Efforts to obtain such information should be documented because, even when unsuccessful, they provide evidence of a reasonable background search.[90] As indicated earlier, criminal information cannot be used for selection decisions unless it is job-related. The rationale for this prohibition is described in the following:

> The leading court cases in this area have held that if an employer's rule against hiring applicants with criminal records has an adverse impact on minorities, the practice violates Title VII unless it is justified by "business necessity."[91]

Nonetheless, circumstances in which customers or employees may be vulnerable to the violent actions of another employee may be the test of business necessity. Further, it appears that it will become easier for employers to check on applicants' criminal records as a result of legislation and better computerized information systems. However, such availability of information may be a two-edged sword, as at least one court has found that "where criminal records were *easily available,* the failure of the employer to check his employee's criminal records can be used as evidence of his negligence."[92] Thus, negligent hiring appears to be another mine field for employers. In order to avoid financial losses, employers must exercise greater diligence in investigating job applicants' backgrounds.

Immigration

The Immigration Reform and Control Act of 1986 (IRCA) directs employers to determine that applicants are legally qualified to be employed in the United States before hiring them. In attempting to determine legal status, employers should be careful to avoid discrimination on the basis of national origin. Nor should they reject applicants because they look like aliens. This can be done by first making *conditional offers of employment* to applicants and then asking for their documentation to determine legal qualification for employment. In making employment decisions, employers should not favor citizens over noncitizens having appropriate work authorization although citizenship can be legally required under some situations by governmental employers and defense contractors. Further, employers having fewer than four employees are not prevented from discriminating against noncitizens. There are also several special business visas authorizing aliens to work in the United States. One of particular interest to companies having operations in other countries is the L-1 visa. This visa permits such companies to transfer foreign managers or specialists, employed in their foreign operations, into the United States. In addition to IRCA, the Immigration Act of 1990 also authorizes a visa for certain highly educated workers.[93]

Employment at Will

An issue of increasing importance to employers is the vitality of the employment-at-will doctrine, as a number of exceptions to the doctrine have developed in recent years.[94] Current estimates indicate that approximately two thirds of U.S. employees work under employment-at-will conditions in which they can readily be terminated from employment.[95] The *employment-at-will doctrine* states that "an employer can legally dismiss an employee for a good reason, a bad reason, or no reason at all, so long as the dismissal does not violate the provisions of a specific statute, such as the National Labor Relations Act or the Civil Rights Act of 1964."[96]

Since employees working under employment-at-will conditions outnumber those afforded protections against arbitrary discharge, it is easier to identify employees having protection against arbitrary discharge. These employees include those covered by collective bargaining agreements. Another such group is governmental employees at the local, state, and federal levels who often work under civil service rules. Such rules mandate due process disciplinary procedures with some form of appeal procedure, often culminating in a hearing before an impartial arbitrator or hearing officer. Frequently governmental employees may have these protections as a result of collectively bargained agreements. University faculty members are often covered by contractual agreements or legislation, which also prevent arbitrary termination. Additionally, the National Labor Relations Act provides protection against discharge where the action is directed against preventing employees from organizing a union. There is also statutory protection against discharge when it results from retaliation against whistleblowers or workers who file charges under such laws as the Fair Labor Standards Act or the Occupational Safety and Health Act. Finally, where discharges result from discrimination against an employee's race, color, national origin, religion, gender, age, or disabilities, other statutory protections exit. Beyond these groups and special conditions, the remaining employees work under the employment-at-will doctrine.[97] Even for employees subject to employment at will, some exceptions to the doctrine have evolved. These include situations where (1) the termination is in *opposition to public policy*. Examples include terminating an employee for refusing to commit perjury, declining to become involved in bribery, and refusing to submit to a polygraph test when such refusal is protected under the Employee Polygraph Protection Act of 1988.[98] Violations of state public policies have also been used for such public policy exemptions, as indicated in the specific example of the *Wagenseller v. Scottsdale Memorial Hospital* case.[99]

> On a company river outing, a nurse refused to "moon" her fellow employees while singing "Moon River" as her boss requested. She was fired as a result. Noting the state's indecent-exposure laws as a statement of public policy, the Arizona Supreme Court approved her right to sue for wrongful discharge as a public policy exception to the state's at-will employment rule.[100]

Another exception to the employment-at-will doctrine is (2) *abusive discharge*. An example is a situation where an employee is fired for refusing to date her boss. An additional exception is where (3) there is an *implied covenant of good faith*. An example of a breach of covenant would be where an employer discharges sales employees to evade obligations to pay earned commissions. Also, (4) statements in personnel handbooks categorizing employees as permanent employees have been interpreted as *implicit contracts*.[101] As a result of litigation on this issue, employers have learned to be careful about such statements and now often include disclaimers in handbooks that explicitly specify employment-at-will status.[102]

Limitations on an employer's ability to discharge employees at will have also evolved in the form of a statute in Montana. The state of Montana has adopted legislation which sets a standard of good cause for employee terminations. Under Montana's Wrongful Discharge from Employment Act, discharges of nonprobationary employees will be considered as wrongful unless there is just cause.[103] In addition, several other states have considered similar legislation that would require just cause for terminations. Such developments have caused some observers to conclude that the employment-at will doctrine has been weakened.[104] Nonetheless, an empirical analysis of California's experience, where there are substantial inroads into the employment-at-will doctrine, concluded the following: "Quantitative analysis of the California experience indicates that the erosion of employment at will has not proceeded nearly as far as is commonly believed."[105] Such laws, the emergence of exceptions to the employment-at-will doctrine, increased litigation over terminations, and large judgments in favor of employees have caught the attention of human resource managers. Nonetheless, there is some evidence that large judgments have involved high-level managerial personnel and are not prevalent among discharged hourly employees.[106]

Finally, companies should consider the impact of employment-at-will policies on potential job applicants' perceptions of the organization as an attractive employer. Catherine Schwoerer and Benson Rosen have found that such policies, when contrasted with policies providing due process grievance and appeals procedures, are associated with significantly lower perceptions of employer attractiveness.[107]

Drug Testing

Since the mid-1980s, drug testing has been a common practice in many companies and governmental agencies, particularly as a preemployment screening process. For example, Exxon Chemical began testing in 1984 while Du Pont started testing job applicants no later than 1986.[108] By 1987, Motorola was testing job applicants and had also begun to test for cause, such as when accidents had occurred. By 1989, Texas Instruments had started testing all of its employees and in 1990 Motorola announced intentions to start testing on a universal basis.[109]

Although companies apparently perceive benefits from drug testing programs, industrial studies of the effectiveness of drug testing typically have not employed experimental designs and, as a result, their impact on desired outcomes cannot be confirmed. However, John Osterloh and Charles Becker's comprehensive literature review found anecdotal evidence of program success. Such successes included reports of reduced accident rates at Southern Pacific Railroad; reduced absenteeism, accidents, and disciplinary actions at General Motors; and drastic reductions in drug incidence in the U.S. Navy.[110] Further, over time the percentage of positive results in preemployment drug testing has been declining. Surveys by the American Management Association (AMA) indicate that the ratio of positive results to applicants declined from 11.4 percent in 1989 to 4.3 percent in 1992. Similar declines have also taken place among current employees, as the ratios of positive results have declined from 8.1 percent in 1989 to 2.5 percent in 1992.[111] One explanation for the decline of positive results in preemployment testing has been that drug users have become aware of companies' testing programs and no longer apply for employment at such companies.

Drug testing appears to be increasing as a 1993 AMA survey found that 84 percent of companies conducted drug testing of some form, a 10 percent increase from the previous year. Additionally, 81 percent of the respondents were testing their current employees, an 18 percent increase from 1992. Reasons credited for the increase in testing include favorable court decisions, federal requirements in transportation and defense industries, and initiatives by insurance companies.[112] These results may overstate the extent of testing current employees as another recent survey of *Fortune* 500 companies found such testing in only 60 percent of the responding companies.[113]

Basically, there are three drug testing approaches for private sector employers. The most prevalent involves the testing of job applicants. The popularity of this *preemployment approach* to testing appears to be a result of its effectiveness and the employer's lower exposure to liability. A second approach, for which there is some legal support, involves testing employees when there is *probable cause* to suspect drug use, such as when there has been an accident. *Reasonable suspicion* of drug use may also fall under this category, as when supervisors observe symptoms of drug intoxication. A third approach of *random testing* of all employees is not as widely used as the first two approaches. Its disadvantages include the uncertainty of its legal standing, its cost, and substantial administrative requirements. When random testing is conducted, it is typically used for employees in environments where safety is an important consideration. Unsurprisingly, random testing is more defensible under such considerations. In fact, private and public sector employees covered by public safety requirements of the U.S. Department of Transportation are required to conduct random drug tests for safety purposes.[114] In the AMA survey noted earlier, 33 percent of the companies reported that they were required to conduct drug tests as a result of these regulations or those of the Department of Defense and other governmental agencies.[115] Accordingly, another AMA survey found that 89 percent of the companies in the transportation industry conduct drug testing.[116]

Drug testing of federal governmental employees is explicitly regulated. Executive Order 12,564 specifies that drug testing of federal employees can take place under four conditions. These include situations of reasonable suspicion, accident investigation, preemployment screening, and as a condition of drug rehabilitation.[117] State and local governments also test employees under similar circumstances. Nonetheless, both public and private employers should take note of the difficulties of establishing reasonable suspicion as justification for drug testing. In two recent court decisions involving governmental employees, observations of erratic or abnormal behavior were rejected as a basis for reasonable suspicion. These rulings noted the absence of a strong link between drug impairment and erratic behavior. They also noted commonplace alternative explanations for such behavior other than drug use.[118]

In order to minimize legal and managerial problems, drug testing programs should conform to a number of requirements. Clearly, steps leading up to the implementation of such programs are critical. One very important requirement is that there should be a well-documented need for testing. Employees should also perceive this need since acceptance of testing programs is expected to correlate with the perceived need for testing, such as in dangerous working conditions.[119] As a result, employees are probably more accepting of both preemployment testing and cause-based testing but are probably much more resistant to universal random testing.

Another requirement for drug testing programs is that the testing should involve a two-step process. The first step should be a *screening test*. All positive results should then be subjected to a *confirmatory test*. Confirmatory tests are typically much more expensive. Privacy issues are also a consideration in such programs and in an employment context, direct observation of the collection of specimens is probably invasive and unnecessary. However, the collection of specimens must be conducted with several precautions to preserve the integrity of the chain of custody. Other requirements include uniform application. For example if preemployment testing is used, all applicants must be tested. Further, when testing is conducted for cause, there must be uniform application without regard to race or gender. There should also be mechanisms for employee challenges, and a provision for employee assistance programs for those found to be using drugs.[120]

Employee acceptance is an extremely important requirement for effective drug testing programs. Because of its importance, the likelihood of litigation or adverse arbitration decisions should be reduced as a result of negotiating agreements with employees on drug testing policies. Such agreements should specify the testing procedures, steps to be taken in collecting specimens, and the consequences of positive results.[121] In addition to litigation, where private and public sector employees are represented by a union or in the public sector where civil service rules apply, grievances over such issues are decided by arbitrators. Arbitrators tend to look for many of these components of drug testing programs before they will uphold employers' actions.

In summary, drug testing involves complicated technical issues and is subject to variations in accuracy. However, as indicated earlier, some drug testing programs have probably produced positive outcomes, such as reductions in accidents.[122] Further, as indicated earlier, employers working under regulations of the U.S. Department of Transportation have no choice in the matter of random drug testing. Nonetheless, a wide array of factors makes drug testing a complex matter. These complexities include the financial risk of exposure to liability, the potential negative impact on employee trust, and the potential negative impact on morale. As a result, the strategic management team must carefully consider the broad implications of drug testing before proceeding.

Safety

The Occupational Safety and Health Act of 1970 (OSHA) requires employers "to provide employees a place of employment free from recognized hazards that are causing, or are likely to cause, death or serious harm to employees."[123] OSHA has a massive set of specific safety standards with which employers are required to comply. Unlike most federal employee relations legislation, there is no minimum size exclusion for small employers. Under OSHA, employers are required to maintain safety records and are responsible for employees' compliance with safety standards. Further, employers are subject to unannounced inspections by OSHA authorities, although some have been successful in requiring search warrants for entry. Additionally, OSHA has the power to level meaningful fines for violations of safety standards. Some of the more controversial aspects of OSHA have been its standards requiring massive financial outlays for compliance without evidence that meaningful reductions in health hazards will be forthcoming. This situation has changed somewhat. OSHA's standards for acceptable levels of exposure to substances, such as airborne toxic materials, must now meet both technological and economic feasibility standards.[124] Nonetheless, there is no requirement that "the cost of a standard bears a reasonable relationship to its benefits."[125]

LABOR RELATIONS AND COLLECTIVE BARGAINING

The National Labor Relations Act (NLRA), also called the Wagner Act, was passed in 1935. Section 7 of this act gave employees the right to form unions and engage in collective bargaining. In order to enforce these rights, section 8(a) of the act prohibited five *employer unfair labor practices:* (1) interfering with employees attempting to unionize or engage in collective bargaining, (2) dominating a union, (3) discriminating on the basis of union status, (4) retaliating against workers charging violations of the act, and (5) refusing to bargain. In order to enforce the law, the act created the National Labor Relations Board (NLRB). Essentially, the first of the unfair labor practices is a general provision particularly relevant to employer conduct when employees are attempting to unionize. This provision is intended to prevent employers from using coercive tactics, such as discharging workers who are attempting to unionize. The second unfair labor practice prevents *company unions.* (In a company union the company might handpick the leaders, provide financial support, and dominate the union in other ways.) Interestingly, worker committees that act on issues similar to those involved in collective bargaining may be viewed as company unions and therefore constitute an unfair labor practice. The third unfair labor practice prevents the employer from treating employees in the bargaining unit differently, depending on whether or not they are members of the union. The fourth and fifth unfair labor practices are self-explanatory.[126]

Following the passage of the NLRA in 1935, unionization increased dramatically, almost quadrupling by 1948. By 1946, a record of 4,985 strikes had occurred, and Congress recognized that unfair labor practices on the union side also needed to be curbed.[127] The Labor Management Relations Act of 1947 (LMRA), also called the Taft-Hartley Act, amended the National Labor Relations Act and sought to restore a balance between the power of unions and employers. Section 8(b) of the act specified a series of *union unfair labor practices:* (1) restraining or coercing employees who are pursuing their rights to bargain collectively, (2) discriminating on the basis of union membership, (3) refusing to bargain, (4) conducting prohibited strikes, (5) charging excessive fees, and (6) requiring employers to provide compensation for services that are not performed. The first of these practices prevents unions from coercing employees who do not want to unionize. The second prevents the union from forcing the employer to terminate an employee, except in cases where he or she refuses to pay union dues where there is a *union shop agreement.* (With union shops an individual must join the union after becoming employed.) It also prevents the union from attempting to induce the employer to favor union members in hiring and outlaws the *closed shop.* (With closed shops an individual must be a member of the union before being hired.) The third union unfair labor practice does not have much meaning because unions want to bargain. The fourth unfair practice basically outlaws *secondary boycotts,* which involve application of coercive economic power to neutral third parties to labor disputes. The fifth unfair labor practice allows unions to charge dues or initiation fees that are reasonable in light of industry practice and the wage level of the job. The sixth provision was intended ostensibly to prevent featherbedding practices, such as requiring overstaffing for certain jobs, but has been largely ineffective.[128]

Another provision of the act is the so called *right-to-work* provision, which allows states to decide whether union shop agreements are legal. Further, the act also requires unions and employers to *bargain in good faith* over mandatory issues such as wages, hours, and other working conditions. Additionally, the Taft-Hartley Act added provisions whereby employees may decertify unions and established a procedure for the resolution of strikes constituting national emergencies.[129]

Because of continuing problems of union corruption and of lack of democratic procedures in the governance of unions, the Labor Management Reporting and Disclosure Act (LMRDA), called the Landrum-Griffin Act, was passed in 1959 and also amended the NLRA. Important provisions of the LMRDA include financial reporting and disclosure requirements for union officers and labor relations consultants, requirements for unions to conduct regular elections, and prohibitions of hot cargo agreements. In *hot cargo agreements* union members refuse to handle materials or components that have previously been processed by nonunion workers or by a company with which the union has a dispute. The act also added a prohibition of recognitional picketing, under certain circumstances, as a seventh union unfair labor practice. Where *recognitional picketing* takes place, expedited representation election procedures may be invoked. Additionally, the NLRA was amended again in 1974. Unions representing employees of health-care institutions are now required to provide 10 days' advance notice of a strike.[130]

Many practitioners refer to the combination of these three pieces of legislation as the act. Employees not covered by the act include supervisors, agricultural workers, domestic servants, employees of parents or spouses, independent contractors, governmental workers, and railroad and airline employees. Further, only the labor relations activities of those private sector employers involved in interstate commerce come under the jurisdiction of the NLRB. Threshold values for NLRB jurisdiction are defined for nonretail companies as $50,000 or more annual input or output across states lines, or in retailing, as $500,0000 or more in annual sales. Additionally, employers not covered by the act include governments, airlines, and railroads. Airlines and railroads are covered by the Railway Labor Act of 1926.[131]

In addition to these federal acts, labor relations is also governed by NLRB policies and decisions as well as court decisions. Unfortunately for unions, the law has not provided effective protection for employees attempting to unionize. Essentially, employers who commit unfair labor practices must provide *"make whole"* remedies to employees whose rights they have violated. For example, an employer might terminate an employee who is attempting to form a union. Upon establishing that the employer has actually committed such an unfair labor practice, the employer would probably be required to reinstate the employee and pay back pay for the wages he or she lost while unemployed. Unfortunately, there is typically a lengthy time period before the remedy is implemented. If the employer's conduct is particularly egregious and a fair representation election cannot be held, the NLRB may order the employer to bargain with the union. Even where the employer commits no unfair labor practices and the union wins the representation election, many unions are never successful in negotiating a contract. Even though the employer is required to bargain in good faith, the sanctions for failure to bargain are not strong. This is another weakness in the law that is particularly troublesome to unions.[132]

Another influence of the legal environment on strategy may be seen in the replacement of strikers. In the 1992 presidential campaign, the Democrats proposed a prohibition of the permanent replacement of strikers.[133] This right of employers has been an enduring principle of labor relations going back to its affirmation by the U.S. Supreme Court in 1938.[134] It is a certainty that such proposed legislation will generate very strong resistance from the business community.

STRATEGIC IMPACT OF THE LEGAL ENVIRONMENT

Whether the increasingly complex and comprehensive regulatory environment of human resources will weaken the competitiveness of U.S. companies in the international marketplace is yet to be determined. Obviously, the legal environment is a major consideration of strategic managers because of the potential exposure to liability, plant location concerns, productivity influences, and other impacts on cost structures. In the future, strategic managers may need to become more proactive in the design of legislation so that the laudable social goals of equal employment opportunity can be obtained simultaneously with organizational growth and efficiency. Without managerial flexibility, some assurance of what the "rules of the game" are, and predictable means of determining when the employer is in compliance with legislation, U.S. companies are not likely to be as productive and efficient as they should be. Conversely, with higher levels of productivity and efficiency, companies are likely to produce a larger economic pie to share with all employees. Given strong economic performance, they should have less difficulty in providing equal employment opportunities. In the absence of these efficiencies and economic growth, companies will be faced with the difficult situation of allocating or rationing employment opportunities to a smaller set of individuals.

A controversial but comprehensive analysis of the economic and legal effects of equal employment opportunity regulation has been conducted by Richard Epstein and published by the Harvard University Press.[135] The major conclusion of his analysis is that substantial economic inefficiency is associated with such regulation. While few of his recommendations for reform are likely to be implemented in the foreseeable future, strategic managers and planners may gain insights from a review of his analysis of the impact of current legislation. Peter Brimelow and Leslie Spencer have also described similar concerns about the legislative environment of human resources as follows:

> Ironically, just as socialism has collapsed across the globe, the leading capitalist power has adopted a peculiarly American neosocialism, putting politics (and lawyers) in command of its workplace, albeit on the pretext of equity rather than efficiency.[136]

While there are costs to equal employment opportunity legislation, as Brimelow and Spencer have pointed out, there are also costs with the alternative of failing to advance members of society who have been subject to prior discrimination. Unfortunately, some of the new legislation appears to have left areas of ambiguity which create greater uncertainty for employers. When employment procedures are made uncertain by ill-conceived legislation and likely targets for even greater litigation are created, rational employers are not likely to be as aggressive in their hiring, as when the legislation is unambiguous and thoughtful of the practical issues involved in running an economically viable business.

SUMMARY

This chapter described the legal environment of human resources, beginning with the equal employment opportunity protections of the Civil Rights Act of 1964, which prohibit discrimination on the basis of race, color, religion, sex, or national origin. Disparate treatment and disparate impact forms of discrimination were explained along with the implications for human resource selection procedures such as those involving the use of tests. The enforcement role of the EEOC in administering the act was also discussed along with the role of the OFCCP. Changes incorporated in the Civil Rights Act of 1991 were also covered including prohibitions against race-norming of test scores, punitive damages for intentional discrimination, and extraterritorial civil rights coverage of expatriate employees of U.S. companies. Prohibitions against discrimination on the basis of age (Age Discrimination in Employment Act), sexual harassment, pregnancy (Pregnancy Discrimination Act), disabilities (Americans with Disabilities Act), and religion were also reviewed. The legal status of discrimination directed at sexual orientation was also discussed.

The regulatory environment governing the administration of compensation and benefit programs was described. Legislation and regulations included in this discussion were the Fair Labor Standards Act, the Employee Retirement Income Security Act, the Equal Pay Act, Financial Accounting Standards Board statement #106 on the financial reporting of obligations to provide health-care benefits for retirees, and the Family and Medical Leave Act.

Other relatively recent legal developments discussed include the establishment of employer liability for negligent hiring, rules governing the employment of immigrants as established by the Immigration Reform and Control Act, exceptions to the employment-at-will doctrine, and drug testing. In addition, the safety requirements of the Occupational Safety and Health Act and the labor relations regulations of the National Labor Relations Act, the Labor Management Relations Act, and the Labor Management Reporting and Disclosure Act were covered. Finally, because of the increased complexity of recent legislation governing human resource management, the economic impact of the legislative environment was examined in terms of decreased managerial flexibility and the uncertainties created by ambiguities in determining compliance.

REFERENCES

1. Hall, Francine S., and Elizabeth L. Hall, "The ADA: Going Beyond the Law," *Academy of Management Executive*, 8, no. 1 (1994), 17–26.
2. Hall and Hall, "The ADA: Going Beyond the Law," 18.
3. Civil Rights Act of 1964 as amended by the Equal Employment Opportunity Act of 1972.
4. Cibon, Patrick J., and James O. Castagnera, *Labor and Employment Law*, 2nd ed. Boston: PWS-Kent, 1993.
5. Miner, Mary G., and John B. Miner, *Employee Selection Within the Law*. Washington, D.C.: Bureau of National Affairs, 1978.
6. Twomey, David P., *Equal Employment Opportunity Law*, 3rd ed. Cincinnati: South-Western, 1994; Arvey, Richard D., and Robert H. Faley, *Fairness in Selecting Employees*, 2nd ed. Reading, Mass.: Addison-Wesley, 1988; Greenlaw, Paul S., "Proving Title VII Discrimination," *Labor Law Journal*, 42, no. 7 (1991), 407–417.
7. *Griggs v. Duke Power Co.*, 401 U.S. 424 (1971).
8. Ibid.
9. Twomey, *Equal Employment Opportunity Law*.
10. Greenlaw, "Proving Title VII Discrimination."
11. Player, Mack A., *Federal Law of Employment Discrimination in a Nutshell*, 3rd ed. St. Paul: West, 1992.
12. Ledvinka, James, *Federal Regulation of Personnel and Human Resource Management*. Boston: PWS-Kent, 1982.
13. *Albemarle Paper Co. v. Moody*, 422 U.S. 405 (1975).
14. Rothstein, Mark A., Andria S. Knapp, and Lance Liebman, *Cases and Materials on Employment Law*, 2nd ed. Westbury, N.Y.: Foundation Press, 1991.
15. Equal Employment Opportunity Commission, *1978 Uniform Guidelines on Employee Selection Procedures*.
16. Arvey and Faley, *Fairness in Selecting Employees*, 80.
17. Robinson, Robert K., Billie Morgan Allen, David E. Terpstra, and Ercan G. Nasif, "Equal Employment Requirements for Employers: A Closer Review of the Effects of the Civil Rights Act of 1991," *Labor Law Journal*, 43, no. 11 (1992), 725–734.
18. Feild, Hubert S., and Robert D. Gatewood, "Matching Talent with the Task," *Personnel Administrator*, 32, no. 4 (1987), 113–126.
19. Robinson, Allen, Terpstra, and Nasif, "Equal Employment Requirements for Employers"; Brimelow, Peter, and Leslie Spencer, "When Quotas Replace Merit, Everybody Suffers," *Forbes*, February 15, 1993, 80–102.
20. *Connecticut v. Teal*, 457 U.S. 440 (1982); Robinson, Allen, Terpstra, and Nasif, "Equal Employment Requirements for Employers."
21. Robinson, Allen, Terpstra, and Nasif, "Equal Employment Requirements for Employers."
22. Cibon and Castagnera, *Labor and Employment Law*.
23. Levin-Epstein, Michael D., *Primer of Equal Employment Opportunity*, 4th ed. Washington, D.C.: Bureau of National Affairs, 1987; Ledvinka, *Federal Regulation of Personnel and Human Resource Management*; Twomey, *Equal Employment Opportunity Law*.
24. Lewis, Anthony, "Double Standards," *Forbes*, with attribution to *The New York Times*, March 1, 1993, 30.

25. Cibon and Castagnera, *Labor and Employment Law*; Dube, Lawrence, E., Jr., "Removing the Cap—Eliminating Mandatory Retirement Under the ADEA," *Employment Relations Today*, 15, no. 3 (1988), 199–204; Player, *Federal Law of Employment Discrimination in a Nutshell*; Twomey, *Equal Employment Opportunity Law.*

26. Dube, "Removing the Cap—Eliminating Mandatory Retirement Under the ADEA"; Player, *Federal Law of Employment Discrimination*; Hassell, Barbara L., and Pamela L. Perrewe, "An Examination of the Relationship Between Older Workers' Perceptions of Age Discrimination and Employee Psychological State," *Journal of Managerial Issues*, 5, no. 1 (1993), 109–120.

27. Twomey, *Equal Employment Opportunity Law*; Mitchell, Charles E., "Waiver of Rights Under the Age Discrimination in Employment Act: Implications of the Older Workers Benefit Protection Act of 1990," *Labor Law Journal*, 43, no. 11 (1992), 735–744.

28. Mitchell, "Waiver of Rights Under the Age Discrimination In Employment Act," 735.

29. Player, *Federal Law of Employment Discrimination in a Nutshell*; Mitchell, "Waiver of Rights Under the Age Discrimination In Employment Act."

30. Crichton, Michael, *Disclosure*, New York: Alfred A. Knopf, 1993.

31. Benton, Debra, "Hands-On Approach Can Get Sticky," *The Wall Street Journal*, March 22, 1993, A14.

32. Schafer, Susanne M., "33 Admirals Are Censured in Tailhook Case," *Fort Worth Star-Telegram*, October 16, 1993, A18.

33. American Broadcasting Company, *ABC News*, October 11, 1993.

34. Twomey, *Equal Employment Opportunity Law.*

35. Equal Employment Opportunity Commission, *Guidelines on Discrimination Because of Sex*, Section 1604.11, November 10, 1980.

36. *Meritor Savings Bank v. Vinson*, 106 S. Ct. 2399 (1986); Koen, Clifford M., Jr., "Sexual Harassment Claims Stem from a Hostile Work Environment," *Personnel Journal*, 69, no. 8 (1990), 90–99.

37. Greenlaw, Paul S., and John P. Kohl, "Proving Title VII Sexual Harassment: The Courts' View," *Labor Law Journal*, 43, no. 3 (1992), 164–171; Koen, "Sexual Harassment Claims Stem from a Hostile Work Environment."

38. Bass, Stuart L., "The 'Reasonable Woman' Standard: The Ninth Circuit Decrees Sexes Perceive Differently," *Labor Law Journal*, 43, no. 7 (1992), 449–455.

39. Slonaker, William M., and Ann C. Wendt, "No Job Is Safe from Discrimination," *HR Magazine*, 36, no. 10 (1991), 69–72.

40. Koen, "Sexual Harassment Claims Stem from a Hostile Work Environment."

41. Hames, David S., "An Actionable Condition of Work-Related Sexual Harassment," *Labor Law Journal*, 43, no. 7 (1992), 430–439; Koen, "Sexual Harassment Claims Stem from a Hostile Work Environment."

42. Twomey, *Equal Employment Law*; Greenlaw and Kohl, "Proving Title VII Sexual Harassment"; Woods, Maureen P., and Walter J. Flynn, "Heading Off Sexual Harassment," *Personnel*, 66, no. 11, (1989), 45–49; Terpstra, David E., and Douglas D. Baker, "Outcomes of Federal Court Decisions on Sexual Harassment," *Academy of Management Journal*, 35, no. 1 (1992), 181–190; Levin-Epstein, Michael D., *Primer of Equal Employment Opportunity*, 4th ed. Washington, D.C.: Bureau of National Affairs, 1987; Koen, "Sexual Harassment Claims Stem from a Hostile Work Environment."

43. Schmid, Pam, "Sexual Harassment Suit Sets Precedent," *Fort Worth Star-Telegram*, February 29, 1992, A3; Koen, "Sexual Harassment Claims Stem from a Hostile Environment."

44. Koen, "Sexual Harassment Claims Stem from a Hostile Work Environment."

45. Terpstra and Baker, "Outcomes of Federal Court Decisions on Sexual Harassment."

46. Terpstra, David E., and Douglas D. Baker, "Outcomes of Sexual Harassment Charges," *Academy of Management Journal*, 31, no. 1 (1988), 185–194.

47. Koen, "Sexual Harassment Claims Stem from a Hostile Work Environment"; Woods and Flynn, "Heading Off Sexual Harassment."

48. *EEOC v. Sage Realty Corp.*, 507 F. Supp. 599 (S.D.N.Y. 1981); Rothstein, Knapp, and Liebman, *Cases and Materials on Employment Law*; Twomey, *Equal Employment Opportunity Law.*

49. Benton, "Hands-On Approach Can Get Sticky," A14.

50. Collins, Eliza G. C., "Managers and Lovers," *Harvard Business Review*, 61, no. 5 (1983), 142–153.

51. Quinn, Robert E., and Patricia L. Lees, "Attraction and Harassment: Dynamics of Sexual Politics in the Workplace," *Organizational Dynamics*, 13, no. 2 (1984), 35–46.

52. Johnston, William B., and Arnold H. Packer, *Workforce 2000: Work and Workers for the Twenty-first Century*. Indianapolis: Hudson Institute, 1987.

53. Slonaker, William M., and Ann C. Wendt, "Pregnancy Discrimination: An Empirical Analysis of a Continuing Problem," *Labor Law Journal*, 42, no. 6 (1991), 343–350; Levin-Epstein, *Primer of Equal Employment Opportunity.*

54. Slonaker and Wendt, "Pregnancy Discrimination."

55. U.S. Department of Labor, "Your Rights Under the Family and Medical Leave Act of 1993." Washington, D.C.: U.S. Department of Labor, Employment Standards Administration, Wage and Hour Division; Barnet, Tim, Winston N. McVea, Jr., and Patricia A. Lanier, "An Overview of the Family and Medical Leave Act of 1993," *Labor Law Journal,* 44, no. 7 (1993), 429–433.

56. Postol, Lawrence P., and David D. Kaude, "An Employer's Guide to the Americans with Disabilities Act," *Labor Law Journal,* 42, no. 6 (1991), 323–342; Kohl, John P., and Paul S. Greenlaw, "The Americans with Disabilities Act of 1990: Implications for Managers," *Sloan Management Review,* 33, no. 3 (1992), 87–90; Bureau of National Affairs, "ADA Americans with Disabilities Act of 1990," *Labor Relations Reporter,* 134, no. 11 (1990), S5–S12; Mello, Jeffrey, "Employing and Accommodating Workers with Disabilities: Mandates and Guidelines for Labor Relations," *Labor Law Journal,* 44, no. 3 (1993), 162–170.

57. Postol and Kadue, "An Employer's Guide to the Americans with Disabilities Act."

58. Mello, "Employing and Accommodating Workers with Disabilities"; Krugel, Charles A., "AIDS and the ADA: Maneuvering Through a Legal Minefield," *Labor Law Journal,* 44, no. 7 (1993), 408–421; Postol and Kadue, "An Employer's Guide to the Americans with Disabilities Act."

59. Snyder, David A., "Qualified Individuals with Disabilities: Defining the ADA's Protected Class," *Labor Law Journal,* 44, no. 2 (1993), 101–109, Postol and Kadue, "An Employer's Guide to the Americans with Disabilities Act."

60. Mello, "Employing and Accommodating Workers with Disabilities."

61. Ibid.

62. Ibid.; Postol and Kadue, "An Employer's Guide to the Americans with Disabilities Act."

63. Frierson, James G., "An Employer's Dilemma: The ADA's Provisions on Reasonable Accommodation and Confidentiality," *Labor Law Journal,* 43, no. 5 (1992), 308–312.

64. Postol and Kadue, "An Employer's Guide to the Americans with Disabilities Act"; Krugel, "AIDS and the ADA"; Frierson, "An Employer's Dilemma."

65. Brady, Teresa, "The Legal Issues Surrounding Religious Discrimination in the Workplace," *Labor Law Journal,* 44, no. 4 (1993), 246–251; *Ansonia Board of Education v. Philbrook,* 479 U.S. 60 (1986); Wermiel, Stephen, "High Court Allows Employers Leeway In Accommodating Workers' Religions," *The Wall Street Journal,* November 18, 1986, 7; Sculnick, Michael W., "Reasonable Accommodation of Religious Observances," *Employment Relations Today,* 14, no. 1 (1987), 9–15.

66. Brady, "The Legal Issues Surrounding Religious Discrimination in the Workplace"; *Trans World Airlines, Inc. v. Hardison,* 432 U.S. 63 (1977).

67. Brady, "The Legal Issues Surrounding Religious Discrimination in the Workplace."

68. Ibid.

69. Ibid., 246.

70. Leonard, Arthur S., "Sexual Orientation and the Workplace: A Rapidly Developing Field," *Labor Law Journal,* 44, no. 9 (1993), 574–583.

71. Jacobs, Roger B., with Cora S. Koch, *Legal Compliance Guide to Personnel Management.* Englewood Cliffs, N.J.: Prentice Hall, 1993.

72. Ibid.

73. Ibid.

74. Rothstein, Knapp, and Liebman, *Cases and Materials on Employment Law;* Milkovich, George T., and Jerry M. Newman, *Compensation,* 2nd ed. Plano, Tex.: Business Publications, 1987.

75. McCaffery, Robert M., *Employee Benefit Programs: A Total Compensation Perspective,* 2nd ed. Boston: PWS-Kent, 1992; Overman, Stephenie. "Wake-up Call on Retiree Health Costs," *HR News,* 11, no. 11 (1992), A3; Jennifer Files, "Big Firms A'Counting: Rule Change Likely to Hurt Retiree Benefits," *Dallas Morning News,* December 17, 1992, D1–D2.

76. Files, "Big Firms A'Counting."

77. Overman, "Wake-up Call on Retiree Health Costs."

78. Files, "Big Firms A'Counting," D2.

79. Rosenbaum, Philip I., "Pension-Rule Pinch," *Fort Worth Star-Telegram,* January 1, 1993, B1–B2.

80. Stautberg, Susan S., "Status Report: The Corporation and Trends in Family Issues," *Human Resource Management,* 26, 2 (1987), 277–290.

81. Morgan, Hall, and Kerry Tucker, *Companies That Care.* New York: Simon & Schuster/Fireside, 1991.

82. Cook, Alice H., "Public Policies to Help Dual-Earner Families Meet the Demands of the Work World," *Industrial and Labor Relations Review,* 42, no. 2 (1989), 201–215; Stautberg, "Status Report: The Corporation and Trends in Family Issues."

83. Stautberg, "Status Report: The Corporation and Trends in Family Issues," 288.

84. U.S. Department of Labor, "Your Rights Under the Family and Medical Leave Act of 1993"; Barnet, McVea, and Lanier, "An Overview of the Family and Medical Leave Act of 1993."

85. Barnet, McVea, and Lanier, "An Overview of the Family and Medical Leave Act of 1993."
86. Ibid., p. 430.
87. Susser, Peter A., and David H. Jett, "Negligent Hiring: What You Don't Know Can Hurt You," *Employment Relations Today*, 14, no. 3 (1987), 279–286; Miller, Gary D., and James W. Fenton, Jr., "Negligent Hiring and Criminal Record Information: A Muddled Area of Employment Law," *Labor Law Journal*, 42, no. 3 (1991), 186–192.
88. Clausing, Jeri, "Children to Receive Millions," *Fort Worth Star-Telegram*, October 3, 1992, 23A, 26A.
89. Susser and Jett, "Negligent Hiring: What You Don't Know Can Hurt You"; Miller and Fenton, "Negligent Hiring and Criminal Record Information."
90. Ibid.
91. Susser and Jett, "Negligent Hiring: What You Don't Know Can Hurt You," 285.
92. Miller and Fenton, "Negligent Hiring and Criminal Record Information," 189.
93. Lake, Monte B., and Lynnette R. Conway, "Avoiding Discriminatory Immigration-Related Employment Practices," *Employment Relations Today*, 15, no. 1 (1988), 49–55; Levin-Epstein, *Primer of Equal Employment Opportunity*; Twomey, *Equal Employment Opportunity Law*.
94. Krueger, Alan B., "The Evolution of Unjust-Dismissal Legislation in the United States," *Industrial and Labor Relations Review*, 44, no. 4 (1991), 644–660.
95. Mandelbaum, Leonard B., "Employment at Will: Is the Model Termination Act the Answer?" *Labor Law Journal*, 44, no. 5 (1993), 275–285.
96. Krueger, "The Evolution of Unjust-Dismissal Legislation in the United States," 644.
97. Mandelbaum, "Employment at Will"; Hauserman, Nancy R., and Cheryl L. Maranto, "The Union Substitution Hypothesis Revisited: Do Judicially Created Exceptions to the Termination-at-Will Doctrine Hurt Unions?" *Marquette Law Review*, 72, no. 3 (1989), 317–348.
98. Twomey, *Equal Employment Opportunity Law*; Naeve, Robert A., *Wrongful Termination*. Walnut Creek, Calif.: Borgman Associates, 1990; Krueger, "The Evolution of Unjust-Dismissal Legislation in the United States"; Mandelbaum, "Employment at Will."
99. *Wagenseller v. Scottsdale Memorial Hospital*, 147 Ariz. 370, 710 P.2d 1025 (1985); Mackey, Daniel M., *Employment at Will and Employer Liability*. New York: American Management Association, 1986.
100. Mackey, *Employment at Will and Employer Liability*, 41.
101. Naeve, *Wrongful Termination*; Krueger, "The Evolution of Unjust-Dismissal Legislation in the United States"; Mandelbaum, "Employment at Will"; Twomey, *Equal Employment Opportunity Law*.
102. Stieber, Jack, and Richard N. Block, "Comment on Alan B. Krueger, 'The Evolution of Unjust-Dismissal Legislation in the United States,'" *Industrial and Labor Relations Review*, 45, no. 4 (1992), 792–799; Mandelbaum, "Employment at Will"; Mackey, *Employment at Will and Employer Liability*.
103. Bierman, Leonard, and Stuart A. Youngblood, "Interpreting Montana's Pathbreaking Wrongful Discharge from Employment Act: A Preliminary Analysis," *Montana Law Review*, 53, no. 1 (1992), 53–74; Krueger, "The Evolution of Unjust-Dismissal Legislation in the United States."
104. Krueger, "The Evolution of Unjust-Dismissal Legislation in the United States."
105. Maltby, Lewis L., "The Decline of Employment at Will—A Quantitative Analysis," *Labor Law Journal*, 41, no. 1 (1990), 51–54.
106. Krueger, "The Evolution of Unjust-Dismissal Legislation in the United States"; Mandelbaum, "Employment at Will"; Stieber and Block, "Comment on Alan B. Krueger, 'The Evolution of Unjust-Dismissal Legislation in the United States.'"
107. Schwoerer, Catherine, and Benson Rosen, "Effects of Employment-at-Will Policies and Compensation Policies on Corporate Image and Job Pursuit Intentions," *Journal of Applied Psychology*, 74, no. 4 (1989), 653–656.
108. Hanson, David J., "Drug Abuse Testing Programs Gaining Acceptance in Workplace," *Chemical and Engineering News*, 64 (June 2, 1986), 7–14.
109. "Motorola Plans Drug Test for All," *Fort Worth Star-Telegram*, May 22, 1990, section 2, 1.
110. Osterloh, John D., and Charles E. Becker, "Chemical Dependency and Drug Testing in the Workplace," *Western Journal of Medicine*, 152, no. 5 (1990), 506–513.
111. American Management Association, "Fewer People Fail as Workplace Drug Testing Increases," *HR Focus*, 70, no. 6 (1993), 24.
112. American Management Association, "Fewer People Fail as Workplace Drug Testing Increases."
113. Gray, George R., and Darrel R. Brown, "Issues in Drug Testing for the Private Sector," *HR Focus*, 69, no. 11 (1992), 15.
114. Osterloh and Becker, "Chemical Dependency and Drug Testing in the Workplace; Weiss, Donald H., *Fair, Square, and Legal*. New York: AMACOM, 1991; Rothstein, Knapp, and Liebman, *Cases and Materials on Employment Law*.

115. American Management Association, "Fewer People Fail as Workplace Drug Testing Increases."
116. Greenberg, Eric R., "Test-Positive Rates Drop as More Companies Screen Employees," *HR Focus,* 69, no. 6 (1992), 7.
117. Rothstein, Knapp, and Liebman, *Cases and Materials on Employment Law.*
118. Liem, Stephen A., "The Fourth Amendment and Drug Testing in the Workplace: Current U.S. Court Decisions," *Labor Law Journal,* 43, no. 1 (1992), 50–57.
119. Osterloh and Becker, "Chemical Dependency and Drug Testing in the Workplace"; Gray and Brown, "Issues in Drug Testing for the Private Sector."
120. Rothstein, Knapp, and Liebman, *Cases and Materials on Employment Law;* Gray and Brown, "Issues in Drug Testing for the Private Sector"; Osterloh and Becker, "Chemical Dependency and Drug Testing in the Workplace."
121. Osterloh and Becker, "Chemical Dependency and Drug Testing in the Workplace"; Weiss, *Fair, Square, and Legal.*
122. Ibid.
123. Jacobs with Koch, *Legal Compliance Guide to Personnel Management,* 303.
124. Jacobs with Koch, *Legal Compliance Guide to Personnel Management;* Ledvinka, *Federal Regulation of Personnel and Human Resource Management;* Cibon and Castagnera, *Labor and Employment Law.*
125. Cibon and Castagnera, *Labor and Employment Law,* 445.
126. Commerce Clearing House, *Labor Law Course,* 26th ed. Chicago: Commerce Clearing House, 1987; Weiss, *Fair, Square, and Legal.*
127. Taylor, Benjamin, and Fred Witney, *Labor Relations Law,* 5th ed. Englewood Cliffs, N.J.: Prentice Hall, 1987.
128. Commerce Clearing House, *Labor Law Course;* Taylor and Witney, *Labor Relations Law.*
129. Commerce Clearing House, *Labor Law Course.*
130. Ibid.
131. Cibon and Castagnera, *Labor and Employment Law.*
132. Ibid.
133. "Promises, Promises, Promises," *Fort Worth Star-Telegram,* January 10, 1993, AA1.
134. Cibon and Castagnera, *Labor and Employment Law.*
135. Epstein, Richard A., *Forbidden Grounds: The Case Against Employment Discrimination Laws.* Cambridge, Mass.: Harvard University Press, 1992.
136. Brimelow and Spencer, "When Quotas Replace Merit, Everybody Suffers," 80.

Case 3

THE LEGAL ENVIRONMENT AS AN INCENTIVE FOR SMALLNESS

In the past, many large companies found that they were not competitive when faced with challenges from smaller companies that responded more quickly to market opportunities and environmental changes. As a result, some downsized and restructured to gain some of the advantages of smaller, more entrepreneurial firms. The inherent properties of smallness—such as flexibility, stream-lined decision-making processes, and closer customer contact—make it more likely that small companies can adapt more quickly to changes in their environments. An example of the efficiencies of smallness is provided by research findings that the highest sales-per-employee ratios are found in companies having fewer than twenty employees. Unsurprisingly, small companies and businesses are becoming an increasingly important source of jobs. Outsourced work from large companies and the emergence of network or unbundled organizations are other important reasons for the growth of employment accounted for by small firms.[1]

U.S. politicians may have become more aware of the job contributions of small businesses. Some may also have recognized the potential impact on such businesses of expanding regulation of human resource management. Such awareness may be reflected in the threshold employment level of fifty employees for coverage by the federal Family and Medical Leave Act of 1993. Such awareness is indicated in the following quotation.

> It has become a mantra of politicians of every hue: small businesses are the engine of growth in jobs, and so deserve special treatment compared with the rest of corporate America. Many laws and regulations (affirmative-action programmes . . . the new Family Leave Act and so forth) exempt businesses with fewer than 50 employees.[2]

Threshold employment levels for coverage by other federal employment laws are 100 for the Worker Adjustment and Retraining Notification Act, twenty for the Age Discrimination in Employment Act, fifteen for the Civil Rights Act of 1964, fifteen for the Pregnancy Discrimination Act, and fifteen for the Americans with Disabilities Act of 1990. (It should be noted that states may have similar laws with lower employment thresholds.)

Aside from the responsiveness and efficiency-related reasons for growth in the importance of small business, the expanding legal environment may also have had an impact on the strategies of entrepreneurs. One need look no further than the daily newspaper to find examples of the extended legal environment. Applications of the Americans with Disabilities Act of 1990 provide some of the latest illustrations. For example, Weight Watchers was sued because of the "company's refusal to offer sign language at its meetings."[3] Regardless of whether such suits against larger organizations are upheld, they probably convince some small business entrepreneurs that federal laws represent a threat. As a result, it has been observed that entrepreneurs may view the threshold employment levels of federal laws as an important determinant of their strategies. They do not want to increase employment to the point where they are covered by federal employment laws.[4] Aside from a strategy to limit employment or substitute capital for labor, an entrepreneur may pursue a growth strategy by adding several small independent entities rather than pursuing a growth strategy within one company. There is precedent for the latter strategy as some unionized construction contractors have established independent companies that operate on a nonunion basis. Further, small companies can outsource activities, such as payroll and accounting functions, in order to keep their employment levels down.

Interestingly, in the high-technology sector, small companies are making use of flexible assembly lines and manufacturing techniques to meet the changing needs of current markets. Such technology requires highly skilled employees.[5] Employees having such skills typically have greater mobility than less-skilled workers. In the absence of legal protections against unfair treatment by their employers, the mobility of such employees may guarantee at least a minimum level of fair treatment as employers will have a strong incentive to preserve their investments in such employees.

Questions

1. Examine the viability of a strategy based on keeping employment levels below the threshold levels for coverage by federal employment laws. What are the threats and opportunities of such strategies?

2. As a result of exclusion of small businesses from coverage by some federal laws, the employees of such businesses have fewer rights than employees of larger companies. Evaluate the fairness of this situation.

3. Explain how the coverage exemptions for small businesses could put larger companies at a competitive disadvantage. Explain how the opposite might be true.

4. It may be argued that employment thresholds for legal coverage provide congressional acknowledgment that employment laws restrict competitiveness and productivity. If this is true, why is the legal regulation of human resource management expanding? Conversely, how could laws such as the Family and Medical Leave Act of 1993 and the Worker Adjustment and Retraining and Notification Act increase productivity?

5. Discuss why employees of small companies or businesses would be more or less likely to be treated unfairly by their employers. Explain the rationale for your answer.

REFERENCES

1. Kanter, Rosabeth M., *When Giants Learn to Dance: Mastering the Challenge of Strategy, Management, and Careers in the 1990s.* New York: Simon & Schuster, 1989; "Ain't Necessarily So," *The Economist,* September 11, 1993, A22–A23; Snow, Charles C., Raymond E. Miles, and Henry J. Coleman, Jr., "Managing 21st Century Network Organizations," *Organizational Dynamics,* 20, no. 3 (1992), 5–20; Phillips, Bruce D., "The Increasing Role of Small Firms in the High-Technology Sector: Evidence from the 1980s," *Business Economics,* 26, no. 1 (1991), 40–47.
2. "Ain't Necessarily So," *The Economist,* A22.
3. Mahlburg, Bob, "Disability Suit Hits Diet Firm," *Fort Worth Star-Telegram,* May 8, 1994, A1.
4. Personal observations reported by John Thompson, Texas Christian University, 1993.
5. Phillips, "The Increasing Role of Small Firms in the High-Technology Sector."

4

STRATEGY FORMULATION

The fourth component in the conceptual framework, strategy formulation, provides direction to the organization. Effective organizational strategies are required for the organization to accomplish its mission while being guided by an investment perspective. After scanning the environment for opportunities and threats and the introspective process of evaluating strengths and weaknesses, the organization is ready for strategy formulation. As noted in the preface, human resource planning may also provide input for strategy formulation although it is sequenced in the conceptual framework after strategy formulation.

This chapter will first discuss the importance of human resource management to strategy formulation. Following this, the theoretical foundations for strategic human resource management will be presented along with strategic concepts and definitions. International strategy, a topic of rapidly growing importance, will then be covered. The chapter examines the contributions that human resources can make to corporate strategy and the interaction between strategy and human resources. After this discussion, strategy-driven role behaviors, human resource strategic types, network organizations, and organizational learning will be examined. Then the integration of strategy and human resource planning will be explored. Finally, personal requirements of strategically oriented roles will be discussed. Although the material presented in this chapter is often expressed in a human resource context, the strategic principles have broad application to all managers.

IMPORTANCE OF HUMAN RESOURCES TO STRATEGY

Human resource management has become more important to general management, largely as a result of its role in providing competitive advantage, the rush to competitiveness, and an awareness of the demands of the technologically advanced environment of the future.[1] Strategist Michael Porter has found that human resource management is a key to obtaining competitive advantage in some industries.[2] In a growing number of organizations human resources are now viewed as a source of competitive advantage. There is greater recognition that distinctive competencies are obtained through highly developed employee skills, distinctive organizational cultures, management processes, and systems. This is in contrast to traditional emphasis on transferable resources such as equipment, which can be purchased by competitors. Increasingly, it is being recognized that competitive advantage can be obtained with a high-quality work force that enables organizations to compete on the basis of market responsiveness, product and service quality, differentiated products, and technological innovation, instead of reliance on low costs.[3] An example of human resource–based competitive advantage is provided by John Deere's efforts to automate its factories. As a result of the development of exceptional talent and expertise in factory automation, the company established a technology division.[4] An indicator of human resource management's importance is provided by ARCO's increased emphasis on human resource management issues in its executive development program.[5] Examples such as these indicate the broader responsibilities and competitive importance of today's more strategically oriented human resource management.

Aside from its role in providing competitive advantage through a quality work force, the necessity of controlling labor costs has also elevated the role of human resource management. As a result of intense pressure to control costs, general managers have gained a greater awareness of the impact of inefficient use of human resources. Managers need look no further than underutilized workers, lack of trust, resistance to change, antagonistic labor–management relations, motivational problems, and restrictive work practices to find causes of lower productivity. Interestingly, resources allocated toward better utilization of human resources may prove to be more cost efficient than investments in plant and equipment. Because of potential cost efficiencies, improved human resource management can play a key role in the organization's competitive strategy and in the development of distinctive competencies.[6]

Economic turbulence has also increased the importance of human resource management's strategic role. Turbulence, globalization, technology, dramatically changing demographics, and differences in work-force values have created almost unprecedented environmental uncertainty. Strategic human resource management and the subprocess of human resource planning are increasingly being seen as means of buffering environmental uncertainty. Unsurprisingly, human resource management is becoming integrated into the strategy formulation and planning process.[7] As human resource management becomes a more important component of a company's competitive strategy, general management has an incentive to insure alignment and consistency between strategy and human resource practices and policies.[8] The first alignment challenge comes with finding the answer to this question: "What kinds of people will be needed to lead the organization in the years to come?"[9] Although there has not been much empirical research on this point to date, organizational performance is expected to improve as a result of alignment or fit. However, one small-scale study of companies in declining industries has confirmed these expectations by finding higher performance to be related to integrated, strategic human resource management.[10] There has also been a recognition of human resource management's contributions to company success in international endeavors. Such success is more likely when international involvement is rewarded and international business training is provided. It is also more likely when managerial selection and promotion criteria incorporate international experience.[11] Nonetheless, before such contributions can be made, a coherent human resource strategy must be developed and linked to the organization's overall strategy.

THEORETICAL FOUNDATIONS

Strategic Concepts and Definitions

In recent years, *strategic human resource management* has become a commonly used term in the management literature. In general, the goal of strategic human resource management is the effective application of such resources to meet organizations' strategic requirements and objectives. When defining the term, practitioners tend to emphasize its implementation role, as revealed in the following definitions:[12]

> ... getting the strategy of the business implemented effectively ... getting everybody from the top of the human organization to the bottom doing things that make the business successful.[13]

Randall Schuler has developed a more comprehensive academic definition of strategic human resource management:

> Strategic human resources management is largely about integration and adaption. Its concern is to ensure that: (1) human resources (HR) management is fully integrated with the strategy and the strategic needs of the firm; (2) HR policies cohere both across policy areas and across hierarchies; and (3) HR practices are adjusted, accepted, and used by line managers and employees as part of their everyday work.[14]

Patrick Wright and Gary McMahan have offered a similar definition of strategic human resource management.[15] Their definition is "the pattern of planned human resource deployments and activities intended to enable an organization to achieve its goals."[16]

Given these definitions, a comprehensive theoretical framework can now be used to organize knowledge of how human resource practices are impacted by strategic considerations. Such a theoretical framework has been developed by Patrick Wright and Gary McMahan and is presented in Figure 4-1. This framework presents six theoretical influences, four of which provide explanations for practices resulting from strategy considerations. (1) The first, the *resources-based view,* explains practices that provide competitive advantage, such as the unique allocation of the firm's resources, organizational culture, and distinctive competence. For example, a firm might allocate its resources to produce superior selection procedures and compensation systems in order to obtain distinctive competence. (2) The second influence, a *behavioral view,* is based on contingency theory. This view explains practices designed to control and influence attitudes and behaviors, and stresses the instrumentality of such practices in achieving strategic objectives. (3) The third draws on *cybernetics systems.* This view explains the adoption or abandonment of practices resulting from feedback on contributions to strategy. When viewed from this perspective, training programs might be adopted to help the organization pursue a strategy and would be

FIGURE 4-1 STRATEGIC HUMAN RESOURCE MANAGEMENT: A THEORETICAL FRAMEWORK

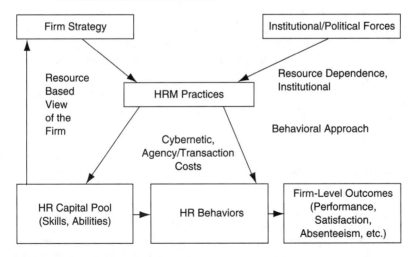

Source: Patrick M. Wright and Gary C. McMahan, "Theoretical Perspectives for Strategic Human Resource Management," *Journal of Management,* 18, no. 2 (1992), 299. Reprinted with permission.

updated according to feedback. (4) The fourth, an *agency/transaction costs view*, explains why companies use control systems such as performance evaluation and reward systems. In the absence of performance evaluation systems linked to reward systems, strategies might not be pursued.[17]

The other two theories provide explanations for personnel practices that are not driven by strategy considerations. (5) *Resource dependence and power theories* explain practices caused by power and political influences such as legislation, unionization, control of resources, and expectations of social responsibility. (6) The final influence, *institutional theory*, explains that practices, such as the use of inappropriate performance evaluation dimensions, may exist because of organizational inertia rather than conscious or rational decision making.[18]

Strategy

The contemporary literature provides a number of different definitions of *strategic management*. James Brian Quinn's definition of strategy focuses on the integration of goals, policies, and action sequences: "A strategy is the *pattern* or *plan* that *integrates* an organization's *major* goals, policies, and action sequences into a *cohesive* whole."[19] Thus, strategy deals with providing direction, coordinating, and providing a decisional framework. Another role of strategy deals with the allocation of resources. The following definition by William Henn focuses on this aspect of strategy: "Strategy is the concentration of resources on selected opportunities for competitive advantage."[20] A similar point is made by the strategist Kenichi Ohmae, "Merely allocating resources in the same way as your competitors will yield no competitive advantage."[21] Henn's and Ohmae's definitions focus on making hard decisions to take resources from less promising product lines, projects, and so forth and concentrating them in areas where the company can obtain a strategic advantage. By failing to be selective about opportunities and failing to make tough decisions about the company's distribution of resources, they are spread too thin across all product lines. As a result, companies that fail to concentrate their resources are at a disadvantage.[22] Thus, strategy performs directional, coordinating, decision-making, and resource allocation functions.

Strategic Planning

Definitions of *strategic planning*, also called the strategy formulation process,[23] differ in their emphasis on rationality and formality. The following is James Craft's description of *rational/comprehensive* strategic planning:

> The rational/comprehensive process, frequently advocated in strategic planning texts and apparently by many practitioners, emphasizes purposeful activity through a logical formulation of goals, examination of alternatives, and delineation of plans prior to actions. It tends to have a long-term orientation and focuses on measurable forces affecting the firm, as well as on quantitative activities and procedures.[24]

The process of formal rational/comprehensive strategic planning is typically comprised of the following steps: (1) development of organizational philosophy and mission statement; (2) environmental scanning; (3) analysis of strengths, weaknesses, opportunities, and threats (SWOT Analysis); (4) formulation of strategic objectives; (5) generation of alternative strategies for achieving objectives; and (6) evaluation and selection of strategies. This series of steps makes no mention of the political aspects of strategic planning. Nonetheless, the formality of the process and its emphasis on logic and quantitative processes, should not obscure the fact that strategic planning is conducted by a dominant coalition. Because of the political nature of the process, some aspects of a plan will be negotiated.[25]

In contrast to formal rational/comprehensive strategic planning, *informal/incremental* strategic planning emphasizes the emergent and temporal nature of strategy and has a shorter-term orientation.[26] According to James Bryan Quinn, to a certain extent the managed or logical incremental approach represents an adaptive process, making changes and adjustments to strategy on the basis of new information. Such planning is not "muddling through," "disjointed," or "unconscious." Further, managed or logical incremental planning is not inconsistent with formal planning but leads instead to quicker implementation and reduces the likelihood of catastrophic errors that might result from rigid adherence to formal rational/comprehensive planning.[27] Logical incrementalism is consistent with adapting to input from organizational subunits and functional areas as information becomes available. This appears to be the case as more of the responsibilities of strategic planning are being shared with line managers.[28]

Although the two types of strategic planning differ, their use is not mutually exclusive as companies tend to employ both approaches. In reality it is probably more useful to think of strategic planning as a balance between rational/comprehensive and incremental planning or a matter of degree.[29] Regardless of the degree of formality versus incrementalism, strategic planning serves a number of vital functions. These functions are presented in Table 4-1.[30]

TABLE 4-1   FUNCTIONS OF STRATEGIC PLANNING

1. Periodic forward scanning
2. Analysis based on longer time frame
3. Communication about goals and resource allocation
4. Framework for short-term plan evaluation and integration
5. Institutionalization of longer-term time horizons necessary for investments such as in research and development
6. Decisional criteria framework for short-term decision making

Source: Adapted from James B. Quinn, "Strategic Change: Logical Incrementalism," *Sloan Management Review*, 30, no. 4 (1989), 45–55.

Planning in Strategic Business Units

To this point, the discussion of strategic planning has been primarily focused at the corporate level. Human resource management also plays an important role at the level of the strategic business unit. This role may be examined in the context of human resources input in the development of strategic alternatives. For example, a strategic business unit's marketing group may identify an opportunity during its planning processes. Marketing planners then develop alternative strategies for exploiting the opportunity. As a part of the planning process, representatives from the functional areas such as production, finance, and human resources make inputs on the strengths, weaknesses, and resource requirements. Human resource management would be expected to provide an analysis of the staffing implications of each alternative. The product of these planning processes is then submitted to the corporate top management team for approval and funding. In many corporations, the vice president for human resources would also be a member of the executive committee making the final decisions on these planning proposals. This representation of human resources by the human resource vice president or senior human resource official would constitute a separate role.[31]

Human Resource Strategy

To this point, the discussion of strategy and strategic planning has focused on the general concept of strategic human resource management and the relatively broad concepts of corporate-level and strategic business unit considerations. The next focal point is *human resource strategy*, which has been defined by Randall Schuler as follows: "HR strategies are essentially plans and programs to address and solve fundamental strategic issues related to human resources management."[32] Human resource strategy focuses on the alignment of the organization's human resource practices, policies, and programs with corporate and strategic business unit plans. Consistent human resource policies and practices are important concerns of general management as well as the human resource function.[33]

Differences in human resource management policies and practices across industries demonstrate that policies and personnel practices vary according to the environment in which companies operate. However, industrial categories do not explain all such differences because variations in company strategies also determine human resource policies and practices. Companies try to avoid excessive emphasis on consistency in attempting to obtain a fit between their strategies and human resources policies and practices. This is because excessive concern with fit can be detrimental, since there must be transition periods during which mismatches will occur. Likewise, too much fit between a company's human resources and its strategies may unnecessarily restrict the range of employee skills, detract from innovation, and limit the capacity to change.[34]

Human Resource Planning

Human resource planning provides input into higher-level strategic planning processes. One benefit of such planning is that, regardless of the accuracy of forecasts involved, the very act of developing forecasts forces managers to reassess the fundamental assumptions under which the organization operates. Other contributions of human resource planning are that it signals the need for change and serves to guide the activities within human resource management toward greater compatibility with the organization. The process of *human resource planning*, in sequential order, includes environmental scanning and an interface with strategic planning, forecasting human resource demand, inventorying the organization's current stock of human resources, forecasting both internal and external supplies of labor, comparing demand and supply forecasts, developing plans for dealing with shortages and surpluses, and feeding back these results in a strategic planning interface.[35] The actual human resource planning process is covered in greater detail in Chapter 5.

INTERNATIONAL STRATEGY

Companies use different strategies to produce products and services that enable them to compete in the global marketplace. These include multinational strategies, global strategies, transnational strategies, and strategic alliances. Nonetheless, as noted in Chapter 2, world-class work forces are required with all of these strategies. Human resource management must be able to identify sources of such labor and plan its use. Even with alliances, human resource management input will be required in both strategy formulation and implementation.[36]

Multinational, Global, and Transnational Strategies

International strategies may be described as multinational, global, transnational, or mixtures of basic strategies. With a *multinational strategy,* companies operate in countries chosen for their individual profit potential. All activities related to design, production, and marketing are then performed in each of these countries. (These are called *value chain* activities.) Such strategies, also called *multidomestic strategies,* customize the product and its marketing to each country's unique preferences. In contrast, *global strategies* produce standardized products with different activities, such as design and production, being located in different countries, depending on labor costs, skills, or other strategic advantages. With *transnational strategies* companies compete in the global marketplace through the use of networks and strategic alliances.[37]

Multinational or multidomestic strategies provide a power advantage where employees are unionized. This is because labor difficulties or other production problems only shut down production and revenue flows from one country's operations, or a small set of countries supplied by these production facilities. However, they do not produce the economies of scale of global strategies. With global strategies, economies of scale are obtained by maintaining only a few different product models. As a result lower costs and higher quality are obtained. An example of a successful application of this strategy is provided by the Japanese automobile manufacturers. A disadvantage of this approach is that standardization does not address all customers' preferences. Likewise, greater coordination is required and marketing may be less effective. A human resource implication of the global strategy is the concentration of resources and talent on a smaller set of activities. Thus, with the global strategy, it is important to locate each of the value chain activities in terms of cost or skills where there is world-class labor. Another human resource implication is that with a global strategy, a company would probably be particularly vulnerable to strikes or labor relations problems at any link in the value chain, since the whole process is dependent on each link. However, with more than one source of manufacturing facilities, the company can shift production to other operating plants.[38]

Strategic Alliances

Companies are increasing their use of *strategic alliances* with foreign companies. Such alliances allow companies to combine their distinctive competencies to gain an advantage in producing or marketing a product. Frequently U.S. companies reduce their labor requirements by forming alliances with foreign firms. However, the history of U.S. companies' experiences with strategic alliances indicates that the arrangement may be fraught with perils. According to David Lei and John Slocum, alliances can be extremely dangerous for companies that outsource manufacturing. The allure of low-cost production, without the costs of investing in product development and new manufacturing technologies, is particularly seductive. Unfortunately, U.S. companies pursuing this strategy have typically ended up being *"deskilled"* or *"hollowed out"* in critical skill areas. Although financial benefits of entering into an alliance may be impressive in the short-run, in the long-run the alliance partner doing the manufacturing typically becomes the dominant player in the market. This occurs as a result of the U.S. partner's diminished manufacturing knowledge and the manufacturing partner's capture of knowledge of the other company's core competencies.[39] Lei and Slocum have concluded the following:

> collaboration may unintentionally open up a firm's entire spectrum of core competencies, technologies, and skills to encroachment and learning by its partners. . . . Alliances can be used as an indirect strategic weapon to slowly "deskill" a partner who does not understand the risks inherent in such arrangements.[40]

A prime example of this is the consumer electronics industry in which U.S. companies such as GE, RCA, and Zenith held dominant positions in all skill areas of the industry. Twenty years after their entry into alliances, virtually no consumer electronics are manufactured in the United States, while alliance partners have become dominant in the industry. More significantly, the alliance partners have used the knowledge gained from these U.S. companies to develop core competencies and take the lead in other areas such as miniature lasers and sensor systems. The greatest danger of transferring such skills occurs in situations where there is frequent interaction and exchange between the organizations' engineering and technical employees. Companies that have outsourced manufacturing in alliances frequently no longer have the skills to compete in manufacturing and may be relegated to marketing the alliance partner's products. Further, because of the integrated design, production, and marketing processes required for today's short product development cycles, the pace of the dependent company's decline may quicken.[41]

Lei and Slocum have concluded that the importance of domestic manufacturing may have been underestimated. For example, companies that have licensed foreign companies to use their manufacturing technologies have placed themselves at future disadvantage. As Lei and Slocum pointed out, "As technology becomes a greater source of competitive advantage, licensing decisions can often radically shift the firm's competitive posture in that industry."[42] An indication of U.S. dependency is provided by the listing of such alliances in Table 4-2.

Human resource managers need to know how to decrease the likelihood of these undesirable outcomes. Measures that may prevent alliances from working to the eventual disadvantage of the company include (1) understanding the real aspirations of the alliance partner, (2) keeping in mind the original purposes of the alliance so that objectives are not redefined to the company's disadvantage, (3) avoiding a false sense of assurance provided by legal control since the real key is knowledge transfer, and (4) keeping alliance interface managers in place over long periods of time so that subtle nuances are understood.[43] Since the latter is often in opposition to the length of management development job rotation cycles, human resource managers may need to lengthen such cycles.

Sustainable Global Competitive Advantage

Interestingly, predictions by some observers that the United States would become an information economy while underdeveloped countries would take on the less-skilled manufacturing roles, appear to have been off the mark. These predictions have underestimated the intellectual resources of such countries and the limited capital investments required for entry into the information industry. For example, the city of Bangalore, India, has high-quality computer programming talent that companies from the United States and other countries are using for development of highly complex computer software. The Indian programmers have the reputation of exceptional ability and the persistence to be able to develop very complex programs.

TABLE 4-2   AREAS OF GROWING U.S. DEPENDENCY

CONSUMER ELECTRONICS	COMPOSITE MATERIALS
GE-Hitachi (TVs)	GE-Asahi Diamond (industrial diamonds)
Westinghouse-Toshiba (TVs)	Corning Glass-NGK Insulators
GE-Samsung (microwave ovens)	(high energy ceramics)
GE-Matsushita (room air conditioners)	Hercules-Toray (specialized chemicals)
RCA-Matsushita (VCRs)	Armco-Mitsubishi Rayon
Kodak-Canon	(composite plastics)
(photographic equipment)	FACTORY EQUIPMENT
Kodak-Matsushita (camcorders)	GE-Fanuc (controllers)
Kodak-Philips (photo-CD players)	GM-Fanuc (robotics)
HEAVY MACHINERY	GM-Hitachi (robotics)
Allis Chalmers-Fiat-Hitachi	Bendix-Murata (machine tools)
(construction equipment)	Cincinnati Milacron (semiconductors,
Ford-Fiat (farm equipment)	automated equipment)
Caterpillar (growing outsourcing)	Kawasaki-Unimation (robotics)
Dresser-Komatsu	Fujitsu-McDonnell Douglas
(construction equipment)	(CAD/CAM systems)
Deere-Hitachi (farm equipment)	IBM-Sankyo Seiki (robotics)
Clark-Samsung (forklift trucks)	Houdaille-Okuma (machine tools)
POWER GENERATION EQUIPMENT	Allen Bradley-Nippondenso
Westinghouse-ABB	(programmable controls)
(heavy power equipment)	Bendix-Yasegawa Tools (robotics)
TGE-Toshiba (nuclear equipment)	OFFICE EQUIPMENT
GE-Hitachi (nuclear equipment)	AT&T-Ricoh (fax machines)
GE-Mitsubishi (steam turbines)	Kodak-Canon (mid-range copiers)
Westinghouse-Mitsubishi	Fuji-Xerox (small copiers)
(motors)	3M-Toshiba (copiers)
Westinghouse-Komatsu	Apple-Toshiba (printers)
(motors, robotics)	RCA-Hitachi (PBX controls)
ABB-Combustion Engineering	Hewlett-Packard-Canon (laser printers)
(power equipment)	Xerox-Sharp (low-end copiers)

Source: David Lei and John W. Slocum, Jr., "Global Strategy, Competence-Building and Strategic Alliances," *California Management Review,* 34, no. 2 (1992), 83. Copyright © 1992 by The Regents of the University of California. Reprinted from the *California Management Review,* Vol. 34, No. 2. By permission of The Regents.

Further, their typical monthly salary of $400, versus $5,000 for comparable labor in the United States, makes them a highly sought-out source of world-class labor.[44] Strategists would do well to avoid a premature dismissal of other countries' long-run capabilities and focus on the factors that provide companies with real and *sustainable competitive advantage* in the global economy.

Likewise, there are other strategy-related, human resource implications of globalization. With greater globalization of markets, it will become more difficult for companies that do not emphasize human resources to compete with companies from other countries that have taken advantage of such resources. For example, Volkswagen has attributed some of its managerial successes to its human resources. Volkswagen maintains a long-term approach which is evident in its training programs that prepare workers for highly automated production systems. Also tied in with its human resource efforts is Volkswagen's extensive involvement in apprenticeship training programs. During one year, 4,500 apprentices were employed by Volkswagen and guaranteed permanent jobs after completion of training, even though unemployment levels in Germany were relatively high.[45] Volkswagen's stock of skilled workers may provide it with a sustainable competitive advantage over its rivals. Nonetheless, Germany's current high wage rates have offset this advantage to some extent.

Globally Competent Managers

A growing area of strategic importance is the recruitment, selection, and development of globally competent managers. Nancy Adler and Susan Bartholomew have studied the human resource requirements for *"transnationally competent managers"* who have global understandings of business and broad cultural knowledge. Such managers have the flexibility to live in different cultural environments, can interact simultaneously with individuals from several different cultures, and have an egalitarian view of colleagues from other countries. A staffing goal would be to have a rich mixture of such managers from different countries, fluent in several languages, who use world-class standards for performance benchmarks. To acquire such managers, human resource managers must hire world-class individuals from throughout the world; develop them through transnational assignments; prepare them for organizational learning roles, such as in strategic alliances; and remove any glass ceiling limitations on promotions based on home country considerations. Unfortunately, Adler and Bartholomew found that most human resource operations in U.S. and Canadian multinational corporations do not meet these requirements.[46]

Location of Production Facilities

In addition to sources of labor, decisions regarding the location of production facilities provide particularly intriguing strategy-related questions. For example, prior to passage of the North American Free Trade Agreement (NAFTA) in 1993, U.S. automobile manufacturers located assembly plants in Mexico in order to have access to the Mexican market. As a result of the passage of NAFTA, by the year 2004 U.S. automobiles can be imported into Mexico without tariffs as long as 62.5 percent of their costs results from North American production.[47] On one hand, there is less incentive to shift production facilities to Mexico because NAFTA will allow automobiles to be imported from U.S. plants without tariffs. On the other hand, lower labor costs in Mexico argue for establishing plants in Mexico to take advantage of them. It is likely that jobs requiring high skills will be retained and created in the United States while those requiring lower skills will be shifted to Mexico until its work force develops such skills.

In addition to the effects of NAFTA, the competitive environment that companies now face in Europe is different than that which existed prior to the 1992 agreements of the European Community. As a result, U.S. and other non–European Community companies have examined mergers, joint ventures, and strategic alliances as means of access to European markets. (An example of such a joint venture is the Whirlpool and Philips arrangement in which Whirlpool appliances carry the Philips brand in European markets.[48]) Another strategic issue is whether the majority of Eastern European countries will become either associate members of the European Community or members of a European free trade zone. Such memberships are important strategic human resource issues because they determine the ease of utilizing human resources across borders, as well as the markets for companies' products.[49] At this point, many of the human resource implications of these developments are uncertain. Additionally, the rapid expansion of markets in Asia has potentially enormous implications.

From this discussion of international aspects of strategy, it is evident that companies' human resource strategies and policies cannot be developed in isolation to those of global competitors. Having human resource strategies or policies superior to those of domestic competitors is no longer sufficient. Companies must scan the regulatory environments of countries in which they wish to manufacture and sell their products in order to determine the human resource implications there. Further, when they locate production facilities in other countries, they must also understand the impact of cultural differences on issues as basic as the compensation mix.[50]

HUMAN RESOURCE CONTRIBUTIONS TO STRATEGY

Human resources can make contributions to strategy and strategic planning in a number of ways. Systems such as performance appraisal, staffing, training, and compensation help enable managers to implement the organization's strategic plan. Human resource planning also links strategic management and business planning with these systems.[51] Most models of strategic human resource management view the function as having an implementation role and it has been less common to find companies using unique human resource capabilities as a primary input in strategy formulation.[52] Nonetheless, more companies are drawing on human resource management in the strategy formulation process. Situations where human resource capabilities serve as a driving force in strategy formulation occur where there are unique capabilities, such as noted earlier with the example of John Deere's creation of a technology division. Another example is Arthur Andersen's unique human resource capabilities in training. The accounting firm's Saint Charles, Illinois, training facility, which resembles a college campus, provides it with a competitive advantage.[53] Thousands of Arthur Andersen employees receive uniform training each year at this facility, which is conducted by the firm's own highly regarded instructional staff. Because of its facilities and in-house instructors, the firm can react quickly to the changing demands of its clients.

Additionally, a recognition of the human resource cost implications of strategies can be brought into the strategy formulation process when human resource management plays an important role. This was not typically the case in the past, until such costs had become extreme. To be sure, goal displacement or means-ends reversal is an outcome to be avoided when human resource capabilities are a primary driver in strategy formulation.[54] However, such dysfunctional side effects can be avoided with periodic reviews of the process.

Environmental Scanning and Corporate Intelligence

Environmental scanning is a prerequisite to strategic planning, and human resource management has a role in environmental scanning, along with finance and marketing. Scanning activities are particularly important in periods of rapidly changing technological and market environments. Typically such scanning efforts focus on trends three to five years into the future and cover developments in demographics, technology, social issues, economics, and the regulatory environment.[55] An example of trends of interest to human resource scanners might be the reactions of competitors to greater access to labor in Mexico resulting from the North American Free Trade Agreement (NAFTA) and whether Japanese auto manufacturers can find a way to assemble cars in Mexico and ship them into the United States duty-free.[56] Another example would be the Battelle Memorial Institute's development of inexpensive biodegradable plastics. Biodegradable plastics have cost as much as $250 per pound while the costs of Battelle's new plastics range from $1 to $2 per pound.[57] Other examples of the trends of interest to human resource scanners were covered in Chapter 2.

One interesting way in which the human resource management function can make additional strategic contributions is in the area of *competitive intelligence* as the function can be an important source of such information. For example, because human resource managers receive résumés from employees at competing firms within the industry, they know who is moving. They also know the skills and types of individuals headhunters and competitors are recruiting. The types of individuals applying for jobs and the trends in their applications can provide information that will help identify the direction being pursued by a competitor.[58] More specifically, human resources can provide the following *corporate intelligence:*

> From public information and legitimate recruiting and interview activities, you ought to be able to construct organization charts, staffing levels and group missions for the various organizational components of each of your

major competitors. Your knowledge of how brands are sorted among sales divisions and who reports to whom can give important clues as to a competitor's strategic priorities. You may even know the track record and characteristic behavior of the executives.[59]

Regardless of the form of linkage between human resources and the strategic planning process, human resource managers must predict the type of people that will be needed to support the strategy.[60]

Implementation of Resource Reallocation Decisions

Although strategy implementation is discussed in Chapters 6 and 7, a major role of human resource management is to assess the feasibility of implementing a strategy and provide such input in the strategy formulation process. Because the essence of strategy is to concentrate resources so that the organization can gain advantage over its competitors, some units, divisions, or product lines must be denied resources. As a result of the denial of resources, human resource management must prevent the demoralization of those not receiving resources. Often times, areas not receiving resources are still critical, at least in the short run, to the success and prosperity of the company. For example, those business areas in which there are opportunities and in which the company has strengths (the star areas) will be provided more resources. These resources would come from areas in which industry opportunities are expected to decline in the future, but in which the company has strength and is making money (cash cows). Resources would also come from those areas characterized by both unattractive industry opportunities and low company strength (dogs). As resources are taken away from the cash cows and the dogs, the manner in which employees from these areas are treated is critical to successful implementation of the strategy. For example, will those in areas facing eventual elimination be allowed to transfer out to the star areas? How will retrenchment or downsizing be handled?[61]

Lead Time for Dealing with Labor Shortages and Surpluses

Another potential contribution of human resource management comes from the lead time produced by human resource planning. The greater lead time provides alternatives for dealing with shortages or surpluses of labor. Additionally, if the organization has included the use of temporary and contingent employees in its staffing strategy, such employees provide a mechanism for strategic maneuvering as this type of labor can sometimes be considered as a variable cost. As a result, employers have more degrees of freedom and flexibility to exercise options.[62] Unfortunately, human resource management does not yet have a strategic role in many organizations and as a result, such lead time apparently is not yet provided in many companies. A survey of the human resource managers of midwestern manufacturing companies, making public statements about financial problems or threats from intense competition, revealed that 94 percent of them had fewer than sixty days to plan downsizing. As a result, other alternatives were seldom considered in these companies.[63]

STRATEGY-DRIVEN ROLE BEHAVIORS AND PRACTICES

Randall Schuler and Susan Jackson have made an important contribution to the literature by explaining how different role behaviors and human resource practices correspond to different strategies. They have explained that role behaviors needed of employees throughout an organization provide a rationale for the linkage between competitive strategies and human resource practices. Drawing on the competitive strategies of innovation, quality enhancement, and cost reduction, Schuler and Jackson have explained that different employee behaviors are needed for successful implementation of different strategies. These behaviors are roles which go beyond skills, knowledge, and abilities.[64]

Essentially, for successful implementation of an innovation strategy, employees probably need to be cooperative because of the interdependencies involved; highly creative; oriented toward the long-term; risk takers, and comfortable with ambiguity. (Companies pursuing such strategies include Johnson & Johnson, 3M, and Hewlett-Packard.) With quality-enhancement strategies, employees need to place emphasis on production or service processes, risk reduction, and predictability. (Examples of companies pursuing quality-enhancement strategies include L. L. Bean, Toyota, and Corning Glass.) For successful implementation of cost-reduction strategies employees should be focused on the short-term, risk-averse, predictable, results-oriented, and comfortable working by themselves.[65]

For each of the different sets of strategies and role behaviors, different human resource practices are required. General categories of such human resource practices include planning, staffing, appraisal, compensation, and training and development. Schuler and Jackson have hypothesized that under *innovation strategies*, the appropriate role behaviors more likely will be obtained with (1) group-oriented, long-term appraisal systems, (2) generalized skill development and broad career paths, (3) compensation approaches accentuating internal equity, and (4) flexible compensation packages including stock ownership. For *quality-enhancement strategies*, they have hypothesized that human resource practices should include (1) employment security guarantees, (2) extensive training programs, and (3) participative decision making. With *cost-reduction strategies*, they have hypothesized that desired role behaviors are more likely with (1) performance appraisal systems emphasizing results in the short-term, (2) virtually no training programs, (3) very specialized jobs, (4) narrow and specialized career paths, and (5) procedures for continual tracking of wage rates in the labor market.[66]

HUMAN RESOURCE STRATEGIC TYPES

Greater understanding of industrial and strategic differences can be obtained by examining different classifications of *strategic types*. Interestingly, principles of enlightened management suggest that companies should develop their employees, strive toward providing employment security, and seek to have supplies of internal candidates prepared for promotion when vacancies occur. Nonetheless, some companies do not manage their human resources in accordance with these principles, nor is there any indication that they should. In fact, promises of job security, committing too much of the company's resources to human resource programs, and placing too much emphasis on employees' feelings about strategic decisions can make the company uncompetitive.[67] An analysis of Digital Equipment Corporation's experience with employment security policies following the plunge of its stock in 1983 revealed the following: "One discovery DEC made was that the provisions of employment security did not automatically motivate employees to learn new skills, change jobs, or relocate to the extent demanded by the crisis."[68] Examples such as DEC's demonstrate that the application of human resource management principles must be tempered by industry differences.

Systematic differences in utilization of human resource practices may be explained by a typology of career systems developed by Jeffrey Sonnenfeld and Maury Peiperl. Companies in this typology are classified as (1) *clubs*, (2) *baseball teams*, (3) *academies*, and (4) *fortresses*. This typology has been overlaid on an earlier typology of strategies developed by Raymond Miles and Charles Snow. In the Miles and Snow typology, the corresponding four basic types of strategies are, respectively: (1) defenders (low-cost producers), (2) prospectors (product differentiators), (3) analyzers (focused operations), and (4) reactors (companies with dysfunctional strategies). Figure 4-2 presents the Sonnenfeld and Peiperl model.[69]

The personnel policies followed by companies in each of these categories provide marked contrasts. For economy of presentation in the following discussion, the characteristics of companies in the Miles and Snow categories are covered within the Sonnenfeld and Peiperl categories.

Club. When the strategy is to be the *low-cost* producer, the focus in on cost control. With cost control as the guiding principle, predictability and a short-term focus are valued.[70] Companies in this category compete by increasing their efficiency in controlling costs, maintaining quality, and providing customer service. Types of companies in the club category include airlines, banks, utilities, and governmental agencies. Club personnel policies emphasize development and training. As new employees are hired only at the entry level, talent is developed within the organization, and higher-level vacancies are filled by promotions from within. There is an expectation that employees will remain with the company for a long period and there is low turnover. In terms of "make" or "buy," these companies make their own

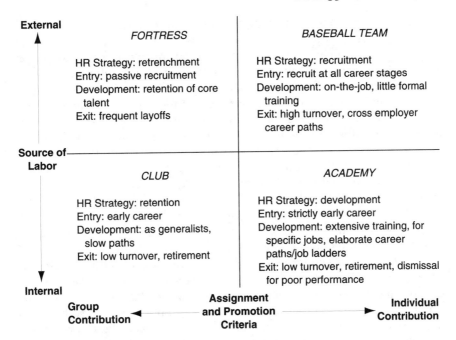

FIGURE 4-2 STRATEGIC STAFFING POLICIES

Source: Modification of figure from Jeffrey A. Sonnenfeld and Maury A. Peiperl, "Staffing Policy as a Strategic Response: A Typology of Career Systems," *Academy of Management Review,* 13, no. 4 (1988), 591. Reprinted with permission.

higher-level employees. A company well-known for its managerial excellence in this category would be Lincoln Electric.[71]

Baseball Team. Sonnenfeld and Peiperl's framework, investment banks, broadcasting companies, software developers, entertainment companies, and biological research companies fit in this category. Professional firms such as law firms, advertising agencies, consulting firms, and accounting firms also fit in this category. Companies in this category may pursue an *innovation* strategy. As such, they design and produce new products and routinely redeploy resources from discontinued products to the development of new ones. Hewlett-Packard is an example of a successful company in this category. When innovation is the strategy, those organizational conditions that foster risk taking and creativity are valued. In such companies there is almost continual redeployment of personnel. Employees are often very talented individuals who have relatively low commitment to the company. There is competition for advancement from talent both within the company as well as individuals external to the organization. Unsurprisingly, companies in this quadrant also tend to have high turnover.[72]

The baseball team brings in talent at any level within the organization and does not place much emphasis on development. Instead there is a "buy" approach to talent. Nonetheless, there may also be development through rapid assignment changes. However, career paths often involve interorganizational moves as individuals take jobs with other companies as they develop and command greater compensation, responsibility, and professional stature. There is employment insecurity and promotion policies are often "up or out" as those passed over are terminated. Unsurprisingly, in such companies, performance appraisals are more results-oriented.[73] The trading of baseball players from one team to another provides a good example of career paths and the high talent and high turnover of the organizations in this category. Another example of career progression in this category might be the local television reporter who moves up to a national news network. Empirical evidence of distinctive make or buy patterns of human resource management practices has been established in a study of MBA students who have accepted offers of employment.[74]

Closer examination of the baseball team quadrant indicates some potential contradictions. Sonnenfeld and Peiperl's category of baseball teams does not correspond completely with Miles and Snow's prospector category since CPA firms and law firms probably do not operate at the same level of innovation as prospectors such as Hewlett-Packard. Firms emphasizing innovation, the prospectors in Miles and Snow's typology, have also been found to place a heavier emphasis on training and development than less innovative companies. There is also a need for lower turnover in such firms because the loss of personnel can be extremely disruptive.[75] Great disruption results from turnover in these firms because their quick rate of learning often leaves organizational knowledge unrecorded. Explanation for this apparent contradiction may require more complex descriptions of baseball teams in Sonnenfeld and Peiperl's typology. Even without considering prospectors, within the baseball team quadrant itself, law firms and CPA firms do indeed have high turnover, but typically it is confined mainly to the lower levels. The employees at the higher levels—the partners—have very low turnover as they are frequently able to reap the financial rewards of managing the efforts of junior professionals.

Academy.   Academies are somewhat of a hybrid in that they are both product innovators and competitors in long-run production roles as well. They attempt to exploit niches in the marketplace. Types of companies in this category include manufacturers of electronics, pharmaceutics, consumer products, and automobiles. Texas Instruments is an example of a successful academy. The personnel policies of the academy, which follows a *focused* strategy, fall between the two extremes of clubs and baseball teams. In this category there is substantial emphasis on development but a few outsiders may be hired to fill higher-level positions. These companies make human resources and have extensive career paths within the companies themselves. Performance appraisal tends to emphasize process.[76] Although the personnel policies of these companies differ, they are consistent with their companies' overall strategies.

Fortress. Companies in this category are in highly competitive markets and are at the mercy of their environments. Examples of the types of companies in this category include those in hotels, retailing, publishing, textiles, and natural resources.[77] Because companies in this category are essentially reactive, there are few systematic strategic implications.

NETWORK ORGANIZATIONS AND STRATEGY

Network organizations were discussed in Chapter 2 as an important development in the human resource environment. Such organizations have developed as a result of advances in communications technology, desires for work-force flexibility, and intensified worldwide competition brought about by financial and economic deregulation. According to Charles Snow, Raymond Miles, and Henry Coleman, *network organizations,* which evolved during the 1980s, readily acquire or divest their organizational units based on their return on assets and outsource activities that other companies or venture partners can produce at a lower cost in less time. Outsourcing enables network organizations to maintain an optimal size and a lower economic risk of ventures into new markets. Essentially, network organizations retain for themselves only those activities in which they have expertise. Several different firms may be involved in a network, with the activities of product design, manufacturing, and distribution being performed by the specialist in each area.[78]

There are differences among network organizations in their degree of permanence and externality. They can even operate internally within giant companies, such as General Motors. In the case of internal networks, efficiencies are sought through the use of market-priced transactions between network components. For external networks, at one end of the spectrum are dynamic networks that have lead companies basically acting as brokers, outsourcing virtually all activities to a changing set of companies. Lewis Galoob toys, with only 100 employees, provides an example of such a network that outsources design, development, manufacturing, distribution, and collection of accounts receivable. At the other end of the external spectrum are stable networks in which one company remains as the central core as an investor and outsources to subsidiaries and other independent companies; BMW provides an example of this. As a result of computer, satellite, and telecommunications technology, components of the network which perform outsourced activities may be located throughout the world.[79]

One strategic implication of network organizations is that lead firms will need employees who have the entrepreneurial skills required for the broker activities of establishing the network. Project management experience across functional areas may help develop the kinds of skills needed. Additionally, the intrapreneurship approaches of firms such as Texas Instruments may also develop the entrepreneurial skills needed to establish networks. Further, because the establishment and operation of networks require contracting skills, construction engineering management and positions requiring negotiation roles may prove to be good sources of network operators. While network lead companies and brokers have fewer permanent employees than more conventional companies, they will have to invest heavily in the training of their permanent core of employees in order to develop and maintain such skills.[80]

ORGANIZATIONAL LEARNING

As noted earlier, one of the problems of international alliances is that one partner may learn more and benefit more from the alliance than the other partner. Companies sometimes become deskilled as a result of the alliance. This has been a problem for U.S. companies, particularly in alliances with Japanese and Korean companies. The problem is especially important because competitive advantage is increasingly being obtained from the invisible assets of *organizational knowledge* and information.[81] This knowledge or know-how is also referred to as *intellectual capital.* Increasingly, intellectual capital is being viewed as a source of competitive advantage. Further, a rate of *organizational learning* faster than competitors is important to maintaining such an advantage. One of the challenges related to intellectual capital is that most companies lack experience in managing it. Nonetheless, less hierarchy, fewer rules, and an absence of barriers to the free exchange of information within organizations appears important to effective management of intellectual capital. One reason why intellectual capital has not received enough emphasis is the difficulty in measuring it.[82] This is unsurprising as intellectual capital may be described as "the sum of everything everybody in your company knows that gives you a competitive edge in the marketplace."[83] Nonetheless, a crude back-door approximation can be obtained by calculating Tobin's q, which is "the ratio between a company's market value (stock price times shares outstanding) and the replacement value of its physical assets."[84]

From a more theoretical perspective, one of human resource management's major roles is to provide control. This control may focus on behavior, such as through use of performance appraisals; outputs, such as accomplishment of goals; and inputs, such as through the selection and training of employees.[85] Because of the difficulty in measuring intellectual capital, organizations will be unable to use controls that require precise measures of organizational learning. It might be speculated that input controls would be appropriate because they avoid the necessity of having precise measures of learning. By selecting employees motivated toward learning and self-control, less emphasis on other controls may be required.

Organizational Learning in International Alliances

Because organizations' abilities to learn from alliance partners is affected by human resource practices and activities, it is critical to companies' own welfare that they are complementary to learning. Several human resource management practices can facilitate organizational learning. These include (1) communicating the strategic goals of the alliance widely within the organization, such as the void of organizational knowledge that necessitated the alliance; (2) forcing the focus of decisions beyond temporary short-run gains to the long-range consequences of outsourced manufacturing capabilities; (3) rewarding organizational learning through career progressions based partially on acquisition of knowledge; (4) not allowing the alliance partner to control human resource management functions, such as staffing the venture; (5) maintaining some slack in staffing on site so that there can be an adequate focus on learning; (6) providing managers and staff members who have language skills and training in the culture; (7) making longer alliance assignments; and (8) monitoring the human resource assignments of the alliance partner, such as where personnel are assigned after they rotate out of the venture.[86]

INTEGRATION OF STRATEGY AND HUMAN RESOURCE PLANNING

The integration of strategy with human resource strategy and planning is particularly important for long-range planning efforts. Furthermore, with the recognition of the potential contributions of human resource planning, line managers have taken on greater responsibilities for these planning efforts.[87] Susan Jackson and Randall Schuler have provided a vivid description of why there needs to be greater integration of the processes:

> Because there is a greater understanding that an organizations's work force cannot be turned around on a dime, long-term human resource planning is gaining currency. It is an activity that demands integration of the skills and knowledge of the human resource planner and all the other executives responsible for strategic planning.[88]

Evolution of Strategy and Human Resource Planning Integration

There are probably four stages in the evolution of linkages between strategic business planning and human resource management. The first stage is called an *administrative linkage* although there is no real linkage. Senior executives operate as if qualified personnel are always available in the labor market and the human resources unit is relegated to a paperwork processing role. The second stage involves a *one-way linkage* in which the human resource function becomes involved only in implementation. In the third stage, there is a *two-way linkage*. This involves a reciprocal relationship in which the human resource function helps implement strategic business plans and also provides input to strategy formulation. The final stage is called an *integrative linkage*. This stage goes beyond the reciprocal relationship to an equal involvement with other functional areas of business in the development of strategic business plans including issues outside of the human resource area. Interestingly, a fully integrated linkage may be described as informal.[89]

Determinants of Integration

The strategy and human resource planning linkage is affected by a number of influences including environmental factors such as intense competition, which often requires productivity enhancements and work-force downsizing; technological change, which requires different employee skills; and changes in the composition of the work force. With greater environmental instability, more integration is needed. Another influence is the level of diversification, as greater integration occurs in companies with one dominant core business as opposed to diversified companies. At the opposite end of the continuum, where an organization's divisions are in different core businesses, a decentralized structure would be likely. Greater integration also occurs where the top human resource executive has equal status with the heads of the other functional areas and has credible line experience. More integration also occurs out of necessity where there are severe skill shortages. Greater integration also occurs where compensation systems reward executives' performance. Likewise, it occurs where line managers perceive that human resource planning can help them implement strategies that will further the goals of the company.[90] One way in which the benefits of human resource planning can be demonstrated is provided by the following practical advice from the director of human resource planning and development at Corning Glass: "Identify the issues that are making it tougher on line managers, then explain how good HR planning can help solve some of those problems."[91]

As noted earlier, changing demands for skills have the potential to affect the degree of integration between strategic planning and human resource planning. With the decline in proportion of employment accounted for by manufacturing and the growth of services, there has been a changing demand for employee skills. Nonetheless, considerable confusion exists about manufacturing and its importance in the United States. The importance of manufacturing to the United States should not be underestimated, even though a smaller proportion of the labor force may be employed in manufacturing in the future because of greater automation, computerization, robotics, and new technologies. In fact, as noted earlier, exports of U.S. manufactured goods more than doubled between 1985 and 1992.[92] In the service industry there is concurrent creation and consumption of the service by the consumer. As a result, service workers must be more involved in controlling quality, must make appropriate adjustments when standards are not met, and must be responsible for more of their own supervision. Such changes dictate that service workers be more involved and committed to the organization. In order to create institutional climates and processes that provide the information and power sharing necessary for employees to operate in this manner, companies must engage in planning and make major changes in organizational direction.[93]

As indicated, the changing composition of the work force may also cause greater integration between strategy and human resource planning. Human resource planning efforts which forecast diversity can help organizations identify the proactive efforts needed to take advantage of the unique perspectives these workers bring to the workplace. As noted earlier, in the future there will be substantially more women, minorities, and immigrants in the U.S. labor force. There will also be more older workers who will be attracted back into the work force, perhaps as a result of various inducements. Further, as a result of the Americans with Disabilities Act of 1990 (ADA), there will probably be more disabled employees on the job. Finally, there will be more diversity involved with coordinating activities that result from the global sourcing of labor.[94]

Mergers and acquisitions may also cause stronger planning and strategy linkages in the future. Their dismal record, in terms of both financial performance and adverse effects on employees, may be improved when human resource issues are planned out before the merger. In companies having recent merger or acquisition experience, human resource managers report that the top-level managerial talent of the firm to be acquired is the most important human resource criterion to be considered prior to a merger.[95] Nonetheless, the reported failures to consider these very issues prior to mergers or acquisitions, indicates that there has been a failure to integrate human resource planning with the strategic planning process.

Conversely, integration is less likely where senior management incorrectly assumes there are qualified employees in the external labor market and specifies that areas such as finance and marketing should have sole responsibility for strategic planning. Integration is also impeded by human resource executives who lack a strategic perspective of the business.[96] Several benefits of linkage and integration are presented in Table 4-3.

TABLE 4-3   BENEFITS OF INTEGRATING HUMAN RESOURCE PLANNING WITH STRATEGIC PLANNING

1. Generates more diverse solutions to complex organizational problems
2. Ensures consideration of human resources in organizational goal setting processes
3. Ensures consideration of human resources in assessment of organization's abilities to accomplish goals and implement strategies
4. Reciprocal integration prevents strategy formulation based on personnel rigidities/preferences
5. Facilitates concurrent consideration of strategic plans and managerial succession

Sources: Adapted from Cynthia A. Lengnick-Hall and Mark L. Lengnick-Hall, "Strategic Human Resources Management: A Review of the Literature and a Proposed Typology," *Academy of Management Review*, 13, no. 3 454–470; James A. Craft, "Human Resource Planning and Strategy," in *Human Resource Management: Evolving Roles and Responsibilities*, ed. Lee Dyer. (1988), Washington, D.C.: Bureau of National Affairs, 1988, 47–87.

Conditions Under Which Integration May Not Be Appropriate

Strategic integration is appropriate only after the human resource management function has progressed through earlier forms of development. In fact, Lloyd Baird and Ilan Meshoulam state that a partial determinant of the effectiveness of an organization's human resource management is the degree to which it matches the organization's developmental stage. For example, without managerial comprehension of such processes as environmental scanning, strategy development, and managerial succession, the resources devoted to strategic integration efforts will be wasted. Additionally, a sophisticated compensation program may fail because the information and administrative systems required for its implementation may be undeveloped. It follows that the stage of development in human resource management should match the stage of development of the parent organization.[97]

The five stages of organizational development are as follows: (1) *initiation,* the start-up or entrepreneurial stage characterized by informality; (2) *functional growth,* the stage at which functional specialization and a more formalized structure develops; (3) *controlled growth,* the stage at which professional management is brought in, product lines are expanded, and productivity and cost control are emphasized; (4) *functional integration,* the stage in which coordination is increased to deal with interdependencies between functions and there is an increase in strategic emphasis; (5) *strategic integration,* the ultimate stage of development in which there is work-force flexibility and adaptability, extensive use of teamwork, broad sharing of human resource responsibilities, and human resource input into strategic decision-making processes. Table 4-4 describes the developmental range of several strategic aspects of human resource management including management's realization of potential contributions of human resources, control and structure of the human resource function itself, human resource program offerings, skills of the human resource staff, information technology, and environmental scanning and awareness.[98]

THE HUMAN RESOURCE MANAGER AND STRATEGIC PLANNING

Frequently human resource management does not play a major role in the organization's strategy formulation process because of the planning inadequacies of human resource executives.[99] However, planning difficulties are not unique to these executives. Indeed, managers from all functional areas have problems with strategic planning. This section will review these general problems and will address the specific implications for human resource management.

Planning Problems

It is well-known that managers are action-oriented, often preferring the action of decision-making or problem-solving interactions. In contrast, part of the planning process is done in isolation. There is a lack of feedback or

TABLE 4-4   STRATEGIC COMPONENTS OF HUMAN RESOURCE MANAGEMENT RELEVANT TO INTERNAL FIT

1. MANAGEMENT AWARENESS

Management awareness ranges from a focus on administrative needs, such as hiring and firing, to a full integration of human resource considerations in all management decision making.

2. MANAGEMENT OF THE FUNCTION

This component includes the structure of the human resources function, and the planning, allocation, and control of its resources. The structure may vary from very loose or nonexistent through matrixed and decentralized.

3. PORTFOLIO OF PROGRAMS

The portfolio of programs ranges from simple salary administration and record-keeping programs to very complex and sophisticated flexible compensation, environmental scanning, and long-range planning programs.

4. PERSONNEL SKILLS

Personnel professionals need appropriate skills. Basic programs and simple information systems require basic skills. The addition of complex programs and growth in size requires more advanced, differentiated, and specialized skills.

5. INFORMATION TECHNOLOGY

Information tools range from manual record-keeping to sophisticated distributed systems with modeling capabilities. Information technologies range from the absence of formal analytical tools to advanced forecasting and simulation based on statistical tools.

6. AWARENESS OF THE ENVIRONMENT

In the initial stage, because of pressures involved in start-up, management does not systematically assess and react to the environment. At . . . [the strategic integration stage], management is very aware of the internal environment and the external environment and their impact. They remain flexible and adjust to opportunities and risks that arise.

Source: Extracted from Lloyd Baird and Ilan Meshoulam, "Managing Two Fits of Strategic Human Resource Management," *Academy of Management Review,* 13, no. 1 (1988), 122–123. Reprinted with permission.

knowledge of results for prolonged periods of time. Further, it is difficult to justify the time needed for planning in relation to more immediate problems that press for solutions. Thus, in spite of its value, many managers do not like to plan. In addition to these general planning problems, there are further problems with strategic planning because it often results in reallocations of resources that determine power and status. Effects of the desire to retain the status quo, through resistance to change, are evident in symptoms such as excessive defense of existing resource allocations, information hoarding, and excessive control of the planning process through manipulation of agendas. Attempts to maintain the status quo may also be evident in symptoms such as padding budgetary requirements.[100]

Other causes of problems in the strategic planning process include mismatches between the tasks of planning and individual managers' skills. Strategic planning requires thinking in terms of the organization as a whole and relationships between the organization and the numerous factors that impact it within its environment. The ability to see patterns at the macro level is more important than processing bits of information to find the solutions to micro-level problems. One of the symptoms of such mismatches is a propensity to slip back into operational issues and the inability to complete tasks. A final problem is lack of top-level executive commitment to the strategic planning process. Symptoms of this problem include managers' attempts to read between the lines to determine top managements' real views on the importance of the process. Compounding these difficulties is the typical absence of rewards for superior planning performance.[101]

Requirements for Strategic Human Resource Managers

Unfortunately, the abilities of human resource executives themselves have sometimes been the cause of the human resource function's failure to take an important role in the strategic planning processes of the company. The personal requirements for those who can operate in strategic human resource management go beyond the requirements of functional competence. Research into the role characteristics reveals the following personal qualifications:

> (a) Information management skills—statistics, analysis, and research; (b) Planning skills—the knowledge of planning and planning methodologies plus statistics techniques; (c) Management skills—skills in the various business functions and environmental analysis; (d) Integration skills—competency at managing organizational interfaces, and skill in assessing the organization plus setting priorities; and (e) Change management skills—the skills of anticipating the future, facilitating changes, and developing organizational activities.[102]

Aside from selecting human resource executives on the basis of these qualifications, weaknesses with current personnel can be overcome even where there are cognitive skill mismatches. For example, the effect of individual cognitive weaknesses may be minimized by pairing planners with offsetting skills and using planning teams. The tasks of planning can also be broken up into phases, some of which can be performed by those whose cognitive skills are not well suited to strategy formulation. For instance, greater responsibilities for information gathering might be assigned to those whose strengths are not consistent with strategic thinking.[103] Using teams to offset weaknesses seems to have appeal as "Although the 'universal manager' may have lost credibility, the 'universal management team configuration' seems to have gained popularity."[104]

SUMMARY

More organizations are recognizing that their human resources provide a source of competitive advantage. This recognition—along with increased environmental uncertainty, greater pressure to control costs, and increased governmental regulation—have elevated the strategic role of human resource management. As a result, there is growing involvement of human resource management in strategy formulation. Where human resources are an organization's source of competitive advantage, human resource management has a critical role of providing "upfront" input in the corporate-level strategic planning process. This chapter has described the theoretical foundations of strategy formulation including concepts and definitions of strategy, strategic planning, planning in strategic business units, human resource strategy, and human resource planning. The latter provides an important linkage with organizational strategy by providing input on the availability of critical labor and by adding lead-time to deal with shortages and surpluses of employees.

The chapter also considered the international aspects of strategy formulation. Multinational, global, and transnational strategies were considered along with strategic alliances and the development of globally competent managers. Aside from deciding such issues as whether to pursue multinational or global strategies, companies must resolve the human resource problem of becoming deskilled as a result of international alliances. In the past, U.S. companies have not learned as quickly as many of their international alliance partners and have been weakened as a result of this deficiency. Human resource practices and policies are critical to international strategies and organizational learning. This chapter pointed out that the relationship between companies' international strategies and human resources should be understood as there can be major differences in the human resource management implications.

Additionally, the chapter pointed out that human resource strategies help align personnel practices, policies, and programs with strategy so that desired employee roles and behaviors will support different strategies, for example, innovation, quality enhancement, and cost reduction. Other strategic inputs of the human resource function include environmental scanning and corporate intelligence.

As discussed, Sonnenfeld and Peiperl's typology provides an explanation of differences in human resource strategies, their relationship to organizational strategies, and differences in personnel practices and policies across industries. Unbundled or network organizations also are of importance to the discussion of human resource strategy because they provide new challenges. While some traditional human resource functions may be unnecessary in such organizations, their core of permanent employees will require extraordinary levels of training and skill development.

In spite of recent developments, in most companies there is still need for a stronger integration of human resource management with organizational strategy formulation. Factors that influence the level of integration include industry differences, shifts in economic activity, changing technology, and changing demographics. Several examples of integration of the processes were provided, along with the barriers that have often limited such integration in the past. Finally, human resource managers must develop the personal skills needed to contribute to the strategy formulation process.

REFERENCES

1. Miles, Raymond E., and Charles C. Snow, "Designing Strategic Human Resources Systems," *Organizational Dynamics*, 13, no. 1 (1984), 36–52; Beer, Michael, Bert Spector, Paul R. Lawrence, D. Quinn Mills, and Richard E. Walton, *Managing Human Assets*. New York: Free Press, 1984; Jackson, Susan E., and Randall S. Schuler, "Human Resource Planning: Challenges for Industrial/Organizational Psychologists," *American Psychologist*, 45, no. 2 (1990), 223–239; Mills, Daniel Q., "Planning with People in Mind," *Harvard Business Review*, 63, no. 4 (1985), 97–105; Porter, Michael E., *Competitive Advantage: Creating and Sustaining Superior Performance*. New York: Free Press, 1985; Schuler, Randall S., and Ian C. MacMillan, "Gaining Competitive Advantage through Human Resource Management Practices," *Human Resource Management*, 23, no. 3 (1984), 241–255; Ulrich, David, "Human Resource Planning as a Competitive Edge," *Human Resource Planning*, 9, no. 2 (1986), 41–50.
2. Porter, *Competitive Advantage*.
3. Quinn, James B., Thomas L. Doorley, and Penny C. Paquette, "Beyond Products: Services-Based Strategy," *Harvard Business Review*, 90, no. 2 (1990), 58–67; Ulrich, David, "Strategic Human Resource Planning: Why and How?" *Human Resource Planning*, 10, no. 1 (1987), 37–56; Kochan, Thomas A., Rosemary Batt, and Lee Dyer, "International Human Resource Studies: A Framework for Future Research," in *Research Frontiers in Industrial Relations and Human Resources*, ed. David Lewin, O. S. Mitchell, and Peter D. Sherer. Madison, Wis.: Industrial Relations Research Association, 1992, 309–337.
4. Dyer, Lee, "Bringing Human Resources into the Strategy Formulation Process," *Human Resource Management*, 22, no. 3 (1983), 257–271.
5. ARCO, *ARCO Annual Report*, 1986.
6. Beer, Spector, Lawrence, Mills, and Walton, *Managing Human Assets*; Rodgers, T. J., "No Excuses Management," *Harvard Business Review*, 68, no. 4 (1990), 84–98; Fombrun, Charles, and Noel Tichy, "Strategic Planning and Human Resource Management: At Rainbow's End," in *Competitive Strategic Management*, ed. R. B. Lamb. Englewood Cliffs, N.J.: Prentice Hall, 1984, 319–332.
7. Jackson and Schuler, "Human Resource Planning"; Tichy, Noel M., Charles J. Fombrun, and Mary Anne Devanna, "Strategic Human Resource Management," *Sloan Management Review*, 23, no. 2 (1982), 47–61; Miles and Snow, "Designing Strategic Human Resources Systems."
8. Beer, Spector, Lawrence, Mills, and Walton, *Managing Human Assets*.
9. Miller, Edwin L., Schon Beechler, Bhal Bhatt, and Raghu Nath, "The Relationship Between the Global Strategic Planning Process and the Human Resource Management Function," *Human Resource Planning*, 9, no. 1 (1986), 12.
10. Fisher, Cynthia D., "Current and Recurrent Challenges in HRM," *Journal of Management*, 15, no. 2 (1989), 157–180; Cook, Deborah S., and Gerald R. Ferris, "Strategic Human Resource Management and Firm Effectiveness in Industries Experiencing Decline," *Human Resource Management*, 25, no. 3 (1986), 441–458.
11. Gómez-Mejía, Luis R., "The Role of Human Resources Strategy in Export Performance: A Longitudinal Study," *Strategic Management Journal*, 9, no. 5 (1988), 493–505.
12. Schuler, Randall S., "Strategic Human Resources Management: Linking the People with the Strategic Needs of the Business," *Organizational Dynamics*, 21, no. 1 (1992), 18–32.
13. Schuler, "Strategic Human Resources Management," 18.
14. Ibid.
15. Wright, Patrick M., and Gary C. McMahan, "Theoretical Perspectives for Strategic Human Resource Management," *Journal of Management*, 18, no. 2 (1992), 295–320.
16. Wright and McMahan, "Theoretical Perspectives for Strategic Human Resource Management," 298.
17. Wright and McMahan, "Theoretical Perspectives for Strategic Human Resource Management."
18. Ibid.
19. Quinn, James B., *Strategies for Change: Logical Incrementalism*. Homewood, Ill.: Richard D. Irwin, 1980, 7.
20. Henn, William R., "What the Strategist Asks from Human Resources," *Human Resource Planning*, 8, no. 4 (1985), 195 (whole article on pp. 193–200).
21. Ohmae, Kenichi, *The Mind of the Strategist*. New York: Penguin Books, 1988, 42.

22. Henn, "What the Strategist Asks from Human Resources."
23. Higgins, James M., and Julian W. Vincze, *Strategic Management: Text and Cases.* Chicago: Dryden Press, 1989.
24. Craft, James A., "Human Resource Planning and Strategy," in *Human Resource Management: Evolving Roles and Responsibilities*, ed. Lee Dyer. Washington, D.C.: Bureau of National Affairs, 1988, 53 (whole chapter on pp. 47–87).
25. Higgins and Vincze, *Strategic Management: Text and Cases*, Walker, James W., *Human Resource Planning.* New York: McGraw-Hill, 1980; Craft, "Human Resource Planning and Strategy."
26. Craft, "Human Resource Planning and Strategy."
27. Quinn, James B., "Retrospective Commentary," *Sloan Management Review*, 30, no. 4 (1989), 55–60.
28. Henn, "What the Strategist Asks from Human Resources."
29. Craft, "Human Resource Planning and Strategy"; Quinn, "Retrospective Commentary."
30. Quinn, James B., "Strategic Change: Logical Incrementalism," *Sloan Management Review*, 30, no. 4 (1989), 45–55.
31. Zabriskie, Noel, and Alan Huellmantel, "Implementing Strategies for Human Resources," *Long Range Planning*, 22, no. 114 (1989), 70–77.
32. Schuler, "Strategic Human Resources Management," 24.
33. Craft, "Human Resource Planning and Strategy"; Beer, Spector, Lawrence, Mills, and Walton, *Managing Human Assets.*
34. Sonnenfeld, Jeffrey, and Maury A. Peiperl, "Staffing Policy as a Strategic Response: A Typology of Career Systems," *Academy of Management Review*, 13, no. 4 (1988), 588–600; Lengnick-Hall, Cynthia A., and Mark L. Lengnick-Hall, "Strategic Human Resources Management: A Review of the Literature and a Proposed Typology," *Academy of Management Review*, 13, no. 3 (1988), 454–470.
35. Walker, James W., *Human Resource Planning.* Milkovich, George L., and Thomas A. Mahoney, "Human Resources Planning and PAIR Policy," in *Planning and Auditing PAIR*, eds. Dale Yoder and Herbert G. Heneman, Jr. Washington, D.C.: Bureau of National Affairs, 1976, 2-1 to 2-29; Middlemist, R. Dennis, Michael Hitt, and Charles R. Greer, *Personnel Management: Jobs, People, and Logic.* Englewood Cliffs, N.J.: Prentice Hall, 1983; Niehaus, Richard J., "Models for Human Resource Decisions," *Human Resource Planning*, 11, no. 2 (1988), 95–107.
36. Pucik, Vladimir, "Strategic Alliances, Organizational Learning, and Competitive Advantage: The HRM Agenda," *Human Resource Management*, 27, no. 1 (1988), 77–93.
37. Yip, George S., "Global Strategy . . . In a World of Nations?" *Sloan Management Review*, 30, no. 4 (1989), 29–41; Adler, Nancy J., and Susan Bartholomew, "Managing Globally Competent People," *Academy of Management Executive*, 6, no. 3 (1992), 52–65.
38. Yip, "Global Strategy . . . In a World of Nations?"
39. Lei, David, and John W. Slocum, Jr., "Global Strategy, Competence-Building and Strategic Alliances," *California Management Review*, 34, no. 2 (1992), 81–97.
40. Lei and Slocum, "Global Strategy, Competence-Building and Strategic Alliances," 82.
41. Lei and Slocum, "Global Strategy, Competence-Building and Strategic Alliances."
42. Lei, David, and John W. Slocum, Jr., "Global Strategic Alliances: Payoffs and Pitfalls," *Organizational Dynamics*, 19, no. 3 (1991), 49 (whole article on 44–62).
43. Lei and Slocum, "Global Strategy, Competence-Building and Strategic Alliances."
44. National Public Radio, "Morning Edition," program broadcast on January 4, 1993.
45. Phillips, Dennis, "How VW Builds Worker Loyalty Worldwide," *Management Review*, 76, no. 6 (1987), 37–40.
46. Adler and Bartholomew, "Managing Globally Competent People."
47. "The Agreement's Key Provisions," *The Wall Street Journal*, November 18, 1993, A14.
48. Kaikati, Jack B., "Europe 1992—Mind Your Strategic P's and Q's," *Sloan Management Review*, 31, no. 1 (1989), 85–92.
49. Cerruti, James L., and Joseph Holtzman, "Business Strategy in the New European Landscape," *Journal of Business Strategy*, 10, no. 5 (1990), 18–23.
50. Townsend, Anthony M., K. Dow Scott, and Seven E. Markham, "An Examination of Country and Culture-Based Differences in Compensation Practices," *Journal of International Business Studies*, 21, no. 4 (1990), 667–678.
51. Wyatt, Larry L., "Adding Value: Future Challenges," *Human Resource Planning*, 8, no. 4 (1985), 229–232.
52. Lengnick-Hall and Lengnick-Hall, "Strategic Human Resources Management."
53. Porter, *Competitive Advantage: Creating and Sustaining Superior Performance.*
54. Dyer, "Bringing Human Resources into the Strategy Formulation Process"; Lengnick-Hall and Lengnick-Hall, "Strategic Human Resources Management."
55. Schrenk, Lorenz P., "Environmental Scanning," in *Human Resource Management: Evolving Roles and Responsibilities*, ed. Lee Dyer. Washington, D.C.: Bureau of National Affairs, 1988, 88–124; Zabriskie and Huellmantel, "Implementing Strategies for Human Resources."

56. Magnusson, Paul, and Stephen Baker, "The Mexico Pact: Worth the Price?" _Business Week_, May 27, 1991, 32–35.
57. Smith, Emily T., "Plastics That Break Down—Without Breaking the Bank," _Business Week_, May 27, 1991, 111.
58. Henn, "What the Strategist Asks from Human Resources."
59. Ibid., 195.
60. Zabriskie and Huellmantel, "Implementing Strategies for Human Resources."
61. Henn, "What the Strategist Asks from Human Resources."
62. Jackson and Schuler, "Human Resource Planning"; Belous, Richard S., "How Human Resource Systems Adjust to the Shift Toward Contingent Workers," _Monthly Labor Review_, 112, no. 3 (1989), 7–12.
63. McCune, Joseph T., Richard W. Beatty, and Raymond V. Montagno, "Downsizing: Practices in Manufacturing Firms," _Human Resource Management_, 27, no. 2 (1988), 145–161.
64. Schuler, Randall S., and Susan E. Jackson, "Linking Competitive Strategies with Human Resource Management Practices," _Academy of Management Executive_, 1, no. 3 (1987), 207–219.
65. Ibid.; Porter, _Competitive Advantage_.
66. Schuler and Jackson, "Linking Competitive Strategies with Human Resource Management Practices"; Porter, _Competitive Advantage_.
67. Lengnick-Hall and Lengnick-Hall. "Strategic Human Resources Management."
68. Kochan, Thomas A., John Paul MacDuffie, and Paul Osterman, "Employment Security at DEC: Sustaining Values Amid Environmental Change," _Human Resource Management_, 27, no. 2 (1988), 139.
69. Miles and Snow, "Designing Strategic Human Resources Systems"; Sonnenfeld and Peiperl, "Staffing Policy as a Strategic Response."
70. Jackson and Schuler, "Human Resource Planning."
71. Sonnenfeld and Peiperl, "Staffing Policy as a Strategic Response"; Miles and Snow, "Designing Strategic Human Resources Systems."
72. Jackson and Schuler, "Human Resource Planning"; Sonnenfeld and Peiperl, "Staffing Policy as a Strategic Response"; Miles and Snow, "Designing Strategic Human Resources Systems"; Jackson, Susan E., Randall S. Schuler, and J. Carlos Rivero, "Organizational Characteristics as Predictors of Personnel Practices," _Personnel Psychology_, 42, no. 2 (1989), 727–786.
73. Miles and Snow, "Designing Strategic Human Resources Systems"; Sonnenfeld and Peiperl, "Staffing Policy as a Strategic Response."
74. Rousseau, Denise M., "New Hire Perceptions of Their Own and Their Employer's Obligations: A Study of Psychological Contracts," _Journal of Organizational Behavior_, 11, no. 5 (1990), 389–400.
75. Jackson, Schuler, and Rivero, "Organizational Characteristics as Predictors of Personnel Practices."
76. Sonnenfeld and Peiperl, "Staffing Policy as a Strategic Response"; Miles and Snow, "Designing Strategic Human Resources Systems."
77. Miles and Snow, "Designing Strategic Human Resources Systems"; Sonnenfeld and Peiperl, "Staffing Policy as a Strategic Response."
78. Snow, Charles C., Raymond E. Miles, and Henry J. Coleman, Jr., "Managing 21st Century Network Organizations," _Organizational Dynamics_, 20, no. 3 (1992), 5–20.
79. Ibid.
80. Ibid.
81. Pucik, "Strategic Alliances, Organizational Learning, and Competitive Advantage."
82. Stewart, Thomas A., "Brainpower," _Fortune_, June 3, 1991, 44–60.
83. Stewart, "Brainpower," 44.
84. Stewart, "Brainpower," 50.
85. Snell, Scott A., "Control Theory in Strategic Human Resource Management: The Mediating Effect of Administrative Information," _Academy of Management Journal_, 35, no. 2 (1992), 292–327.
86. Pucik, "Strategic Alliances, Organizational Learning, and Competitive Advantage."
87. Ulrich, "Human Resource Planning as a Competitive Edge."
88. Jackson and Schuler, "Human Resource Planning," 233.
89. Golden, Karen A., and Vasudevan Ramanujam, "Between a Dream and a Nightmare: On the Integration of the Human Resource Management and Strategic Business Planning Processes," _Human Resource Management_, 24, no. 4 (1985), 429–452.
90. Golden and Ramanujam, "Between a Dream and a Nightmare." Buller, Paul F., "Successful Partnerships: HR and Strategic Planning at Eight Top Firms," _Organizational Dynamics_, 17, no. 2 (1988), 27–43. Thompson, James D., _Organizations in Action_. McGraw-Hill, 1967; Craft, "Human Resources Planning and Strategy."

91. McManis, Gerald L., and Michael S. Leibman, "Integrating Human Resource and Business Planning," *Personnel Administrator,* 33, no. 6 (1988), 36 (whole article on 32–35).
92. Flint, Jerry, "The Myth of U.S. Manufacturing's Decline," *Forbes,* January 19, 1993, 40–42.
93. Jackson and Schuler, "Human Resource Planning"; Jackson, Schuler, and Rivero, "Organizational Characteristics as Predictors of Personnel Practices."
94. Jackson and Schuler, "Human Resource Planning"; Johnston, William B., and Arnold H. Packer, "Work and Workers in the Year 2000," in *Workforce 2000: Work and Workers for the Twenty-first Century.* Indianapolis: Hudson Institute, 1987, 75–103; American Association of Retired Persons, *The Aging Work Force: Managing an Aging Work Force.* Washington, D.C.: American Association of Retired Persons, 1990; Machan, Dyan, "Cultivating the Gray," *Forbes,* September 14, 1989, 127–128; Morrison, Peter A., "Applied Demography: Its Growing Scope and Future Direction," *The Futurist,* 24, no. 2 (1990), 9–15; Bureau of National Affairs, "ADA: Americans with Disabilities Act of 1990," *Labor Relations Reporter,* no. 11 (1990), 5–12.
95. Schweiger, David A., and Yaakov Weber, "Strategies for Managing Human Resources During Mergers and Acquisitions: An Empirical Investigation," *Human Resource Planning,* 12, no. 2 (1989), 69–86.
96. Craft, "Human Resource Planning and Strategy"; Baird, Lloyd, and Ilan Meshoulam, "Managing Two Fits of Strategic Human Resource Management," *Academy of Management Review,* 13, no. 1 (1988), 116–128.
97. Baird and Meshoulam, "Managing Two Fits of Strategic Human Resource Management."
98. Ibid.
99. Burack, Elmer H., "Linking Corporate Business and Human Resource Planning: Strategic Issues and Concerns," *Human Resource Planning,* 8, no. 3 (1985), 133–145.
100. Bedeian, Arthur G., *Management,* 2nd ed. Chicago: (Dryden Press, 1989; Lenz, R. T., and Marjorie A. Lyles, "Managing Human Problems in Strategic Planning Systems," *Journal of Business Strategy,* 6, no. 4 (1986), 57–66.
101. Lenz and Lyles, "Managing Human Problems in Strategic Planning Systems."
102. Baird and Meshoulam, "Managing Two Fits of Strategic Human Resource Management," 126–127.
103. Lenz and Lyles, "Managing Human Problems in Strategic Planning Systems."
104. Lengnick-Hall and Lengnick-Hall, "Strategic Human Resources Management," 459.

CASE 4

INTEGRATING STRATEGY AND HUMAN RESOURCE MANAGEMENT

The experiences of several organizations provide good examples of the integration of strategy and human resource management. One example is provided by the experiences of Peoples' Bank, a regional bank headquartered in Bridgeport, Connecticut. Massive changes began to take place in the business environment of banking with deregulation and relaxation of ceilings on interest. Money markets began to drain off funds that ordinarily went into banks' deposits, forcing them to rely on more expensive sources of funds. Further, the money center banks began to compete in the same middle markets as regional banks. As a result of these changes, Peoples' changed its strategy from a product orientation to one directed toward markets. With a product orientation, products are developed and then markets are sought out in which to sell the product. Conversely, a market orientation involves an opposite approach in that market demands are determined and then products developed to serve the market. In five years, Peoples' doubled the number of branches to sixty, increased its asset base from $1.3 billion to $4 billion, established a discount brokerage service, acquired savings and loan associations, added a credit-card operation, and entered the commercial lending field.[1]

Because of major changes in Peoples' strategy, there was a recognition that new organizational structures would be needed to accommodate the changes. The organization was decentralized, hierarchical levels removed, strategic business units formed, and new senior vice presidencies created within a matrix structure. The bank then conducted a study of the types of employees that would be needed with the new strategy's skill and organizational requirements. Major changes were undertaken as a result of the audit. For example, the performance appraisal system was revised. The revised system emphasized goal-setting, linked individual goal accomplishment and rewards with the attainment of the bank's objectives, and placed greater emphasis in performance appraisal on marketing and sales. Further, human resource planning was more fully integrated with the strategic planning process through synchronization of its scanning processes with the bank's overall environmental scanning process.[2]

The experiences of the U.S. Navy provide another example of the integration of strategy and human resource management. As a result of its linkage of strategic planning with human resource management, the Navy was able to pursue a proactive strategy which provided lower labor costs. In the Navy's case, its human resource planners analyzed the labor cost savings of a strategy involving its civilian employees, which would substitute local wage policies for national wage policies. By developing human resource forecasts to determine labor market reactions to these changes, planners could determine whether sufficient labor supplies would be available with the cost savings strategy. In this example, the planners also examined the impact of the reduction of private sector middle management positions and found that higher-quality employees could be hired.[3]

Ingersoll-Rand's experiences with one of its divisions also provides a good example of the outcome of a strong linkage between strategy and human resource management. Ingersoll-Rand's rock drilling division was experiencing rapid growth and had shortages of labor. It also needed to train its employees to work with new technology and wanted to control labor costs. The outcome of integrating its human resource capabilities with its strategic planning process was that the company implemented a number of programs, including gain sharing and employee involvement teams. It also had employees participate in decisions on the purchase of new technology and made a major commitment to technological training.[4]

A final example of the integration of strategy and human resources is provided by Maid Bess, a manufacturer of uniforms. The company faced intense competition from foreign manufacturers and control of labor costs became very critical. Because of its labor intensity, the company closely integrated human resource management with the strategic planning process. As an outcome of the integrated strategic planning process, the company's executive vice president designed a compensation program incorporating bonuses that enhanced productivity, increased employee wages, and reduced turnover.[5]

Questions

1. Based on these descriptions of the experiences of Peoples' Bank, Ingersoll-Rand, and Maid Bess, what is the unifying theme of the role played by human resource management?
2. How does the strategic role of human resource management in the U.S. Navy case differ from the others?
3. What were the environmental influences stimulating the actions described for each of these organizations?
4. What managerial trends are indicated in the experiences of these organizations?
5. The Ingersoll-Rand case indicates that its solutions to its problems were based largely on employee empowerment approaches. Explain how employee empowerment can provide a valuable source of competitive advantage to be considered in strategic decision making.

REFERENCES

1. Coleman, Sharon M., Martin Leshner, and C. Chase Hewes, "Human Resources Planning: A Tool for Strategic Change," *The Bankers Magazine*, 169, no. 6 (1986), 39–44.
2. Ibid.
3. Atwater, D. M., E. S. Brees, III, and R. J. Niehaus, "Analyzing Organizational Strategic Change Using Proactive Labor Market Forecasts," in *Creating the Competitive Edge through Human Resource Applications*, eds. Richard J. Niehaus and Karl F. Price. New York: Plenum Press, 1988, 119–136.
4. McManis, Gerald L., and Michael S. Leibman, "Integrating Human Resource and Business Planning," *Personnel Administrator*, 33, no. 6 (1988), 32–35.
5. Ibid.

5

HUMAN RESOURCE PLANNING

As indicated in the conceptual framework presented in the preface, conventional wisdom has been that organizations conduct human resource planning after strategy formulation as a means of implementation. However, as also indicated in the framework, where human resource planning is fully integrated with strategy or has a reciprocal relationship, it provides input in the formulation process. In such an evolving role, human resource planning may identify competitive advantages of the organization's human resources, or it may be used to assess the feasibility of various strategic alternatives in terms of human resource capabilities. This chapter will begin with a discussion of the growing strategic role of human resource planning. Next, it will explore the topic of human resource planning by providing an overview of human resource planning and the managerial issues involved. It will then examine factors that influence the selection of forecasting techniques, discuss specific supply and demand forecasting techniques, and provide examples of their application.

THE STRATEGIC ROLE OF HUMAN RESOURCE PLANNING

Human resource planning is linked in several ways with strategy formulation and implementation. One such linkage is its developmental role.

Developmental Planning for Strategic Leadership

Recently a management development expert observed that there is currently more interest in succession planning today than there has been during the past thirty years. Because of the rapidly changing environments in which companies must compete, a concern is that there will be a shortage of individuals with the requisite skills and talents who can lead companies into the next century. Given the significant costs of leadership failures at the highest organizational levels, it is important to have qualified replacements for high-level executives. Succession planning, a form of human resource planning discussed later, is an important part of the solution to the successorship problem. Such planning, as well as other forms of human resource planning, are becoming more critical to the successful formulation and implementation of strategies. Succession planning is quite challenging in today's rapidly changing environment because the skills that will be needed after the turn of the century are not well defined. Nonetheless, the potential strategic contributions of succession planning are substantial.[1]

Assessment of Strategic Alternatives

As organizations' human resources are utilized more frequently as sources of competitive advantage, human resource planning and forecasting will become more central to the strategic planning process. It will be essential for human resource executives or other executives to be able to forecast the future availability of employees having knowledge in such critical areas as technology. Companies that have a developing critical mass of employees who are knowledgeable or skilled in a particular technology may constitute an evolving potential source of competitive advantage. Similarly, information regarding critical employee knowledge bases provides important input for strategy formulation. Conversely, given a particular strategic alternative, it is useful for human resource executives as well as other executives to be able to forecast the human resources necessary to carry out various strategies.

Adding Value

The literature often states that human resource planning is becoming more important to organizations. While some observers have noted the difficulties of planning during turbulent periods and have downplayed the current role of human resource planning, there is indication that some organizations are placing major emphasis on succession planning for top-level executives, as well as other forms of planning. Reasons cited for human resource planning include shifting demographics, the proportion of total costs accounted for by labor costs, and the competitive pressures of the global economy.[2] There is also some empirical evidence that strategic planning is positively related with financial performance. Although various studies provide mixed evidence on this relationship, methodological problems appear to be responsible for some inconsistencies in results.[3] More specifically, it has also been hypothesized that human resource planning is related to profitability. Although there is good reason to expect such planning efforts to increase profitability, methodological limitations have also prevented the empirical validation of this hypothesis. Establishing such an empirical relationship is very difficult because of the many potential indirect effects of human resource planning and the time required for its effects to be manifested in profitability. Nonetheless, recent empirical research has found a positive relationship between succession planning for chief executive officers' positions and company profitability.[4]

Unfortunately, difficulties in quantifying value added are somewhat common in human resource management. The results of some human resource programs and policies undoubtedly have major impacts on morale and motivation although they are not easily translated into dollars and cents. On the other hand, many human resource programs probably do not add value and do not conform to the investment perspective advocated in this book. Fortunately, as indicated in Chapters 1 and 8, some progress has been made in the area of measurement with such techniques as utility analysis.[5]

Contribution to Strategic Human Resource Management

Aside from anecdotal evidence on the strategic importance of human resource planning, surveys of company practices also provide an indication of its increasing importance for strategic applications. A survey during the mid-1980s asked human resource executives from 137 companies to indicate why their companies engaged in human resource forecasting, a major component of human resource planning. The top three reasons were for developing their human resources (77.6 percent), for avoiding personnel shortages (73.1 percent), and to obtain information for decisions (73.1 percent). A second set of reasons for human resource forecasting included the following: affirmative action efforts (63.6 percent), budgeting (62.1 percent), and career planning (59.7 percent). Interestingly, the study, which also compared similar responses from four to five years earlier, found an increase of over 20 percent in the proportion of companies citing affirmative action as a reason for human resource planning. Forecasts are probably needed for the development of estimates of when affirmative action goals can be reached.[6] Similarly, another survey has found an association between the development of affirmative action strategies and human resource planning.[7]

Strategic Salary Planning

As noted, survey results indicate that over 60 percent of companies conduct human resource planning for budgetary purposes. A related budgetary issue is strategic salary planning. Interestingly, compensation systems are one of the few business systems that have remained relatively static over the past years. Nonetheless, for effective implementation, such systems must change if they are not compatible with organizational strategies. (New compensation systems are discussed in Chapter 7.) While the importance of having compensation systems that are compatible with organizational goals is well-known, in reality such compatibility is often not obtained. Strategic salary planning goes beyond insuring compatibility and draws on the rationale of the essence of strategy.[8] As noted in Chapter 4, strategic management rejects the notion of allocating resources in the manner of competitors and instead advocates concentration of resources.[9] This rationale for strategic salary planning is demonstrated in the following quotation.

> Realistically, few employers can justify above-average workers in all positions. An organizations's business strategy leads to a staffing strategy and that, in turn, provides a basis for developing the compensation strategy. It may be that "world-class" experts are needed in just a few key positions. If the organization's success is dependent, for example, on its marketing expertise, this may justify higher pay levels in this function.[10]

Thus, strategic salary planning, which is based on input from human resource plans, provides another example of the strategic role of human resource planning.

OVERVIEW OF HUMAN RESOURCE PLANNING

Although a brief definition of *human resource planning* was provided in Chapter 4, a more comprehensive definition is appropriate for in-depth treatment of the process. Human resource planning encompasses the following steps: (1) interfacing with strategic planning and scanning the environment, (2) taking an inventory of the company's current human resources, (3) forecasting the demand for human resources, (4) forecasting the supply of human resources both from within the organization and in the external labor market, (5) comparing forecasts of demand and supply, (6) planning the actions needed to deal with anticipated shortages or overages, and (7) feeding back such information into the strategic planning process.[11] (Step 4 could precede step 3.) This chapter will place emphasis on broad planning issues as well as forecasting techniques.

Planning in a Context of Change

Because the major themes of this book deal with the strategic aspects of human resource management, a longer-range time perspective has been adopted. Since strategy and planning are essentially forward-looking activities, they are critical responsibilities of general managers. Although planning and strategy are sometimes neglected because of the press of current demands, at times these planning activities also take on an unwarranted sense of importance and can distract managers from the real goals of the organization. The rational and proactive nature of the process, uncluttered by the very real problems of implementation, may cause their planners to forget that they are dealing with changing phenomena.

The dangers of having a plan chiseled in granite and lesser forms of inflexibility are well-known. The rapidity and scope of environmental changes that can affect human resource strategy and plans are formidable and should not be forgotten. As example of such effects on human resources was provided a few years ago by Iraq's invasion of Kuwait. On the day following the invasion, there was a decline in the sales of Pier 1 Imports. One week later, when U.S. troops were ordered to the area of conflict, there was another decline. As a result, Pier 1, which was planning an eighty-four-store expansion, cut its expansion plans by eighteen stores.[12] The war was soon over and the conditions affecting Pier 1 Import's sales were transitory. Although in hindsight, the actions of Pier 1 seemed premature, at the time few observers would have predicted the stunning quickness with which the war was brought to a conclusion. Nonetheless, this example illustrates the extreme range of factors that can affect planned staffing levels and provides a good demonstration of the flexibility that should be combined with any planning process.

Responsibility for Human Resource Planning

In early practice, human resource planning was often the responsibility of a specialist in the human resource area. Often this planning was conducted with little involvement of others in the organization. Unsurprisingly, when planning was conducted in this manner, the data supplied for use in forecasting were often inaccurate. Managers were asked to take the time to supply information for something that they did not understand. Because they did not see how forecasts could help their job performance, the value of forecasts was not appreciated. These earlier experiences reveal that when the planning process is complex and cumbersome, as is more likely on a centralized basis, its value to managers is not as readily apparent. Further, when planning is concentrated in a single corporate planning unit, other management personnel may be demotivated by their exclusion from the strategic planning process. The weaknesses of centralized planning are even more apparent in large companies having diverse operating divisions. In these companies, decentralized human resource planning seems much more appropriate.[13]

Fortunately, the thrust of human resource planning has changed. There is evidence of much greater line management involvement in human resource planning and thus greater strategic impact. Surveys of planning practices reveal that greater emphasis is being placed on the use of simple forecasting techniques with line management involvement as opposed to heavy reliance on centralized planning and forecasting practices based on sophisticated quantitative forecasting techniques.[14] Even with extensive line management "ownership" of the process and recognition of its value, extensive staff involvement is still required to facilitate the process. Martin Greller and David Nee have pointed out the requirement for balancing of responsibilities between line and staff in the following two statements: "(1) The manager knows what needs to be done and has control of the day-to-day assignments that allow real development to occur. (2) Human resource planning requires that someone pay consistent attention to the process, year in and year out, not just when there is a crisis."[15]

Failure to Plan for Human Resources

There are a number of examples where the failure to plan for human resources has had a major adverse effect on organizations. For example, General Electric encountered difficulties in the mid-1970s because of a mismatch between the skills of its engineering staff and the work that needed to be done. At the time, General Electric had 30,000 electromechanical engineers whose skills were becoming largely irrelevant because the company's needs were shifting toward the skills possessed by electronics engineers. Eventually, the company recognized that its difficulties were caused by a failure to plan in earlier years. By the end of the 1970s, problems such as these prompted General Electric's chairman to urge his managers to conduct human resource planning. A similar example is provided by a multinational corporation that planned a technologically advanced smelter for construction in Brazil. Because the company did not assess the availability of computer technicians and service workers in the geographic area, it had to make expensive changes in its plans in order to match the plant with the available labor supply.[16] Another example is provided by public accounting firms as some of their problems have been attributed to the failure to plan for the succession of top managers. Part of this failure of planning appears to be related to the unique nature of the partnership form of these organizations.[17]

The public sector has not been immune from these problems. An example of a failure to plan is provided by the construction of an expensive, state-of-the-art jail facility in Fort Worth, Texas, as a solution to severe problems of inmate overcrowding. Well into the actual construction phase of the project, officials were shocked to learn that the facility, which had incorporated recent innovations in design, would be much more expensive to operate than they had assumed because the design required high staffing levels. Since labor costs are the most important cost in operating a jail, the effects of this oversight were profound.[18]

Other causes for failure to plan or failures in planning are related to inadequacies in organizations' broader strategic management processes. A survey has indicated that the most common problem in human resource planning is a lack of precision in business operating plans.[19] An example is provided by the following quotation from the vice president of personnel for the Quaker Oats Company who stated that "Little is gained by grafting a HR plan to an unreliable business plan."[20] Quinn Mills has reported a similar response from an executive:

> "I've told my staff to quit talking to me about human resource planning," said one executive. "We can't plan for people because we do a miserable job of business planning. And I don't want another nest of strategic planners in the company."[21]

Although the literature had advocated that companies should place increased emphasis on human resource planning, there was still a lack of enthusiasm for the process by the 1970s. Nonetheless, by the late 1970s human resource planning activity appeared to have increased. Some observers of the turning point cited a reactive response to the need to comply with equal employment opportunity legislation and a greater recognition of the contribution of human resources to the performance and profitability of companies.[22] As noted earlier, in order to comply with affirmative action goals and timetables, some planning is a practical necessity. The experiences with the jail project just described can be contrasted with the experiences of the U.S. Navy's shipyards operations in which a total work force of 80,000 was reduced to 72,000. Because of forecasting, alternative actions enabled the Navy to achieve these reductions while having to release only 58 employees.[23] Similarly, survey results reveal that companies doing extensive human resource planning have been able to minimize layoffs during a recession.[24]

MANAGERIAL ISSUES IN PLANNING

Several important managerial issues are critical to human resource planning. Among the most important are the personal implications for planners as well as its acceptance by the organization and challenges to planning efforts.

Personal Implications

Aside from the reasons noted earlier for human resource planning and the associated benefits, there is another pragmatic reason of individual importance to managers. This reason is related to the fact that the planning process will have normally required the human resource manager to communicate with other managers, senior executives, and staff members about the future human resource environment and the associated staffing issues. It will also have forced the human resource manager and other managers with planning responsibilities, to have thought through these staffing issues and to have examined their operating assumptions. Although there are limitations and abuses of planning and there has been resistance to human resource planning in the past, there are benefits as well. An important benefit from the planner's perspective is that senior management will be more comfortable with the knowledge that the manager has a plan.[25] As such, senior managers have greater confidence that the manager has thought through the implications of potential demand and supply relationships and there is less chance that the company will be unprepared in the future.

Changing Receptivity Toward Planning

As will be noted in this chapter, a paradox of planning is that it is difficult to conduct when it is most needed. The turbulent business environment in which companies currently operate is obviously a difficult time in which to plan. Nonetheless, substantive evidence exists that companies have increased their emphasis on human resource planning. It is evident that some corporate-wide planning objectives require centralized, sophisticated human resource planning processes. However, as noted earlier, there has been a trend toward the use of more simple planning and forecasting techniques on a decentralized basis by line managers. This trend has developed at a time when planning has been difficult and long-term planning horizons seem to some like a relic of a foregone era. As the human resource function's role shifts from direct involvement to greater indirect and shared involvement, it will need to take on a greater strategic role in environmental scanning and more responsibility for assisting in the development of pools of talent for the new jobs of the future. Further, the human resource function will need to help redesign organizations to meet the demands of the future, such as being able to respond to customer preferences more quickly, provide higher quality, make faster decisions, and be more cost competitive.[26] The interplay of the current trend toward organizational restructuring and redesign will have to be integrated with strategic human resource planning efforts.

Implications of the European Experience

It is interesting to speculate whether the growing restrictions in the United States on employers' abilities to lay off employees will also serve as an additional incentive for human resource planning. In the future, if layoffs in the United States become more restricted by legislation, as in Europe, U.S. companies may place greater emphasis on human resource planning as a means of avoiding employee surpluses. This may be an interesting hypothesis to consider as some European companies had developed sophisticated human resource planning programs prior to the 1980s. C.J. Verhoeven, a Dutch researcher, has pointed out the importance of employment security policies as a factor encouraging human resource planning:

> In some countries—for instance, in the Netherlands—the commitment of many organizations toward their personnel is high, which means that protection from dismissal exists as well as good career opportunities, good work circumstances, and the like. This is partly in contrast to the United States, where people can be fired on short notice in many organizations.[27]

Guvenc Alpander has provided a similar perspective on Dutch firms in an example of the Philips Company's human resource planning efforts for a new plant. Because of its responsibilities to an immobile work force, Philips assumed employment responsibilities from twenty to thirty years into the future. Consequently, Philips forecasters attempted to link the plant's technology to its work force for the next twenty years.[28] Whether such firms will be able to maintain commitments to their employees in the future remains to be seen. During the 1990s European firms have experienced strong pressures to downsize.

It is also interesting to speculate on whether there will be more restrictions on terminations and layoffs in the United States, as in Europe, or whether the Europeans will move toward the U.S. model as their companies seek the productivity gains made possible by greater flexibility. Verhoeven

has also identified concerns over irregular age distributions, such as disproportionate numbers of younger or older employees, as a reason for human
resource planning.[29] Although there is little in the literature on the effects of
irregular age distributions in the United States, as noted in Chapter 2, some
companies with disproportionately older work forces have incurred higher
health-care costs, which have challenged their cost competitiveness. Such
challenges will probably grow in importance and will consume more of the
planning time and attention of general managers.

SELECTING FORECASTING TECHNIQUES

Several factors influence the choice of techniques used to forecast either the
supply or demand for human resources.

Purpose of Planning

One such factor is related to the purpose of human resource forecasting.[30] If
the purpose is to forecast the supply of human resources in order to identify
and eliminate bottlenecks in the career paths of promising managers,
replacement charts or Markov analysis may be used. Conversely, if the purpose is to forecast the future age distribution of a company's work force in
order to estimate its likely health-care costs, it would be better to use some
form of renewal analysis in which specific numbers of employees in various
individual jobs, job categories, or job families would be relatively unimpor-
tant. In the former case, detailed data would be required on movements
through the various jobs while in the latter case, the data requirements
might be limited to employment data, current age distributions, turnover,
and retirement trends.

Organizational Characteristics

Several other factors influence the selection of forecasting techniques, one
being the size of the organization. For example, minimum numbers of
incumbents in the various positions are necessary to develop reliable probabilities of transitions from one position to another. Nonetheless, companies
having as few as 2,000 employees have developed effective human resource
forecasting models. Size is also related to the sophistication of forecasting
techniques, with larger companies tending toward greater sophistication,
although industry and planning horizons also affect the relationship.
Human resource forecasting also varies in sophistication across divisions
within large companies. Another factor in selection of forecasting techniques
is the complexity of the organization. With greater complexity there are
more differences in model parameters and fewer common assumptions that
can be applied. Further, another factor is that with longer-range forecasting
horizons, there is a tendency to use more sophisticated forecasting techniques.[31]

Industry Characteristics

The type of industry also affects technique utilization as companies in regulated industries tend to use more sophisticated forecasting techniques. These industries are normally subject to less change and, as a result, forecasts can be quite accurate. Unsurprisingly, forecasts in utilities, insurance companies, and railroads have often been highly accurate. This accuracy could be contrasted with an industry, such as high-fashion women's clothing, where forecasts can be off by a wide order of magnitude. Regardless of the planning technique employed, a *paradox of planning* in general is that it is probably the most difficult to conduct in circumstances where it is most needed. Since human resource planning is undertaken to reduce uncertainty, the resultant need for planning is greatest in industries facing the greatest environmental change.[32]

Environmental Turbulence

Some general trends in the use of various human resource forecasting techniques are also evident. Consistent with the decentralization theme mentioned previously, a survey of forecasting techniques by Quinn Mills indicates that the most prevalently employed techniques are relatively unsophisticated ones that can be readily understood and used by line managers.[33] Many of these relationships are also explained by forecasters' perceptions of the level of uncertainty in the environment. Thomas Stone and Jack Fiorito have developed a *perceived uncertainty model* which explains the selection of forecasting techniques. Their model's predictions are consistent with Mills' findings as it predicts lower utilization of sophisticated techniques such as Markov analysis, operations research, and computer simulation under conditions of moderately high and high perceived uncertainty. Essentially, their model indicates that sophisticated techniques cannot be used effectively in such environments because they require greater stability for accurate predictions. Such conditions describe the current environment of many companies and many explain the trend toward use of less sophisticated techniques.[34]

The trend toward increasing economic turbulence began during the 1980s and has continued through the 1990s. The level of turbulence has also posed difficulties for economic forecasters. Interestingly, economic forecasting, which thrived during the 1950s and 1960s when conditions were much more stable, began to lose credibility during the 1980s. By the 1990s companies such as Eastman Kodak, Citibank, Xerox, Equitable Life, and Chemical Bank had eliminated their economic forecasting staffs.[35] This loss of credibility is illustrated in the results of studies by Stephen McNees:

> Stephen McNees . . . has made a specialty of comparing economic forecasters' predictions against what has actually come to pass. His data show that the forecasters have made huge errors around virtually every major recent turning point of the economy—recessions as well as recoveries—including 1973–75, 1978–79 and 1981–82.[36]

In spite of the decline in credibility of macro-level economic forecasting, many economic forecasters have made a successful transition to more micro-level applications, such as forecasting the behavior of industries or specific companies.[37] Thus, although the value of macro-level forecasting may have declined, more micro-oriented applications, such as human resource forecasting, currently have greater credibility and value.

Other Considerations

The sheer number of forecasting techniques can also pose problems for those who must make decisions on which ones to use. Several factors should be considered in making these decisions, including time horizon, level of technical or mathematical sophistication required of the forecaster, cost, whether appropriate data are available, and the stability of the data on which forecasts will be based. Other factors include accuracy, whether the technique is effective at identifying turning points, whether the forecast output includes a measure of central tendency, and an indication of the breadth of potential outcomes. One precaution regarding forecasting horizons is that the desire to extend the forecast far out into the future should be tempered with a recognition that with long-range time horizons, the process will become more complex and time-consuming. The costs may also increase disproportionately to the forecast's value. A general recommendation for improving forecasting, which appears to have a great deal of validity, is to use a combination of techniques in order to offset their different disadvantages.[38] The basis of this recommendation is revealed in the following account:

> The research on combining forecasts to achieve improvements (particularly in accuracy) is extensive, persuasive, and consistent. The results of combined forecasts greatly surpass most individual projections, techniques, and analyses by experts . . . combining forecasts—particularly with techniques that are dissimilar—offers the manager an assured way of improving quality.[39]

A general guide to the selection of forecasting techniques has been prepared by David Georgoff and Robert Murdick. Their guide covers twenty different techniques and includes a set of questions to which the forecaster provides answers for guidance in selecting the most appropriate technique.[40] The following sections provide greater detail on several techniques that have potential applicability in human resource planning and forecasting. Since demand and supply forecasting are interchangeable in the planning sequence, and supply forecasting may be easier to understand, the discussion will begin on the supply side.

FORECASTING THE SUPPLY OF HUMAN RESOURCES

Techniques used to forecast supplies of human resources may be classified as either *qualitative* or *quantitative*, although the distinction is sometimes unclear. Further, some forecasting techniques may be used to forecast both the supply and demand of human resources. Thus, classifications of techniques as either supply or demand, as well as qualitative or quantitative, must be arbitrary to some extent. With these limitations in mind, the category of qualitative supply forecasting techniques includes *replacement charts, succession planning,* and *supervisory estimates.* Occasionally, human resource inventories will be categorized as planning or forecasting techniques. However, they are not really forecasting techniques even though inventories provide the data base from which forecasts of internal supplies of human resources are derived.[41] The category of quantitative techniques includes *Markov analysis* or *network flow models, attrition analysis models, renewal models, computer simulation,* and *operations research techniques.* This section will describe replacement charts, succession planning, Markov models, renewal models, and computer simulation. In addition, the current utilization of these techniques will be discussed.

Replacement Charts

Replacement charts describe a company's organizational structure in terms of individuals occupying various managerial and professional positions. For each position incumbent, potential replacements are identified along with such information as their individual potential for advancement and numbers of years' experience needed before being qualified for the next higher position. The individual's age may also be included for estimating retirement dates.[42] For each potential replacement, the potential replacements for that individual are also listed with similar information. Thus, the replacement chart, which is likely to be computerized, provides a description of how vacancies can be filled from the internal labor market. It also shows the associated cascading effects.

In determining the time when potential managerial replacements will be ready to take on higher-level responsibilities, an assessment of their current skills must be conducted and matched against those required for higher-level positions. Two organizational dimensions should guide such assessments: (1) the hierarchical or vertical level of various jobs and (2) where the job falls in a continuum from basically individual contributions to managing the efforts of others. Thus, the assessment should include not only the skills that will be required for vertical moves but also the skills to move horizontally, typically toward the broader orientation and responsibilities of general management. Movement upward often entails a shift toward the managerial end of the continuum. Beginning with the individual contributor end of the continuum and moving toward the managerial end, employees would be assessed against skill requirements for the following tracks: technical development, technical application, technical management, operations management, and business management.[43]

Another aspect of the utilization of replacement charts to forecast supplies of human resources involves the assessment of the organization's current employees' abilities and qualifications to take on future positions. Before the number of qualified replacements for a current or future position can be determined, there must be a means of comparing potential replacement candidates with the position's requirements. Robert Gatewood and Wayne Rockmore have provided an extensive description of an electric utility's systems and procedures that have enabled the company to evaluate this matching activity. One important component of the company's system is its human resource inventory, which is based on supervisory estimates of individual employees' capabilities of performing various job tasks. In this company, supervisory evaluations of their subordinates' capabilities are obtained with a lengthy questionnaire. The job requirements, in terms of tasks and employees' characteristics and capabilities to perform these tasks, are combined in a document called a talent bank, similar to a replacement chart. Self-assessments, instruments administered by the human resource staff, information from the talent bank, and assessment center data are used to guide the training and developmental efforts needed to prepare employees for future and current needs. An interesting side benefit of the company's system is that career paths have become better understood and the company now does a better job in career counseling.[44]

Succession Planning

Although similar to replacement planning and the use of replacement charts, *succession planning* tends to be directed toward a longer-range time horizon and is more focused on development. It is also more concerned with the development of pools of potential replacements as opposed to individuals. Succession planning involves more elaborate planning for skill development of potential replacements, is more systematic in the assessment of potential replacements and their developmental needs, and generally applies to higher levels of managerial positions.[45] For example, at Air Products and Chemicals, Inc., which has annual sales in excess of a billion dollars, the succession plan involves only approximately 300 key jobs.[46]

An example of succession planning is provided by one of Scott Paper Company's divisions which has a policy of internal promotions. Succession planning in this case has involved the assessment of managers occupying positions as plant managers. As a result of succession planning and associated developmental efforts, the division has been able to solve its productivity problems. Prior to these efforts, the division suffered from problems related to employee dissatisfaction, autocratic management styles, and the aftermath of downsizing. The assessment procedures, conducted by an outside consulting firm, involved administration of a battery of tests and personality assessments by psychologists. Following the assessment, managers were provided detailed individual feedback on areas in which they needed further development. One of the keys to success in this succession planning effort was the emphasis placed on detailed specification of the skills and requirements needed for performance as plant managers.[47]

In some companies succession planning also incorporates developmental planning for high potential managers while they are still in lower-level positions. This is especially prevalent for minorities and women who are likely to become long-range successors. Additionally, succession planning may also be concerned with the future requirements of executive positions since the necessary personal skills and characteristics may differ substantially from current requirements. Given the growing interdependencies across functional areas in many companies, one promising approach for developing potential successors for positions of the future may be to assign them leadership responsibilities in cross-functional teams. Unsurprisingly, current executives may be hesitant to make selection decisions on the basis of projections of future skill requirements which are difficult to quantify.[48] A related difficulty is revealed in the following account.

> It becomes extremely difficult for top management to have confidence that they are selecting successors with this new profile when there are no data they can trust. Before, when executives were selecting successors in their own image, the data were less important, since they could use their own intuition, a sense that "he's one of us." (And he usually was a he.)[49]

To the extent that succession planning is participatory and plans are incorporated into career development sessions, there may be reduced turnover of valued managers. For those informed that they are next in line for a position, there may be a motivational effect as well as an enhanced likelihood that they will remain with the organization.[50]

Of course, events such as acquisitions and mergers can make such plans meaningless and increase the level of top management turnover.[51] In this regard, James Walsh has found that "59 percent of each *company's* top management team departs within 5 years of a merger."[52] In cases where change in the strategic direction of the organization is needed, succession plans become less important. The rationale is that organizations are more likely to obtain such changes in strategy with outsider successor executives. Such executives are less likely to be subject to the influences of escalating commitment and are more inclined to have a different vision. Empirical research is consistent with this reasoning as it supports the notion that outsiders are more likely than insiders to change an organization's strategy.[53]

Markov Analysis

In the past, some researchers observed that companies tended to have greater expertise and placed greater emphasis on forecasting the demand for human resources than for their supply. However, the application of *Markov analysis* to human resource forecasting changed the situation by providing a practical and versatile technique for forecasting internal supply. As such, the technique can serve the strategic purpose of evaluating the availability of human resources required for different strategies. Markov models have an advantage of being relatively simple to understand although they can be quantitatively sophisticated.[54]

In setting up Markov models, the forecaster must account for all possible moves or flows of employees in an organization. Such moves include moves into the organization, moves from one job to another, and exit moves.

Moves between jobs can be upward moves in hierarchical level as well as moves across functions. Essentially, Markov models begin with distributions of the number of employees in various job categories at a starting point in time. These distributions are then transformed by a *transition probability matrix* into a forecasted distribution of employees across these same job categories one period later. (A Markov model is presented in Figure 5-1.) The transition probabilities in each row of the matrix must total to 1. The diagonal set of transitional probabilities, after excluding the column representing exit moves, represents the proportion of employees remaining in the same job from time 1 to time 2. Markov models cannot take into account more than one move per time period.[55]

For purposes of illustration, the Markov model in Figure 5-1 contains only five different jobs and an exit move. Although not reflected in this example, the jobs could also be arrayed in terms of their hierarchical level, with job 1 being lower in the job hierarchy than job 2, and so forth. The forecasted distribution of employees for period 2 is obtained by multiplying the initial distribution of employees by each column of transition probabilities. The number of employees for each job in the forecasted distribution is the sum of each of these levels of employment as multiplied by the column's transition probabilities.[56] Although any time period can be used, time periods of one year are relevant for many applications.

The transition probabilities for Markov models are typically derived from historical data on the movements of employees between jobs, as well as exit moves from the organization. For example, transition probabilities from job 1 to job 2 might be determined by computing the percent of employees in job 1 who make such a move over a one-year time period. An important consideration for the use of Markov models is that with small numbers of job incumbents, the transition probabilities become unstable. For example, if there are only two employees in a job and one leaves, a transition probability

FIGURE 5-1   MARKOV MODEL FOR FORECASTING SUPPLY

	Employees	Transition Matrix					
	Job 1 27	.66	.11	.09	.03	.02	.09
Distribution	Job 2 41	.15	.60	.08	.06	.01	.10
of Employees	Job 3 55	.03	.08	.55	.13	.10	.11
in Time 1	Job 4 64	.00	.09	.18	.54	.03	.16
	Job 5 73	.00	.08	.10	.17	.45	.20
		26	44	55	57	41	37
		Job 1	**Job 2**	**Job 3**	**Job 4**	**Job 5**	**Exit**

Distribution of Employees in Time 2

Note: Numbers of employees in each job in Time 2 are rounded off to the nearest whole number.

based on the number remaining would be only .50, which could be very misleading.[57]

Another problem is that the probabilities derived from such percentages may not be stable if based on only the moves in one single year. Accordingly, the forecaster may want to compute an average percentage of employees making such moves over several years, for example from three to five years, in order to obtain a more stable transition probability. The positive aspect of the trade-off is that, with probabilities based on percentages derived from several years of data, they are less subject to spurious influences. Unfortunately, the downside is that the impact of recent trends will be muted to the extent that such recent data are averaged in with data from earlier years. On the other hand, with transition probabilities based on only one or two years of historical data, employee movements between jobs will track more quickly and recent trends will be more heavily represented in the forecast.

Human resource forecasters can obtain the proper balance between slower and quicker tracking transition probabilities through a process of trial and error. For example, a forecaster may attempt to forecast the movements of employees between jobs which occurred *last* year. He or she could experiment with transition probabilities based on movements for one year prior to that, an average of the two previous years, an average of the three previous years, and the like, and compare these forecasts with what actually happened. In this manner, the forecaster can determine the particular number of years that produces transition probabilities which will result in the most accurate forecast. Of course, any use of historical data assumes that certain conditions of the past will remain in the future, which may not be true.

In addition to forecasts of an organization's internal supply of human resources one year into the future, Markov analysis can be used for longer-range forecasts. Herbert Heneman and Marcus Sandver have pointed out that, through applications of matrix algebra, forecasts for multiple years into the future can be developed. Additionally, they have explained that such forecasts can incorporate new hires in the various jobs for individual years.[58] Iterative approaches provide an alternative for extending Markov analysis forecasts several years into the future. With an iterative approach, the forecasted distribution of employees across job categories is used as the input for the next year's employee distribution, which is then used with the transition probabilities to derive the next forecasted distribution. This process is repeated for a forecast of another year into the future and can be performed on computerized spreadsheets. Forecasters must bear in mind that the validity of the transition probabilities will probably be lower as the forecast is extended further into the future since more conditions are likely to change.

Aside from use in forecasting, Markov analysis can also be used for audits of the human resource function to determine whether there are any irregularities in the flow of employees through an organization's different positions. This can be done by constructing separate Markov transition matrices for minorities and females and comparing their similarity.

Likewise, Markov analysis may have applicability in the development of affirmative action goals because it can be used to forecast the internal supply of minorities and females that will be available in various positions at some point in the future. Additionally, the technique may be useful for identifying career paths and mobility patterns that may be helpful in career planning and development. Researchers have also demonstrated the feasibility of using a combination of Markov analysis and human resource accounting to forecast and depreciate the future value of an acquired firm's human resources.[59]

Although Markov models are classified here as a supply forecasting technique, they can also be used in conjunction with specifications of future demand. An example of such an application of Markov models is provided by a large computer manufacturer that has conducted human resource planning since the 1960s.[60] When combining Markov analysis with specified levels of demand, the forecaster begins by specifying the desired future distribution of employees in various job categories, typically in higher-level positions. By working backward, the forecaster then determines the magnitude of the transition probabilities that will be needed to create the flow of employees from the existing distribution into the desired future distribution. Promotion rates and termination rates are examples of human resource policies that would be adjusted to obtain the desired flow of human resources through the company to achieve the desired future distribution of employees. Transition rates can also be changed to reflect changes in such policies. By running the models with different transition rates, corresponding to policy changes, the impact on human resource flows between jobs and hierarchical levels can be determined.[61]

Another example of an application of Markov analysis is provided by the experiences of the Weyerhaeuser Company. In this example, the model was first developed during a growth phase of the company. The model was used to forecast the number of employees in a specialty, on a corporate-wide basis, that would be available from the company's internal labor supply. In the event that internal supplies were forecasted to fall short of demand, accelerated programs were instituted to provide the training needed to qualify current employees to take on the responsibilities for the positions where shortages were anticipated. During this phase, the model was used for decisions on a daily basis. Following this period, there was a recession which changed the situation from shortages to surpluses of employees and the company needed to reduce the number of employees by 700. Fortunately, information from the model helped decision makers discover that the solution to the problem could come from attrition of current employees. By modeling human resource flows through Markov analysis, Weyerhaeuser was able to reduce its employee surplus within fifteen months through attrition rather than layoffs. In subsequent years, the company used the technique to examine flows of exempt personnel within its separate divisions.[62]

Renewal Models

Another category of human resource forecasting techniques consists of *renewal models*. These models reflect the movement or flow of employees through companies as they are "pulled" upward to fill vacancies in higher-level job categories. An advantage of renewal models is that since they involve simple mathematics, they are readily understood by managers. Renewal models, in their simplest form, can use age cohorts of employees as the focus of analysis. As the level of incumbent employees in an age group is projected forward into the future, the group is "aged" by one year. When greater rates of change are expected, shorter time periods may be used. The aged cohort is then adjusted for losses of employees due to various forms of attrition. Rates of attrition can be obtained from historical data and typically differ across the age cohorts. Typically attrition would be relatively high with younger workers, such as recent college graduates, and for age cohorts close to retirement.[63]

In addition to "aging" employee cohorts and adjusting age cohorts for attrition, renewal models may also be configured in accordance with the job classification hierarchy and may also reflect the hiring of new employees and the promotions of current employees into different job categories. The numbers of employees in each job category may be adjusted during the process to reflect needs for growth or contraction which is dictated by the company's strategic plan. Starting with the top of the job hierarchy, the human resource planner can work downward through each job category, in a stepwise manner, to determine the number of employees that must be promoted from the lower classifications and the flow policies that will be needed to supply such numbers. For example, in addition to promotion rates, needs for external hiring can be identified, as well as needs for training programs for specific job categories predicted to have shortages.[64]

Renewal models can also be run with different specifications of promotion rates so that their differential impacts can be determined. The models can also be run with different attrition rates and other planning assumptions. Additionally, renewal models can also be applied to specific populations, such as minorities and females, so that a company's future affirmative action status may be forecasted.[65]

Computer Simulation

It is sometimes stated that *computer simulations* are the most useful forecasting techniques for guiding business decisions. Simulations have the advantage of allowing the forecaster to create a number of different future scenarios by altering the values of the simulation's parameters. Through this process, the forecaster can determine variations in forecasted values according to different formulations of future conditions and can plan alternative courses of actions to reduce uncertainty and manage risk. Further, computer simulations allow planners and forecasters to assess the sensitivity of the simulation model's parameters to alternative specifications. By running *sensitivity analyses*, forecasters can gain an understanding of the impact of inaccurate assumptions. With the rapidly increasing power of personal computers and advances in software, computer simulations are likely to grow in importance as human resource planning and forecasting techniques.[66]

An example of a strategic application of a combination of computer simulation and *attrition analysis* to forecast supplies of human resources is provided by the experiences of two public school districts in British Columbia. In this application, the current inventory of teachers was projected into the future after reductions for attrition. Attrition estimates were based on historical rates which differed according to age cohorts and by school district.[67] The following account describes the outcomes of this planning effort.

> The most important outcome of these applications of manpower planning was that the analysis encouraged school administrators to think strategically about the manpower resources they managed. By using specific procedures to estimate the supply and demand for teachers, those factors which influenced the district's ability to balance supply and demand became more visible and explicit. . . . A second aspect of this strategic orientation to manpower management was that school administrators concentrated on the importance of the relative rates of manpower flows into, through, and out of their organizations.[68]

Utilization of Supply Forecasting Techniques

A survey mentioned earlier also determined utilization rates for various forecasting techniques, as well as any significant changes between the late 1970s and mid-1980s. The results of this survey for the mid-1980s are presented in Table 5-1 in terms of the percentage of companies using such supply forecasting techniques. As indicated in Table 5-1, the two most frequently used techniques are *succession planning techniques* or *replacement charts* (66.7 percent) and *human resource inventories* (66.7 percent). At the other end of the spectrum, only 7.6 percent of the companies used *regression analysis* while 6.1 percent used *Markov analysis/network flow models*. There was a marked decline in the proportion of companies using *Markov analysis/network flow models* compared to the earlier time period (down from 21.7 percent). This is consistent with the trend, reported earlier, toward simpler, less sophisticated and often nonquantitative techniques that can be used by line managers.[69]

Nonetheless, many companies have human resource forecasters, often with Ph.D. degrees who do sophisticated, large scale organization-wide forecasts of their organizations' internal supplies of human resources. These forecasts are not necessarily replaceable by the trend toward greater human resource planning at the managerial level and typically serve separate functions. For these applications, *Markov models* are probably still very important forecasting techniques. In addition, although 7.6 percent of the responding

TABLE 5-1   SUPPLY FORECASTING TECHNIQUES

	PERCENT OF COMPANIES USING TECHNIQUE
Succession planning or replacement charts	66.7
Personnel inventories	66.7
Supervisor estimates	48.5
Rules of thumb or nonstatistical formulas	27.3
Computer simulation	12.1
Renewal models	9.1
Regression analysis	7.6
Markov or network flow models	6.1
Exponential smoothing or trend extrapolation	6.1
Operations research techniques	4.5

Source: Extracted from Charles R. Greer, Dana L. Jackson, and Jack Fiorito, "Adapting Human Resource Planning in a Changing Business Environment," *Human Resource Management,* 28, no. 1 (1989), 110. Copyright © 1989 by John Wiley & Sons, Inc. Reprinted by permission of John Wiley & Sons, Inc.

companies reported the use of *regression analysis* for forecasts of human resource supplies, the technique's direct applicability as a supply forecasting technique is not readily apparent and its use in this application may be overstated.

FORECASTING THE DEMAND FOR HUMAN RESOURCES

There are a number of practical difficulties in forecasting the demand for human resources. For example, a common constraint on the value of forecasts, based on extrapolations of current labor and output relationships, is ignorance of whether current staffing levels are appropriate. The massive reductions in labor utilization in the 1990s by companies facing intense competition have highlighted this problem. With the strategic moves toward leaner organizations, there have been labor cuts beyond those prompted by the efficiencies of new technology. Interestingly, along this same line, some companies implementing *total quality management* (TQM) programs have found that they need fewer employees. Thus, human resource planners must use appropriate *learning curve parameters*, which reflect expected productivity improvements, in order to avoid overestimating the demand for human resources.[70]

Table 5-2 presents productivity data from the U.S. manufacturing sector as well as the entire business category. As the data indicate, in manufacturing, productivity increased from an index value of 100 in 1982 to 129.3 in 1992. In contrast, only modest gains were made in productivity in the entire business sector, which includes services. In this sector the productivity index increased over the same time period from 100.0 to 113.3. Data for specific industries, where even greater differences are evident, are presented

TABLE 5-2 TRENDS IN U.S. PRODUCTIVITY

YEAR	MANUFACTURING OUTPUT PER HOUR	BUSINESS OUTPUT PER HOUR
1982	100.0	100.0
1983	102.2	102.3
1984	105.6	104.6
1985	106.8	106.3
1986	109.6	108.5
1987	116.7	109.6
1988	119.4	110.7
1989	120.0	109.9
1990	121.5	110.1
1991	123.6	110.2
1992	129.3	113.3

Sources: Data extracted from Bureau of Labor Statistics, U.S. Department of Labor, "Current Labor Statistics," *Monthly Labor Review,* 116, no. 1 (1993), 104; and Bureau of Labor Statistics, U.S. Department of Labor, "Current Labor Statistics," *Monthly Labor Review,* 116, no. 7, (1993), 107. For output indices, 1982 is the base year.

in Table 5-3. For example, productivity in semiconductors increased from an index of 100.0 in 1982 to 206.8 in 1990 while there was virtually no change over the same period for hotels and motels. In that labor-intensive service industry, the index declined from 100.0 in 1982 to 97.0 in 1990. Further, it should be noted that these are highly aggregated productivity averages. At greater levels of industry specificity, there may be even larger variances in productivity and learning curves.

Additionally, in forecasting demand, forecasters must choose predictor variables (independent variables) that are linked with variations in the underlying level of business activity.[71] This requirement for forecasting is evident in the experiences of a computer manufacturer that utilizes computerized productivity models to predict the demand for human resources. These models, which are based on statistical correlations between workload and staffing levels, enable the company to forecast the demand for human resources in its manufacturing divisions, as well as in marketing and services. In some other departments, where such relationships are less systematic, more qualitative techniques are used.[72]

An interesting forecasting example is provided by the case of maintenance workers. In forecasting the demand for maintenance workers, the reliability of the equipment to be repaired is an important predictor variable. With equipment that is to be maintained, forecasters can use such factors as the mean-time-between-failure of components as indicators of the number of maintenance workers needed. In the case of maintenance work, these estimates of the demand for maintenance workers can be considered in conjunction with decisions to purchase equipment. In cases where a stable employment level of maintenance workers is desired, purchases of equipment can be phased over

TABLE 5-3   TRENDS IN U.S. PRODUCTIVITY IN SELECTED INDUSTRIES

YEAR	SERVICES OUTPUT PER HOUR			MANUFACTURING OUTPUT PER HOUR		
	COMMERCIAL BANKS	EATING & DRINKING PLACES	HOTELS & MOTELS	PETROLEUM REFINING	SEMICONDUCTORS AND RELATED DEVICES	STEEL
1981	97.4	100.3	103.2	105.4	86.8	123.2
1982	100.0	100.0	100.0	100.0	100.0	100.0
1983	108.9	99.0	108.8	102.7	107.1	128.7
1984	112.0	95.3	115.6	116.3	116.5	144.3
1985	117.8	92.6	112.4	128.8	105.1	153.3
1986	120.0	95.6	109.9	142.6	110.1	156.3
1987	124.9	96.1	110.9	143.4	152.3	167.6
1988	129.3	98.3	109.6	151.9	166.7	184.8
1989	127.8	97.0	101.8	157.8	193.5	179.5
1990	135.7	97.6	97.0	157.5	206.8	184.8
1991	—	101.0	—	155.4	—	177.5

Sources: Extracted from Bureau of Labor Statistics, U.S. Department of Labor, "Current Labor Statistics," *Monthly Labor Review*, 116, no. 1 (1993), 105–106. For the output index, 1982 is the base year. Data for 1991 were extracted from Bureau of Labor Statistics, U.S. Department of Labor, "Current Labor Statistics," *Monthly Labor Review*, 116, no. 3 (1993), 99–100.

time so that expected failures will not occur all at once, necessitating higher levels of maintenance workers. With phased purchasing, all equipment does not need maintenance at the same time and lower levels of maintenance workers can be maintained, who have a steady amount of work to perform.[73]

It should also be noted that with some potential predictors of demand, a doubling of business activity may not necessarily translate into a doubling of the need for employees in a particular job category.[74] For example, the number of kilowatt hours generated by an electric power plant could double while there is no greater need for safety inspectors or billing clerks.

As indicated earlier, some forecasting techniques have both supply and demand applications. Replacement charts and renewal models have demand implications because they also indicate vacancies when replacements are promoted into vacancies at higher levels. Computer simulations may also be used for both supply and demand forecasting. These techniques have already been covered in detail and will not be addressed in this section. This section will briefly describe the qualitative techniques of rules of thumb, heuristics, and the Delphi technique. It will focus more extensively on the quantitative techniques involving management science and operations research applications and regression analysis.

Rules of Thumb, Heuristics, and the Delphi Technique

Rules of thumb are simple guidelines used to predict demand for human resources. For example, a retailing chain may have developed a heuristic which specifies that for every twelve new stores, another regional manager will be hired. *Heuristics* are conceptual frameworks, often expressed as diagrams, that help human resource forecasters organize relevant conceptual relationships and trace through the outcomes of various personnel action alternatives. Using the retail chain example, forecasters might consider the strategic plans for the number of new stores the next year, then diagram the interaction of factors affecting the number of regional managers that will be needed. One common qualitative approach for forecasting the demand for human resources is the *"bottom-up" approach* in which unit managers estimate their specific human resource needs for the next period. These estimates are then combined into aggregate forecasts for the whole company.[75] The *Delphi technique,* an iterative judgment-refinement technique based on the collection of expert opinion, is sometimes categorized as a qualitative demand forecasting technique. This technique can approach the accuracy of quantitative techniques and does not require a historical data base. Nonetheless, the Delphi technique is used for such purposes by only a very small number of organizations.[76]

Operations Research and Management Science Techniques

Such techniques as *linear programming, integer programming,* and *network optimization techniques* are generally considered as operations research or management science techniques. These techniques can be used to determine optimal personnel flows through organizations. Personnel flows can be managed through specification of time-in-grade requirements for promotions, rates of turnover, and the like. Managed flows can produce desired stocks of personnel in various positions or ranks at points in the future. A further extension of *linear programming,* called *goal programming,* allows human resource planners to take into consideration, sequential and multiple managerial goals or constraints, such as maximum headcounts, budgetary limitations, and so on. Goal programming has been used in human resource planning models that incorporate equal employment opportunity considerations.[77]

The use of such planning techniques runs counter to the trend toward greater use of less sophisticated approaches. However, such techniques are still very important in that they affect the service capability and profitability of major corporations and governmental organizations. Human resource planning systems based on these techniques require mathematical sophistication and complex computer programs. They are also expensive to develop. Nonetheless, they are often key systems in large organizations which produce savings of millions of dollars in labor costs. Such systems are developed by human resource planning specialists. Although they are developed and maintained on a centralized basis, they may be used on computerized networks by line managers for applications such as the development of optimal work-force schedules.[78]

An example of the application of such techniques is provided by the United Airlines Station Manpower Planning System. This system has been used to develop work schedules for several thousand United customer service agents and reservation sales representatives. While the system is used primarily for short-range planning, it does enable managers to forecast the number of employees needed to maintain desired service levels a few weeks and months into the future. It also allows industrial relations specialists to formulate the costs of various negotiated configurations of contract settlements. The system has been used to optimize the utilization of customer service agents at its airport operations. Through the specification of optimal staffing levels, sufficient numbers of agents are available to handle customer demand, but not so many that employees are underutilized. Managers and schedulers at each airport are able to use the computerized system to develop work schedules that take into account the unique demands of operations and employee preferences. Additionally, the system provides an optimal schedule standard for the minimization of labor costs. Managers of United's airline ticket reservations centers also make similar use of the system.[79]

Aside from the benefits already noted for this computerized simulation system, the complexity of airline operations necessitates the use of such systems. Several modules in United's system are needed to handle this complexity. Specifically, forecasts of demand for reservations representatives are determined on the basis of historical data through application of regression analysis and moving averages. The system's demand module takes a queuing approach to build in management's specification of customers' acceptable waiting times, and employs a Poission distribution to simulate the frequency and spacing of incoming calls for reservations. A similar approach, drawing on aircraft arrival trends and passenger loads, is used to forecast the demand for customer service agents. Aside from the system's demand forecasting module, other modules deal with starting times, scheduling, days off, and reports. Specific techniques employed in some of these modules include linear programming, continuous linear programming, and network assignment models.[80]

A practical managerial problem of user resistance was encountered when United's system was being implemented. Because the developers of the system needed to bring it on line quickly in order to meet the demands of business, potential users were not sufficiently involved in the system's development. As a result, the users perceived that the system did not meet all of their needs. This resistance was overcome by involving the potential users in refinements of the system and by making it more flexible to their locations' specific needs. Benefits of the system have included approximately $6,000,000 in annual labor costs savings, increased employee satisfaction with scheduling, and better customer service.[81] The overall impact of the system is captured in the following quotation from a United manager: "Just as the (customer) lines begin to build, someone shows up for work; and just as you begin to think you're overstaffed, people start going home."[82]

Regression Analysis

Regression analysis is a robust statistical technique having applicability to forecasting demand for human resources. Although its greatest applicability may be for centralized human resource forecasting at the corporate level by planning specialists, its wide availability as a feature of computerized spreadsheets makes it a potential technique for widespread adoption by line managers as well. *Multiple regression analysis* allows the forecaster to control for a number of potential influences on the number of employees needed in a particular specialty.

An example of the use of regression analysis for predicting demand is provided by an application at the New York Power Authority (an electric power utility). In this application, regression analysis was used to predict such dependent variables as the overall staffing level and staffing levels for various categories of employees, for example, professionals, managers, technicians, craft workers, service, and maintenance workers. The predictor or independent variables used in the models include such variables as the number of kilowatt hours produced, operating revenues, sales, and the capital budget. A limitation of this application is that the variables are only of a general nature and therefore, inappropriate for predicting the demand for specific jobs, such as the various professional or managerial specialties. Another aspect of this application of regression analysis is the stability of the utility's environment. Since utilities are typically characterized by stable environments, assumptions of stable relationships between the predictor

TABLE 5-4 DEMAND FORECASTING TECHNIQUES

	PERCENT OF COMPANIES USING TECHNIQUE
Supervisor estimates	69.7
Succession planning or replacement charts	65.2
Rules of thumb or nonstatistical formulas	37.9
Computer simulation	18.2
Exponential smoothing or trend extrapolation	12.1
Regression analysis	9.1
Delphi technique	3.0

Source: Extracted from Charles R. Greer, Dana L. Jackson, and Jack Fiorito. "Adapting Human Resource Planning in a Changing Business Environment," *Human Resource Management*, 28, no. 1 (1989), 110. Copyright © 1989 by John Wiley & Sons, Inc. Reprinted by permission of John Wiley & Sons, Inc.

variables and the dependent variable are more likely to be valid than in many environments characterized by turbulence.[83]

Utilization of Demand Forecasting Techniques

The two-period comparative survey of techniques cited earlier also examined the utilization rates for demand forecasting techniques. The mid-1980 results, as indicated by the percentage of companies utilizing the various techniques, are reported in Table 5-4. As indicated in Table 5-4, the simple techniques of *supervisor estimates* (69.7 percent) and *succession planning techniques* or *replacement charts* (65.2 percent) are the most heavily utilized techniques. At the other end of the distribution are *regression analysis* (9.1 percent) and the *Delphi technique* (3.0 percent). Significant differences between the mid-1980s and the late 1970s in the utilization of techniques include a marked decline in the use of *regression analysis* (down from 30.1 percent).[84] However, although line managers may rely extensively on simpler techniques, corporate-level specialists in human resource planning, who do large-scale organization-wide forecasting, probably make extensive use of *regression analysis*.

SUMMARY

This chapter has reviewed the changing environment which has increased both the strategic importance and difficulty of human resource planning. Organizations are concerned about having an adequate supply of successors for their top-level positions who will have the experiences and skills needed to provide leadership into the next century. With the recognition of human resources as a source of competitive advantage, human resource planning will have a larger strategic role in the future. Along with increasing strategic importance, there has also been a trend toward decentralization of the responsibilities for human resource planning to line managers.

Aside from the benefits of such planning, the problems that organizations incur when they fail to plan were also discussed. Such problems include having shortages or surpluses of employees with various skills and experiences, as well as higher operating costs which result from failures to include staffing projections in strategic plans. A number of managerial issues related to planning were also discussed. These issues included planning's importance for individual human resource managers, the changing receptivity toward human resource planning, and the paradox of the value of planning. Additionally, implications of European experiences with human resource planning were discussed.

Forecasting techniques were also discussed, beginning with the factors that determine the utilization of different techniques. These factors include the purpose of planning; organizational characteristics such as size and complexity; industry characteristics; the level of environmental turbulence; and other considerations such as data availability, forecasting horizon, the user's mathematical sophistication, and accuracy requirements. The discussion of supply forecasting techniques included replacement charts, succession planning, Markov analysis, renewal models, and computer simulation. Trends in the utilization of the various supply forecasting techniques were also reviewed. Techniques for forecasting the demand for human resources were also discussed including the general category of rules of thumb, heuristics, and the Delphi technique; operations research and management science techniques; and regression analysis. Differences in the utilization of these techniques were also discussed.

REFERENCES

1. Eichinger, Robert W., Comments to the Metroplex Human Resource Planning Society. Plano, Texas, April 7, 1994.
2. Meehan, Robert H., and S. Basheer Ahmed, "Forecasting Human Resource Requirements: A Demand Model," *Human Resource Planning,* 13, no. 4 (1990), 297–307.
3. Wood, D. Robley, Jr., and R. Lawrence LaForge, "The Impact of Comprehensive Planning on Financial Performance," *Academy of Management Journal,* 22, no. 3 (1979), 516–526; Pearce, John A., II, Elizabeth B. Freeman, and Richard B. Robinson, Jr., "The Tenuous Link Between Formal Strategic Planning and Financial Performance," *Academy of Management Review,* 12, no. 4 (1987), 658–675.
4. Zajac, Edward J., "CEO Selection, Succession, Compensation and Firm Performance: A Theoretical Integration and Empirical Analysis," *Strategic Management Journal,* 11, no. 3 (1990), 217–230.
5. Nkomo, Stella M., "Human Resource Planning and Organizational Performance: An Exploratory Analysis," *Strategic Management Journal,* 8, no. 4 (1987), 387–392.
6. Greer, Charles R., Dana L. Jackson, and Jack Fiorito, "Adapting Human Resource Planning in a Changing Business Environment," *Human Resource Management,* 28, no. 1 (1989), 105–123.
7. Nkomo, Stella M., "The Theory and Practice of HR Planning: The Gap Still Remains," *Personnel Administrator,* 31, no. 8 (1986), 71–84.
8. Risher, Howard W., "Strategic Salary Planning," *Compensation and Benefits Review,* 25, no. 1 (1993), 46–50.
9. Henn, William R., "What the Strategist Asks from Human Resources," *Human Resource Planning,* 8, no. 4 (1985), 193–200.
10. Risher, "Strategic Salary Planning," 47.
11. Walker, James W., *Human Resource Planning.* New York: McGraw-Hill, 1980; Milkovich, George L., and Thomas A. Mahoney, "Human Resources Planning and PAIR Policy," in *Planning and Auditing PAIR,* eds. Dale Yoder and Herbert G. Heneman, Jr. Washington, D.C.: Bureau of National Affairs, 1976,

2-1 to 2-29; Middlemist, R. Dennis, Michael A. Hitt, and Charles R. Greer, *Personnel Management: Jobs, People, and Logic.* Englewood Cliffs, N.J.: Prentice Hall, 1983; Niehaus, Richard J., "Models for Human Resource Decisions," *Human Resource Planning,* 11, no. 2 (1988), 95–107.

12. Murray, Alan, "Mideast Turmoil Jolts Business Confidence in Widening Sectors," *The Wall Street Journal,* September 28, 1990, 1, A9.

13. Baytos, Lawrence M., "A 'No Frills' Approach to Human Resource Planning," *Human Resource Planning,* 7 (1984), 39–46.

14. Greer, Jackson, and Fiorito, "Adapting Human Resource Planning in a Changing Business Environment"; Mills, D. Quinn, "Planning with People in Mind." *Harvard Business Review,* 63, no. 4 (1985), 97–105.

15. Greller, Martin M., and David M. Nee, *From Baby Boom to Baby Bust: How Business Can Meet the Demographic Challenge.* Reading, Mass.: Addison-Wesley, 1989, 124.

16. Mills, "Planning with People in Mind."

17. Goldstein, Michael, "Management Succession—Plan Now or Pay Later," *The CPA Journal,* 62, no. 8 (1992), 14–20.

18. Mahlburg, Bob, "New Jail to Entail High Costs," *Fort Worth Star-Telegram,* September 7, 1989, 19, 21.

19. Greer, Jackson, and Fiorito, "Adapting Human Resource Planning in a Changing Business Environment."

20. Baytos, "A 'No Frills' Approach to Human Resource Planning," p. 39.

21. Mills, "Planning with People in Mind," 99.

22. Burack, Elmer H., and Thomas G. Gutteridge, "Institutional Manpower Planning: Rhetoric Versus Reality," *California Management Review,* 20, no. 3 (1978), 13–22.

23. Niehaus, "Models for Human Resource Decisions."

24. Mills, "Planning with People in Mind."

25. Carter, Norman, Development Systems International, personal communication with the author, 1990.

26. Greer, Jackson, and Fiorito, "Adapting Human Resource Planning in a Changing Business Environment"; Tichy, Noel M., "Editor's Note," *Human Resource Management,* 27, no. 4 (1988), 365–367; Mills, "Planning with People in Mind."

27. Verhoeven, C.J., *Techniques in Corporate Manpower Planning.* Boston: Kluwer-Nijhoff, 1982. 3–4.

28. Alpander, Guvenc G., *Human Resources Management Planning.* New York: AMACOM, 1982.

29. Verhoeven, *Techniques in Corporate Manpower Planning.*

30. Bechet, Thomas P., and William R. Maki, "Modeling and Forecasting Focusing on People as a Strategic Resource," *Human Resource Planning,* 10, no. 4 (1987), 209–217; Niehaus, "Models for Human Resource Decisions."

31. Niehaus, "Models for Human Resource Decisions"; Walker, James W., "Human Resource Planning, 1990s Style," *Human Resource Planning,* 13, no. 4 (1990), 229–240; Fiorito, Jack, Thomas H. Stone, and Charles R. Greer, "Factors Affecting Choice of Human Resource Forecasting Techniques," *Human Resource Planning,* 8, no. 1 (1985), 1–17; Walker, James W., *Human Resource Strategy.* New York: McGraw-Hill, 1992; Wikstrom, Walter S., *Manpower Planning: Evolving Systems.* New York: The Conference Board, 1971.

32. Niehaus, "Models for Human Resource Decisions"; Walker, "Human Resource Planning, 1990s Style"; Fiorito, Stone, and Greer, "Factors Affecting Choice of Human Resource Forecasting Techniques"; Walker, *Human Resource Strategy;* Wikstrom, *Manpower Planning.*

33. Mills, "Planning with People in Mind."

34. Stone, Thomas H., and Jack Fiorito, "A Perceived Uncertainty Model of Human Resource Forecasting Technique Use," *Academy of Management Review,* 11, no. 3 (1986), 635–642.

35. Linden Dana W., "Dreary Days in the Dismal Science," *Forbes,* January 21, 1991, 68–71.

36. Linden, "Dreary Days in the Dismal Science," 68.

37. Linden, "Dreary Days in the Dismal Science."

38. Georgoff, David M., and Robert G. Murdick, "Manager's Guide to Forecasting," *Harvard Business Review,* 64, no. 1 (1986), 110–120.

39. Georgoff and Murdick, "Manager's Guide to Forecasting," 119.

40. Georgoff and Murdick, "Manager's Guide to Forecasting."

41. Niehaus, "Models for Human Resource Decisions"; Greer, Jackson, and Fiorito, "Adapting Human Resource Planning in a Changing Business Environment"; Greer, Charles R., and Daniel Armstrong, "Human Resource Forecasting and Planning: A State-of-the-Art Investigation," *Human Resource Planning,* 3, no. 2 (1980), 67–78.

42. Milkovich and Mahoney, "Human Resources Planning and PAIR Policy."

43. Hoffman, William H., Larry Wyatt, and George G. Gordon, "Human Resource Planning: Shifting from Concept to Contemporary Practice," *Human Resource Planning,* 9, no. 3 (1986), 97–105.

44. Gatewood, Robert D., and B. Wayne Rockmore, "Combining Organizational Manpower and Career Development Needs: An Operational Human Resource Planning Model," *Human Resource Planning,* 9, no. 3 (1986), 81–96.

45. Walker, *Human Resource Planning.*

46. Wagel, William H., "Planning for Tomorrow's Human Resource Needs," *Personnel,* 63, no. 11 (1986), 4–9.

47. Stahl, Robert J., "Succession Planning Drives Plant Turnaround," *Personnel Journal,* 71, no. 9 (1992), 67–70.

48. Dyer, Lee, "Human Resource Planning at IBM," *Human Resource Planning,* 7, no. 3 (1984), 111–125; Hall, Douglas T., "Dilemmas in Linking Succession Planning to Individual Executive Learning," *Human Resource Management,* 25, no. 2 (1986), 235–265; Petrock, Frank, "Planning the Leadership Transition," *Journal of Business Strategy,* 11, no. 6 (1990), 14–16.

49. Hall, "Dilemmas in Linking Succession Planning to Individual Executive Learning," 239.

50. Greller and Nee, *From Baby Boom to Baby Bust.*

51. Walsh, James P., "Top Management Turnover Following Mergers and Acquisitions," *Strategic Management Journal,* vol. 9, no. 2 (1988), 173–183.

52. Walsh, "Top Management Turnover Following Mergers and Acquisitions," 180.

53. Wiersema, Margarethe F., "Strategic Consequences of Executive Succession Within Diversified Firms," *Journal of Management Studies,* 29, no. 1 (1992), 73–94.

54. Rowland, Kendrith M., and Michael G. Sovereign, "Markov-Chain Analysis of Internal Manpower Supply," *Industrial Relations,* 9, no. 1 (1969), 88–99; Heneman, Herbert G., III, and Marcus G. Sandver, "Markov Analysis in Human Resources Administration: Applications and Limitations," *Academy of Management Review,* 2, no. 4 (1977), 535–542.

55. Rowland and Sovereign, "Markov-Chain Analysis of Internal Manpower Supply"; Heneman and Sandver, "Markov Analysis in Human Resources Administration."

56. Heneman and Sandver, "Markov Analysis in Human Resource Administration"; Bechet and Maki, "Modeling and Forecasting Focusing on People as a Strategic Resource"; Middlemist, Hitt, and Greer, *Personnel Management.*

57. Heneman and Sandver, "Markov Analysis in Human Resource Administration."

58. Ibid.

59. Hopkins, David S. P., "Models for Affirmative Action Planning and Evaluation," *Management Science,* 26, no. 10 (1980), 994–1005, Ledvinka, James, "Technical Implications of Equal Employment Law for Manpower Planning," *Personnel Psychology,* 28, no. 3 (1975), 299–323; Heneman and Sandver, "Markov Analysis in Human Resource Administration"; Flamholtz, Eric G., George T. Geis, and Richard J. Perle, "A Markovian Model for the Valuation of Human Assets Acquired by an Organizational Purchase," *Interfaces,* 14, no. 6 (1984), 11–15.

60. Dyer, "Human Resource Planning at IBM."

61. Bechet and Maki, "Modeling and Forecasting Focusing on People as a Strategic Resource"; Buller, Paul, and W. R. Maki, "A Case History of a Manpower Planning Model," *Human Resource Planning,* 4, no. 3 (1981), 129–137.

62. Buller and Maki, "A Case History of a Manpower Planning Model."

63. Walker, *Human Resource Planning;* Burack, Elmer H., and Nicholas J. Mathys, *Human Resource Planning: A Pragmatic Approach to Manpower Staffing and Development.* Lake Forest, Ill.: Brace-Park Press, 1980.

64. Burack and Mathys, *Human Resource Planning.*

65. Ibid.

66. Sheridan, James A., "Forecasts and Projections: Drawing Implications from Changes in Employee Characteristics," in *Human Resource Forecasting and Strategy Development: Guidelines for Analyzing and Fulfilling Organizational Needs,* eds. Manuel London, Emily S. Bassman, and John P. Fernandez. New York: Quorum Books, 1990, pp. 91–98.

67. Pinfield, Lawrence T., and Steven L. McShane, "Applications of Manpower Planning in Two School Districts," *Human Resource Planning,* 10, no. 2 (1987), 103–113.

68. Pinfield and McShane, "Applications of Manpower Planning in Two School Districts," 113.

69. Greer, Jackson, and Fiorito, "Adapting Human Resource Planning in a Changing Business Environment."

70. Frantzreb, Richard R., "Confessions of a Manpower Modeler," in *Manpower Planning for Canadians,* 2nd ed., eds. Larry F. Moore and Larry Charach. Vancouver, Canada: Institute of Industrial Relations, University of British Columbia, 1979, 480–489; Barrier, Michael, "Small Firms Put Quality First," *Nation's Business,* 80, no. 5 (1992), 22–32; Wikstrom, *Manpower Planning.*

71. Wikstrom, *Manpower Planning.*

72. Dyer, "Human Resource Planning at IBM."

73. Malmborg, Charles J., and Gene R. Simons, "Planning Maintenance Human Resource Requirements over the Life Cycle of a Repairable Equipment Population," *Human Resource Planning*, 9, no. 1 (1986), 25–39.
74. Wikstrom, *Manpower Planning*.
75. Bryant, Don R., Michael J. Maggard, and Robert P. Taylor, "Manpower Planning Models and Techniques," *Business Horizons*, 16, no. 2 (1973), 69–78; Milkovich, George L., and Thomas A. Mahoney, "Human Resource Planning Models: A Perspective," *Human Resource Planning*, 1, no. 1 (1978), 19–30; Niehaus, "Models for Human Resource Decisions."
76. Milkovich, George L., Anthony J. Annoni, and Thomas A. Mahoney, "The Use of Delphi Procedures in Manpower Forecasting," *Management Science*, 19, no. 4 (1972), 381–388; Greer and Armstrong, "Human Resource Forecasting and Planning"; Greer, Jackson, and Fiorito, "Adapting Human Resource Planning in a Changing Business Environment."
77. Niehaus, "Models for Human Resource Decisions"; Thornton, Billy M., and Paul Preston, *Introduction to Management Science: Quantitative Approaches to Managerial Decisions*. Columbus, Ohio: Charles E. Merrill, 1977; Middlemist, Hitt, and Greer, *Personnel Management*.
78. Holloran, Thomas J., and Judson E. Byrn, "United Airlines Station Manpower Planning System," *Interfaces*, 16, no. 1 (1986), 39–50.
79. Holloran and Byrn, "United Airlines Station Manpower Planning System."
80. Ibid.
81. Ibid.
82. Holloran and Byrn, "United Airlines Station Manpower Planning System," 49.
83. Meehan and Ahmed, "Forecasting Human Resources Requirements."
84. Greer, Jackson, and Fiorito, "Adapting Human Resource Planning in a Changing Business Environment."

Case 5

HUMAN RESOURCE PLANNING SUPPORT SYSTEMS

The description of United Airlines' short-range Station Manpower Planning System presented in Chapter 5 indicates the importance of having appropriate computer systems to support such efforts. Although the United system's forecasting range is on the short-range end of the spectrum, its computerized system has an obviously important financial impact in cost savings. While some human resource forecasting approaches are qualitative rather than quantitative and therefore require minimal computer support, many others require sophisticated software. As indicated in Chapter 5, because organizations' human resources are utilized more frequently today as sources of competitive advantage, human resource planning inputs will become more critical in the strategy formulation process. As a result, both human resource executives and other senior managers will need timely information on the future availability of critical human resources. Similarly, they will need timely information on the staffing requirements of a particular strategic alternative. Interestingly, even in the most traditional area of human resources, that of labor relations, computerized systems are already being used in union contract negotiations to provide on-the-spot cost evaluations of proposals and counterproposals.

Fortunately, a number of computer software packages are available for strategic human resource applications. For example, specialized software can be obtained for succession planning, human resource forecasting, and modeling human resource flows. In managing the software acquisition and implementation process, several factors need to be considered. One suggestion is that the software evaluation team should include representatives from end-user groups, management information systems (MIS), and any other support groups. Because of the greater decentralization of human resource planning in many organizations, users' perceptions of the user friendliness and usefulness of software should be even more critical. As line managers take on more responsibilities for succession planning, human resource planning, and forecasting, there will be increased need for systems they can use without great difficulty. Along this line, efforts to educate line managers on use of these software packages should enhance the ultimate success of the company's human resource planning and forecasting efforts. While adequate representation from these groups is critical, the evaluation team should be small enough to perform its task in a timely manner. A second suggestion is that the evaluation team should develop a set of initial screening procedures for use in narrowing down the list of packages to a smaller set for in-depth evaluation. Potential screening procedures include checking the software's functionality against a requirements list, checking with human resource contacts in other companies using the software, viewing vendor presentations, and obtaining recommendations from industry associations.[1]

A third suggestion pertains to the in-depth examination phase. The assessment in this phase should assign highest priority to the mandatory requirements. Beyond whether the software performs the required functions, other components of this phase include an assessment of the technical compatibility of the software with the organization's hardware and other software systems; the software's functionality or types of operations it performs; the adequacy of documentation; ease of enhancing the software as future requirements and business conditions change; ease of maintenance; the level of training that will be needed for users; and an assessment of the vendor's staying power and the likelihood of satisfactory service in the future. More detailed checklists of factors for software evaluation are available in the practitioner literature.[2]

Although there is growing availability of human resource planning software, managers should remember that user dissatisfaction is still a problem with various software packages. Such dissatisfaction often results because the complexity of software has been underestimated and insufficient resources have been allocated to its implementation.[3]

Questions

1. What typical organizational groups should be represented on a committee that will develop the requirements list against which human resource planning software should be evaluated? Why should each of these groups be included?

2. What would be some critical parameters or assumptions in software used to forecast an organization's internal supply of human resources? How would you determine the sensitivity of the software to inaccuracies in these parameters?

3. Which of a company's computerized data bases should be integrated with a computerized succession planning system? Which ones should not? Explain your reasoning.

4. What factors could prevent a company from realizing the benefits of an investment in human resource planning software? Explain how each would detract from the investment.

5. Identify a commercially available human resource planning software package and describe its capabilities, its data requirements, its hardware requirements, and the time needed to become proficient with it. Outline a plan for evaluating it.

REFERENCES

1. TenEyck, Gretchen, "Software Purchase: A to Z," *Personnel Journal*, 69, no. 10 (1990), 72–79; Walker, Alfred J., "New Technologies in Human Resource Planning," *Human Resource Planning*, 9, no. 4 (1986), 149–159.

2. TenEyck, "Software Purchase: A to Z"; Frantzreb, Richard B., ed., *Microcomputers in Human Resource Management: A Directory of Software*. Roseville, Calif.: Advanced Personnel Systems, 1985.

3. Mandell, Mel, "Managing the Human Assets," *Computerworld*, April 6, 1992, 128.

6

STRATEGY IMPLEMENTATION
Work-Force Utilization and Employment Practices

The sixth component in the conceptual framework is strategy implementation. In order to accomplish their missions, organizations formulate requirements for returns on investments, scan the environment for opportunities and threats, formulate strategies, plan human resource requirements, and then implement their strategies. Unfortunately, implementation is usually the most difficult part of management and has often been overshadowed by the emphasis on strategy formulation. Fortunately, there is growing awareness of the actions needed for strategy implementation and literature on the topic is expanding. This chapter will cover several areas of implementation, beginning with the efficient utilization of human resources through work-force flexibility. Such efficiencies have become increasingly important because of pressures to control labor costs. Next, approaches for dealing with employee shortages and surpluses will be discussed. The chapter concludes with approaches for dealing with some special implementation challenges. Because of the breadth of this topic, the reward and developmental aspects of strategy implementation will be discussed in Chapter 7.

EFFICIENT UTILIZATION OF HUMAN RESOURCES

Several managerial practices have the potential to provide for more flexibility in work-force utilization. More recently, such flexibility has been obtained by cross-training and other innovative practices. A more traditional approach involves operating on a nonunion basis.

Cross-Training and Flexibility in Assigning Work

Flexibility in work assignment is a key to efficient utilization of human resources. One of the most extreme examples of the efficiencies that can be obtained is provided by Chaparral Steel in Midlothian, Texas. Chaparral, which was established in 1973 as a start-up operation, has only two job classifications in its production operations: one dealing with production activities and the other with maintenance. It has obtained flexibility in work-force utilization through extensive cross-training and by operating on a nonunion basis. By paying skill-based or knowledge-based pay, Chaparral has motivated its employees to master a broad range of skills which enable them to perform wide-ranging activities. Examples of efficient work-force utilization include having security guards perform computer data entry functions, serve as paramedics, and perform safety functions such as checking fire extinguishers. In addition to efficient utilization of human resources, Chaparral has achieved its position as one of the world's most efficient producers of steel through heavy emphasis on technological innovation and computerization.

Interestingly, most of Chaparral's research and development efforts come from its production employees, as it views technological innovation as a responsibility of production personnel. Because of heavy emphasis on profit sharing and the avoidance of individualized suggestion systems, which discourage teamwork and information sharing, the company's employees are motivated to work together in developing technological advancements in production. Although Chaparral's research and developmental efforts come from its production employees, these employees are well-trained. Chaparral's production employees who have only a high school education go through two years of training in such areas as electronics, hydraulics, and statistical process control. Further, there is very high representation of college-trained engineers at Chaparral, such as those running the furnaces, and the CEO has a Ph.D. in materials science from MIT.[1] Admittedly, Chaparral has a production advantage in producing steel from scrap. However, its efficiencies are remarkable considering that with fewer than 1,000 employees, Chaparral's annual production of approximately one and one-half million tons of steel comprises about one and one-half percent of the steel produced in the United States.[2]

Interestingly, although Chaparral has achieved much of its productivity through technology, its managerial approach has also made substantial contributions. This is because the company's industry leadership in technological innovation is, in part, a result of its unique work environment. Major characteristics of this environment include encouragement of risk taking; challenge in the form of specific, reachable goals; the freedom to question; trust; and an absence of policies.[3] In fact, Chaparral has a "no fault" absence policy in which "an employee can be absent for a good reason, no reason, or a bad reason."[4] Interestingly, with this policy, "the daily absence rate is less than one percent."[5] Chaparral's CEO, Gordon Forward, has explained the company's rationale for the absence of policies as follows:

> We don't have policies. . . . We felt that a lot of the procedures in many organizations were designed to catch the 3 percent who were trying to cheat in one way or another. We decided to design out rules for the 97 percent we can trust. The others would stand out like sore thumbs, we figured, and they'd eventually leave. That's exactly what happened.[6]

The efficiencies made possible by technological innovation and human resource flexibility are also evident in the experiences of Frost, Inc., a small manufacturer in Grand Rapids, Michigan. Frost wanted to diversify its product line and decided that it needed greater flexibility in both its production facilities, and its employees and managers. At the time it had machinery and employees who could perform only very limited numbers of functions. Frost replaced outdated machining equipment with robots and numerically controlled machine tools, introduced an automated inventory control system, and automated its office functions. Specific managerial and human resource changes included broadening employees' skill and job responsibilities, making each employee a stockholder of the company, with options to purchase additional stock through its 401(k) plan, moving all hourly employees to salaried status, educating its employees on the new technology, eliminating perks such as reserved parking places, and eliminating several layers in the management hierarchy. Other changes included widely disseminating company information, adding quarterly bonuses driven by the company's productivity, and increasing the level of employee participation in decision making. The productivity increases made possible by these changes and a reduction in the number of employees to approximately 120, enabled the company to increase the level of sales per employee from $80,000 to $200,000.[7]

Commonalities in the approaches of Frost, Inc. and Chaparral include broadened employee job scope and responsibility, lean staffing, small size, informality, information availability, financial incentives based on company performance, and a flat organizational structure. It is important to note that the efficiencies obtained at Chaparral and Frost, Inc. through flexible work assignment and broadened jobs, were accompanied by corresponding changes in involvement in decision making, compensation, informality, and education.[8]

Operating on a Nonunion Basis

In order to gain greater flexibility, companies commonly pursue strategies of operating on a nonunion basis. Such strategies are sometimes a major determinant of the organization's structure, affecting divisional composition, plant size, and plant location.[9] Anil Verma has studied some large multiplant firms that have both union and nonunion operations. One strategy he found among firms desiring to reduce their exposure to labor relations problems was the approach of building small new plants that operate on a nonunion basis rather than investing in increased capacity in existing unionized plants.[10] Emerson Electric, which has both unionized and nonunion plants, provides an example of such strategies as it has an effective organizational structure for economical manufacturing. This structure has also reduced the likelihood of unionization in some of its plants. Some Emerson divisions carry well-known product line names, such as Skil tools, Insinkerator kitchen appliances, Dremel hobby tools, and Ridgid tools. As a result of locating its plants in small rural communities and organizing by divisions having strong name identification, stronger employee commitment and lower costs have been obtained, as well as an increased likelihood of remaining nonunion.[11] In addition to these organizational characteristics, numerous other variables affect the likelihood of unionism such as the individual characteristics of the work force, job content, compensation, industry, job satisfaction, perceptions of union instrumentality, characteristics of unions, governmental regulation, and macroeconomic influences. Because of space limitations, a detailed discussion of these influences cannot be provided here.[12]

DEALING WITH EMPLOYEE SHORTAGES

The demographic-based predictions of labor shortages for the 1990s had not materialized by the middle of the decade. For the United States as a whole, the problem of the 1990s has been one of a lack of jobs instead of a shortage of workers. Nonetheless, downturns and upturns are permanent features of the economy and individual employers may experience skill shortages of qualified personnel at a particular point in time. Many companies deal with such shortages by strategic recruiting, special recruiting for minorities and females, and flexible retirement policies.

Strategic Recruiting

Because companies must have the appropriate human resources to pursue specific strategies, recruiting must be aligned with their strategies. Empirical evidence backs up the importance of such alignment. An analysis of human resource practices of good and poor performing companies found that the good performing companies in the retailing industry were much more strategic in their orientation to selection and recruiting. One of these good performing companies, as a part of a major strategic change, broke with its traditional human resource practices by using a front-end strategy of combining higher selectivity with higher salaries, as an alternative to reliance on an attrition approach for elimination of marginal employees.[13]

One suggestion for effective recruiting is to focus on those sources providing the greatest number of desirable employees. Along this line, a number of studies have evaluated different recruiting sources to identify differences in important work-related outcomes such as performance, turnover, attitudes, and absenteeism. For example, one study focused on a company's research personnel who had bachelors, masters, or doctoral degrees in chemistry or biology. For these types of employees, those making recruiting contact with the company through newspaper ads and college placement offices, had lower performance than those responding to professional journal/convention ads or contacting the company on their own volition. Employees who responded to newspaper ads also had higher absenteeism rates. Further, those recruited through college placement offices had the lowest levels of job satisfaction. These results indicate that for research employees, newspaper ads and college placement offices are less desirable recruiting sources.[14] Unfortunately, as with most of the research in this area, it is difficult to generalize from such results. In this case the subjects were highly educated research personnel. Employees having doctorates are often active in professional associations that have well-developed job placement services at their annual conventions. Such employees might likely have a training deficiency if they do not understand how placement works in the professional discipline.

On the other hand, the study pointed out a potentially interesting explanation for differentials in recruiting source success, namely that the various recruiting sources provide differing amounts of information about companies and jobs. Those sources associated with greater applicant information produced better results because self-selection led to better job and applicant matching.[15] However, a recent study by Charles Williams, Chalmer Labig, and Thomas Stone was unable to lend support to the differential knowledge and self-selection explanation. Because of the equivocal nature of the literature and a failure to find any relationships between recruiting sources and performance, this same study concluded that it is probably counterproductive to attempt to identify differentials in success rates across various sources of recruits. Instead, the study recommended that companies focus on those characteristics of individual applicants that are stronger predictors of job performance.[16]

Another strategy-related recruiting issue is the extent to which the company should rely on internal or external recruiting, or a mixture of the two. Some well-managed companies hire externally only at the entry level and fill all higher-level positions from within the firm; examples of such companies include Merck, 3M, and IBM. The advantages associated with internal recruiting include having more reliable information on internal applicants, the motivational impact of employees' knowing that promotions will be filled from within the company, less recruiting and selection expense, quicker response time, and a shorter adjustment period in the new job because of the internal applicant's familiarity with the company. Unfortunately, internal recruiting may lead to managerial inbreeding, which may be particularly disadvantageous in rapidly changing environments where old strategies may be ineffective. Further, external recruiting has advantages of providing fresh ideas, requires less internal employee development, and may facilitate affirmative action.[17]

Employee shortages may not even require recruiting. Aside from the obvious approach of assigning more overtime, another alternative to recruiting is provided by temporary help firms. As indicated in earlier chapters, in addition to reduced recruiting responsibilities, temporary workers provide greater strategic flexibility in matching staffing with workload requirements. Because of heavy reliance on temporary workers, some companies have even created temporary worker programs within their own companies. For example, Fidelity Investments has 300 temporary employees who cover about 90 percent of the company's needs for temporaries. Fidelity's program provides temporary employees with some stability in work although it is not guaranteed. A benefit to Fidelity is that it obtains quality temporaries who are knowledgeable about its procedures.[18]

Special Recruiting for Minorities and Females

Organizations often have shortages of minorities and females. Recruiting in this area is affected by a company's public image. Companies that have created positive public images through their leadership in developing diverse work forces have an advantage in attracting females and minorities.[19] Companies such as "Merck, Xerox, Syntex, Hoffman-La Roche, and Hewlett-Packard have been aggressively using favorable publicity to recruit women and racioethnic minorities."[20] Typically such companies have introduced greater flexibility in work assignment and have provided support services such as child-care facilities, which also reduce turnover.[21] Pepsico is another company that has placed heavy emphasis on diversity. As a result, it has an excellent representation of minorities and females throughout its top-level positions. As a part of its efforts, the company has provided attractive scholarships and summer internships for talented minority MBA students. Pepsico has been very successful in recruiting these talented individuals upon graduation. In addition to these actions, Pepsico has also provided leadership as a corporate citizen. After the Los Angeles riots in 1992, Pepsico was one of the first companies to go back into the burned-out areas to demonstrate their commitment to the minority community. Pepsico has also been active in sponsoring diversity management workshops for business professors.

Many companies have moved beyond the requirements of affirmative action and are now focusing on the management of diversity, addressed later in this chapter. Nonetheless, for this to be a meaningful emphasis, there must first be an adequate representation of minorities and females, at least at entry level. Thus, affirmative action is a prerequisite. For those companies that have been successful in obtaining good representations of minorities and females at entry level, their next concerns are how to retain and facilitate the advancement of minorities and females to top positions. Thus, companies seeking to get maximum production out of their work forces should identify and remove barriers that limit individual employees' contributions. Much of what is meant by the term *management of diversity* is directed toward increasing productivity.[22]

Flexible Retirement Policies

With an aging population, it seems likely that labor shortages may be partially addressed by extending the number of years employees work before retirement. On the other hand, during the 1980s and first half of the 1990s, many companies had too many employees and were sometimes offering attractive packages for early retirement. Thus, encouraging more employees to stay on the job was not generally a pressing issue. Nonetheless, in the future, a number of factors may motivate older workers to remain on the job, some of which are limited retirement benefits or inadequacies in health-care benefits for retirees.

As indicated in Chapter 2, the larger older age cohorts and smaller younger age cohorts may create a labor shortage.[23] Because of this shortage, more older people may need to work to provide needed goods and services. This may be a fortuitous situation because the psychological well-being of older persons is enhanced if they are allowed options for *flexible retirement.* This could be implemented with *phased retirement* or a reduced number of working days, instead of total retirement. Because of the centrality of work to our lives, the opportunity to continue working could provide great benefit. Surveys of managers and executives indicate a desire to work more years through various flexible approaches, such as phased retirement, transfers, and job redesign. Nonetheless, even though mandatory retirement at a given age is prohibited for most types of employees, human resource managers receive very little support from senior executives for flexible retirement approaches. Some of this resistance may be related to the difficulties involved in individually determining who should be allowed to continue working. Determinations of fitness for continued employment would presumably be based on performance and medical evaluations. It is easy to visualize the greater difficulty of telling a long-time, loyal employee that he or she must retire because of performance inadequacies, instead of letting an impersonal policy serve as the standard. In addition to executive opposition to flexible approaches, a large number of older workers favor early retirement, in the interests of the organization as well as of the employee.[24]

> We were surprised to find that older respondents, compared to younger respondents, were more likely to agree that it is in the best interests of both the organization and the employee for senior exempt employees to retire at age 65 or even earlier.[25]

DEALING WITH EMPLOYEE SURPLUSES

As discussed in Chapter 1, there are several methods by which companies may reduce the likelihood that they will have to lay off employees. These included both short-range and long-range approaches. Several of these approaches need further explanation, two of these are redeployment and retraining, with the latter often being required before employees can be redeployed.

Retraining and Redeployment

The prevention of skill obsolescence and career plateauing were covered in Chapter 1. Unfortunately, obsolescence is not always prevented and retraining may be required. With the increased rate of technological change and potential for skill obsolescence, *retraining* may become more important. As a result, many companies provide retraining for managers whose skills have become obsolete. A critical determinant in the success of such programs are managers' self-efficacy beliefs, or expectations that they will be successful in mastering the new skills. Interestingly, some companies send the wrong message.[26]

> Executives often adopted a "slash and burn" strategy when retraining efforts failed to realize objectives, laying off managers who did not acquire new competencies, behaviors, and attitudes. Layoffs following retraining programs may send a message to the workforce that retraining is a futile endeavor.[27]

A few companies currently provide extensive retraining for employees who will be *redeployed* within the company. One is IBM, which provides retraining for professionals being internally redeployed. However, most companies do not provide retraining for the employees they lay off. A study by Leana and Feldman found that less than 10 percent of laid-off workers receive such assistance from their former employers. Since governmental agencies provide various retraining programs, the response of most companies is to leave such training to these agencies. However, there are exceptions, one being the Ford Motor Company, which funds and operates the National Development and Training Center. Laid-off workers going through the center receive individualized retraining, specific to their needs.[28]

Early Retirement

In dealing with overages of employees, companies frequently offer *early retirement* incentives in which employees currently ineligible for retirement receive additional years' credit and a bonus payment that enhances pension benefits. Major concerns with this practice are the effects on the company's pool of talent and the impact on early retirees. A longitudinal study by Ann Howard of AT&T and Bell System managerial employees addressed these concerns. One of the study's major conclusions was that there were no significant differences at the twentieth-year mark, in the performance ratings of managers who took early retirement versus those who did not.[29] The study concluded the following:

> Thus, the companies suffered no loss in quality of management talent as a result of the early retirements . . . there are no indications that the most capable mangers leave the company if a golden handshake for those nearing retirement age is offered. Nor, of course, are the least capable most likely to leave.[30]

The same study also investigated other characteristics of managers taking early retirement and those remaining. Although performance ratings at their twentieth years were not significantly different for those retiring early, work had a lower priority in their lives, they were less conscientious about quality work, they perceived lower likelihood of future promotion, and they were more dissatisfied with their present jobs. In addition, they were more dissatisfied with their supervisors and the company. Further, they were more dissatisfied with the company a number of years before they retired. In retrospect, some of this greater dissatisfaction may have been manageable because there were warning signs of its development. Nonetheless, the overall evaluation of the early retirement program was that the more highly motivated managers who had better work and company attitudes remained.[31]

On the other side, from the perspective of those taking early retirement, these managers seemed to be motivated by an instrumentality rationale. They had fewer financial concerns and stronger life interests outside of work, such as hobbies and socializing. Nonetheless, there was some dissatisfaction with the manner in which the early retirements were handled. A particularly troublesome issue was a change in the performance appraisal approach, as it was perceived as a means of shoving them out of the company.[32] The following quotation from one manager describes this perception.

> About the time they introduced the new benefit plan, they also introduced a new appraisal plan. I had always been rated above average, but the new appraisals were done by managers upstate. I became the bottom of the list. My boss and I both broke into tears. Rather than face another unsatisfactory rating, I decided to leave the company.[33]

A reaction such as this indicates that abrupt changes in performance appraisal approaches are likely to be viewed as deceptive and may create ill will. Thus, one guideline for downsizing through the use of early retirements is that abrupt changes in performance appraisal should be avoided. Further, a truly voluntary approach is preferred because coercive approaches will be seen for what they are.[34] To protect themselves from charges of age discrimination, employers downsizing through voluntary early retirement programs typically request that employees sign waivers against claims under the Age Discrimination in Employment Act (ADEA). As indicated in Chapter 3, several specific conditions must be met before these waivers will constitute valid defenses against such charges.[35]

Of course it is sometimes more desirable to focus on eliminating the poorer performers, which necessitates another approach. From the standpoint of employee welfare, those opting for early retirement will probably be better prepared from a financial standpoint. Since some retirees indicate that they would like to work to maintain contact and earn extra money, the company should also consider providing part-time employment. Finally, the early retiree's contributions to the company should be recognized with a demonstration of the company's appreciation. Although performance may have declined at some point, an employee's many years of service to the company merit recognition and the conclusion of a long career should not carry the stigma of a forced retirement.[36]

Retreat from Employment Security Policies

As noted in Chapter 1, layoffs have become a fact of life in the United States. From the late 1980s to the mid-1990s, structural changes in the economy, increases in productivity resulting from technology, computerization, and intense global competition led scores of companies to abandon employment security policies and downsize their work forces. Although a recession also accounted for some layoffs, many were the result of permanent structural changes as companies were able to accomplish the same or more work with fewer employees. Many companies that had maintained no-layoff policies in the past reverted to layoffs. In early 1990, the list of companies that maintained no-layoff policies included Delta Airlines, Digital Equipment Corporation, Federal Express, IBM, S. C. Johnson, Lincoln Electric, Mazda Motor, Motorola, National Steel, New United Motor, Nissan Motor, Nucor, and Xerox.[37] Layoffs came earlier at AT&T, Eastman Kodak, and Polaroid.[38] By 1991, Digital signaled its first layoffs with an announcement that it would lay off some 3,500 employees. Although the company had spent $550 million during the previous year in voluntary severance pay and retraining costs, not enough employees elected to leave.[39]

IBM, which had long maintained a no-layoff policy, announced plans in 1989 to reduce employment by 10,000 but planned to avoid layoffs through use of a financial-incentive program.[40] Nonetheless, by 1992 the company found that it had to reduce its employment by 40,000 during that year alone. In total, IBM reduced its employment by 100,000 between 1985 and 1992. Also in 1992, Digital Equipment eliminated 18,000 jobs. IBM tried to become more responsive by shifting to semiautonomous or free-standing units, a process called deconstructing. Essentially, IBM tried to obtain some of the quickness and accountability advantages of rapidly responding, personal computer and workstation manufacturers such as Sun Microsystems and Dell.[41] By the middle of the 1990s, IBM had made massive cuts in its work force.

During 1990 Boeing planned to lay off employees while having a huge backlog of orders.[42] By 1992, some of these orders had been canceled as a result of the difficulties of the airline industry. By 1994, Delta announced its intentions to reduce employment by as much as 15,000 by 1997.[43] The business press reported that "The promise of 'employment security,' not long ago a bright hope for curing America's competitive problems, has faded."[44] Nonetheless, job security or income security is still a goal of major importance to employees. In the 1990 negotiations between the United Auto Workers and General Motors, a major bargaining issue involved guaranteed wages and benefits during layoffs.[45] Nonetheless, downsizing and layoffs have become a strategy implementation reality.

Downsizing and Layoffs

Before conducting *layoffs,* there should be a careful analysis of their effects in the long run, as well as in the short run. For example, if a company conducts layoffs in response to short-term losses, it may find that its long-term survivability is endangered. A short-term problem may only be symptomatic of a larger problem that is not addressed by layoffs, such as lack of adaptability. In reality, layoffs, such as in the research and development area, may place a company in the position of mortgaging its future. Such cuts may prevent a company from pursuing its intended strategies because it has focused on short-term tactical moves to the detriment of strategy. Thus, before conducting layoffs, companies should seek an appropriate balance between short-term and long-term demands, as well as between the goals of work-force stability and organizational adaptability. Downsizing strategies are also more effective when the most effective performers can be retained. In some instances the performance evaluation system may need improvement for accurate identification of such individuals. Further, the reward system may require modification to obtain the flexibility needed to retain them. Such flexibility is necessary because resource scarcities often prompt downsizing strategies. Even with resource scarcities, effective performers may be retained by future-oriented rewards such as stock ownership and profit sharing.[46]

Companies must also be aware that even their short-term problems may not be solved by downsizing because of the loss of skills resulting from the departure of experienced employees who are offered early retirement options or severance packages. An example of poor results is provided in Cook and Ferris' study of declining industries which found that "The poor performers [companies] looked at their actions (e.g., layoffs or early retirements) as individual events without considering the long-term consequences."[47] As noted in Chapter 1, it has been hypothesized that organizations having previous experience with layoffs will reduce their work forces through less severe methods. This is because their managers are predicted to have more timely insight of surpluses. With this recognition, they should take remedial action more quickly and should be in a position to rely more on attrition or redeployment. It has also been hypothesized that companies having less slack in their resource base are more likely to reduce employment by resorting to more severe approaches such as layoffs.[48]

An example of short-term problems related to layoffs is provided by the Carlson Travel Network, a large travel agency that had conducted layoffs. One important client, who had planned to travel to Taiwan after completing business in Japan, found that while in Japan he could not travel to Taiwan without a visa. This necessitated his flying back to Minnesota before going on to Taiwan. A mistake had been made by an inexperienced agent. Eventually, Carlson's quality of service improved to desired levels and the company obtained desired efficiencies. However, this and other problems occurred during the learning period.[49] As noted earlier, companies must be careful in conducting layoffs not to deplete their knowledge base such that their distinctive competencies are lost.[50]

Another problem with downsizing is that it often begins a vicious cycle. Typically, the cycle is initiated by more intensified competition that cuts into the company's revenues. Lower revenues then lead to efforts to quickly cut costs and some employees are laid off. Although the company is left with fewer employees, the workload remains constant. Overwork, stress, frustration, and declining morale are experienced by the "survivors" who often find themselves in a crisis management mode in which they attend only to immediate problems. Additionally, remaining employees also tend to become more risk-averse and narrow-minded. As a result, insufficient workers are available to examine the underlying causes of problems, and fewer resources are available for research and developmental efforts. Because of these detrimental effects, customer satisfaction wanes, causing revenues to decline further, thus precipitating another round of layoffs to cut costs. Another problem with downsizing strategies is that companies frequently do not obtain the benefits of reduced expenses, profitability, and increased return on investment which they had hoped to achieve. Cost savings are also wasted when consultants have to be hired to supply the expertise lost from staff layoffs. Some observers have even estimated that replacements eventually have to be hired for 10 to 20 percent of those employees who were laid-off.[51]

Nonetheless, after all alternatives have been exhausted and there are no others, layoffs sometimes become unavoidable. To enhance the likelihood of success, downsizing needs to be viewed more systematically. Typically downsizing strategies need to be accompanied by changes in other factors that have an impact on organizational efficiency, such as the design of the organization and the elimination of redundancies.[52] Some key findings about the conduct of layoffs are presented in Table 6-1.

TABLE 6-1   KEY FINDINGS ABOUT DOWNSIZING

Far too many companies are not well prepared for downsizing, they begin with no retraining or redeployment policies in place, and they fail to anticipate the kinds of human resource problems that develop subsequently.

Six months to a year after a downsizing, key indicators often do not improve: expense ratios, profits, return-on-investment to shareholders, and stock prices.

Survivors' syndrome is a common aftermath. Be prepared to manage it. Better yet, to try to avoid it by actively involving employees in the planning phase of any downsizing effort.

Recognize that downsizing has exploded the myth of job security and has accelerated employee mobility, especially among white-collar workers. It has fundamentally altered the terms of the psychological contract that binds workers to organizations.

To bring about sustained improvements in productivity, quality, and effectiveness, integrate reductions in headcount with planned changes in the way that work is designed.

Downsizing is not a one-time, quick-fix solution to enhance competitiveness. Rather, it should be viewed as part of a process of continuous improvement.

Source: Extracted from Wayne F. Cascio, "Downsizing: What Do We Know? What Have We Learned?" *Academy of Management Executive,* 7, no. 1 (1993), 103. Reprinted with permission.

Unfortunately, layoffs too frequently have been conducted without sufficient regard for employees. In order to minimize the adverse consequences to employees, managers should consider the guidelines presented in Table 6-2, a discussion of which follows.

(1) Companies should give employees advance notice that they are going to be laid-off. Reasons for not providing notice are based on fears that employees will sabotage equipment or quit, leaving the company without workers to complete production prior to the plant's closure. In a study of layoffs in the steel industry and work related to NASA programs, researchers found that less than 50 percent of employees had received advance notice.[53] There is evidence that employers' concerns about the dangers of providing advance notice are unfounded as there are no associated declines in productivity or greater instances of sabotage. In contrast, companies actually benefit by providing advance notice because they are likely to be perceived more positively by the public.[54] Further, those companies having 100 or more employees are covered by the Worker Adjustment and Retraining Notification Act (WARN). Under the act, employers must provide sixty days' advance notice of plant closings to employees, unions, and officials at state and local levels when fifty or more employees will lose their jobs.[55] Additionally, employees tend to receive other benefits from advance notice, one being that early notification enables employees to prepare for their departure from the company.[56] Another is that their period of unemployment may be shorter. Empirical evidence indicates that the period of unemployment for those who receive advance notice is shorter than for those who do not.[57]

(2) Those being laid-off should receive severance pay, and benefits should be extended. Aside from humanitarian reasons, providing severance pay may preserve the company's relationship with the employee and enhance its chances of rehiring the employee after business improves. Additionally, severance pay may be perceived to reduce the likelihood of litigation.[58]

(3) Make outplacement services available to employees. Outplacement services tend to stimulate laid-off workers to pursue retraining opportunities and to relocate. Likewise, they provide opportunities for building social support. Although the effectiveness of outplacement services probably varies by employee level and needs, their role in providing a base of operations for contacting employers appears to be uniformly valuable. Additionally, employees' perceptions of fair treatment are probably enhanced by outplacement services. Although the research evidence has not definitively established that outplacement programs are effective in helping workers become reemployed, such programs may have an additional major benefit of facilitating employees' psychological adjustment to the loss of their jobs and in helping them regain their self-confidence.[59]

Other suggestions for carrying out layoffs include (4) supplying additional training, particularly where declines in industries have made employees' skills obsolete, (5) attending to the morale of remaining employees, such as by not making derogatory remarks about those laid-off, and (6) displaying social responsibility by helping to defray the costs incurred by the community in which layoffs or plant closures are conducted. (7) A final suggestion is to avoid preferential treatment of minorities and women even for the affirmative action objective of retaining utilization of such employees. Such treatment has not been well received by the courts, particularly where seniority systems are circumvented.[60]

The impact of layoffs on remaining employees or survivors should be taken into account when conducting layoffs. Further, the basis on which employees are selected for layoffs appears to have an impact on survivor's work performance. While in reality few layoffs are conducted on the basis of a random criterion, the results of a laboratory study of such circumstances provide some interesting insights on survivors' behavior. The laboratory study, which drew on the tenants of equity theory, demonstrated that subjects who survived layoffs conducted on a random basis were more productive in terms of quantity after the layoffs. The theoretical basis for this finding is that the survivors of a random layoff will experience positive inequity because survivors would see their ratio of outcomes to inputs to be more favorable than those laid-off. This is because their performance or inputs were no greater, but the outcomes of those laid off—losing their jobs—were less. In order to restore equilibrium and to reduce feelings of guilt, the survivors worked harder and produced more. Experimental conditions ruled out an alternative explanation, that the survivors' increased productivity may have resulted from feelings of anxiety regarding future layoffs.[61]

Regardless of the layoff strategy used, the impact in human terms will be considered by all but the most cold-blooded managers. The human cost of a layoff or termination may be assessed, in part, in terms of the anticipated length of the period of unemployment. Clearly, the morale of remaining employees will be adversely affected by prolonged periods of unemployment of those laid-off or terminated, except in the most extreme cases of misbehavior. Unfortunately, it is difficult to predict the average length of time

TABLE 6-2 GUIDELINES FOR CONDUCTING LAYOFFS

Give early warnings/announcements of layoffs

Soften the impact with compensation and benefits

Utilize the services of outplacement firms

Supply retraining services

Insure supportive treatment of survivors

Maintain a cooperative approach with unions

Uphold obligations to the community

Provide equitable and decent treatment of laid-off employees

Source: Adapted from Daniel C. Feldman and Carrie R. Leana, "Managing Layoffs: Experiences at the Challenger Disaster Site and the Pittsburgh Steel Mills," *Organizational Dynamics,* 18, no. 1 (1989), 52–64.

employees will remain unemployed as there are numerous explanatory factors. However, a New York outplacement firm has used a sixty variable formula to predict the period of unemployment for its clients.[62] A rule of thumb also exists. Although its predictive accuracy is unknown, the rule predicts that a terminated manager will remain unemployed for "one month for every $10,000 of income."[63]

Termination Strategies

Although terminations may be indicative of deficiencies in other human resource management systems, they are often required for organizational change and have even been categorized as an organizational development process. As such, terminations may be critical for the implementation of a shift in the strategic direction of an organization. Terminations of managers have been necessary in organizational evolutions where managers, who can work effectively within its informal structure, cannot adapt to the more formal structure required with growth in size. Terminations have also been used where entrepreneurs who were effective in founding companies could not make the transition to the different managerial requirements of a bureaucratic environment.[64]

Companies should develop approaches that assure employees that termination will be for just cause and that the performance appraisal, coaching, and counseling systems will have warned them that their performance must improve or that certain behaviors are unacceptable. On the other hand, companies must also terminate employees in a manner which communicates that substandard performance and inappropriate behaviors will result in termination. Companies need an approach that eliminates unsatisfactory performers while allowing competent employees to feel secure in their jobs, committed to the company, capable of taking reasonable risks, and deserving of their loyalty. In the absence of such an approach, the company will not have a performance culture nor will it have employee commitment. Interestingly, experienced outplacement consultants have observed that managerial terminations are usually due to personality-related conflicts with the terminated employee's manager. In contrast, less than 5 percent of managerial terminations are based on the grounds of incompetence.[65]

In terminating unsatisfactory performers, U.S. employers have an advantage over many European competitors as they have much greater latitude. For example, in Italy, governmental regulations require an employer to pay up to $130,000 in benefits to terminate an employee forty-five years of age who has been employed for twenty years. Termination costs are not as expensive in all European countries as the cost in Ireland would be $13,000 under the same circumstances.[66]

Unfortunately, even with an appropriate balance between employment security and the maintenance of performance and behavioral standards, the implementation of termination strategies often leaves much to be desired. In recent years terminations have been conducted too frequently with little regard for employees' dignity. Employees are frequently told of the termination, escorted by security personnel to their desks to pick up their personal property, and then taken to the door. Although often related to fears that the terminated employee will sabotage a computer system or other company assets, this rationale is not always applicable.[67] The following examples are more typical of termination actions than they should be.

> A supervisor at a tractor plant in Dubuque, Iowa, got the ax while he was on vacation. "He got a call at home. Company officials told him to meet them in the parking lot of a local fast-food restaurant. He got in his boss's car and [his boss] read him a brief notice," says Earl Payson, a lawyer who represented the client in an age-discrimination suit against the same company. "They wouldn't answer any questions. My client had been with the company for over 25 years."[68]
>
> My own son was terminated [recently] by an advertising company with a note on the door. It said, "You're fired. Come and see me." It was signed by his boss.[69]

Although the literature on terminations is largely prescriptive and anecdotal, there are some practical guidelines. One is that terminations should be conducted as business decisions. Employees should be told that the termination is an irrevocable business decision. In contrast to the advice offered by some attorneys, employees should be told the reasons for their termination.[70] Some attorneys advise that providing the reason for the termination simply gives the employee another rationale for initiating litigation. Nonetheless, such advice hardly meets the standard of fairness which managers themselves should apply, as well as the expectations of fairness held by other employees.

Outplacement services should be provided to help the employee make the adjustment from ending the employment relationship to beginning the search process. This adjustment process is sometimes equated to a grieving process in which the employee goes through predictable steps. It has been suggested by some observers that these steps are analogous to the Kubler-Ross five stages of dying: "denial, anger, bargaining, depression, and acceptance."[71] Outplacement counselors may be of assistance in helping the terminated employee work more quickly through these stages to acceptance, at which point constructive steps can be taken toward obtaining a new job. Career counseling and realistic assessments of strengths and weaknesses may also be helpful in shortening the period of time before the employee can obtain a new job. Employees receiving outplacement assistance feel more fairly treated by the company.[72]

Another suggestion is to exercise care in the timing of terminations. Employees frequently want to take positive action to obtain another job as quickly as possible. Therefore, terminating employees before a weekend or during a holiday may be unduly stressful because they cannot pursue job search activities at this time. Further, during these times the employee may have too much time to brood over the termination. Managers should also consider the impact of a termination on other employees because how a co-worker is terminated may have a lasting impact on employees' perceptions of the company. Terminations should be conducted only after prior warning, after real attempts to improve the employee's performance or correct unacceptable behavior, and after a thorough investigation surrounding the last straw incident. Nonetheless, managers often delay too long before terminating employees. One reason for delay is that managers tend to feel guilty about terminating employees and may blame the employees' failures on themselves.[73]

In conducting the termination session, the manager should describe the conditions of the separation, benefits, and the nature of recommendations the company is willing to make. A practical suggestion is that the severance package and explanation of benefits should be in writing since the employee may not "hear" the information during such a traumatic time. In the termination session, the manager should cover the essential information, convey appropriate appreciation for the employee's contributions, and treat the employee with respect and as humanely as possible, but the session should not be a debate and should be fairly short, usually about fifteen minutes.[74]

SPECIAL IMPLEMENTATION CHALLENGES

Several developments in the area of employment practices and policies provide special implementation challenges. One of the most important challenges to strategies requiring a mobile labor force is provided by the dual-career couple. Another is related to the problem of nepotism.

Dual-Career Couples

Increasingly, companies are facing challenges in transferring employees because of the rising number of dual-career couples. Two-income families are now involved in approximately 60 percent of transfers. Further, women are more frequently the employee who is being transferred. In 1989, of employees transferred, 13 percent were women, up from 5 percent in 1980. By 2000, women are expected to comprise 24 percent of those transferred. With women now comprising a large percentage of the professional occupations, it is not surprising that they are increasingly the employee being transferred. An obvious problem companies face in transferring employees involved in dual-career situations is the spouse's ability to find a commensurate position. Such fears are well grounded, as a few years ago spouses were averaging between four and six months before finding a new job.[75]

Another problem encountered with dual-career couples is their frequency of turnover when the spouse works for another large employer that transfers employees. For women employees, there is a perception, whether valid or not, that they may be more susceptible to turnover in such circumstances. This perception is as follows: "Because the female manager is seen as more often following her spouse in a relocation decision, her dual-career family status is considered more of a liability."[76] A related problem concerns travel requirements. Where both individuals have jobs that necessitate extensive travel, there are difficult problems with caring for children and in finding enough time for the couple to be together.[77]

Most employees in dual-career situations have a strong desire for assistance in obtaining employment for their spouses. Fortunately, companies' human resource personnel are in an advantageous position to provide such assistance, as they are the most attuned to job opportunities and are frequently networked with other area employers. One such example is an employer network in Columbus, Ohio, comprised of over forty organizations.[78] As specific examples, General Motors provides referrals and counseling assistance for spouses and IBM provides similar assistance.[79] More specific examples of employer assistance are the following:

> Atlantic Richfield Company, The Dow Chemical Company, Eastman Kodak, IBM, Merck & Co., Procter & Gamble, US Sprint, and Warner-Lambert will all help spouses find jobs. Many will give serious consideration to hiring them.[80]

Aside from obtaining another job for the spouse, another problem faced by dual-career couples is the details of moving. In the past, these details have been handled by the spouse who was not employed, typically the wife. Further, family support systems now handle more duties such as child care, housekeeping, and assistance with elderly parents. These support systems must be reestablished with a move to a different geographic location. With dual-career couples, the details involved with transfers have increased and cannot be handled by a spouse who is not employed. As a result, more time is required for the transfers, along with earlier notice.[81]

A related issue of greater importance in recent years, is requests for transfer assistance when the other half of the dual-career couple is not a spouse. A survey in 1988 revealed that almost 20 percent of companies furnish relocation assistance in such situations.[82]

> However, there are a number of problems companies face in these situations, such as, "How significant does the other have to be to be considered a partner? Is the length of time the relationship has existed a factor in defining partners? What about same-gender couples?"[83]

In response to problems such as these, more companies are adapting their policies to deal with the special issues involved with dual-career couples. A survey of nepotism policies indicates that of the companies planning to change their nepotism rules, 58 percent intended to make them more liberal. Companies at the forefront in liberalizing policies to accommodate dual-career couples are in high-tech industries.[84] It is not surprising that high-tech industries offer more liberal nepotism rules since these industries must attract high-quality talent and, therefore, will bypass traditional approaches. A specific example is provided by a software company, Lotus Development, where over 40 percent of married employees are from dual-career families.[85] As indicated in Chapter 2, women have benefited from the progressive policies of such companies and have made great strides into the managerial ranks of high-tech firms because these firms have strong needs for talent.[86]

Nepotism

The increasing number of dual-career couples—defined as both individuals working as professionals, administrators, or managers—has caused organizations to reconsider their rules on nepotism.[87] However, there is wide variance in *nepotism policies*. In some of the largest publicly held companies where there is substantial family ownership, there is nepotism in high positions. Examples include Anheuser-Busch, Corning Glass Works, Ford Motor Company, W. R. Grace, Lowes, Marriott, McDonnell Douglas, Weyerhaeuser, and Winn-Dixie. Privately held companies in which nepotism exists at the highest managerial levels include Koch Industries, Levi Strauss, Mars, and Milliken and Company. Herman Miller Inc. hires relatives of employees up to mid-level management because of the family feeling produced. However, nepotism is precluded in its top management positions.[88]

Some companies provide more extreme examples of nepotism and with remarkable success. For example, Mrs. Baird's Bakeries, Inc., in Fort Worth, Texas, employs several members of the Baird family. The following quotation captures their degree of success:

> "We have 19 family members involved in this business," said Baird, chairman of the board of Mrs. Baird's Bakeries Inc., which has 650 Tarrant County employees. "Part of that 19 is fifth-generation, and we're still in business after 80 years."[89]

Benefits of nepotism are that top managers may have longer-range strategic perspectives, family executives can pursue more risky decisions because of personal job security, there is greater job security for employees, the companies can respond more quickly to opportunities or threats because of simplified decision processes, and family members may be more committed to the company.[90] Companies run by family members may also place greater emphasis on quality. As Ivan Lansberg has stated, "They worry a helluva lot more about quality because the boss's name is on the product."[91] The downside of nepotism is that it is often demoralizing to higher-level managers who are passed over for promotion because of the son or daughter of the chief executive officer. Also, there are power struggles within the family when the relative is not extremely competent.[92]

Because of such problems, nepotism is prohibited in many companies. Unfortunately, these prohibitions go too far in some situations and fears about nepotism are often unfounded.[93] As a result, dual-career couples may be unfairly penalized. The newspaper industry provides an example of approaches toward nepotism. The following passage describes the origins of nepotism rules in this industry. Although industry-specific, this passage also details some concerns of managers in other industries.

> The original rationale for nepotism rules at most news organizations was to erect a barrier against the editor's half-literate son or the publisher's unscrupulous nephew. As more women became reporters, there was concern that newsroom marriages would be, well, messy—although editors were equally uncomfortable with a spouse working for the rival paper, lest the competition get wind of a big scoop.[94]

With the increase in dual-career couples, there has been pressure to relax the rules. Some newspapers have relaxed their nepotism prohibitions as editors have found synergies from both partners being employed by the same paper. Newsroom couples also have a supportive understanding of reporters' "fairly bizarre lifestyle."[95] In 1991, the *Houston Chronicle* had sixteen couples in its newsroom. In contrast, during the same year prohibitions against nepotism still existed at the *Philadelphia Inquirer,* the *St. Petersburg Times,* and the *Washington Post.* In the case of newspapers, these rules are particularly burdensome for dual-career couples because journalists are frequently married to journalists and there may be only one newspaper in the cities in which they live.

Although there has been a trend toward relaxation of anti-nepotism rules in the private sector, the trend is not nearly as evident in the public sector. Anti-nepotism rules are still common in the public sector, although they vary in the breadth of their prohibitions. The least stringent prevent elected officials from hiring relatives, while the most restrictive preclude the employment of family members in the same department or organization. Although these rules have been increasingly litigated by dual-career couples, the courts have generally been sympathetic to the position of management. It has been argued that anti-nepotism rules work to the particular disadvantage of women. Because of child-rearing activities, the woman is likely to join the job market later than her husband. Accordingly, anti-nepotism rules deny employment to women more frequently than men because the husband is more likely to be already employed by the organization. Federal courts have rejected this and similar arguments; however, state courts have been somewhat more likely to rule against nepotism rules. While the courts have supported anti-nepotism rules, their rulings also commend accommodative efforts on the part of management, such as providing transfers.[96] Nonetheless, in public universities, the author's own observations are that the rules against nepotism have been relaxed to preclude only the supervision of one spouse by the other.

A survey of public sector organizations found that a relatively small percentage of public sector organizations prevent family members from being employed in the same organization. More public sector organizations will not allow family members or spouses to be employed in the same office.

TABLE 6-3   ANTI-NEPOTISM RULES IN PUBLIC SECTOR ORGANIZATIONS

	PERCENTAGE REPORTING RULES				
TYPE OF RULE	*FEDERAL AGENCIES (N=19)*	*STATE AGENCIES (N=49)*	*COUNTY/ LOCAL AGENCIES (N=101)*	*UNIVERSITY SYSTEMS (N=43)*	*NONPROFIT ORGANIZATIONS (N=20)*
Prohibits families/spouses working in same organization	5.3	10.2	17.8	2.3	20.0
Prohibits families/spouses working in same office	21.1	12.2	53.0	9.3	30.0
Prohibits family member/spouse supervising another family member/spouse	73.7	57.1	71.7	46.5	30.0

Source: Extracted from Christine M. Reed, "Anti-Nepotism Rules and Dual Career Couples: Policy Questions for Public Personnel Administrators," *Public Personnel Management*, 17, no. 2 (1988), 227. Reprinted with permission, *Public Personnel Management*, International Personnel Management Association, Alexandria, Virginia.

A majority of public sector organizations prevent family members from occupying positions where they supervise one another.[97] The results of the survey are presented in Table 6-3.

SUMMARY

This chapter has covered methods by which companies obtain the efficiencies needed for implementation of their strategies. Employers have become more efficient and flexible by broadening the duties and responsibilities of their employees. Cross-training has been used effectively in these efforts to gain flexibility in making work assignments that more efficiently utilize employees' time. In addition to producing benefits for the organization, cross-training has appeal for employees when combined with skill-based pay systems, which are discussed in Chapter 7. Organizational cultures emphasizing trust appear to promote flexibility through such practices as the elimination of rules. Approaches for operating on a nonunion basis were also discussed as means of obtaining flexibility.

Several methods for dealing with shortages of employees and skills were discussed. These included strategic recruitment from both internal and external sources and special recruiting for minorities and females. Suggestions were provided for the conduct of flexible retirement programs as a means of dealing with employee shortages. Methods for dealing with employee surpluses were also reviewed including retraining and redeployment within the organization and early retirement. A brief description of the abandonment of employment security policies in the United States was also provided. Problems of downsizing and layoffs were then examined in some depth along with means for eliminating some of the dysfunctional effects of these actions. In addition, termination problems were discussed as were suggestions for improving the effectiveness of these personnel actions.

Finally, the special challenges to strategies requiring a mobile work force were discussed. Some of the most important of these challenges are encountered when dealing with dual-career couples. The obstacles to strategy implementation resulting from nepotism rules were also examined. Several suggestions for dealing with these issues were also provided.

REFERENCES

1. Forward, Gordon E., "Wide-Open Management at Chaparral Steel," *Harvard Business Review*, 64, no. 3 (1986), 96–102; Luthans, Fred, "Conversation with Gordon Forward," *Organizational Dynamics*, 20, no. 1 (1991), 63–72; personal conversations of the author with Gordon Forward, CEO; Dennis Beach, vice president for administration; and Larry Clark, vice president for finance.
2. Forward, "Wide-Open Management at Chaparral Steel"; United States Bureau of the Census, *Statistical Abstract of the United States: 1990*, 110th ed.; Washington, D.C.: U.S. Government Printing Office, 1990; Greer, Charles R., and Robert T. Rhodes, "A Contrasting View of the Effect of Foreign Competition on Labor Unionism in the United States," *West Virginia Law Review*, 93, no. 4 (1991), 945–955; Luthans, "Conversation with Gordon Forward."
3. Luthans, "Conversation with Gordon Forward."
4. Forward, Gordon E., Dennis E. Beach, David A. Gray, and James Campbell Quick, "Mentofacturing: A Vision for American Industrial Excellence," *Academy of Management Executive*, 5, no. 3 (1991), 36, (whole article on pp. 32–44).
5. Forward, Beach, Gray, and Quick, "Mentofacturing: A Vision for American Industrial Excellence," 36.
6. Luthans, "Conversation with Gordon Forward," 69.
7. Galante, Steven P., "Frost Inc. Technological Renewal and Human Resource Management: A Case Study," *Human Resource Planning*, 10, no. 1 (1987), 57–67.
8. Ibid.
9. Mills, Daniel, *Labor-Management Relations*. New York: McGraw-Hill, 1978; "Emerson Electric's Rise as a Low-Cost Producer," *Business Week*, November 1, 1976, 47–48.
10. Verma, Anil, "Relative Flow of Capital to Union and Nonunion Plants Within a Firm," *Industrial Relations*, 24, no. 3 (1985), 395–405.
11. Mills, *Labor-Management Relations*; "Emerson Electric's Rise as a Low-Cost Producer," *Business Week*.
12. Fiorito, Jack, Daniel G. Gallagher, and Charles R. Greer, "Determinants of Unionism: A Review of the Literature," in *Research in Personnel and Human Resources Management*, eds. Kendrith M. Rowland and Gerald R. Ferris. Greenwich, Conn.: JAI Press, 1986, pp. 269–306.
13. Cook, Deborah S., and Gerald R. Ferris, "Strategic Human Resource Management and Firm Effectiveness in Industries Experiencing Decline," *Human Resource Management*, 25, no. 3 (1986), 441–457.
14. Breaugh, James A., "Relationships Between Recruiting Sources and Employee Performance, Absenteeism, and Work Attitudes," *Academy of Management Journal*, 24, no. 1 (1981), 142–147.
15. Ibid.
16. Williams, Charles R., Chalmer E. Labig, and Thomas H. Stone, "Recruitment Sources and Posthire Outcomes for Job Applicants and New Hires: A Test of Two Hypotheses," *Journal of Applied Psychology*, 78, no. 2 (1993), 163–172.
17. Breaugh, James A., *Recruitment: Science and Practice*. Boston: PWS-Kent, 1992.
18. Bassett, Joan, "Recruitment: Fidelity Investments Brings Temporary Employment In-House," *Personnel Journal*, 68, no. 12 (1989), 65–70.
19. Cox, Taylor H., and Stacy Blake, "Managing Cultural Diversity: Implications for Organizational Competitiveness," *Academy of Management Executive*, 5, no. 3 (1991), 45–56.
20. Cox and Blake, "Managing Cultural Diversity," 49.

192 / *Chapter Six*

21. Cox and Blake, "Managing Cultural Diversity," Cox, Taylor, Jr., "The Multicultural Organization," *Academy of Management Executive*, 5, no. 2, (1991), 34–47.
22. Thomas, R. Roosevelt, "From Affirmative Action to Affirming Diversity," *Harvard Business Review*, 68, no. 2 (1990), 107–117.
23. Fullerton, Howard W., "Evaluation of Labor Force Projections to 1990," *Monthly Labor Review*, 115, no. 8 (1992), 3–14, Fullerton, Howard W. "New Labor Force Projections, Spanning 1988 to 2000," *Monthly Labor Review*, 112, no. 11 (1989), 2–12.
24. Rosen, Benson, and Thomas H. Jerdee, "Retirement Policies: Evidence of the Need for Change," *Human Resource Management*, 28, no. 2 (1989), 87–103.
25. Rosen and Jerdee, "Retirement Policies," 99.
26. Hill, Linda, and Jaan Elias, "Retraining Midcareer Managers: Career History and Self-Efficacy Beliefs," *Human Resource Management*, 29, no. 2 (1990), 197–217.
27. Hill and Elias, "Retraining Midcareer Managers," 213.
28. Leana, Carrie R., and Daniel C. Feldman, "Job Loss and Employee Assistance: Joint Efforts to Help Displaced Workers," in *Human Resource Forecasting and Strategy Development*, eds. Manual London, Emily S. Bassman, and John P. Fernandez. New York: Quorum Books, 1990, 127–140.
29. Howard, Ann, "Who Reaches for the Golden Handshake?" *Academy of Management Executive*, 2, no. 2, (1988), 133–144.
30. Howard, "Who Reaches for the Golden Handshake?" 134.
31. Howard, "Who Reaches for the Golden Handshake?"
32. Ibid.
33. Howard, "Who Reaches for the Golden Handshake?" 140.
34. Howard, "Who Reaches for the Golden Handshake?"
35. Player, Mack A., *Federal Law of Employment Discrimination in a Nutshell*, 3rd ed. St. Paul: West, 1992; Mitchell, Charles E., "Waiver of Rights Under the Age Discrimination in Employment Act: Implications of the Older Workers Benefit Protection Act of 1990," *Labor Law Journal*, 43, no. 11 (1992), 735–744.
36. Howard, "Who Reaches for the Golden Handshake?"
37. Hoerr, John, and Wendy Zellner, "A Japanese Import That's Not Selling," *Business Week*, February 26, 1990, 86–87.
38. Kochan, Thomas A., John Paul MacDuffie, and Paul Osterman, "Employment Security at DEC: Sustaining Values Amid Environmental Change," *Human Resource Management*, 27, no. 2 (1988), 121–143.
39. Wilke, John R., "Digital Equipment, in Its First Layoffs, to Dismiss About 3,500 Workers by July," *The Wall Street Journal*, January 10, 1991 A3.
40. Burke, Steven, "PC Operations Spared the Worst of IBM's Cost-Cutting Programs," *PC Week*, December 11, 1989, 1, 6.
41. Verity, John W., "Deconstructing the Computer Industry," *Business Week*, November 23, 1992, 90–100.
42. Uchitelle, Louis, "Boeing Plans Worker Cuts at Factories," *The New York Times*, January 19, 1990, 33, 36.
43. Piller, Dan, "Carrier Breaks Long Tradition with Latest Work-Force Cuts," *Fort Worth Star-Telegram*, April 29, 1994, 1–2.
44. Hoerr and Zellner, "A Japanese Import That's Not Selling," 86.
45. Patterson, Gregory A., "GM's New Contract with UAW May Be Ratified by Sunday," *The Wall Street Journal*, September 28, 1990, B4.
46. Greenhalgh, Leonard, Robert B. McKersie, and Roderick W. Gilkey, "Rebalancing the Workforce At IBM: A Case Study of Redeployment and Revitalization," *Organizational Dynamics*, 14, no. 4 (1986), 30–47; Ferris, Gerald R., Deborah A. Schellenberg, and Raymond F. Zammuto, "Human Resource Management Strategies in Declining Industries," *Human Resource Management*, 23, no. 4 (1984), 381–394.
47. Cook and Ferris, "Strategic Human Resource Management and Firm Effectiveness in Industries Experiencing Decline," 448.
48. Greenhalgh, Leonard, Anne T. Lawrence, and Robert I. Sutton, "Determinants of Work Force Reduction Strategies in Declining Organizations," *Academy of Management Review*, 13, no. 2 (1988), 241–254.
49. Harper, Lucinda, "Hazardous Cuts: Travel Agency Learns Service Firms' Perils in Slimming Down," *The Wall Street Journal*, March 20, 1992, A1, A6.
50. Greer, Charles R., and Timothy C. Ireland, "Organizational and Financial Correlates of a 'Contrarian' Human Resource Investment Strategy," *Academy of Management Journal*, 35, no. 5 (1992), 956–984.
51. Schneier, Craig E., Douglas Shaw, and Richard W. Beatty, "Companies' Attempts to Improve Performance While Containing Costs: Quick Fix Versus Lasting Change," *Human Resource Planning*, 15, no. 3 (1992), 1–25; Cascio, Wayne F., "Downsizing: What Do We Know? What Have We

Learned?" *Academy of Management Executive*, 7, no. 1 (1993), 95–104.

52. Cascio, "Downsizing: What Do We Know? What Have We Learned?"
53. Feldman, Daniel C., and Carrie R. Leana, "Managing Layoffs: Experiences at the Challenger Disaster Site and the Pittsburgh Steel Mills," *Organizational Dynamics*, 18, no. 1 (1989), 52–64.
54. Feldman and Leana, "Managing Layoffs"; Leana, Carrie R., and John M. Ivancevich, "Involuntary Job Loss: Institutional Interventions and a Research Agenda," *Academy of Management Review*, 12, no. 2 (1987), 301–312.
55. Rothstein, Mark A., Andria S. Knapp, and Lance Liebman, *Cases and Materials on Employment Law*, 2nd ed. Westbury, N.Y.: Foundation Press, 1991.
56. Leana and Ivancevich, "Involuntary Job Loss."
57. Feldman and Leana, "Managing Layoffs"; Love, Douglas O., and William Torrence, "The Value of Advance Notice of Worker Displacement," *Southern Economic Journal*, 55, no. 3 (1989), 626–643.
58. Feldman and Leana, "Managing Layoffs."
59. Ibid., Leana and Ivancevich, "Involuntary Job Loss."
60. Feldman and Leana, "Managing Layoffs"; Kleiman, Lawrence S., and Robert H. Faley, "Voluntary Affirmative Action and Preferential Treatment: Legal and Research Implications," *Personnel Psychology*, 41, no. 3 (1988), 481–496.
61. Brockner, Joel, Jeff Greenberg, Audrey Brockner, Jenny Bortz, Jeanette Davy, and Carolyn Carter, "Layoffs, Equity Theory, and Work Performance: Further Evidence of the Impact of Survivor Guilt," *Academy of Management Journal*, 29, no. 2 (1986), 373–384.
62. Hymowitz, Carol, and Timothy D. Schellhardt, "After the Ax: Formula Aims to Predict Length of a Fired Manager's Job Search," *The Wall Street Journal*, October 20, 1986, 25.
63. Ibid.
64. Morin, William J., and Lyle Yorks, *Outplacement Techniques: A Positive Approach to Terminating Employees*. New York: AMACOM, 1982.
65. Ibid.
66. Conte, Christopher, "Labor Letter," *The Wall Street Journal*, May 12, 1992, A1.
67. Alexander, Suzanne, "Firms Get Plenty of Practice at Layoffs, but They Often Bungle the Firing Process," *The Wall Street Journal*, October 14, 1991, B1, B3.
68. Alexander, "Firms Get Plenty of Practice at Layoffs, but They Often Bungle the Firing Process," B1.
69. Ibid.
70. Coulson, Robert, *The Termination Handbook*. New York: Free Press, 1981; Dessler, Gary, *Personnel Management*, 4th ed. Englewood Cliffs, N.J.: Prentice Hall, 1988.
71. Rice, F. Philip, *Human Development: A Life-Span Approach*. New York: Macmillan, 1992; Kubler-Ross, Elisabeth, *Questions and Answers on Death and Dying*. New York: Macmillan, 1974.
72. Morin and Yorks, *Outplacement Techniques*.
73. Dessler, *Personnel Management*; Coulson, *The Termination Handbook*.
74. Alexander, "Firms Get Plenty of Practice at Layoffs, but They Often Bungle the Firing Process"; Coulson, *The Termination Handbook*; Dessler, *Personnel Management*; Morin and Yorks, *Outplacement Techniques*.
75. Collie, H. Cris, "Two Salaries, One Relocation: What's a Company to Do?" *Personnel Administrator*, 34, no. 9 (1989), 54–57.
76. Guinn, Stephen L., and Lori G. Russell, "Personnel Decisions and the Dual-Career Couple," *Employment Relations Today*, 14, no. 1 (1987), 84 (whole article on pp. 83–89).
77. Guinn and Russell, "Personnel Decisions and the Dual-Career Couple."
78. Collie, "Two Salaries, One Relocation."
79. Taylor, Alex, III, "Why Women Managers Are Bailing Out," *Fortune*, 114, no. 4 (1986), 16–23.
80. Morgan, Hal, and Kerry Tucker, *Companies That Care*. New York: Simon & Schuster, 1991, 333.
81. Collie, "Two Salaries, One Relocation"; Guinn and Russell, "Personnel Decisions and the Dual-Career Couple."
82. Collie, "Two Salaries, One Relocation: What's a Company to Do?"
83. Collie, "Two Salaries, One Relocation: What's a Company to Do?" 55.
84. Newgren, Kenneth E., C.E. Kellogg, and William Gardner, "Corporate Responses to Dual-Career Couples: A Decade of Transformation," *Akron Business and Economic Review*, 19, no. 2 (1988), 85–96.
85. Taylor, "Why Women Managers Are Bailing Out."
86. Naisbitt, John, and Patricia Aburdene, *Megatrends 2000: Ten New Directions for the 1990's*. New York: William Morrow, 1990.
87. Reed, Christine M., "Anti-Nepotism Rules and Dual Career Couples: Policy Questions for Public Personnel Administrators," *Public Personnel Management*, 17, no. 2 (1988), 223–230.
88. Toy, Stewart, "The New Nepotism: Why Dynasties Are Making a Comeback," *Business Week*, April 4, 1988, 106–109.

89. Hicks, Lesli, "Working Together: Employers Moving Toward More-Relaxed Nepotism Rules," *Tarrant Business,* August 15–21, 1988, 18.
90. Toy, "The New Nepotism: Why Dynasties Are Making a Comeback."
91. Toy, "The New Nepotism: Why Dynasties Are Making a Comeback," 107.
92. Toy, "The New Nepotism: Why Dynasties Are Making a Comeback."
93. Ibid.; Guinn and Russell, "Personnel Decisions and the Dual-Career Couple,"
94. Kurtz, Howard, "Married . . . with Press Pass: Journalist Couples, Competing Papers and Nepotism," *Washington Post,* November 3, 1991, C1.
95. Ibid.
96. Reed, "Anti-Nepotism Rules and Dual Career Couples"; Reed, Christine M., and Linda J. Cohen, "Anti-Nepotism Rules: The Legal Rights of Married Co-Workers," *Public Personnel Management,* 18, no. 1 (1989), 37–44.
97. Reed, "Anti-Nepotism Rules and Dual Career Couples."

Case 6

HEALTH-CARE EMPLOYMENT

The health-care industry is undergoing major structural changes in order to become more efficient. Such efforts were underway for several years prior to the Clinton Administration's initiatives in 1994 which were directed at cost containment and providing universal access to health care.[1] Accordingly any projections of future employment in this industry must be balanced with skepticism. Nonetheless, the growing size of older age cohorts is a real phenomenon which will have an important impact on the demand for employees in this industry.[2] Projections of the demand for medical care prior to the initiation of attempts to reform health care indicated increases in future health-care employment. Such increases were well underway in the previous decade. With older age cohorts using disproportionately greater amounts of medical services, the increase in the size of these cohorts has been expected to have a major impact on the demand for medical care. An indication of the impact of these older age cohorts may be obtained by examining their projected growth. By 2000, the 75 to 84 age cohort will increase to 12 million while those in the over 85 cohort will increase to 4.6 million.[3]

In spite of these projections, health-care reform, managerial innovations, and mergers of hospitals or health-care corporations may result in lower levels of employment than projected.[4] By 1994 there had already been layoffs in the health-care industry because of efficiencies resulting from streamlined delivery systems. Some anecdotal evidence even indicated reversals in local job markets from chronic undersupply to surpluses of health-care specialists, such as registered nurses. At the time this book was being written, it was too early to determine the impact of efficiencies resulting from anticipatory actions on the part of health-care organizations to the prospects of health-care reform legislation.

Aside from overall industry projections, the demand for the various health-care specialties has also been forecasted. For example, the number of jobs for registered nurses has been forecasted to increase. Part of this growth is expected as a result of increasingly sophisticated medical technology and cost containment moves in which registered nurses will perform more expanded tasks. Medical assistants' jobs are expected to increase by 90 percent, partly as a result of the economy and of their supporting role for health professionals. Almost as much growth is expected for physical therapists. Employment of health-care technicians is also expected to show strong growth. Even with the expansion of the duties of registered nurses, the number of physicians has also been projected to increase during this period.[5] The health-care needs of an aging population will obviously affect the demand for physicians and other health-care specialties, although as indicated earlier, reforms and managerial innovations may reduce the projected growth in demand.

Questions

1. Strategic actions by health-care organizations, such as mergers and shifts to preventative approaches, have had differential impacts on employment across the various health-care specialties. Describe some of these impacts. How have you or members of your family been affected? What are some of the human resource management implications of these strategic actions?

2. Some health-care organizations are now placing greater emphasis on marketing strategies. There is anecdotal evidence that some are hiring MBAs for marketing responsibilities while laying off registered nurses. Discuss the implications of these developments.

3. Given the uncertainty of the demand for health-care workers, how can health-care organizations be prepared to meet their future needs for such employees? How can they help their employees prepare for their employment futures?

4. Interview someone from the health-care industry about the changes in utilization of human resources that have taken place during the 1990s. What are the major changes? What are his or her personal views about the value of these changes? How does this person view the effectiveness of the implementation of these changes?

5. Will layoffs in the health-care industry have a different impact on employees and organizations than might be expected in other industries? Explain.

REFERENCES

1. Priest, Dana, "Now for the Nitty Gritty of Legislating Health Reform," *Washington Post National Weekly Edition*, May 16–22, 1994, 31–32.
2. Personick, Valerie A., "Industry Output and Employment: A Slower Trend for the Nineties," *Monthly Labor Review*, 111, no. 11 (1989), 25–41.
3. Ibid.; Thurow, Lester C., "From the Post-Industrial Era to the New Industrial Era," *Fort Worth Star-Telegram*, September 7, 1989, 25.
4. Fuquay, Jim, "Hospital Giants Plan Merger," *Fort Worth Star-Telegram*, October 3, 1993, A1–A14.
5. Silvestri, George T., and John M. Lukasiewicz, "A Look at Occupational Employment Trends to the Year 2000," in Bureau of Labor Statistics, *Projections 2000*, Bulletin 2302. U.S. Government Printing Office U.S. Department of Labor, 1988, 44–61.

7

STRATEGY IMPLEMENTATION
Reward and Development Systems

The seventh component of the conceptual framework presented in the preface deals with strategy implementation through the use of reward and development systems. Reward systems provide the incentives and reinforcement for work-force behaviors that contribute to the implementation of strategies while development systems provide the work-force skills required for implementation. This chapter begins with a discussion of performance measurement systems, which provide the information required for allocation of rewards and identification of developmental needs. Next, following coverage of the limitations of traditional compensation systems, there is a discussion of strategically oriented compensation systems including skill-based pay, broad banding, team-based pay, variable compensation, and executive compensation. The chapter then covers employee development approaches including various training programs and methods, apprenticeships, management development approaches, management development for international assignments, and the strategic fit dilemma of whether to focus on development or selection of managers.

STRATEGICALLY ORIENTED PERFORMANCE MEASUREMENT SYSTEMS

The strategic importance of performance measurement systems is indicated in the following quotation by Clinton Longenecker and Dennis Gioia:

> A shipping firm executive captured his personal credo in the phrase: "You get what you measure." And we might add: "You measure what you value." If

the organization values short-term results, that is what it will measure and get. If it values executive development, a different emphasis emerges.[1]

Various approaches to performance measurement are available to help assess the degree to which the behavior of employees at all organizational levels contribute to the implementation of strategies. Measures of performance are necessary for the functioning of reward systems, covered in the next section. All methods of performance measurement and evaluation are potentially useful means of providing feedback on the degree to which behaviors are congruent with organizational strategies. Likewise, to varying degrees they all are potentially useful means of informing reward systems of the extent to which employees are deserving of increased compensation, promotions, recognition, and so forth. Further, they all are potentially valid sources of guidance for future developmental efforts, although their appropriateness in this regard differs.

Performance Measurement Approaches

A number of evaluation approaches have been traditionally used for performance measurement, some of the most common being management by objectives, graphic rating scales, and narratives. The most advanced performance evaluation systems are those utilizing behaviorally anchored rating scales. These approaches will be discussed in the following section.

Management by objectives

Management by objectives (MBO) is a traditional performance evaluation approach. The linkage with the implementation of strategies is easy to establish in MBO because the objectives can be specified as outcomes or milestones in the strategy implementation process. In the initial phase of MBO, the subordinate typically generates goals or objectives to be accomplished over the next time period. As a part of this process, the subordinate specifies the measures by which accomplishment of such objectives will be determined and outlines action plans he or she will use to achieve these objectives. The superior also generates objectives for the subordinate and then meets with the subordinate to work out a joint agreement. At the end of the next time period, the subordinate is evaluated on the extent to which the objectives were accomplished and the existence of factors beyond the subordinate's control which may have affected objective accomplishment. Unfortunately, as with all performance evaluation approaches, MBO has disadvantages as well. Objectives for some jobs are more difficult to write, such as for staff jobs, and problems occur when objectives are not well thought-out. Further, the process may be viewed with cynicism if higher-level executives are not evaluated by MBO.[2] As with all evaluation approaches, organizations sometimes offset their disadvantages and take advantage of the strengths of various evaluation approaches by combining MBO, graphic rating scales, narratives, and other approaches.

Graphic rating scales

Graphic rating scales, the most frequently used rating approach, involve a format of multiple-interval response scales carrying numerical values with short descriptive anchors. For example, a seven-point scale might be used for an item tapping an employee's quality of work. At the low end of the scale the blank carrying a value of 1 might be anchored by a characterization of "low quality of work" while the high-end blank carrying a value of 7 would be anchored by a characterization of "high quality of work." Graphic rating scales differ in whether their anchors are absolute (as in the example just provided) or relative. An example of a scale constructed with relative anchors would be where the low end of the scale would be anchored with "one of the lowest quality producers" while the top end would be anchored with "one of the highest quality producers." There is some evidence that anchors expressed in relative terms are superior to those expressed in absolute terms.[3]

Unfortunately, although graphic rating scales can be improved with the use of anchors expressed in relative terms, they are typically not anchored in terms of behaviors and often have items that measure only traits. However, an advantage of graphic rating scales is that their lack of behavioral specificity provides a standardized performance evaluation approach that can be used across large numbers of jobs. Organizations often find standardized approaches useful for comparison purposes, such as in developing a list of employees to be laid-off on the basis of performance. However, because evaluators differ in the degree to which they are strict or lenient raters, some means of converting individual evaluators' ratings into a standardized score is required when evaluations are to be used for comparison purposes. Finally, the results of graphic rating scales are fairly easily translatable into numerical indices which can then be used to determine raises. However, they have somewhat limited value for use in developmental counseling.[4]

Narratives

Another traditional approach to performance evaluation is the *narrative description* of performance written by an employee's supervisor. Such approaches, which can be highly individualistic according to the unique aspects of the employee's job, are sometimes used with higher-level professionals and managerial personnel. Disadvantages to this approach are the writing skills required on the part of the evaluator and the time taken to write thoughtful narratives. Further, it is difficult to translate narratives into increases in compensation. Nonetheless, they are very useful in developmental counseling.

Behaviorally anchored rating scales

One of the most advanced of the approaches to performance evaluation is called behaviorally anchored rating scales (BARS). With BARS approaches, job incumbents are evaluated according to their performance on a relatively small set of job dimensions. This approach's major advantage is that for each dimension, specific anchor points on the rating scale are provided in the form of observable behaviors. Thus, the evaluator is not forced to choose between the ambiguous meanings of adjective or numerical scale values. For example, in rating an employee's performance as a consumer credit representative in handling denials of credit, the rater does not have to decide whether the employee merits a rating of a 6 or a 7 on a 10-point scale. With the BARS approach, the evaluator typically chooses among an array of observable behaviors for the most representative one. In the case of the credit representative, such behaviors might range from "tactfully informs the customer that credit cannot be extended at this time and encourages the customer to reapply at a later date" to "tells customer that he or she is a bad credit risk and that it would be pointless to reapply." Because the evaluator is reporting observations, rather than making inferences about the mental processes of an employee, there may be increased validity and less likelihood of bias. Unfortunately, research to date on BARS has not yet demonstrated their superiority to other rating approaches in inter-rater reliability or in reducing leniency or halo errors. (Halo errors occur when an outstanding rating on one dimension of performance carries over to affect ratings on other dimensions.)[5]

In spite of the failure of research to demonstrate the superiority of BARS, the greatest contribution of the BARS approach may be through its role as a feedback mechanism. Because of its focus on behaviors, the use of BARS may be less likely to lead to employee defensiveness and the feedback may be heard. Likewise, the BARS format produces ratings that are directly useful in developmental counseling because the employee knows the behaviors that should be adopted or discontinued. Further, its behavioral anchors carry numerical values which can be summed across performance dimensions to provide an index translatable into merit increases in compensation. Unfortunately, BARS are applicable only to the specific jobs for which they are developed. As a result, it is practical to use them only for jobs having large numbers of incumbents because of their considerable developmental expense and the statistical expertise required. And yet, further up the job hierarchy there are ordinarily fewer job incumbents at the managerial and professional levels. However, large organizations may have sufficient numbers of managers at lower levels, such as sales managers and store managers, to justify their development. Likewise, many organizations have lower-level professional jobs with many incumbents, such as staff accountants, insurance claims adjusters, and registered nurses, who could be evaluated with BARS.[6]

Performance Evaluation of Executives

In spite of the value of performance evaluation systems, Longenecker and Gioia have found that such systems are not used very frequently for executives. More specifically, "the higher one rises in an organization the less likely one is to receive quality feedback about job performance."[7] Several questionable beliefs or myths are apparently responsible for the low regard for performance evaluation at the executive level. These myths are that performance evaluation is (1) not needed nor desired by executives, (2) inconsistent with an executive's dignity, (3) too time-consuming for the schedules of the superiors of executives, (4) detrimental to executive creativity and autonomy, (5) irrelevant since executives must meet "bottom line" criteria, and (6) ineffective because executive performance is too intangible for description. Nonetheless, Longenecker and Gioia found that these myths lack a factual basis. In marked contrast, their research found that executives desire feedback and that even though bottom line results are critical for executives, they still need process-type feedback. Further, when executive performance is considered too intangible for description, the vacuum of explanation may be filled by political explanations. Some suggestions may be helpful in encouraging the use of performance evaluation at executive levels. For example, the process should utilize written narratives instead of standard rating forms because of the highly individualistic nature of executive work. It should also include clarification of organizational goals, discussions of how success will be defined, and assessment of the executive's management style. Also, the process should be a regularly occurring activity based on both process considerations as well as outcomes.[8]

Effectiveness of Performance Measurement

Human resource managers are sometimes criticized for the attention they place on the format of evaluation instead of on the management of the evaluation process. Even the most unsophisticated evaluation approach can be effective while the most sophisticated can be ineffective. When employees understand the dimensions of performance on which they will be evaluated, know that they are being evaluated on relevant aspects of their jobs, view the evaluation process as valid, feel that their evaluations are fair, and see reward contingencies, they will "buy in" to the evaluation system. At this point, the evaluation system can help strategy implementation. Further, performance evaluation will have a greater impact on strategy implementation when evaluators make meaningful distinctions among different levels of performance. Unfortunately, there have always been political aspects of performance evaluation that reduce its effectiveness, such as when evaluators rate subordinates lower than they deserve in order to establish managerial authority, encourage them to leave, or establish a convincing paper trail in the event that they are terminated.[9]

STRATEGICALLY ORIENTED COMPENSATION SYSTEMS

One of the critical means by which organizations implement their strategies is to reward employees for behaviors that are consistent with strategic goals. Reward systems provide the ability to reinforce desired behaviors and serve the traditional functions of attracting and maintaining a qualified work force. Because of the centrality of compensation to strategy, the following discussion will focus only on rewards distributed through compensation systems. As indicated earlier in this chapter, a critical determinant of whether a strategy will be successfully implemented is the degree of flexibility of the work force. In order to gain more flexibility from their work forces, many organizations have implemented new compensation approaches. Four of the better-known compensation innovations are (1) skill-based pay, (2) broad banding, (3) team-based pay, and (4) variable compensation. These approaches will be examined in this section along with executive compensation. However, a review of traditional compensation systems should be helpful before examining these approaches.

Traditional Compensation Systems

Millions of employees are compensated through traditional job-based pay systems. Such systems typically use *job analysis* to determine the knowledge, skills, and abilities required to perform jobs. Job analysis information is then incorporated into the process of *job evaluation*, which determines the relative standing of each job in the salary or wage hierarchy of an organization. Essentially, the process of job evaluation involves a review of each job to determine the extent to which *compensable factors* are present. Typically jobs are evaluated on only a small set of compensable factors such as knowledge, know-how, accountability, effort, and problem solving. The *point system* is a common job evaluation approach which uses a job evaluation manual to assign points to each job on the basis of compensable factors. Another job evaluation system is the *factor comparison system,* a rather complicated approach of comparing jobs directly with each other to determine differences in the presence of compensable factors. Hybrid systems, which often involve a combination of the point system and factor comparison system, are also widely used. An example of a hybrid system is the *Hay Guide Profile Method.* Traditional approaches involving job evaluation are used to determine *internal equity* or fairness in compensation among jobs in an organization. Salary surveys are used to determine *external equity* with market rates. Managers then set rates of compensation by balancing considerations of internal and external equity.[10]

Strategic Inadequacies of Traditional Compensation Approaches

Unfortunately, traditional compensation systems leave much to be desired from a strategic perspective. One of the strongest criticisms involves the evaluation of jobs on compensable factors such as problem solving or know-how. By assigning differential points to various jobs on the basis of these factors, the process tells job incumbents—whose jobs are evaluated as low on problem solving or know-how—that they are not being paid to solve problems or think. A further criticism is that because of the job-based focus, each employee is compensated only for the performance of a specific job. Thus, the compensation system introduces constraints on managers' flexibility in utilizing the work force. When a person is asked to perform work outside of his or her job classification, there are problems in assignment of a pay rate. The presence of a union complicates this further as the pay rates for the various job classifications are the result of collective bargaining. Additionally, traditional compensation systems do not work well with managers and professionals as the job-based focus of traditional systems conflicts with the individualized nature of the work. With increasing professionalization of the work force, the importance of this problem will be magnified. To summarize, when compensation systems limit work-force flexibility and discourage workers from using their intelligence, they cannot facilitate the implementation of today's competitive strategies.[11]

Skill-Based Pay

In contrast to traditional compensation approaches, *skill-based pay* or *knowledge-based pay* focuses on the individual, not the job. In fact, with skill-based pay employees perform a number of jobs and receive the same pay rate, irrespective of the job. As noted earlier, in Chaparral Steel's application of skill-based pay, there are only two general job classifications in its production environment. With skill-based pay, employees are able to increase their compensation as they acquire a broader range of skills; thus, they have a strong incentive to learn. With the rapid rate of change in today's business environment and the need for flexible work assignments, an obvious need exists for employees to develop or broaden their skill repertoires.[12] The flexibility of skill-based pay is revealed in the following description of its application in a container plant.

> For example, a plant technician at the top of the skill range may work on electrical assignments when such work needs to be done or may be assigned to quality assurance or to operate a specific machine if no electrical problems require attention.[13]

Because of such characteristics, companies dealing with stiff foreign competition have a higher propensity to implement skill-based pay approaches. Likewise, in those companies where promotional opportunities have been reduced because of the delayering of organizational structures, there are also higher propensities to implement skill-based pay.[14] The extent of skill-based pay usage is revealed by a survey conducted in 1990 which found that 51 percent of responding companies had implemented the approach, up from approximately 40 percent in 1987. However, companies generally apply this pay approach to less than 20 percent of their employees.[15]

Because of the advantages of skill-based pay, numerous companies have adopted this approach. For example, General Mills, Northern Telecom, and Honeywell have substantial experience with skill-based pay. Skill-based pay approaches have been frequently implemented in high-involvement manufacturing settings, and they are also used in service environments. Although there are variations in how skill-based pay is implemented, employees typically start out at a base rate and increase their compensation as they master a sequence of skill blocks. Typically, employees take several years to master the content of all skill blocks, which are generally fairly broad. For example, at a General Mills plant, all of the production processes are contained in four skill blocks. One of the more difficult aspects involved in the administration of skill-based pay involves the determination of the amount of pay to assign to skill blocks. Nonetheless, market survey data are often used to establish the range and average values for skill blocks.[16]

Skill-based pay is also often implemented in conjunction with semiautonomous work teams. In such applications, employees master the skills required for a job and then rotate into another job in the team until its skills are mastered, and then into the next, and so forth. Upon completion of the rotation, the employee can then move into another team and acquire more skills by rotating through its various jobs. Certification and recertification of skill block mastery is assessed through various approaches, one being testing approaches that often involve sample observations of work, written tests, and oral examinations. Other certification approaches include assessment by multiple evaluators such as supervisors, peers, technical experts, management committees, and human resources personnel. Skill-based pay's focus on compensation for skills is also contained in approaches used with professional employees paid according to maturity curves. In maturity curve approaches, with increasing experience and development following the completion of formal education, professionals receive increased compensation.[17]

Aside from the flexibility advantages already noted, skill-based pay also has some other desirable effects although average wage rates tend to be higher. An important advantage is that the costs of higher wages are offset by higher productivity and increased quality. Other advantages include employees' heightened motivation for training, greater task variety, employee-induced pressures on companies to provide training, and increases in employees' self-esteem which accompany the acquisition of skills. With skill-based pay it is also easy to fill in for absences because of the availability of cross-trained employees. Skill-based pay also tends to give employees a broader understanding of production processes. Because employees gain compensation increases by expanding their skill sets, seniority is not the determinant of progression to higher-paying jobs. Another advantage of skill-based pay is its provision of greater job security for employees because they can perform a wider range of jobs.[18]

Skill-based pay is often implemented in conjunction with total quality management (TQM) programs because higher quality often requires more highly skilled employees. It is also implemented frequently in participative environments, and as noted earlier, in conjunction with semiautonomous work groups or self-managed teams. With teams, participative management, and high involvement environments, employees can make meaning-ful contributions that result from their broader understanding of the pro-duction environment.[19]

Although there are numerous benefits of skill-based pay, there are also problems, as with any other compensation approach. One problem involves compensating employees who have topped out on the skill progression. For these employees, some observers have recommended incentives in the form of gain sharing, in which benefits from cost reductions or increased produc-tivity are passed on to employees. Another problem is that training is fre-quently insufficient to support skill-based pay approaches. Some mangers have even been reluctant to release sufficient funds from their training bud-gets to support skill-based pay.[20]

Broad Banding

In contrast to skill-based pay, *broad banding* retains some of the components of the traditional approaches described earlier, such as a job focus and some utilization of job evaluation for *key jobs*. (Key jobs are visible jobs having identifiable market wage rates.) However, like skill-based pay, broad band-ing can be helpful in strategy implementation because it is directed toward obtaining greater flexibility. Typically broad banding involves a reduction in the number of salary bands (pay grades). Interestingly, General Electric was able to reduce its number of bands to five for all employees. With broad banding the organization might reduce its salary bands for white-collar employees to three. For example, the first band for professionals might range from $30,000 to $66,000, the second for management might range from $33,000 to $96,000, and a third for leadership might range from $85,000 to $180,000. As these salary levels indicate, the salary ranges within each band cover a wide range of compensation: The advantage of maintaining fewer bands is that employees' salaries can be raised substantially even without a promotion. Likewise, employees' salaries could conceivably be reduced without resort to a demotion.[21]

Broad banding is frequently used along with other changes that facili-tate strategy implementation. For example, it may be used with reengineer-ing, delayering of organizational hierarchies, employee empowerment efforts, and cross-functional approaches. Although a very different compen-sation approach than skill-based pay, it also encourages skill acquisition and development. With broad banding, an employee who is paid the market value for a job, such as $36,000 for the professional band, can earn more by acquiring more skills. A second-generation version of broad banding aban-dons most of the traditional compensation system components, such as job evaluation, and shifts to an individual focus rather than a job focus. For example, the second-generation approach would develop a market value for an individual based on his or her individual skills.[22]

In moving toward a broad banding approach, some of the same advice applies as with conventional compensation systems: there must be sufficient employee understanding of the salary determination process, trust, a culture that emphasizes performance, and sufficient communication. Employees must also be aware of the skills that must be mastered for increased compensation as well as the means for their acquisition.[23]

Team-Based Pay

With the growing importance of work teams noted in earlier chapters, compensation systems are needed to reward team members for behavior that facilitates strategy implementation. *Team-based pay* is being used more frequently in such settings. Typically, team-based pay is operationalized by specifying a goal or desired outcome and then allocating to all team members a reward for its accomplishment. Objective goals or outcomes are commonly specified, such as production levels, cost savings, or project completions, although goals may also be some form of subjective executive assessment. A wide variety of rewards may be used such as cash bonuses, stock ownership, trips, and time off from work.[24]

Team-based pay offers a number of advantages, one being that it overcomes the difficult problem of measuring individual contributions. Another advantage is that it is also likely to facilitate cooperation. Further, bonuses to teams, such as for the completion of a major project, can be given very shortly after the event, thereby strongly linking desired behaviors with desired rewards. A further advantage of team approaches to compensation may occur where team rewards are linked to the development of skills. In situations were the team reward is not given until all team members are cross-trained, the team members may help train or motivate those who have not yet acquired the necessary skills.[25]

One type of team setting likely to appear more frequently in the future is the research and development team. Fortunately, there is evidence that team-based pay systems have worked well in such settings. One study of research scientists and engineers specifically examined the effectiveness of team-based bonuses. The study examined the impact of such pay on several criteria of effectiveness including performance on projects as well as individual performance, satisfaction with pay, and a cognitive withdrawal or propensity to leave measure. The study found that team pay was superior to individual-based bonuses and merit pay when evaluated according to these criteria. In contrast, the individual-based forms of compensation were not significantly related with the criteria. Further, other aggregate compensation in the form of stock ownership plans and profit sharing tended to enhance the retention of employees. With any group or team-based pay system, there is always a concern that some individuals may not do their share of work, preferring instead to be free riders on the efforts of more productive members. Interestingly, this study found that team members did not become free riders. Potential explanations for the absence of such behaviors include the combination of challenging work and the intrinsic motivation of professional employees.[26]

Team-based pay often involves some form of *gain sharing*. However, unlike gain sharing approaches such as the Scanlon Plan or Rucker Plan, the gains to be shared are sometimes linked to the accomplishment of strategic objectives. Some strategic objectives tend to be more ambiguous than tactical objectives and require commitment from employees because desirable performance on their part may also be difficult to specify. The Fibers Department at Du Pont is an example of a very large scale team-based approach which incorporated gain sharing. The department wished to increase the emphasis on participation and team work and decided to pursue a goal of increasing annual earnings by 4 percent.[27] The plan was operationalized as follows:

> The Achievement Sharing Program is being phased in over approximately five years. At the end of this period, Fibers Department employees will be earning 6 percent less in their base pay than their counterparts elsewhere in the company. If the department meets its annual profit, the employees will collect the 6 percent difference; if profits fall below 80 percent of the goal, they will receive a 3 percent bonus, and at 150 percent they will receive a 12 percent bonus.[28]

Unfortunately, the Du Pont plan, which also constituted a form of variable pay, was terminated two years after its implementation. The plan failed because of poor business conditions which severely restricted or eliminated bonuses and employees' failure to cope with the downside risk. The plan also conflicted with Du Pont's centralized culture and strategy by compensating employees for departmental results. The plan's failure highlights the necessity of careful planning and preparation for successful implementation of such compensation programs. In contrast to Du Pont's experience, Nucor Steel's gain sharing plan has been in existence for over twenty-five years. Part of the success of Nucor's plan is probably due to its compatibility with the company's "no frills" culture.[29]

Because of the broad application of gain sharing, its impact on the productivity of white-collar workers has been the subject of recent research. An office of a Big Six public accounting firm operationalized gain sharing as a percentage of labor savings, which were determined by subtracting actual labor costs from allowable labor costs. The study found that gain sharing increased productivity and that employees worked "smarter."[30]

Variable Compensation

Variable pay plans have been implemented by a number of companies, such as Xerox, Westinghouse, and Nucor Steel. A major purpose for such plans has been to create a sense of shared destiny among employees. Such plans seek to accomplish this by linking a portion of employee compensation to various performance measures. A common element of such plans is having a portion of employees' compensation "at risk."[31] The rationale for variable compensation is appealing and, at first glance, seemingly uncomplicated. However, there is a level of complexity to these programs which must be understood.

An important consideration of variable pay plans is the form they will take. The first form is an increment to base pay which is frequently called "add-on." Bonuses based on company performance would constitute a form of add-on variable pay. The second is "at-risk" pay, which is normally operationalized by reducing employees' base pay by a certain percentage and then allowing them to receive various amounts of that percentage and more, depending on performance measures. The third form, "potential base pay at risk," is related to the second; it might be operationalized in situations where the company has a tradition of steady raises, for example, averaging approximately 6 percent per year. This practice would be changed by allocating only 3 percent as a regular raise. The remaining 3 percent is set aside to be obtained along with greater increases if performance targets are met or exceeded. While there are no strict guidelines for identifying the circumstances in which these forms of variable pay are implemented, companies encountering heavy pressure to reduce labor costs are more likely to use at-risk variable pay. Companies might use add-on pay to pave the way for a later introduction of other forms of variable pay. They might also use add-on pay for very high performance standards.[32]

Another element of complexity with variable pay involves the measures of performance to which pay is to be linked. Unfortunately, the use of some seemingly rational performance measures can lead to very dysfunctional results. For example, if one links variable pay to the profitability of an insurance company, claims representatives may not pay customer accident claims as they should. On the other hand, if these same representatives are paid according to customer satisfaction, they may be too generous in the settlement of claims. In any event, the measures should reflect the organization's overall strategies. The range of measures may include profitability, improvements in quality, various financial ratios, and customer satisfaction. It is recommended that the measures not be defined in too narrow a fashion since some units could receive pay increases while the company becomes unprofitable.[33] Several recommendations regarding measures are presented in the following advice.

> Therefore, even though different goals are used, it is best that these measures not pay off unless the organization gains real bottom-line results. This is central to new variable pay. Productivity measures may be used at the team level as long as they do not result in awards when the organization's profit performance and quality have not improved. . . . It is best for plans to generate awards only if both profit and productivity measures are satisfied.[34]

Aside from creating a feeling of shared destiny, another potential benefit is better labor cost control.[35] Further, such plans may help provide employment security because with part of employees' compensation being derived from the company's profitability, with declines in business conditions and profits, total labor costs decline and employees may not need to be laid-off.

Executive Compensation

The human resource function has been criticized for its failure to provide compensation systems that support companies' strategies. Probably the first and most important step needed to obtain alignment between strategy and compensation systems involves designing the system for compensating executives.[36] The impact of executive compensation systems has been described by Luis Gómez-Mejía and David Balkin as follows:

> Executive pay is perhaps the most crucial strategic factor at the organization's disposal. It can be used to direct managerial decisions and indirectly channel the behavior of subordinates. Because most organizations follow a pyramidal structure, whatever is rewarded at the top is likely to have a multiplier effect throughout all segments of the business . . . mechanisms used to reward executives are likely to have an enormous effect on the company's future.[37]

The approaches used for executives are obviously critical to the implementation of strategies. Unfortunately, the problems of executive compensation, particularly with CEOs, continue to be particularly troublesome in the United States and are a frequent subject of controversy to both employees and the public alike, particularly when executive compensation seems to run to excess. Regardless of the controversy, there is still need for sound executive compensation systems. For many years, executive compensation systems have involved a myriad of bonus systems, stock options, deferred compensation, and an elaborate set of perquisites. Nonetheless, there is increasing skepticism whether separate systems should exist for executives. Rosabeth Moss Kanter has described this problem as follows:

> Every year routine company surveys of employees find greater skepticism about the fairness of traditional pay practices. Every year the numbers seem to get worse, possibly because traditional practices are skewed toward rewarding the climb to high positions rather then [than] the contribution to organizational success.[38]

As a result of problems with compensation and the notion that compensation should be directed toward employees' contributions instead of their positions, Kanter has recommended that "large executive bonuses or stock options should not be allowed at all unless comparable bonus systems exist for employees in general."[39] If Kanter's recommendations are an indicator of future reality, executive compensation systems will be largely indistinguishable from those of lower-level employees except for the magnitude of differentials based on contributions. In accordance with the compensation innovations presented in this chapter, lower-level employees are also likely to receive a larger component of their compensation in the form of variable pay and gain sharing.

EMPLOYEE DEVELOPMENT

Several approaches are available for the development of work-force skills that are needed for strategy implementation. The discussion of employee development will begin with training programs.

Training Programs

Companies having an investment perspective of human resource management view training as an opportunity to increase long-term productivity. Training may also be viewed as the solution to a number of problems such as substandard quality resulting from skill deficiencies and voluntary turnover of employees seeking more rewarding jobs. It may also reduce involuntary turnover of employees who are terminated because of skill deficiencies and provide a means of preventing skill obsolescence. Aside from training's value in enhancing productivity and helping companies to avoid these problems, it is also a means for avoiding shortages of qualified workers.

At the lowest-level jobs in the skill hierarchy, there is a need for training in basic skills. Even the most basic skills of reading and writing cannot be taken for granted in today's environment. Because of these skill inadequacies, when there are labor shortages companies may become more involved in remedial teaching. Further, with high levels of immigration, there will be a need to train immigrant workers in U.S. cultural norms, values, and job expectations. Managers may also need training, such as in the immigrants' language and culture. Further, the disadvantaged and traditionally unemployed may need training in basic skills such as work norms.[40]

In addition to training at the lower end of the skill hierarchy, workers in today's information age, need more training in thinking skills or analytical skills. Workers need to have skills in drawing inferences, synthesizing, categorizing, and generalizing from data.[41] Professor Edward de Bono of Cambridge University has developed programs for teaching thinking skills and has trained thousands of individuals through these programs, including executives from major corporations. An interesting outcome of the information age has been that although we now have vastly more information, we will never have enough time to teach it. Therefore, we need to be better thinkers to benefit from this information.[42] John Naisbitt and Patricia Aburdene have summarized this need as follows:

> The more information we have, the more we need to be competent thinkers. This is the quandary of the information society: We have an overabundance of data. But we lack the intelligence, the thinking ability, with which to sort it all out. That is why thinking is now as basic as reading.[43]

Unfortunately, training programs often focus on mid- to upper-level managers with little emphasis on lower-level employees.[44] The survey results in Table 7-1 indicate that salespeople, professionals, and first-line supervisors receive the most training, 40.7, 35.5, and 35.4 hours per year, respectively. Further, middle managers, first-line supervisors, and executives are the most likely to receive training with 75.9, 73.3, and 67.3 percent of companies providing such training, respectively. In contrast, production workers are the least likely to receive training, as only 33.3 percent of organizations provide such training.[45]

210 / *Chapter Seven*

TABLE 7-1 DISTRIBUTION OF TRAINING BY JOB CATEGORY

JOB CATEGORY	PERCENT OF ORGANIZATIONS PROVIDING TRAINING	MEAN NUMBER OF HOURS DELIVERED
Middle managers	75.9	35.1
Professionals	59.6	35.5
Executives	67.3	32.9
Salespeople	40.4	40.7
First-line supervisors	73.3	35.4
Senior managers	58.5	31.2
Production workers	33.3	30.7
Customer service people	45.0	33.0
Office/administrative workers	66.7	19.0

Source: Extracted from Jack Gordon, "Where the Training Goes," *Training*, 27, no. 10 (1990), 52. Reprinted with permission from the October issue of *Training* magazine. Copyright 1990. Lakewood, Minneapolis, Minnesota. All rights reserved. Not for resale.

Aside from an uneven distribution of training across job categories, the extent to which companies provide training over time is also irregular. During good economic times, many corporations invest heavily in training their employees. Even though the cyclical nature of training is well-known, in the 1980s some observers became convinced of the commitment of U.S. companies to training. For example, trend forecasters Naisbitt and Aburdene concluded the following:

> The recognition that people are a company's critical resource—and its greatest storehouse of knowledge—is creating a boom in corporate training and education. Corporations are finally willing to invest in people and their skills through training and education to the degree that they have always invested in equipment.[46]

Unfortunately, while this may have characterized the training environment of the boom period of the 1980s, this commitment faded quickly with the recession of the 1990s, and many companies slashed their training outlays. Thus, the commitment that Naisbitt and Aburdene observed in 1985 appears to have been illusory. An additional problem is that training needs to be systematic and continuous to be most effective. Companies that conduct training on a "boom and bust" basis are unlikely to develop the kinds of human resources they need to gain a competitive advantage. Nonetheless, there are excellent companies that demonstrate a genuine commitment to their human resources, such as Motorola. A sense of this commitment is provided by comment from a previous chief executive officer of Motorola who stated that people are "the ultimate high technology."[47] Further, such comments are more than just rhetoric at Motorola. For example, the company is teaching automated production concepts to its production employees, even those who have previously performed only manual assembly work. In this training, employees learn concepts of computer-integrated manufacturing (CIM) and receive hands-on experience in programming robots.[48] "One of Motorola's goals is for manufacturing employees at all levels to achieve literacy in modern automated factory concepts."[49] Similarly, Corning, Inc. is investing heavily in training its employees, particularly as a part of its efforts to improve quality. All of Corning's employees have received two days of training in quality, and each year 5 percent of each employee's hours are devoted to training. Corning is convinced that these investments in employee training have paid off in improved quality.[50]

Training Methods

Training covers a broad area of human resource activities. Because of its breadth and importance, medium- and larger-sized companies typically have specialized training staffs. Although training is an area of specialization, general managers should be acquainted with several general training methods and instructional approaches. The methods discussed in this section include orientation training, socialization of new employees, coaching, mentoring, computer-based training, and computer-assisted instruction. It also considers job rotation as a component in management development programs.[51] Apprenticeships and management development will be covered later in greater depth. Many specifics of both on-the-job training and management development have already been covered in Chapter 1 as part of a discussion of an investment perspective toward human resources.

Most larger organizations have some type of *orientation program* for new employees. This training is important because it provides the first real work contact with the company and the first opportunity for new employees to develop an understanding of the company's culture, norms, and values. One useful suggestion for orientation and socialization is to assign an experienced employee to be the sponsor of each new employee. Because of its importance, some companies are very careful about the content and approach of their orientation programs so as to impart a particular impression. In designing orientation programs it is probably advisable to place greater emphasis on imparting the company's values to new employees, with less emphasis on details such as the technical issues of health-care programs and retirement plans. With respect to the latter, employees should be given "survival skills," or only enough information to get them through the first few weeks of employment. When there is more time and less chance for information overload, more details can be provided at a more leisurely pace.[52]

Socialization of new employees is extremely critical as it can have a major impact on employees' understandings of such basic cultural norms as the company's performance expectations. Socialization is also important because turnover often occurs during the early months of employment.[53] Such turnover frequently occurs because there are delays before new employees become "permanent" members of work groups. In their permanent work groups new employees form friendships, begin to make real contributions to the company, gain acceptance and learn "how things really work."[54] Unfortunately, quick entry into a permanent work group is at odds with job rotational approaches for new managerial employees. In rotational program approaches, trainees may be rotated from one functional area to another after assignments for two or three months. Only after completion of the rotational phase, are trainees given a permanent assignment. The logic of such approaches is that the trainees will have a broader understanding of the company and how the components fit together. One means of reducing the turnover associated with rotational programs is to move new trainees in pairs or small groups to each new temporary assignment. In this manner they have some peer group support and can begin to develop permanent friendships and support systems within their group. They should also be assigned "real" work which provides a challenge and receive frequent and timely feedback.[55]

Coaching consists of the day-to-day feedback, instruction, and advice provided by the employee's supervisor. Some observers have noted that the first supervisor is very critical to an employee's career. This is because basic values, performance standards, confidence in one's proficiency, and skills are developed by the first supervisor. Unfortunately, the importance of this assignment is often overlooked and opportunities are lost when new employees are assigned to mediocre supervisors.[56]

Mentoring is another important method for training managers and professionals. Many subtle skills needed to advance to the highest-level positions are learned through mentoring relationships. Aside from providing viable role models, candid feedback, instruction, insights into the company's politics, advice, and other support, mentors also serve in other valuable capacities. Mentors are frequently in the position of sponsors who help their protégés gain visibility and responsibility. One of the barriers to the advancement of women to the top positions of their companies has probably been the lack of women mentors in male-dominated career fields. Although men are sometimes the mentors of women and women the mentors of men, mixed genders introduce special complexities such as concerns about how others may perceive the relationship.[57] An example of problems of perceptions and their heavy toll on those involved is the case of Mary Cunningham and Bill Agee at the former Bendix Corporation, now Allied Signal.[58]

Aside from providing an invaluable service to the developing manager or professional and the organization, mentoring can provide a great deal of satisfaction to the mentor. Mentors are usually eight to fifteen years older than the junior employee. Given the age and experience requirements, mentoring would be expected to begin at the midpoint of managers' and professionals' careers. Nonetheless, contrary to intuition, both younger managers in their thirties and managers over fifty appear to have stronger interests in serving as mentors than those in the mid-stages of their careers. An interesting explanation is that mid-career individuals are not as available for mentoring roles because they themselves are often preoccupied with mid-life crisis and the accompanying self-doubts and anxieties about the future. Mentoring can be a particularly valuable role for a manager who has reached a relatively high level in the company but who will not be promoted further. Likewise, mentoring may be a very important role for those in the latter part of their career cycles who may have stepped down from the highest positions. Finally, in contrast to expectations, mentoring activity tends to increase during times of corporate stress, such as during downsizing. This is because for the mentor, the activity provides a source of esteem perhaps not otherwise available because of curtailed opportunities for advancement and the junior employee may seek out mentors during such times for coaching and guidance.[59]

Computer-based training or instruction involves computer-generated presentation of material, through video and audio media, with interaction on the part of the student. For example, material may be presented in a format that requires the student to respond. The student's correct responses then receive positive reinforcement from the computer and incorrect responses are diagnosed, followed with additional instruction until the correct response is learned.[60] An example of such training is provided by the American Airlines Flight Academy, which uses such training for transition training in which pilots and flight engineers learn to operate another type of aircraft. It is also used for upgrade training, such as in the case of flight engineers preparing for copilot duties.[61] An example of this training is provided in the following:

> American's Flight Academy, adjacent to Dallas/Ft. Worth International Airport, has 85 microcomputer high-resolution, color touch-screen monitors linked with audio tapes and slide projectors to present coursework and testing for pilots' transition training. . . . A pilot beginning the day goes to the library and pulls the binder containing the program he or she is to work on that day . . . tapes, a slide tray, and a script. . . . There are generally about 60–70 programs for a transition course, each lasting about 8–10 min., explaining the nature of a specific aircraft system or set of controls. . . . After each presentation, with the pace controlled by the pilot, the crew member is tested to determine whether he or she can do what is required, such as set up the hydraulic panel using the touch screen. A correct response lets the program proceed. If the pilot answers incorrectly, the system will set up the panel correctly, and the slide device and audio tape come on to explain why the answer was incorrect.[62]

This computer-based instruction is in addition to the very complex and expensive flight simulation training that American Airlines conducts on twenty flight simulators. These simulators are designed for specific aircraft, such as the Boeing models 767 and 727, McDonnell Douglas models MD-80, DC-10, and the Airbus A300-600R. American's training operations are extensive. In a recent year the company expected to conduct over 100,000 pilot days of training at the academy.[63]

214 / *Chapter Seven*

Another example of computer-based instruction is one for training sales personnel which builds in role playing:

> Using a video camera mounted above the monitor, the student is filmed interacting with the customer segments, contained on a laser disk. The interface is an IBM Info-Window monitor with a touch screen. The final tape merges the student's and customer's responses for review.[64]

Interestingly, computer-based instruction or training has low delivery costs but is expensive to develop. In contrast, the lecture instructional approach involves low development costs but is very expensive to deliver. In the past, developmental expenses and the computing power required for sophisticated multimedia software limited computer-based instruction. However, with rapid gains in microcomputer power during the 1990s there should be fewer impediments to computer-based instruction. The advantages of computer-based instruction are meaningful. It can be readily available and accessible on demand at the student's convenience, allows for self-pacing, and provides for active involvement through the interactive features of computerization. It also provides in-progress testing, reinforcement, remedial training based on incorrect responses, and can be operated on a stand-alone basis. Such training also provides standardized training that can be widely disseminated within an organization and can provide realistic simulation of pragmatic work situations.[65]

Another training approach is called *computer-assisted instruction.* In this approach, the computer may not be the primary instructional mode but may be used to augment more conventional training. The distinction between the terms is somewhat blurred as they sometimes are used interchangeably. Nonetheless, computer-assisted instruction seems to have a more general connotation. In recent years, there has been a substantial amount of research in the management information systems literature on how to design human–computer interfaces in computer-assisted training so as to obtain active involvement of the student. One important finding is that the design can have a significant impact on learning effectiveness.[66]

Apprenticeships

Apprenticeship programs are not used extensively in the United States. Currently they involve a very small proportion of the work force, estimated to be only 0.16 percent. In contrast, apprenticeships involve 6.5 percent of the work force in Germany.[67] Apprenticeship programs are most highly developed in Germany where they lead to examination and certification in approximately 400 occupations.[68] As institutionalized in Germany, "About 65 percent of each class of middle school graduates enter apprenticeship training in fields ranging from skilled manufacturing to office work. Over 3 years, these would-be-apprentices spend 4 days per week in on-the-job training and at least 1 day per week at a state-supported vocational school."[69] The majority of students involved in the apprenticeship program, also called dual training, begin when they are fifteen or sixteen years old and finish in three years.[70]

German students not going on to college see the value of making good grades because scholastic performance is one of the factors employers consider in selecting apprentices. Further, students see that completing an apprenticeship and passing the examination for certification leads to a good job with attractive compensation. Following completion of their training programs, large German manufacturing companies retain approximately 80 to 90 percent of their apprenticeships as regular, long-term employees and placement rates are high for all sizes of companies. At six months after successful completion of their certification examinations, 68 percent of German apprentices have jobs in the occupations in which they apprenticed. In contrast, in the United States unless one is going on to college, the grades one makes in elementary school and high school are not an important determinant of employment as the jobs typically require only low skill and provide low pay. Therefore, there is little incentive to do well in school.[71]

German employers spend approximately twice as much on worker training than their counterparts in the United States. Further, their investments in apprenticeship training, are partially funded by the German government. However, they usually do not pay apprentices the regular wage rate, typically lower than one third of the regular rate. German firms also benefit from apprenticeships through the increased productivity of their work force as well as stronger relationships among workers and supervisors. Supervisors and managers tend to understand the jobs of their subordinates because many of them were trained in apprenticeship programs.[72]

Unfortunately, there are a number of barriers or arguments in opposition to the adoption of German-type apprenticeship programs in the United States. One anticipated argument is that students will be forced to make the critical decision whether to pursue a vocational or university track while they are too young. Clearly there will be a need for greater career awareness so that students can make informed decisions. Another argument is that because of the narrower focus of apprenticeship programs, students will not have sufficient breadth in their educations. A counter to this is that many students are already dissatisfied with school at a relatively early age and drop out under the current system. A further argument is that, because of the specificity of the training, the skills learned will become obsolete too quickly. This is not necessarily true as some skills can have broad applications. A final argument is that disadvantaged students, who are more likely to be minorities, will be disproportionally represented in the vocational track. As a result, they will have limited occupational mobility and truncated career paths. Unfortunately, the current reality is that the occupational outlook for disadvantaged youth is already abysmal and limited by the absence of networking relationships for good jobs. Apprenticeship programs provide employment relationships, networks, and mentorships that help build good work habits and self-esteem.[73]

Interestingly, as the prospects for jobs for young people in the United States have become increasingly bleak, more attention is being focused on apprenticeship programs. U.S. employers facing competition from Germany and Japan have great need for technically qualified work forces and may become the champions of apprenticeship programs. For example, Sears has been involved in a pilot apprenticeship program in appliance repair. In the program students attend high school half of the day and then participate in an apprenticeship training program designed by Sears during the other half. The program is paid for by their high school and a federal grant through the National Alliance of Business. Other apprenticeship programs are being conducted for surgical technicians, medical secretaries, metalworkers, accountants, and printers. Such programs should counter employer complaints that high school graduates do not have the knowledge required in today's more technological work environment. Some indication of increased interest in apprenticeships was evident in the 1992 presidential campaign in which Bill Clinton advocated a national apprentice network, while George Bush announced plans for demonstration apprenticeship programs. Unfortunately, in the United States, as contrasted with Germany and Britain, there is no comprehensive system for administering apprenticeship training. The German program is well-integrated into the educational system, and in Britain, students of ages sixteen and seventeen who have discontinued their schooling are guaranteed two years of such training.[74]

Management Development

Approaches to management development commonly emphasize *job rotation* through successively more responsible positions. As mentioned in Chapter 2, one challenge resulting from the massive organizational changes of the 1980s and 1990s is how to groom managers for top-level positions after much of the middle-management training ground has been eliminated. Indeed, between 1989 and 1991, 17 percent of those laid-off were middle managers although they represented only 5 to 8 percent of the work force.[75] As a result, in the future there may be more management development efforts that utilize rotating leaderships of task forces or product development teams.

However, one of the most commonly used approaches of management development is still the rotation of managers through successively more responsible positions or a combination of broadening assignments and vertical assignments. A departure from these traditional rotational programs involves *cross-functional assignments.* An important insight into these assignments is provided in the following description.

> While expertise-oriented managers are the bedrock of any organization, they succumb to Peter Principle traps when in leadership positions. . . . But if one moves a manager who is thought to have leadership potential to another area of expertise, that person is obligated to develop leadership skills in delivering results through people who have more expertise. The duration of this cross-

functional job should be at least 3–4 years (contrary to the practice of many firms)—otherwise people will only develop skills in starting things off, not in implementation and execution.[76]

A good description of management training practices is provided by a study that surveyed training practices for managerial personnel in 611 companies having at least 1,000 employees. Although systematic assessment of formal training would seem prudent, the study found that only 27 percent of the responding companies reported having needs assessment procedures. On the other hand, needs assessment and company size were significantly correlated as larger companies are more likely to have needs assessment procedures. A number of other important aspects of training were also found to be related to company size. Larger companies were more likely to involve their managerial employees in formal training programs, more likely to use job rotation as a training or development approach, and more likely to conduct career planning. There were also some significant industry differences as service industry companies were least likely to use job rotation as a management training approach and also least likely to send their managers through university management development programs.[77]

One of the major results of the study was that the respondents expected to do more managerial training in the future in order to update managers' skills. The respondents also expected more managerial training in the future because of more corporate-level emphasis. Furthermore, managerial participation in such training was required by written policies in 22 percent of the companies.[78] Another study provides empirical evidence of performance-related differences in approaches toward training and development in the retailing industry. In this study, one of the good performers implemented a major change in strategy during a period of decline. As part of the change, the company increased its emphasis on training, particularly of a strategic nature, such as competitor analysis. In contrast, the poor performers either stopped or scaled back their programs.[79]

In addition to future changes in the amount and type of training, the speed of development has already changed. From the 1960s through the 1990s, exceptionally talented individuals were developed for the highest positions through fast-track management development programs. For example, over a period of thirty-two years Edgar S. Woolard, Jr., moved through twenty jobs before he became the chief executive officer of Du Pont. While his tenure in these jobs ranged from only five months to three years, his experience was not unusual for fast-trackers as promotions came after an average of eighteen to twenty-four months on the job. Because of reductions in the numbers of middle management jobs and the age bulge of the baby boomers, the rate of promotions has slowed dramatically.[80]

In spite of developmental slowdowns and a reduction in the middle management training ground, there are still means for developing high-talent managers. One approach is to use lateral moves. By making *lateral assignments* of both average performers and stars, there is less chance that the assignment will be perceived as dead end. Increases in the span of supervision and magnitude of responsibility without vertical movement can also promote development. Specific examples are Pepsico's use of lateral assignments for approximately 60 percent of its management-track assignments, and Hughes Aircraft's use of lateral moves in which electrical engineers are assigned to quality control. An obvious advantage of these lateral moves and the "*slow track*" approach is that the manager develops a broader understanding of the company and is on the job long enough to see more of the fruits of his or her efforts. Another example of an alternative developmental approach is Du Pont's assignment of managers to overseas posts as a prerequisite to top management positions.[81]

Management Development for International Assignments

The use of overseas assignments for development is in sharp contrast to the past when managers having poorer prospects for higher positions were relegated to international assignments, as indicated by the following quotation: "At Du Pont, where nearly half the sales are foreign, overseas tours are becoming *de rigueur* for eventual moves up."[82] Unfortunately, U.S. companies have often failed to provide adequate training for expatriate assignments and have been dissatisfied with cross-cultural training. Nonetheless, such training can be more effective if it is supported by top management, is based on adequate resources, and is of sufficient duration. Where extensive cultural fluency is necessary, an immersion approach to training may be needed. Such approaches involve the use of field experiences, simulations, comprehensive training in languages, and sensitivity training.[83] There may also be greater support in the future from top management for such training. As early as the mid-1980s, Motorola was providing strategically oriented training on various countries in its senior-level executive development program.[84] A related issue is that in order to obtain world-class labor, human resource managers and executives must acquire the skills to recruit, hire, and develop managers and professionals from other countries for global operations.[85]

Product Life Cycles and Managerial Fit: Development versus Selection

Earlier discussions have noted the importance of aligning human resource practices with the organization's overall strategy. A related issue concerns the importance of matching types of managers with the organization's strategies. Some strategists have proposed that different types of managerial skills or personalities are required for the different stages of product life cycles or different corporate strategies. Although there is no common agreement on the life cycle stages, a common typology includes introduction, growth, maturity, and decline. Broader strategy categories might include steady-state and evolutionary stages. In the case of product life cycles, it is argued that in the introduction stage, a manager should be a risk taker or entrepreneur while in the decline stage, the manager should be risk-averse and focused on cost containment. Problems with product life cycle models stem from ambiguities in stage identification, the validity of prescribed styles or personalities needed for each stage, and inaccuracies in style and personality measurement. However, they have value in focusing attention on alignment through either hiring, development, or the use of reward systems. With the limitations of these approaches in mind, a careful contingency approach to matching or fit may have some value.[86]

Along this line, Jeffrey Kerr and Ellen Jackofsky have argued that with companies pursuing steady-state strategies, more effective matching will be obtained by placing greater emphasis on development rather than selection. With steady-state strategies, growth is achieved through internal expansion and managers must have a broad understanding of the business. Conversely, in organizations pursuing evolutionary strategies, selection should provide a more effective matching approach. Because evolutionary strategies rely on acquisitions and mergers for growth, the managerial talent needed to staff an unrelated acquisition can be obtained more easily through external selection.[87] These results indicate that for companies growing through internal expansion, management development will be an important means of aligning managers' talent with organizational strategies.

SUMMARY

This chapter has discussed the role of reward and development systems in strategy implementation. Because performance measures are necessary for assessment of employees' contributions to the implementation of strategies, various measurement approaches were discussed as antecedents to reward and development systems. Management by objectives was covered along with graphic rating scales, narrative descriptions of performance, and behaviorally anchored rating scales. Additionally, the lack of performance evaluation at executive levels was discussed. The absence of such formal evaluation for executives was attributed to several unfounded beliefs or myths. Suggestions were offered for increased application of performance evaluation to executives.

Following the discussion of performance measurement, reward systems were considered from a compensation perspective. Traditional job-based pay systems were described along with their inability to provide the flexibility needed for today's competitive environment. Because of compensation's critical role in new work systems and organizational structures, several innovative compensation approaches were discussed. These included skill-based pay, which focuses on the individual as opposed to the job. Because work forces with high skill levels will be needed to obtain future competitive advantages, the alignment of rewards with skill acquisition can be critical to successful strategy implementation. The new compensation approach of broad banding was also examined. Broad banding, like skill-based pay, facilitates efficient work-force utilization. Also discussed was team-based pay, which rewards cooperative efforts, and variable compensation. Variable compensation is becoming more widely adopted because it helps to create a sense of shared destiny among all employees. Such plans may place a portion of employees' compensation at risk and then link that portion to the achievement of overall performance goals. Variable compensation also has the potential to contribute to employment security. The role and current status of executive compensation were also examined.

Following the discussion of compensation systems, employee and management development were discussed as means of strategy implementation. Several training methods were examined, including both traditional and evolving approaches. These included new employee orientation, socialization, coaching, mentoring, computer-based training, and computer-assisted instruction. The training approaches of apprenticeships, which may receive greater emphasis in the future, and management development were covered in detail. Management development was examined in terms of job rotation, cross-functional assignments, and lateral assignments.

REFERENCES

1. Longenecker, Clinton O., and Dennis A. Gioia, "The Executive Appraisal Paradox," *Academy of Management Executive*, 6, no. 2 (1992), 26 (whole article on pp. 18–28).
2. Richards, Max D., *Setting Strategic Goals and Objectives*, 2nd ed. St. Paul, Minn.: West, 1986.
3. Cardy, Robert L., and Gregory H. Dobbins, *Performance Appraisal: Alternative Perspectives*. Cincinnati, Ohio: South-Western, 1994.
4. Ibid.
5. Ibid.
6. Ibid.
7. Longenecker and Gioia, "The Executive Appraisal Paradox," 18.
8. Longenecker and Gioia, "The Executive Appraisal Paradox."
9. Longenecker, Clinton O., Henry P. Sims, and Dennis Gioia, "Behind the Mask: The Politics of Employee Appraisal," *Academy of Management Executive*, 1, no. 3 (1987), 183–193.
10. Gómez-Mejía, Luis R., and David B. Balkin, *Compensation, Organizational Strategy, and Firm Performance*. Cincinnati, Ohio: South-Western, 1992; Milkovich, George T., and Jerry M. Newman, *Compensation*, 4th ed. Homewood Ill.: Richard D. Irwin, 1993; Emerson, Sandra M., "Job Evaluation: A Barrier to Excellence?" *Compensation and Benefits Review*, 23, no. 1 (1991), 39–51.
11. Emerson, "Job Evaluation: A Barrier to Excellence?" Tosi, Henry, and Lisa Tosi, "What Managers Need to Know About Knowledge-Based Pay," *Organizational Dynamics*, 14, no. 3 (1986), 52–64; Gómez-Mejía and Balkin, *Compensation, Organizational Strategy, and Firm Performance*.
12. Ledford, Gerald E., Jr., "Three Case Studies on Skill-Based Pay: An Overview," *Compensation and Benefits Review*, 23, no. 2 (1991), 11–23; Lawler, Edward E., III, Gerald E., Ledford Jr., and Lei Chang, "Who Uses Skill-Based Pay, and Why," *Compensation and Benefits Review*, 25, no. 2 (1993), 22–26.
13. Tosi and Tosi, "What Managers Need to Know About Knowledge-Based Pay," 57.
14. Ledford, "Three Case Studies on Skill-Based Pay"; Lawler, Ledford, and Chang, "Who Uses Skill-Based Pay, and Why."
15. Lawler, Ledford, and Chang, "Who Uses Skill-Based Pay, and Why."
16. Ledford, "Three Case Studies on Skill-Based Pay."
17. Ibid.; Tosi and Tosi, "What Managers Need to Know About Knowledge-Based Pay", Lawler, Ledford, and Chang, "Who Uses Skill-Based Pay, and Why."
18. Ibid.

19. Lawler, Ledford, and Chang, "Who Uses Skill-Based Pay, and Why"; Tosi and Tosi, "What Managers Need to Know About Knowledge-Based Pay."
20. Tosi and Tosi, "What Managers Need to Know About Knowledge-Based Pay"; Ledford, "Three Case Studies on Skill-Based Pay."
21. Hofrichter, David, "Broadbanding: A 'Second Generation' Approach," *Compensation and Benefits Review,* 25, no. 5 (1993), 53–58.
22. Ibid.
23. Ibid.
24. Gómez-Mejía and Balkin, *Compensation, Organizational Strategy, and Firm Performance.*
25. Gómez-Mejía, Luis R., and David B. Balkin, "Effectiveness of Individual and Aggregate Compensation Strategies," *Industrial Relations,* 28, no. 3 (1989), 431–445; Gómez-Mejía and Balkin, *Compensation, Organizational Strategy, and Firm Performance.*
26. Gómez-Mejía and Balkin, "Effectiveness of Individual and Aggregate Compensation Strategies."
27. Ost, Edward J., "Team-Based Pay: New Wave Strategic Incentives," *Sloan Management Review,* 31, no. 3 (1990), 19–27.
28. Ost, "Team-Based Pay," 22.
29. Gross, Steven E., and Jeffrey P. Bacher, "The New Variable Pay Programs: How Some Succeed, Why Some Don't," *Compensation and Benefits Review,* 25, no. 1 (1993), 51–56.
30. Bowie-McCoy, Susan W., Ann C. Wendt, and Roger Chope, "Gainsharing in Public Accounting: Working Smarter and Harder," *Industrial Relations,* 32, no. 3 (1993), 432–445.
31. Gross and Bacher, "The New Variable Pay Programs;" Hogarty, Donna Brown, "New Ways to Pay," *Management Review,* 83, no. 1 (1994), 34–36.
32. Schuster, Jay R., and Patricia K. Zingheim, "The New Variable Pay: Key Design Issues," *Compensation and Benefits Review,* 25, no. 2 (1993), 27–34.
33. Ibid., Kerr, Steven, "On the Folly of Rewarding A While Hoping for B," *Academy of Management Journal,* 18, no. 4 (1975), 769–783.
34. Schuster and Zingheim, "The New Variable Pay," 31.
35. Gross and Bacher, "The New Variable Pay Programs."
36. Henn, William R., "What the Strategist Asks from Human Resources," *Human Resource Planning,* 8, no. 4 (1985) 193–200; Gómez-Mejía and Balkin, *Compensation, Organizational Strategy, and Firm Performance.*
37. Gómez-Mejía and Balkin, *Compensation, Organizational Strategy, and Firm Performance,* 221.
38. Kanter, Rosabeth Moss, *When Giants Learn to Dance: Mastering the Challenge of Strategy, Management, and Careers in the 1990s.* New York: Simon & Schuster, 1989, 237.
39. Kanter, *When Giants Learn to Dance,* 368.
40. Magnus, Margaret, "Training Futures," *Personnel Journal,* 65, no. 5 (1986), 61–71.
41. Ibid.; Naisbitt, John, and Patricia Aburdene, *Re-inventing the Corporation: Transforming Your Job and Your Company for the New Information Society.* New York: Warner Books, 1985.
42. Naisbitt and Aburdene, *Re-inventing the Corporation.*
43. Ibid., 127.
44. Gordon, Jack, "Where the Training Goes," *Training,* 27, no. 10 (1990), 51–69; Peters, Tom, *Thriving on Chaos: Handbook for a Management Revolution.* New York: Harper & Row, 1987.
45. Gordon, "Where the Training Goes."
46. Naisbitt and Aburdene, *Re-inventing the Corporation,* 165.
47. Ibid.
48. Cheng, Alex F., "Hands-On Learning at Motorola," *Training and Development Journal,* 44, no. 10 (1990), 34–35.
49. Cheng, "Hands-On Learning at Motorola," 34.
50. Hammonds, Keith H., "Corning's Class Act," *Business Week,* May 13, 1991, 68–76.
51. Magnus, "Training Futures"; Wexley, Kenneth N., and Gary P. Latham, *Developing and Training Human Resources in Organizations,* 2nd ed. New York: HarperCollins, 1991; Goldstein, Irwin L., *Training in Organizations: Needs Assessment, Development, and Evaluation,* 2nd ed. Monterey, Calif.: Brooks/Cole, 1986.
52. Ivancevich, John M., and William F. Glueck, *Foundations of Personnel: Human Resource Management,* 4th ed. Homewood, Ill.: Richard D. Irwin, 1989; Cherrington, David J., *Personnel Management: The Management of Human Resources,* 2nd ed. Dubuque, Iowa: William C. Brown, 1987; Dessler, Gary, *Personnel Management,* 4th ed. Englewood Cliffs, N.J.: Prentice Hall, 1988.
53. Ivancevich and Glueck, *Foundations of Personnel.*
54. Schein, Edgar H., *Career Dynamics: Matching Individual and Organizational Needs.* Reading, Mass.: Addison-Wesley, 1978, 117.

55. Wexley and Latham, *Developing and Training Human Resources in Organizations;* Schein, *Career Dynamics.*
56. Schein, *Career Dynamics.*
57. Ibid.; Hunt, David M., and Carol Michael, "Mentorship: A Career Training and Development Tool," *Academy of Management Review,* 8, no. 3 (1983), 475–485.
58. Velasquez, Manuel, Dennis J. Moberg, and Gerald F. Cavanagh, "Organizational Statesmanship and Dirty Politics: Ethical Guidelines for the Organizational Politician," *Organizational Dynamics,* 12, no. 2 (1983), 65–80.
59. Wexley and Latham, *Developing and Training Human Resources in Organizations;* Hunt and Michael, "Mentorship: A Career Training and Development Tool;" Kram, Kathy E., and Douglas T. Hall, "Mentoring as an Antidote to Stress During Corporate Trauma," *Human Resource Management,* 28, no. 4 (1989), 493–510; Schein, *Career Dynamics.*
60. Wexley and Latham, *Developing and Training Human Resources in Organizations.*
61. Shirfrin, Carole A., "American Meets Pilot, Fleet Increase with Computer-Intensive Instruction," *Aviation Week and Space Technology,* June 13, 1988, 139–141.
62. Shirfrin, "American Meets Pilot, Fleet Increase with Computer-Intensive Instruction," 139. Copyright © 1988 by McGraw-Hill. Reprinted by permission of McGraw-Hill.
63. Shirfrin, "American Meets Pilot, Fleet Increase with Computer-Intensive Instruction."
64. Booker, Ellis, "Grading High-Tech Teaching," *Computerworld,* February 19, 1990, 114.
65. Booker, "Grading High-Tech Teaching." Granger, Ralph E., "Computer-Based Training Works," *Personnel Journal,* 69, no. 9 (1990), 85–91.
66. Goldstein, *Training in Organizations,* Gal, Graham, and Paul John Steinbart, "Interface Style and Training Task Difficulty as Determinants of Effective Computer-Assisted Knowledge Transfer," *Decision Sciences,* 23, no. 1 (1992), 128–143.
67. Hilton, Margaret, "Shared Training: Learning from Germany," *Monthly Labor Review,* 114, no. 3 (1991), 33–37.
68. Lerman, Robert I., and Hillard Pouncy, "The Compelling Case for Youth Apprenticeships," *The Public Interest,* 101, (Fall 1990), 62–77.
69. Hilton, "Shared Training," 33.
70. Rachwalsky, Klaus, *Vocational Training—Investment for the Future: The Dual Training System in the Federal Republic of Germany.* Cologne, Carl Duisberg Gesellschaft, 1983.
71. Lerman and Pouncy, "The Compelling Case for Youth Apprenticeships."
72. Hilton, "Shared Training;" Phillips, Dennis, "How VW Builds Worker Loyalty Worldwide," *Management Review,* 76, no. 6 (1987), 37–40; Lerman and Pouncy, "The Compelling Case for Youth Apprenticeships."
73. Lerman and Pouncy, "The Compelling Case for Youth Apprenticeships."
74. Wartzman, Rick, "Learning by Doing: Apprenticeship Plans Spring Up for Students Not Headed to College," *The Wall Street Journal,* May 19, 1992, A1, A6.
75. Cascio, Wayne F., "Downsizing: What Do We Know? What Have We Learned?" *Academy of Management Executive,* 7, no. 1 (1993), 95–104.
76. Evans, Paul A. L., "Management Development as Glue Technology," *Human Resource Planning,* 15, no. 1 (1992), 93.
77. Saari, Lise M., Terry R. Johnson, Steven D. McLaughlin, and Denise M. Zimmerle, "A Survey of Management Training and Education Practices in U.S. Companies," *Personnel Psychology,* 41, no. 4 (1988), 731–743.
78. Saari, Johnson, McLaughlin, and Zimmerle, "A Survey of Management Training and Education Practices in U.S. Companies."
79. Cook, Deborah, and Gerald R. Ferris, "Strategic Human Resource Management and Firm Effectiveness in Industries Experiencing Decline," *Human Resource Management,* 25, no. 3 (1986), 441–457.
80. Weber, Joseph, Lisa Driscoll, and Richard Brandt, "Farewell, Fast Track," *Business Week,* December 10, 1990, 192–200.
81. Ibid.
82. Weber, Driscoll, and Brandt, "Farewell, Fast Track," 196.
83. Mendenhall, Mark E., Edward Dunbar, and Gary R. Oddou, "Expatriate Selection, Training and Career-Pathing: A Review and Critique," *Human Resource Management,* 26, no. 3 (1987), 331–345.
84. Bolt, James F., "Tailor Executive Development to Strategy," *Harvard Business Review,* 63, no. 6 (1985), 168–176.
85. Hambrick, Donald C., James W. Fredrickson, Lester B. Korn, and Richard M. Ferry, "Preparing Today's Leaders for Tomorrow's Realities," *Personnel,* 66, no. 8 (1989), 23–26.
86. Galbraith, Jay R., and Robert K. Kazanjian, *Strategy Implementation: Structure, Systems, and Process,* 2nd ed. St. Paul, Minn.: West, 1986; Kerr, Jeffrey, "Assigning Managers on the Basis of the Life Cycle," *Journal of Business Strategy,* 2, no. 4 (1982), 58–65; Szilagyi, Andrew D., Jr., and David M. Schweiger,

"Matching Managers to Strategies: A Review and Suggested Framework," *Academy of Management Review,* 9, no. 4 (1984), 626–637.
87. Kerr, Jeffrey L., and Ellen F. Jackofsky, "Aligning Managers with Strategies: Management Development Versus Selection," *Strategic Management Journal,* 10 (1989), 157–170.

Case 7

CEO COMPENSATION

Many readers probably have had the experience of being asked by a neighbor or colleague to explain the extremely high compensation of some CEOs. A notable example includes the Walt Disney Corporation's CEO who received $203 million in one year.[1] Others include stock option gains of $125.9 million to the CEO of HCA Hospital Corporation of America, and $58.5 million to the CEO of U.S. Surgical Corporation.[2] Graef Crystal, a noted critic of CEO compensation, has spent a great amount of time studying the subject. For example, in his study of CEO compensation in healthcare organizations, in which there is great variance in compensation, he found no rationale according to organizational performance or size. Further, he discredited supply and demand explanations and attributed CEOs' high compensation to other sources of power.[3] Some of Crystal's conclusions are as follows:

> So is there any rhyme or reason to explain the huge variation of CEO pay levels? Short answer: Forget it. . . . There's no justifiable theory on a shortage of CEO talent to drive up CEO pay. But there is a creditable theory at work, the theory of CEO power. Pack the board with your friends, hire consultants who are good at blowing smoke, float a lot of statistics about how other companies offer their CEOs a ton of money, and, voila, you, too, can make a lucrative sum no matter how you perform, and see your pay rise at a rate faster than people who fill other important jobs in the organization.[4]

On the other hand, there are defenders of current levels of CEO compensation. Consultants Ira Kay and Rodney Robinson have argued that the pay of CEOs is justified by the performance of their companies. Further, they have pointed out that academic research studies using time series methodologies provide the basis for such conclusions.[5] Even Crystal has found a small positive relationship between performance, in the form of shareholder returns, and CEO compensation. On the other hand, he has found that such performance explains only 19.8 percent of the variance in their compensation, which leaves approximately 80 percent to other factors.[6] Further, other critics have pointed out the vast differences between the United States and other countries in ratios of CEO compensation to the average worker's compensation. Randall Schuler and Vandra Huber, who cited some of Crystal's earlier work, have noted that, "In 1992 there was a ratio of 40 to 1 in the U.S. between the pay of CEOs and rank and file employees, compared with 17 to 1 in Germany and only 10 to 1 in Japan."[7]

Because of the problem of excessive compensation, several recommendations have been proposed. Some very high-level policy recommendations would require legislation. One such recommendation is that the U.S. Glass-Steagall Act of 1933, which prohibits bankers from sitting on their customers' boards of directors, should be amended to permit such practices. Presumably, such bankers would be more cost conscious. A more radical policy recommendation is that the United States should move to a German style of code-termination system in which worker representatives sit on boards of directors. In contrast, another recommendation is to avoid solutions based on legislation since they are likely to introduce even more problems.

Several other recommendations are directed toward implementation at the organizational level. One is to link CEO pay to long-term profitability. A second is to put more stockholders and workers on boards of directors. A related recommendation is directed toward members of company boards of directors, it maintains that board members should ignore self-serving surveys that portray CEOs as underpaid in comparison to other CEOs. They should also be very skeptical of assessments which conclude that CEOs are mobile. Still another recommendation is to use succession planning to develop an internal pool of qualified CEO candidates and thereby avoid seeking expensive replacements from the external labor market.[8] A final recommendation would attack the problem in a more indirect manner. In response to the problems of excessive CEO compensation, as well as other factors, the Financial Accounting Standards Board (FASB) has proposed that stock option grants be reflected on financial statements as a charge to earnings.[9] Without such a requirement, stock option grants to executives, which may eventually take on millions of dollars in value, are never reflected in financial statements.

Questions

1. Explain the potential adverse impacts on strategy implementation when the CEOs of companies receive extremely high compensation.
2. Discuss the merits of the various recommendations for solutions to the problem of extremely high CEO compensation. Which are more likely to be adopted?
3. What nonregulatory pressures are most likely to bring excessively high CEO salaries more in line with realistic levels?
4. Evaluate the argument that pay for performance justifies the level of compensation paid to the CEOs noted in the examples.
5. Evaluate the argument that the problem of excessive CEO compensation should not be addressed through legislation. Provide examples of situations where legislation directed at solving a problem had the unanticipated consequence of creating new problems.

REFERENCES

1. Hardy, Eric S., "Marathon Men," *Forbes*, May 23, 1994, 140–142.
2. Crystal, Graef, "Inefficient Market for CEOs in Health Care," *Compensation and Benefits Review*, 25, no. 5 (1993), 74–75.

3. Ibid.
4. Crystal, "Inefficient Market for CEOs in Health Care," 75.
5. Kay, Ira T., and Rodney F. Robinson, "Misguided Attacks on Executive Pay Hurt Shareholders," *Compensation and Benefits Review,* 26, no. 1 (1994), 25–33.
6. Crystal, Graef "Speaking My Mind," *Compensation and Benefits Review,* 26, no. 1 (1994), 34–37.
7. Schuler, Randall S., and Vandra L. Huber, *Personnel and Human Resource Management,* 5th ed. St. Paul, Minn.: West, 1993, 437.
8. Wilhelm, Paul G., "Application of Distributive Justice Theory to the CEO Pay Problem: Recommendations for Reform," *Journal of Business Ethics,* 12, no. 6 (1993), 469–482.
9. Kay and Robinson, "Misguided Attacks on Executive Pay Hurt Shareholders."

8

HUMAN RESOURCE EVALUATION

The eighth and final component of the conceptual framework is human resource evaluation. With the increasing emphasis placed on strategic contribution, competitiveness, and cost control, there has been a greater need to justify the existence of human resource programs and activities. As will be noted in this chapter, the evaluation of human resource programs has not been a high priority in most organizations. Nonetheless, because of the increased need to demonstrate efficient utilization of resources, evaluation will be more important in the future. This chapter will deal with several aspects of evaluation beginning with an overview. It then will describe major evaluation approaches and the prevalence of evaluation. In addition, the chapter will examine approaches for evaluating the strategic contributions of traditional human resource areas as well as emerging areas. Finally, there will be a discussion of macro-level evaluation of human resource effectiveness.

Several human resource theorists and practitioners have presented compelling arguments for the evaluation of human resource management and the human resource function. Such evaluations have been advocated for a number of reasons including (1) promotion of the human resource function, for example, through demonstration of bottom line contributions through reduced turnover; (2) the demonstration of accountability in

Author's Note: Although this chapter draws on many sources, the numerous works of Anne Tsui and Luis Gómez-Mejía were particularly helpful in its development and are cited several times. Similarly Wayne Cascio's and Irwin Goldstein's works on the evaluation of training were also particularly helpful and are cited several times. Those readers desiring to learn more about evaluation are referred to the extensive works by these authors.

utilization of resources; (3) promotion of change by identifying strengths and weaknesses; (4) introduction of financial assessment as a decision tool in human resource program selection, (5) highlighting key human resource practices, (6) gauging the performance of the human resource function, and (7) demonstrating the function's role in the accomplishment of company goals.[1] The intensive emphasis of the 1990s on cost control, efficient allocation of resources, contributing to the bottom line, and capability of human resources to provide a competitive advantage appear likely to result in more emphasis on evaluation.[2]

AN OVERVIEW OF EVALUATION

Before evaluating human resource management, a suitably comprehensive definition of evaluation must be accepted, as well as the criteria and measurement approach. From an organizational perspective, *organizational effectiveness* is generally viewed as a multidimensional construct and typically involves multiple criteria, such as productivity and flexibility. *Productivity measures* sometimes tap efficiency, quantity, and quality while *flexibility measures* may also tap the effectiveness with which the organization deals with schedule changes, crash programs, or emergencies. In some instances, adaptability is operationalized separately and includes measures of problem anticipation, knowledge of new technology, and adaptation to change. Because of the multidimensionality of the effectiveness concept, policy capturing statistical procedures have been developed for constructing multiple measures of subunit effectiveness.[3]

Within the narrower confines of human resource management, there has been substantial progress in the evaluation literature. Although dozens of effectiveness measures have been proposed for evaluation of the function, including composite indexes, the literature has suffered from a lack of an organizing, theoretical framework. This void has since been filled by Anne Tsui and Luis Gómez-Mejía's comprehensive conceptual framework. Their framework differentiates between outcomes or processes affected by line management and those under control of the human resource management function. In order to evaluate broader human resource performance, a company might examine turnover, grievance rates, or workers' compensation claims, which are largely affected by the actions of the company's line managers.[4] Tsui and Gómez-Mejía's conceptual model of human resource effectiveness is presented in Figure 8-1.

In contrast, more narrow evaluations of human resource management would focus on the function's efficiency in administering a benefit program or recruiting and screening applicants. With more broadly focused evaluations, the company's efficient use of human resources would be affected by the efficiency of the company's line managers, while the effectiveness of the human resource management function would be affected mostly by the man-

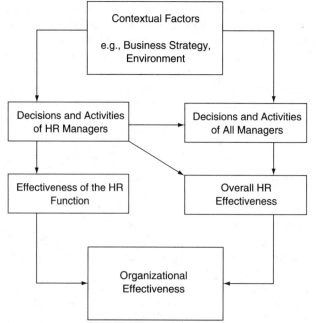

FIGURE 8-1
MODEL OF HUMAN
RESOURCE
EFFECTIVENESS

Source: Anne S. Tsui and Luis R. Gómez-Mejía. "Evaluating Human Resource Effectiveness," in *Human Resource Management: Evolving Roles and Responsibilities,* ed. Lee Dyer. Washington, D.C.: Bureau of National Affairs, 1988, 1–211. Reprinted with permission, 1–211 from *Human Resource Management Evolving Roles and Responsibilities,* edited by Lee Dyer. Copyright © 1988 by the Bureau of National Affairs, Inc., Washington, D.C. 20037.

agers and employees in the human resource function. Human resource departments are somewhat unique in that their activities and responsibilities apply to all managers and employees in all departments.[5] Along this line, Donald Jarrell has cautioned that isolated evaluations of human resource departments run the risk of communicating that others have no responsibilities in the area. Since all managers and departments affect the quality of human resource management and have related responsibilities, this would be an undesirable side effect of evaluation.[6]

Another aspect of human resource evaluation is that the nature of the process is changing from a reactive focus on how well a problem is solved or how successful a program has been to an emphasis on the organizational and employee impact of human resource policies, programs, and activities. For example, in contrast to past evaluation practice where a company might have examined criteria such as turnover rates, a more strategic approach would examine whether it is losing high performers. Essentially, more strategic approaches to evaluation have moved from narrow determinations of whether human resource activities are working to broader analyses of their contributions.[7]

Another dimension of evaluation involves the *level of analysis,* which is the level of aggregation or level within the organizational structure. Tsui and

Gómez-Mejía have identified three levels of analysis in human resource management evaluation: strategic, management, and operational. The objective of evaluation at the strategic level is to determine whether human resource policies and programs are consistent with the company's strategy. At the management level the focus is on control, such as the cost effectiveness of a benefit program. At the operational level the focus is on the quality of human resource services and programs. Since there are multiple constituencies at this level, the service provided and level of satisfaction with the human resource department may vary across these constituencies.[8]

In another comprehensive study, Anne Tsui identified criteria by which the effectiveness of human resource departments can be assessed. Her results emphasize that the various constituencies of human resource departments have differing views of the importance of the various services provided. Results of factor analytic statistical procedures indicate five clear categories of effectiveness criteria for human resource departments: (1) responsiveness, (2) managing cost and negative performance, (3) proactivity and innovativeness, (4) training and development, and (5) affirmative action accomplishments.[9]

Another of Tsui's findings is that the *level of constituents* has a major impact on the effectiveness criteria they apply. Managers and nonsupervisory employees tend to place importance on the department's ability to provide services on matters of immediate or short-term importance. Operating line executives, who have production responsibilities, hold similar views. In contrast, when corporate-level human resource executives evaluate human resource departments, they tend to place greater importance on such activities as organizational development and human resource planning, which have strategic implications. Thus, human resource departments are subject to incompatible expectations which need to be taken into account in an evaluation strategy.[10]

APPROACHES TO EVALUATION

There are a number of general approaches to human resource evaluation, as well as various measures and criteria of effectiveness. Some of the classifications of these components of evaluation are not mutually exclusive as they may fit several categories.

Audit Approaches

In addition to different evaluative foci, criteria, and levels of analysis, two general approaches have also been traditionally used in human resource evaluation. The first is the *audit* approach, which relies on (1) personnel indices, such as per-capita recruiting costs, absenteeism rates, or workers' compensation experience rates, or (2) service/user reactions, such as the perceived equity of the job evaluation system. Typically, data pertaining to the latter would be obtained through the use of surveys or interviews.[11] Usually, items for such surveys can be obtained from published sources. Audit approaches may also be referred to as stakeholder approaches to human resource evaluation. Stakeholder approaches determine the satisfaction of key users or consumers of human resource services. Such stakeholders may be individuals or units within the organization. There may also be external stakeholders such as unions, community organizations, or suppliers. An example of a stakeholder approach to evaluation is provided by Honeywell's Aerospace and Defense Division, which has used the process to clarify the human resource department's role in the company.[12]

Analytical Approaches

The second approach is *analytical* and involves either (1) experimental designs, such as the pretest-posttest control group design, which will be discussed later regarding evaluation of training, or (2) cost-benefit analysis, such as utility theory discussed in Chapter 1 and considered in more detail in this chapter. Although the cost-benefit analytical approach has been used with success, the valuation of benefits is sometimes difficult in human resource applications. *Utility analysis* is a specific type of cost-benefit analysis, that applies to human resource evaluation. It has the advantage of expressing evaluations in economic terms, which are probably more understandable by decision makers from other functional areas. Several human resource activities have been evaluated with utility analysis including appraisal systems, equal employment policies, recruiting, selection, training, and turnover. Although utility analysis has broad applicability and represents a quantitatively superior means of evaluating human resource activities, the process is quite difficult for some applications. As a result of these difficulties and the amount of resources and effort required for analysis, its use has been limited to selected applications only. (An example of an application of utility analysis to a selection problem is provided later in this chapter.) Human resource practices such as succession planning and career development, which may have greater strategic value, often defy quantitative measurement.[13]

Quantitative and Qualitative Measures

Other evaluation issues are whether to use *quantitative* or *qualitative* measures. A number of quantitative and qualitative measures can be constructed to measure the effectiveness of a company's human resources or the human resource function. Quantitative measures can sometimes be combined in the form of composite indices and, as indicated earlier, weighting schemes necessary for such indices can be developed through policy-capturing approaches. Further, the human resource function can also be evaluated as a cost center. Additionally, the benefits resulting from human resource management programs, such as reduced turnover or improved percentages of good hires, can sometimes be determined in dollar values. In such cases the effectiveness of the function can be measured as a profit center. It is worth noting that an inordinate emphasis on quantitative evaluation measures can become dysfunctional. This occurs when the focus on goals, as operational-ized in terms of such measures, does not contribute to accomplishment of strategic goals. On the other hand, changes in the attitudes of an organiza-tion's work force can sometimes provide a partial indication of the effective-ness of the human resource function. These indicators, although inherently more qualitative than many other organizational characteristics, can be cap-tured in measures that allow them to be subjected to statistical analysis.[14]

Outcome and Process Criteria

A final evaluation issue is whether the criteria will involve *outcomes* or *processes*. The distinction between the two types of criteria is that outcomes are results or end products of work while processes concern behaviors or how activities are performed. An example of an outcome criterion might be productivity ratios for a company's work force. In spite of the appeal of their link to production activity, ease of measurement, and objective nature, out-come or output criteria are often contaminated by external factors unrelated to the activity being evaluated.[15] For example, high turnover rates could be more indicative of low unemployment rates in the local labor market than weaknesses in a company's selection or compensation system.

Conversely, an example of a process criterion could be whether a unit meets affirmative action milestones according to a schedule, such as com-pleting a utilization analysis by the end of the first quarter, conducting an availability analysis by the end of the next quarter, and so on. The author's experience has been that many managers experience difficulties in defining objectives in terms of processes. When they have difficulty in articulating a desired process by which an activity should be performed, it is sometimes useful to reverse the question and ask them if they can describe how the activity should not be performed. Almost without exception they can describe how the activity should not be performed, which then helps to stimulate and organize their thinking on desired or efficient processes.

A matrix of these two categories of evaluative criteria is presented in Figure 8-2, with separate breakdowns for evaluations of the effectiveness of the company's human resources and the human resource management func-tion itself.

Benchmarking

Another general evaluation approach which has been applied to human resource practices in recent years is called benchmarking.[16] The origination of benchmarking in the United States is generally credited to Xerox, which used the approach to reduce its manufacturing costs. In essence, bench-marking involves studying how competitors, and sometimes even compa-nies in unrelated industries, are better at certain activities. For example, Ford studied 400 different features of the automobiles of competing manufactur-ers, with the goal of designing and producing a car that would be better than, or at least as good as, the best competitor in each feature.[17]

FIGURE 8-2   EFFECTIVENESS CRITERIA MATRIX

	Overall HR Effectiveness		HR Function Effectiveness	
	Quantitative	**Qualitative**	**Quantitative**	**Qualitative**
Process	Cell 1	Cell 2	Cell 5	Cell 6
	-Absenteeism rate -Minority turnover -Grievances -Job acceptance rate	-Lack of conflict -Innovativeness -Union relations -Flexibility	-Average time to fill jobs -Cost per employee -No. of minority applicants -Training hours per employee	-Time to answer inquiries -Quality of HR services -Cooperativeness of HR staff -Quality of HR programs
Outcome	Cell 3	Cell 4	Cell 7	Cell 8
	-Revenue per employee -New inventions -Productivity -Loss of key employees	-Employee morale -Stakeholder approval -Company reputation for HR	-Value added on HR investment -HR budget per employee -No. of new ER programs -Personnel ratio	-Executive satisfaction -Line manager satisfaction -Employees' opinion of HR

Source: Anne S. Tsui and Luis R. Gómez-Mejía, "Evaluating Human Resource Effectiveness," in *Human Resource Management: Evolving Roles and Responsibilities*, ed. Lee Dyer. Washington, D.C.: Bureau of National Affairs, 1988, 1–213. Reprinted with permission, 1–213 from *Human Resource Management Evolving Roles and Responsibilities*, edited by Lee Dyer. Copyright © 1988 by the Bureau of National Affairs, Inc., Washington, D.C. 20037.

Similarly, *benchmarking* in human resource applications involves the collection of information about specific human resource practices, from large numbers of respondents across many companies. At a macro-analysis level, Dave Ulrich, Wayne Brockbank, and Arthur Yeung at the University of Michigan collected information on twenty-one human resource practices in the general areas of staffing, development, performance appraisal, rewards, communication, and organizational design. Questionnaires comprised of five-interval response scale items (where 1=low ... 5=high) were used to measure these practices. The questionnaires were completed by 10,300 respondents in 91 companies. Of the respondents, 1,315 were human resource professionals while 8,985 were from associates of these professionals from various functional areas throughout their companies. The data provided by this large number of respondents provide benchmarks for various human resource practices in ten different industries. Much of the data concerns practices and perceptions of the human resource function's competencies in such areas as recruitment, training, and designing benefit programs. The data also provide benchmarks of perceived competencies across the various other functional areas—for example, finance, marketing, research and development—and allow a comparison with the human resource function on competencies in such areas as business knowledge, change management, and so on.[18]

Through benchmarking a company can compare its human resource practices and competencies with other companies. In addition to some of the benefits of evaluation noted earlier, benchmarking can also enable a company to see how its competencies in human resource practices have improved over time when longitudinal data are collected. An implication of benchmarking of particular relevance to human resource management's strategic role is that it enables a company to better concentrate its resources so that it can obtain a competitive advantage.[19]

> Benchmarking HR practices provides the means of focusing attention on highest value-added HR activities—those practices which are more likely to be practiced by successful companies. Rather than fall into the trap of trying to do everything well and please everyone with insufficient resources—which results in no one being satisfied—HR professionals could use benchmarking to focus limited resources on critical activities.[20]

Industry Influences

One important consideration in evaluating human resources is industry differences. What may constitute effective human resource practice in one setting may be ineffective in another. A study of high technology entrepreneurial start-up firms provides some good examples of industry differences in effective human resource practices. This study points out that the entrepreneurial and high-technology literatures provide contradictory guidance in the areas of human resource planning, compensation, and the work environment. For example, in high-technology industries, higher company performance is associated with the use of internal sources for managerial recruitment. Extrapolating from this relationship, the researchers reasoned that human resource planning would be needed to insure the availability and development of internal sources of talent. Thus, they hypothesized that in high-technology companies human resource planning is associated with company performance. In contrast, the entrepreneurial literature suggests that there is insufficient time for such planning, relative to other demands, and that planning is inconsistent with the rapid rate of change and flexibility required in entrepreneurial companies.[21]

The researchers also examined compensation issues. The high-technology literature argues that high-technology firms should exercise salary leadership in order to attract talent. While the entrepreneurship literature recognizes these benefits, it maintains that cash flow problems in entrepreneurial firms typically preclude salary leadership practices. The high technology literature also argues that since its key employees—scientists and engineers—adhere to norms of autonomy, an autonomy-oriented work environment will be associated with company performance. On the other hand, the entrepreneurial literature argues that a control-oriented work environment is necessary to focus employees' efforts on short-term goals.[22]

The study, which tested the hypotheses in high-technology entrepreneurial start-up companies, found no relationship between human resource planning and performance. In contrast, compensation leadership was found to be related to sales growth and measures of innovation, as predicted by the high-technology literature. Also, as predicted by the high-technology literature, work environments emphasizing professional autonomy were found to be associated with company performance.[23] An important conclusion from this study is the following:

> Researchers interested in the effects of HR policies and practices on organizational effectiveness are advised to take into account such contingencies as industrial setting, stage in the lifecycle, and business strategy. Failure to do so may result in prescriptions which are inapplicable or inappropriate in particular settings.[24]

PREVALENCE OF EVALUATION

In spite of advocacy for evaluation, a relatively small proportion of companies conduct human resource management evaluations. Likewise, few companies express the results of their evaluations in economic terms. Even with billions of dollars being spent on training every year, many companies do not even evaluate training.[25] Tsui and Gómez-Mejía's survey results found the following: "Systematic, periodic evaluation of HR effectiveness does not occur frequently in American business organizations."[26] Several potential explanations exist for this difference between the normative views of the human resource literature and industry practice. These include human resource executives' fears of the outcomes of evaluation, difficulties in obtaining meaningful and valid measures of human resource activity, and lack of a meaningful evaluative framework. Nonetheless, important variables are positively correlated with the conduct of such evaluation, including financial performance, aggressiveness in marketing strategy, economically oriented goals, and top-level involvement of human resource executives in setting the strategic direction of their companies.[27] Because of these positive contributions of evaluation and the cost consciousness resulting from the pressures of the global economy, evaluations should become more prevalent in the future.

EVALUATING STRATEGIC CONTRIBUTIONS OF TRADITIONAL AREAS

As indicated in Figure 8-2, many areas within the traditional functions of human resource management should probably be evaluated. Major human resource functions of obvious strategic importance are human resource planning, staffing, performance evaluation, compensation and reward systems, training and development, and labor relations.[28] The first to be considered is human resource planning. The potential strategic contributions of human resource planning have already been discussed in earlier chapters and the evaluation of this area should be of importance to general managers.

Human Resource Planning

The effectiveness of human resource planning can be viewed from a behavioral perspective. This includes the degree to which managers accept human resource planning as an activity that helps them perform their jobs. Line management's willingness to supply information to be used in the development of forecasts and actually use human resource forecasts in their own planning provides other indicators of human resource planning effectiveness. Even when forecasts are inaccurate, the human resource planning process has value. This is because, as noted in Chapter 5, in any planning effort, the process of forecasting is often more valuable than the forecast itself as managers are forced to reexamine fundamental operating assumptions.[29] Such reexamination and resultant communications are often valuable side effects.

From a quantitative perspective, for companies that have strong preferences to fill vacancies from internal sources, the extent to which the organization must hire in the open labor market, instead of from its internal labor market, may be an indicator of the effectiveness of the human resource planning process. To the extent that shortages in certain skill areas are forecasted and prepared for with the development of employees, the organization has less need to hire externally. Companies that hire from the external market only at entry levels must have effective human resource planning programs. The failure to plan is probably no more obvious than in professional sports when a team finds itself with a roster of aging athletes and then must endure years of rebuilding because it did not have an effective planning process for bringing in younger players.

Another standard or criterion of human resource planning and development effectiveness is provided by the concept of *just-in-time talent* which means that vacancies can be filled quickly from within the company by a person qualified for promotion. The promoted individual should have been developed by previous assignments and training but should not have to wait in a holding pattern where his or her skills are underutilized.[30] The concept of just-in-time talent has a great deal of appeal because, from the company's standpoint, during the period in which the individual is underutilized, the company is not obtaining a return on its investment in development. From the individual's perspective, there is the obvious advantage of not having to spend time in positions which underutilize one's talents. Such situations lead to turnover, which has costly implications for the company as well.

At a macro level, the forecasted labor shortages for the 1990s had not developed by the middle of the decade. Although demographic trends provided a basis for these predictions, some researchers, even in the late 1980s, were skeptical about the development of such shortages. For example, some labor economists pointed out that demographic factors play a much smaller role in the creation of labor shortages than economic factors and that one such factor, productivity in manufacturing, grew at a robust 4.3 percent annually during most of the 1980s.[31] Another critic of the forecasts of shortages argued that the technological changes of the 1990s would not produce massive labor shortages of skilled workers because, while some jobs would require more skills, others would be deskilled.[32] In addition, as noted in Chapter 2, there were 846,000 immigrants in 1992, the most in any one year since 1914.[33] Obviously, a record level of immigration could have helped eliminate shortages of labor.

It is at least interesting to speculate about another potential cause for the inaccuracies of forecasts that had predicted labor shortages to materialize by the midpoint of the 1990s. This explanation points to the rationale for planning. Although paling in comparison to the effects of global recession and intensified international competition, at the micro level individual companies probably planned for the forecasted shortages. For example, many companies invested heavily in labor-saving equipment. This was particularly evident in manufacturing in which, as noted earlier, productivity grew rapidly. Such investments helped U.S. companies meet international competitive pressures by increasing their employees' productivity. Manufacturing employment should remain fairly stable through 2000 although manufacturing output should increase substantially. It is reasonable to assume that, while gearing up to meet the productivity challenges brought on by intensified international competition, companies were aware of the forecasted labor shortages for the 1990s. Thus, increased investment in labor-saving equipment could have been influenced to some extent by companies' awareness of forecasted labor shortages through their environmental scanning activities. At least in some small portion, forecasted labor shortages may not have materialized because companies did human resource planning and took appropriate actions.

This speculative explanation is also consistent with a general description of an effective human resource management function. James Walker has explained this as follows:

> One company suggested that the most effective function is the one that ensures that there are no pressing human resource issues to concern management. The most proactive, strategic approach to managing resources anticipates and addresses emerging issues before the "pain" is felt. Because conditions continually change, however, there are always issues to be addressed. Through human resource planning, the function may bring these issues to management's attention and create a sense of urgency for action.[34]

Staffing

Obviously, a company's recruiting and selection procedures are critical to its ability to acquire the human resources needed to obtain competitive advantage. Further, as indicated in the Tsui and Gómez-Mejía model in Figure 8-1, human resource effectiveness is influenced by factors outside the human resource function. Accordingly, evaluation approaches for staffing functions must control these other influences before valid assessments can be obtained. In addition to the traditional approaches to selection, which attempt to match applicants with job requirements, some new views of selection may pose different evaluation challenges. For example, David Bowen has pointed out that some companies are now placing primary emphasis in matching applicants with the characteristics or culture of the organization instead of the job.[35] Thus future evaluations may need to focus on developing measures of staff compatibility with organizational characteristics.

Several measures can be used in the evaluation of recruiting effectiveness—for example, cost per hire, number of résumés received, and recruiter activities.[36] In turn, the effectiveness of recruiting has an impact on the effectiveness of a company's staffing. To the extent that a company performs staffing functions poorly, the impact may be potentially manifested in problems such as excessive turnover, line management dissatisfaction, poor quality, litigation, under-representation of minorities and women, and the like, which detract from human resource effectiveness. *Utility analysis* may be used for assessing the effectiveness of selection processes. An interesting feature of the utility analysis approach to cost-benefit analysis is that it can be linked with capital budgeting processes. In turn, this link with capital budgeting may make such evaluation of much greater interest to general managers. Like capital budgeting, utility analysis of selection procedures deals with projected cash flows, such as in the form of savings from increased productivity. The results of the utility analysis of such cash flows can be expressed as net present values.[37]

Application of Utility Analysis to Selection

Neal Schmitt and Richard Klimoski have used the approach of Frank Schmidt, M. J. Mack, and John Hunter to provide a relatively straightforward explanation of the application of utility analysis. Schmitt and Klimoski's explanation of the determination of the utility for a new selection test has been modified in this presentation for application to sales personnel. In this example, a company has decided to pursue a strategy of increasing its market share. To implement this strategy, it needs fifteen additional sales persons this year. The company's current selection procedures are based solely on interviews which have a validity coefficient of .15 while the new test will produce a validity coefficient of .30. Validity coefficients indicating the accuracy of selection procedures range in value from .0 to 1.0, with values of 1.0 indicating perfect prediction.[38]

Since the new test holds out the prospect of making better selection decisions—that is selecting a higher percentage of applicants who turn out to be better salespersons—an estimate of the dollar value of better performance is needed to determine the benefit of the new procedure. The company knows the contribution margin for each salesperson, which is sales minus all variable costs including costs of goods sold and his or her compensation. Based on these data the company determined that the value of better performance is $20,000.

Given the $20,000 value of better performance, utility analysis then involves comparison of the associated costs with the benefits. In order to make comparisons, the company has determined that its current interviewing costs are $100 per applicant and that the new test, which requires special scoring, will cost $250 per applicant. It also knows that salespersons stay with the company for an average of three years. If the company chooses the top 10 percent of all applicants, the formula provided by Schmitt and Klimoski indicates that the utility of the new test would be approximately $215,000. The cash flows from such utility gains can then be projected out into the future and then discounted to arrive at a net present value of investing in the new test. However, the period of time over which such gains will be accrued will be reduced by changes in the jobs which reduce the validity coefficient. (For readers who desire to probe further into the details of methods for determining the value of better performance or the standard deviation of dollar contributions, selection ratios, standardized scores, validity, and the formula used in this example, books by Schmitt and Klimoski and Wayne Cascio provide excellent reference sources.)[39]

Training

As noted earlier, one of the most neglected areas in human resource management is the evaluation of training effectiveness. Such failures to evaluate training have been identified by Steven Kerr as a classic example of misdirected reward structures, or "rewarding A while hoping for B." In a typical scenario, the proponent of the training, who championed the financial outlay, will collect anecdotes and testimonials that provide "evidence" of the success of the program.[40]

> The last thing many desire is a formal, systematic, and revealing evaluation. Although members of top management may actually *hope* for such systematic evaluation, their reward systems continue to *reward* ignorance in this area.[41]

There is probably a great deal of truth in Kerr's comments even today. Scott Tannenbaum and Steven Woods even go as far to suggest that with expensive training programs, strong forms of evaluation are sometimes unlikely because of personal risk to the proponent of the program, in the event of failure. The alternative in such cases is a trade-off of risk for a weaker form of evaluation, such as participants' reactions or satisfaction with the program.[42]

However, as noted earlier, because of international competition and increased focus on costs, human resource programs have been subjected to greater scrutiny. Consequently, human resource managers have had to become more sophisticated in justifying their programs because the costs of investments in training can be substantial. For example, during one year in the 1980s training costs for both IBM and the Bell System were more than $2 billion.[43] Thus, conducting credible evaluations of training effectiveness should be more important in the future.

Although training should normally be expected to contribute to increased productivity, reduced expenses, reduced turnover, improved morale, and the like, training is also conducted for other reasons that may be difficult to quantify. For example, training is sometimes conducted in attractive off-site locations to reward performance and to communicate to those being trained that they are important to the organization. It may also be conducted to allow employees to build informal relationships and to develop personal networks which facilitate communication and coordination. Training may also be conducted for the purpose of allowing a managerial coalition to propagate its views at the expense of another or for other political purposes that cannot be acknowledged in assessment measures.[44] Further, some companies' cultures may require objective data before an evaluation will have any credibility, while in others, elaborate evaluations of training employing objective measures may be rejected because they are incompatible with the company's culture.[45]

Nonetheless, in spite of such difficulties, training can normally be evaluated with relevant, acknowledgeable criteria. Traditional levels of evaluative criteria are (1) reaction, (2) learning, (3) behavior, and (4) results. In addition, some researchers consider attitude change as another category of evaluative criteria.[46]

Measures of *reaction criteria* typically tap participants' satisfaction with training or their perceptions of its quality or relevance.[47] Student evaluations of professors are examples of such measures. Whether reaction criteria actually provide valid standards of effectiveness is arguable as they may only indicate satisfaction. In most industrial settings, some level of satisfaction with training probably is a necessary although insufficient condition for effectiveness. The essence of this intuitive interpretation has been supported by a recent empirical study which found no linear relationship between reactions and learning. Instead, the study found that reactions moderate the training motivation and learning relationship and that reactions have a complex relationship with other facets of training and effectiveness criteria. In fact, the best training results occur where trainees are highly motivated to learn and have a positive reaction to the training.[48]

Learning criteria are concerned with whether participants have absorbed the concepts or content of training. As such they are concerned with whether the trainees have learned facts, information, techniques, strategies, and so on.[49] An application of this criterion would be a test to determine whether stockbroker trainees have learned the content of training on Security Exchange Commission regulations.

Behavior criteria go a step beyond whether the trainee has learned the relevant concepts. These criteria are concerned with whether the lessons of the training program are translated into changes in the behavior of the trainee on the job. For example, there should be changes in the managerial behavior of employees who have completed a management training program. Unlike the other criteria, a period of time is usually needed for the training to become manifested in behaviors. Therefore, a minimum of three months between the completion of training and measurement of behavior is recommended.[50]

Finally, *results criteria* are bottom line criteria. Measures of such criteria might be breakage and scrap rates that are affected by the skill levels of production workers. Similarly, measures of turnover and morale could be relevant applications of results criteria for managerial training programs.[51] With results criteria it is easy to visualize potential contaminants of broader or more global outcomes such as morale, since a multitude of factors other than training may impact morale.

Criteria can also be classified as internal or external. *Internal criteria* are reactions, attitude change, and learning, while *external criteria* are behavior and results. External criteria have an advantage of going beyond the measurement of satisfaction with training or learning of material as they provide information on whether the training has an impact on job performance.[52] A final point on evaluation criteria is that when measuring the effectiveness of training methods, such as lectures, behavioral modeling, role plays, and the like, the choice of evaluative criterion makes a difference. In other words, the effectiveness of different training methods depends on the type of criterion to be measured in the evaluative process. For example, a comprehensive meta-analysis of seventy studies by Michael Burke and Russell Day found that when objective performance standards are applied, evaluations of general management training indicate that they are usually quite effective. These findings differ from the conclusions of evaluations applying learning and subjective behavioral criteria.[53]

In addition to the criteria used, it is critical to have an appropriate and practical research design guiding the collection of data and the choice of measures of the evaluative criteria. The potential contaminants to valid measurement of training effectiveness must be eliminated or controlled through the use of an appropriate research design. Both experimental and quasi-experimental designs can be used in a wide range of evaluative applications. Two experimental designs have particular relevance to the assessment of training effectiveness in many organizational settings. Experimental designs are presented in Table 8-1.

The first is called the *pretest-posttest control group design* as there are both experimental and control groups. Assignment of participants to these groups is based on random selection in order to control for such contaminants as differences in ability, experience, and so forth. Prior to the commencement of training, both groups are pretested on the effectiveness criteria, such as knowledge of concepts and skill levels. The experimental group then receives the training while the control group does not. After completion of the training and

TABLE 8-1   EXPERIMENTAL DESIGNS

PRETEST-POSTTEST CONTROL GROUP DESIGN				
ASSIGNMENT	*GROUP*	*PRETEST*	*TRAINING*	*POSTTEST*
Random	Experimental	Yes	Yes	Yes
Random	Control	Yes	No	Yes
POSTTEST-ONLY CONTROL GROUP DESIGN				
ASSIGNMENT	*GROUP*	*PRETEST*	*TRAINING*	*POSTTEST*
Random	Experimental	No	Yes	Yes
Random	Control	No	No	Yes

Sources: Adapted from Donald T. Campbell and Julian C. Stanley, *Experimental and Quasi-Experimental Designs for Research.* Boston: Houghton Mifflin, 1966; and Wayne F. Cascio, *Applied Psychology in Personnel Management,* 4th ed. Englewood Cliffs, N.J.: Prentice Hall, 1991.

any appropriate time lags for behaviors to be manifested, both groups are posttested. The statistical approach for assessing the significance of results involves the computation of gain scores, in which each individual participant's pretest score is subtracted from the posttest score. Mean values of gain scores are computed within the experimental group and the control group. The significance of the difference in means of the gain scores between the two groups can then be tested with a *t*-test. In realistic company settings, a control group should not be too difficult to obtain. Its members can be employees who may even participate in the same training at some point in the future, after its effectiveness has been determined. Nonetheless, when assigning employees to control groups, evaluators must be able to provide justifications as to why control group members are not being trained when they know that another group is receiving training. Another aspect of control groups, of which evaluators should be aware, is the group's knowledge of the training. In work settings it is often likely that members of the control group may receive substantial information about the training through discussions with other employees.[54]

The second experimental design is the *posttest-only control group design.* This design also utilizes experimental and control groups with random assignment of participants. Unlike the pretest-posttest control group design, there is no pretest. With randomization and sufficient sample size, the two groups may be assumed to have equivalent characteristics, such as ability and experience. This design is useful where a pretest cannot be used because it may sensitize employees to a subtle objective of the training and therefore defeat its purpose.[55] An example might be where "asking questions of the members of the control group regarding their management style might cause them to become sensitized to this aspect of their behavior and, inadvertently, cause them to change their style in some systematic way."[56] Further, the statistical testing with this design is straightforward, as the significance of the difference in the means between the experimental and control groups is determined with a *t*-test. Unfortunately, the researcher may have nagging doubts as to whether the experimental and control groups are truly equivalent.[57] This is an important point because decision makers, who must be convinced of the value of the training, may not truly understand randomization and research design.

Although these two experimental designs should be adequate for most evaluation needs, the *Solomon four-group design* can eliminate other threats to the validity of evaluation.[58] However, the exceptions which require this level of analysis are probably beyond the scope of interest for most general managers.

A final research design appropriate to the assessment of training programs may be the *quasi-experimental design* based on a time series. This design may be appropriate in situations where no control group can be obtained. The essence of the approach is to obtain measures of the evaluation criterion at repeated intervals, such as every month for six months, prior to the conduct of training. After the training, the measures would be collected again at repeated intervals. Unfortunately, analysis of the significance of the results is not as straightforward as with the two experimental designs because of the nonindependence of observations.[59] In some cases, the interpretation of the results may rest on a simple visual examination of trend lines.

The CIGNA Corporation has used the quasi-experimental design to assess the effectiveness of its basic management skills training program. In one unit, repeated measures of productivity were collected for several months prior to and after the training in order to assess the program's effectiveness. In another unit, measures of outstanding collectibles were collected in the same manner. Additionally, in this unit projections of collectibles were also developed to indicate the performance that would have occurred in the absence of the training. These projections allowed the calculation of financial returns on the training investment. The comprehensiveness of CIGNA's evaluation approach is indicated by other aspects of its program. In addition to these results evaluations based on the time series quasi-experimental design, the company also used reaction, learning, and behavioral criteria to assess training effectiveness. In the case of assessments of behaviors, the company had the participants' supervisors assess their managerial behaviors prior to and after the training on such dimensions as leadership, setting standards, and planning.[60]

Performance Evaluation Systems

Unfortunately, in response to complaints and unfavorable comments, many organizations may respond in a technical manner by changing their performance evaluation format instead of addressing more basic problems, such as inadequate training for evaluators, absence of linkage between ratings and rewards, or failures to consider strategic contributions. Maintaining an effective performance measurement system requires training for evaluators, adequate time to perform evaluations, adequate time to conduct performance counseling, and rewards to distribute according to performance. Periodic surveys of managers' views on these aspects of the performance evaluation system can provide indicators of its effectiveness. Another effectiveness indicator can be obtained by correlating employees' ratings with their percentage merit increases in compensation. Although structural adjustments for external equity or other adjustments can sometimes legitimately alter the relationship, on average there should be a positive correlation. While it is hoped that an effective performance evaluation system will reduce the frequency of litigation, another indicator of effectiveness may be its track record in litigation.

Compensation Systems

As indicated in Chapter 7, the human resource function has been faulted for the existence of compensation systems that are not congruent with organizational strategies. Several aspects of compensation systems need to be evaluated in order to determine their value in strategy implementation. The *compensation mix* is a critical issue that needs monitoring. Unfortunately, in the United States the compensation mix does not promote work-force stability as it does in Japan. In the United States, most employees receive fixed levels of salaries or wages over time, regardless of the performance of their companies or the state of the economy. When demand for their company's product diminishes or performance factors cause profits to decline, employees are laid-off. When it is considered that during the prosperous years of 1983–1989, approximately 5 million workers having at least three years' tenure on their jobs were laid-off, the magnitude of the problem is evident. As discussed in Chapter 7, one means of providing more employment stability is to change the compensation mix by building in a larger proportion of variable compensation, such as profit sharing or bonuses, which is the approach used in Japan. When profitability and demand decline, compensation costs also decline, making it less necessary to lay off employees.[61]

Another critical issue in evaluating the effectiveness of compensation systems is their flexibility. Unfortunately, as indicated in Chapter 7, traditional compensation systems based on job evaluation and determination of internal equity among jobs tend to be inflexible. As noted, the process of job evaluation, commonly performed according to the point system, assigns different numbers of points for various levels of characteristics, such as "know-how," which refers to operational knowledge of different jobs. Unfortunately, for some nonmanagerial jobs, there are no know-how points in the evaluation system. Thus, the job evaluation system categorizes some employees as being in "nonthinking" positions. One consequence of placing employees in such pigeonholes is that some tend to stop thinking and maintain a level of ignorance in order to conform with the job requirements. Another consequence is that some employees dissatisfied with the nonthinking requirements proceed on their own to develop other knowledge. As a result of these employees' initiatives, managers attempt to have their positions upgraded, which introduces another source of distortion to the wage structure.[62]

In addition to these major issues, several other aspects of compensation should be evaluated for their contribution to the company's strategic goals. These may include subjective measures of the extent to which the compensation system provides for internal equity; conforms with legal requirements for race, gender, and age; and provides pay satisfaction. Objective measures of compensation system effectiveness may include overtime utilization, payroll complaints, and comparisons of the company's wages for various jobs with those in relevant labor markets.[63]

Labor and Employee Relations

It is important for unionized companies to evaluate the effectiveness of their labor relations functions and line managers' conduct of labor relations. For unionized companies, there are numerous indicators of labor relations effectiveness, such as the frequency or length of work stoppages, the restrictiveness of collective bargaining agreements, the degree of cooperation between the union and management, the managerial flexibility in work assignment, the ability to impose reasonable work rules, other management prerogatives, the discretion to promote or lay off on the basis of ability or merit, the ease of administering the labor agreement, and the company's grievance experience. In the case of grievances, caution must be used in drawing inferences of effectiveness, as there are a multitude of potential influences on the incidence of grievances. Such influences include managerial behavior, the technology of the workplace, the personality and motivation of union representatives, the company's relationship with the union, and individual employee characteristics.[64]

It is also important for nonunion companies to evaluate the effectiveness of their employee relations functions. For such companies, the prospects of unionization should not be discounted even though union membership has declined to approximately 16 percent of the employed labor force. (In 1991, union members accounted for 16.1 percent of the employed labor force.[65]) One reason is that job security has become a major concern for many U.S. workers. As noted in Chapter 1, in the past several industry leaders such as Hewlett-Packard, IBM, and Digital Equipment maintained no-layoff approaches or employment security policies.[66] Such approaches and policies were probably a major reason why these companies were able to remain nonunion. However, because of competitive pressures, many such companies have abandoned these policies.[67] In addition, the casual approach of many companies to downsizing and the emergence of unbundled or network organizations have probably reduced employee loyalty to the extent that more employees may be willing to unionize in order to gain job security. The question remains whether employees will see unionization as instrumental to their job security or as a futile effort.

In the past, unions were often able to confine layoffs to the most junior employees, as the vast number of layoffs were conducted according to inverse seniority.[68] They were successful to the extent that they could organize extensively in an industry and make all competitors pay the same wages and offer similar working conditions. Their strategy was to "take wages out of competition."[69] The cost of wage increases and favorable terms of employment were then largely passed on to consumers in the form of price increases. However, with today's international marketplace, the power of unions has declined. Unions cannot organize all international manufacturers in a given industry, as demonstrated by abortive attempts at multinational union cooperation.[70] As a result, there will be disemployment to the extent that employment security agreements put domestic manufacturers at a disadvantage to international competitors. Further, unions seem unable to prevent domestic manufacturing companies from shifting production facilities to other countries. It will be interesting to see whether unions will be able to devise strategies to help employees obtain greater job security.

Regardless of the eventual direction of unionization in the future, unionization is very much a reality in many industries. Nonunion companies should not become complacent to the prospects of unionization and should evaluate periodically their organizational climate and human resource policies in order to determine whether they may encourage unionization.

EVALUATING STRATEGIC CONTRIBUTIONS IN EMERGING AREAS

There are a number of challenges from emerging areas related to human resource management which have major consequences for most companies. Two of the most important of these are (1) equal employment opportunity and management of diversity, and (2) quality readiness. The following sections will cover these areas in some detail.

Equal Employment Opportunity and Management of Diversity

The relevance of the *management of diversity* to the topic of evaluating human resource effectiveness is that effective management in this area enables organizations to tap the potential of their work forces. Thus management of diversity can be related to the effectiveness with which companies avoid labor shortages. For example, black employees tend to have higher turnover.[71] By correcting those factors leading to the turnover of blacks, companies should be able to reduce their labor shortages. Evaluations of effectiveness in this area should measure turnover of minority and female employees.

Corning, Inc. provides an example of a company that has had considerable success in this area. It has made remarkable progress in increasing the number of black and female managers, both in total numbers and in their representation in executive positions. This accomplishment is all the more impressive when it is noted that the company is located in a small company town in upstate New York. One specific example of Corning's approach was to take a leadership position in making the local area more attractive to black managers and professionals. Attrition of blacks declined from 15.3 to 11.3 percent between 1987 and 1990. Additionally, over the same time period, the attrition of females declined from 16.2 to 7.6 percent.[72]

Some suggestions from the emerging literature appear to have value in enabling organizations to be more effective in the management of diversity. One suggestion deals with the advancement of minorities and females. Advancement to upper-level positions requires information that is obtained through informal networks from which minorities and females are often excluded. Because the pathway to promotion for companies' highest-level jobs becomes more subtle and ill-defined with moves up the organizational hierarchy, it is desirable for organizations to devote more attention to these subtleties. Being networked and acquiring upward pull from a mentor are critical before minorities and females can rise to the top.[73] Roosevelt Thomas has explained this process as follows:

> Another widespread assumption, probably absorbed from American culture in general, is that "cream will rise to the top." In most companies, what passes for cream rising to the top is actually cream being pulled or pushed to the top by an informal system of mentoring and sponsorship.[74]

Unfortunately, performance evaluation processes frequently do not provide managers with the feedback that they need to advance to the highest-level positions. This weakness of performance evaluation systems is often offset by informal feedback through personal mentoring or networks. When lack of access to networks deprives an individual of honest feedback, performance appraisal systems must be improved for increased effectiveness.[75]

A second suggestion for improved effectiveness is that, where the problems of minorities and females are unrelated to prejudice, remedial efforts should facilitate the advancement of all groups of people. In contrast, when remedial programs give special consideration only to particular groups, they become enormously time-consuming and are inconsistent with the spirit of diversity. A third suggestion is that, since the management of diversity is not an exact science, mistakes will be made and setbacks will occur. Accordingly, in the interests of fairness, managers should not be penalized for their efforts. A fourth suggestion is that the focus of the management of diversity should be a broad one, extending even to education, personality, background, and age. Such a broad orientation should facilitate the development of a heterogeneous culture instead of attempting to assimilate those who differ into the dominant culture of white males.[76] A fifth suggestion is to conduct training courses on diversity which may deal with communication style differences, increase self-awareness, and reduce biases through skill-building exercises. Leading companies in this type of training include Hewlett-Packard, McDonnell Douglas, and Ortho Pharmaceuticals. Such training can be evaluated with the approaches discussed earlier. A sixth suggestion is to incorporate management of diversity into the company's performance evaluation and reward system so that those managers doing a good job in this regard are rewarded. Companies providing leadership in this area include Baxter Health Care, Coca-Cola, and Exxon.[77]

Quality Readiness

Although *total quality management* (TQM) has received a great deal of attention, the importance of the role of human resource management is not well-known. Christopher Hart and Leonard Schlesinger have pointed out that TQM is relevant to the evaluation of human resources in at least three respects: (1) The quality that can be achieved by a company's work force is in part determined by its motivation and training; (2) the quality of the activities and services of the human resource function are evaluated in TQM approaches; and (3) the Malcom Baldrige National Quality Award framework provides a TQM guide for evaluation of human resources. Interestingly, human resource management and development make up one of the seven major components on which companies are evaluated for the Baldrige Award, comprising 150 of the total of 1,000 points. The importance of the Baldrige framework, however, is not attributable to its role in the granting of awards for quality. Instead, its importance lies with its usefulness in providing a guide to obtaining quality and its value in evaluation or assessment.[78]

Under TQM, the ultimate objective is to provide customer satisfaction. By satisfying customers, a company increases its market share and enhances the likelihood of increased profitability. The traditional objectives of the human resource function, which seek to improve performance, productivity, employee satisfaction, and motivation, are indirectly related to customer satisfaction. This is because employee retention and a well-trained work force are required for the production of quality goods and services. Since TQM emphasizes the importance of a systematic, comprehensive approach toward quality, the interrelated role of the human resource function and its indirect impact on the work force make it critical to this objective. One outcome of TQM is that a stronger case is made for the importance of funding training.[79]

As a model for evaluation, the Baldrige guidelines make several important points. Among those most relevant to human resource management are its emphasis on (1) the use of objective performance data and (2) benchmarking based on external comparisons or based on the company's own performance in earlier time periods. Hart and Schlesinger have noted that the guidelines also deal with the specifics of assessment, such as described in the following.[80]

> What Baldrige examiners look for, though, is objective evidence, like job definitions that include clearly delineated quality responsibilities. The criteria ask, among other things, for "indicators, benchmarks, or other bases for evaluating

and improving organizational structure" (1.2.b), and "key methods and key indicators the company uses to evaluate and improve awareness and integration of quality values at all levels of management and supervision" (1.2.d).[81]

By using the Baldrige framework as a questionnaire, a company can use the guidelines as the award examiners do to evaluate its strengths and weaknesses in quality. This assessment would be a first step toward adoption of TQM and improvement of quality. Following this evaluation or assessment, a triage process would be undertaken in which priorities would be established for actions to be taken. One practical suggestion is to fix first those problems that have easy solutions or pick the "low-hanging fruit" first. Another TQM-related suggestion is that the human resource function should adopt a perspective similar to that of an independent contractor providing services to a customer. When viewed from this perspective, those in the human resource function would begin to ask themselves whether the customer, the company, would renew their contract; thus, the importance of customer satisfaction is more evident.[82]

Finally, the use of the Baldrige framework as a guide for evaluation and its emphasis on objective data deserve comment. Many important organizational phenomena may not meet all parties' definitions of objective. Dysfunctional results occur when important phenomena are ignored because they cannot be expressed in an objective format.

MACRO-LEVEL EVALUATION OF HUMAN RESOURCE EFFECTIVENESS

Although the focus of this chapter has been to describe approaches, methods, and criteria of evaluation, two end results of macro-level human resource effectiveness evaluations deserve mention. The first concerns differences in effectiveness across industries. The Ulrich, Brockbank, and Yeung benchmarking study, discussed earlier, reached the following conclusions: One is that "HR professionals demonstrate higher competencies in service, aircraft, and electronics industries, and lower competencies in manufacturing, utilities, and petroleum industries."[83] One explanation for such results may be that human resource management plays a more strategic role in the service, aircraft, and electronics industries because competitive advantages in these industries are based more on human resources. Interestingly, their findings also suggest that top-level general managers perceive greater competencies in human resource professionals than do executives and managers in other functional areas.[84]

The second macro-level finding is from Anne Tsui's examination of human resource departmental effectiveness. Her investigation found greater satisfaction among line executives than among operating managers, probably because of the human resource department's "tendency to 'cater' to the needs of the more powerful constituencies."[85] One implication of this result is that human resource managers need to devote more attention to the remainder of the company's managers and employees, for example, they need to obtain these managers' and employees' input on the content of human resource programs.[86] This finding is somewhat ironic, given the history of human resource management. In the past human resource professionals decried their inability to gain the confidence of their top executives and to participate in the strategic management process. Human resource managers must not forget the importance of generating user satisfaction throughout the middle and lower levels of the organizational hierarchy as well.

SUMMARY

This chapter has reviewed concepts related to the evaluation of effectiveness from a strategic management perspective. As a part of this discussion, the Tsui and Gómez-Mejía framework was utilized to illustrate the interrelated nature of human resource management with other functional areas and the necessity of considering (1) the impact of line management on human resource measures and (2) the level of analysis at which evaluation is directed. Methodological aspects of evaluation were reviewed including audits, analytical approaches, quantitative and qualitative measures, outcome and process criteria, benchmarking, and industry influences. In spite of the logical appeal of evaluation, human resource evaluation was not a widespread practice in the past. Nonetheless, the cost and competitive pressures of today's global economy and the focus on quality will probably serve as a stimulus for more evaluation in the future.

Greater attention was devoted to the evaluation of strategic human resource management contributions in the traditional areas. Specific approaches were described for evaluating human resource planning, which is likely to take on greater importance with growing human resource strategic contributions. Measures for assessing the effectiveness of staffing were discussed, along with an example of utility analysis applied to staffing issues. Effectiveness measures and research designs were also presented for evaluating the effectiveness of training. Although training has not received the evaluation attention warranted, the financial resources that will be required for training in the future will also serve as a strong incentive for more evaluation. Evaluation needs and approaches for assessment of performance measurement systems and compensation systems were also discussed along with evaluation of labor and employee relations.

Beyond the traditional areas of human resource management, evaluation approaches in two newer areas of strategic importance were discussed. These were (1) equal employment and management of diversity and (2) quality readiness. Although the management of diversity literature is still evolving, some important insights have been developed for evaluating effectiveness in this area. Finally, the contributions of human resource management to quality were discussed along with approaches for evaluating such contributions.

REFERENCES

1. Tsui, Anne S., and Luis R. Gómez-Mejía, "Evaluating Human Resource Effectiveness," in *Human Resource Management: Evolving Roles and Responsibilities*, ed. Lee Dyer. Washington, D.C.: Bureau of National Affairs, 1988, 187–227; Ulrich, Dave, "Assessing Human Resource Effectiveness: Stakeholder, Utility, and Relationship Approaches," *Human Resource Planning*, 12, no. 4 (1989), 301–315; Gómez-Mejía, Luis R., "Dimensions and Correlates of the Personnel Audit as an Organizational Assessment Tool," *Personnel Psychology*, 38, no. 2 (1985), 293–308.
2. Ulrich, "Assessing Human Resource Effectiveness."
3. Steers, Richard M., "Problems in the Measurement of Organizational Effectiveness," *Administrative Science Quarterly*, 20, no. 4 (1975), 546–558; Mott, Paul E., *The Characteristics of Effective Organizations*. New York: Harper & Row, 1972; Hitt, Michael A., and R. Dennis Middlemist, "A Methodology to Develop the Criteria and Criteria Weightings for Assessing Subunit Effectiveness in Organizations," *Academy of Management Journal*, 22, no. 2 (1979), 356–374; Hitt, Michael A. R., Dennis Middlemist, and Charles R. Greer, "Sunset Legislation and the Measurement of Effectiveness," *Public Personnel Management*, 6, no. 3 (1977), 188–193.
4. Tsui and Gómez-Mejía, "Evaluating Human Resource Effectiveness"; Tsui, Anne S., "Personnel Department Effectiveness: A Tripartite Approach," *Industrial Relations*, 23, no. 2 (1984), 184–197.
5. Tsui and Gómez-Mejía, "Evaluating Human Resource Effectiveness"; Tsui, "Personnel Department Effectiveness."
6. Jarrell, Donald W., *Human Resource Planning: A Business Planning Approach*. Englewood Cliffs, N.J.: Prentice Hall, 1993; Peterson, Donald J., and Robert L. Malone, "The Personnel Effectiveness Grid (PEG): A New Tool for Estimating Personnel Department Effectiveness," *Human Resource Management*, 14, no. 4 (1975), 10–21.
7. Portwood, James D., "Process Management vs. Problem Solving: Choosing an Appropriate Perspective for Evaluating Human Resource Systems," in *Creating the Competitive Edge through Human Resource Allocations*, eds. Richard J. Niehaus and Karl F. Price. New York: Plenum Press, 1988, 181–191.
8. Tsui and Gómez-Mejía, "Evaluating Human Resource Effectiveness"; Tsui, "Personnel Department Effectiveness:"
9. Tsui, Anne S., "Defining the Activities and Effectiveness of the Human Resource Department: A Multiple Constituency Approach," *Human Resource Management*, 26, no. 1 (1987), 35–69.
10. Ibid.
11. Tsui and Gómez-Mejía, "Evaluating Human Resource Effectiveness"; Peterson and Malone, "The Personnel Effectiveness Grid (PEG)"; Phillips, Jack J., and Anson Seers, "Twelve Ways to Evaluate HR Management," *Personnel Administrator*, 34, no. 4 (April 1989), 54–58.
12. Ulrich, "Assessing Human Resource Effectiveness."
13. Tsui and Gómez-Mejía, "Evaluating Human Resource Effectiveness"; Phillips and Seers, "Twelve Ways to Evaluate HR Management"; Steffy, Brian D., and Steven D. Maurer, "Conceptualizing and Measuring the Economic Effectiveness of Human Resource Activities," *Academy of Management Review*, 13, no. 2 (1988), 271–286; Ulrich, "Assessing Human Resource Effectiveness."
14. Hitt and Middlemist, "A Methodology to Develop the Criteria and Criteria Weightings for Assessing Subunit Effectiveness in Organizations"; Phillips and Seers, "Twelve Ways to Evaluate HR Management."
15. Tsui and Gómez-Mejía, "Evaluating Human Resource Effectiveness"; Schmitt, Neal W., and Richard J. Klimoski, *Research Methods in Human Resources Management*. Cincinnati, Ohio: South-Western, 1991.
16. Ulrich, Dave, Wayne Brockbank, and Arthur Yeung, "Beyond Belief: A Benchmark for Human Resources," *Human Resources Management*, 28, no. 3 (1989), 311–335.
17. Jorgensen, Les, "How to Steal the Best Ideas Around," *Fortune*, October 19, 1992, 102–106.
18. Ulrich, Brockbank, and Yeung, "Beyond Belief."
19. Ibid.
20. Ibid., p. 312.
21. Bamberger, Peter, Samuel Bacharach, and Lee Dyer, "Human Resources Management and Organizational Effectiveness: High Technology Entrepreneurial Startup Firms in Israel," *Human Resource Management*, 28, no. 3 (1989), 349–366.
22. Bamberger, Bacharach, and Dyer, "Human Resources Management and Organizational Effectiveness."
23. Ibid.
24. Bamberger, Bacharach, and Dyer, "Human Resources Management and Organizational Effectiveness," pp. 362–363.

25. Tsui and Gómez-Mejía, "Evaluating Human Resource Effectiveness"; Phillips and Seers, "Twelve Ways to Evaluate HR Management"; Petersen and Malone, "The Personnel Effectiveness Grid (PEG)"; Cascio, Wayne F., "Responding to the Demand for Accountability: A Critical Analysis of Three Utility Models," *Organizational Behavior and Human Performance*, 25, no. 1 (1980), 32–45; Tannenbaum, Scott I., and Woods, Steven B., "Determining a Strategy for Evaluating Training: Operating Within Organizational Constraints," *Human Resource Planning*, 15, no. 2 (1992), 63–81.

26. Tsui and Gómez-Mejía, "Evaluating Human Resource Effectiveness," 200.

27. Tsui and Gómez-Mejía, "Evaluating Human Resource Effectiveness"; Peterson and Malone, "The Personnel Effectiveness Grid (PEG)."

28. Butler, John E., Gerald R. Ferris, and Nancy K. Napier, *Strategy and Human Resources Management*. Cincinnati, Ohio: South-Western, 1991.

29. Mills, D. Quinn, "Planning with People in Mind," *Harvard Business Review*, 63, no. 4 (1985), 97–105; Robbins, Stephen P., *Management*, 3rd ed. Englewood Cliffs, N.J.: Prentice Hall, 1991.

30. Walker, James W., *Human Resource Strategy*. New York: McGraw-Hill, 1992.

31. Levitan, Sar A., and Frank Gallo, "The Shortsighted Focus on Labor Shortages," *Challenge*, 32, no. 5 (1989), 28–32.

32. Mangum, Stephen L., "Impending Skill Shortages: Where Is the Crisis?" *Challenge*, 33, no. 5 (1990), 46–52.

33. Usdansky, Margaret L., "256,561,239 Live in the USA," *USA Today*, December 31, 1992, 1A.

34. Walker, *Human Resource Strategy*.

35. Bowen, David E., Gerald E. Ledford, Jr., and Barry R. Nathan, "Hiring for the Organization, Not the Job," *Academy of Management Executive*, 5, no. 4 (1991), 35–51.

36. Cascio, Wayne F., *Applied Psychology in Personnel Management*, 4th ed. Englewood Cliffs, N.J.: Prentice Hall, 1991.

37. Ibid.; Cronshaw, Steven F., and Ralph A. Alexander, "One Answer to the Demand for Accountability: Selection Utility as an Investment Decision," *Organizational Behavior and Human Decision Processes*, 35, no. 1 (1985), 102–118; Schmitt and Klimoski, *Research Methods in Human Resources Management*; Boudreau, John W., "Economic Considerations in Estimating the Utility of Human Resource Productivity Improvement Programs," *Personnel Psychology*, 36, no. 3 (1983), 551–576.

38. Schmitt and Klimoski, *Research Methods in Human Resources Management*; Schmitt, Frank L., Murray J. Mack, and John E. Hunter, "Selection Utility in the Occupation of U.S. Park Ranger for Three Modes of Test Use," *Journal of Applied Psychology*, 69, no. 3 (1984), 490–497.

39. Schmitt and Klimoski, *Research Methods in Human Resources Management*; Schmitt, Mack, and Hunter, "Selection Utility in the Occupation of U.S. Park Ranger for Three Modes of Test Use"; Cascio, Wayne F., *Costing Human Resources: The Financial Impact of Behavior in Organizations*, 3rd ed. Boston: PWS-Kent, 1991.

40. Kerr, Steven, "On the Folly of Rewarding A While Hoping for B," *Academy of Management Journal*, 18, no. 4 (1975), 769–783.

41. Kerr, "On the Folly of Rewarding A While Hoping for B," 774.

42. Tannenbaum and Woods, "Determining a Strategy for Evaluating Training."

43. Ibid.

44. Boettger, Richard D., and Charles R. Greer, "The Wisdom of Rewarding A While Hoping for B," *Organization Science*, 5, no. 4, (1994), in press.

45. Tannenbaum and Woods, "Determining a Strategy for Evaluating Training."

46. Cascio, *Applied Psychology in Personnel Management*; Goldstein, Irwin L., *Training in Organizations: Needs Assessment, Development, and Evaluation*, 2nd ed. Monterey, Calif.: Brooks/Cole, 1986; Tannenbaum and Woods, "Determining a Strategy for Evaluating Training."

47. Cascio, *Applied Psychology in Personnel Management*, Goldstein, *Training in Organizations*.

48. Mathieu, John E., Scott I. Tannenbaum, and Eduardo Salas, "Influences of Individual and Situational Characteristics on Measures of Training Effectiveness," *Academy of Management Journal*, 35, no. 4 (1992), 828–847.

49. Cascio, *Applied Psychology in Personnel Management*; Goldstein, *Training in Organizations*; Tannenbaum and Woods, "Determining a Strategy for Evaluating Training."

50. Cascio, *Applied Psychology in Personnel Management*; Goldstein, *Training in Organizations*.

51. Ibid.

52. Cascio, *Applied Psychology in Personnel Management*.

53. Burke, Michael J., and Russell R. Day, "A Cumulative Study of the Effectiveness of Managerial Training," *Journal of Applied Psychology*, 71, no. 2 (1986), 232–245.

54. Campbell, Donald R., and Julian C. Stanley, *Experimental and Quasi-Experimental Designs for Research.* Boston: Houghton Mifflin, 1966; Tannenbaum and Woods, "Determining a Strategy for Evaluating Training."

55. Campbell and Stanley, *Experimental and Quasi-Experimental Designs for Research;* Cascio, *Applied Psychology in Personnel Management.*

56. Schmitt and Klimoski, *Research Methods in Human Resources Management.* 385.

57. Campbell and Stanley, *Experimental and Quasi-Experimental Designs for Research;* Cascio, *Applied Psychology in Personnel Management.*

58. Campbell and Stanley, *Experimental and Quasi-Experimental Designs for Research;* Cascio, *Applied Psychology in Personnel Management;* Goldstein, *Training in Organizations.*

59. Campbell and Stanley, *Experimental and Quasi-Experimental Designs for Research.*

60. Paquet, Basil, Elizabeth Kasi, Laurence Weinstein, and William Waite, "The Bottom Line," *Training and Development Journal,* 41, no. 5 (1987), 27–33.

61. Gómez-Mejía, Luis R., and David B. Balkin, *Compensation, Organizational Strategy, and Firm Performance.* Cincinnati, Ohio: South-Western, 1992; Henn, William R., "What the Strategist Asks from Human Resources," *Human Resource Planning,* 8, no. 4 (1985), 193–200.

62. Emerson, Sandra M., "Job Evaluation: A Barrier to Excellence?" *Compensation and Benefits Review,* 23, no. 1 (1991), 39–51.

63. Gómez-Mejía, "Dimensions and Correlates of the Personnel Audit as an Organizational Assessment Tool."

64. Labig, Chalmer E., and Charles R. Greer, "Grievance Initiation: A Literature Survey and Suggestions for Future Research," *Journal of Labor Research,* 9, no. 1 (1988), 1–27; Allen, Robert E., and Timothy J. Keaveny, "Factors Differentiating Grievants and Nongrievants," *Human Relations,* 38, no. 6 (1985), 519–534.

65. U.S. Department of Commerce, *Statistical Abstract of the United States, 1992,* 112th ed. Washington D.C.: U.S. Government Printing Office, 1992.

66. Hewlett-Packard Corporation, *Hewlett-Packard Annual Report,* 1985; Peters, Tom, *Thriving on Chaos: Handbook for a Management Revolution.* New York: Harper & Row, 1987; Hoerr, John, and Wendy Zellner, "A Japanese Import That's Not Selling," *Business Week,* February 26, 1990, 86; Burke, Steven, "PC Operations Spared the Worst of IBM's Cost-Cutting Programs," *PC Week,* December 11, 1989, 1, 6.

67. Hoerr and Zellner, "A Japanese Import That's Not Selling"; Wilke, John R., "Digital Equipment, in Its First Layoffs, to Dismiss About 3,500 Workers by July," *The Wall Street Journal,* January 10, 1991, A3; Burke, "PC Operations Spared the Worst of IBM's Cost-Cutting Programs."

68. Freeman, Richard B., and James L. Medoff, *What Do Unions Do?* New York: Basic Books, 1984.

69. Mitchell, Daniel J. B., *Human Resource Management: An Economic Approach.* Boston: PWS-Kent, 1989.

70. Northrup, Herbert R., and Richard L. Rowan, "Multinational Union Activity in the 1976 U.S. Rubber Tire Strike," *Sloan Management Review,* 18, no. 3 (1977), 17–28.

71. Cox, Taylor H., and Stacy Blake, "Managing Cultural Diversity: Implications for Organizational Competitiveness," *Academy of Management Executive,* 5, no. 3 (1991), 45–56.

72. Hammonds, Keith H., "Corning's Class Act," *Business Week,* May 13, 1991, 68–76.

73. Thomas, R. Roosevelt, "From Affirmative Action to Affirming Diversity," *Harvard Business Review,* 68, no. 2 (1990), 107–117.

74. Thomas, "From Affirmative Action to Affirming Diversity," 114.

75. Thomas, "From Affirmative Action to Affirming Diversity."

76. Ibid.

77. Cox, Taylor, Jr., "The Multicultural Organization," *Academy of Management Executive,* 5, no. 2 (1991), 34–47.

78. Hart, Christopher, and Leonard Schlesinger, "Total Quality Management and the Human Resource Professional: Applying the Baldrige Framework to Human Resources," *Human Resource Management,* 30, no. 4 (1991), 433–454.

79. Ibid.

80. Ibid.

81. Hart and Schlesinger, "Total Quality Management and the Human Resource Professional," 442–443.

82. Hart and Schlesinger, "Total Quality Management and the Human Resource Professional."

83. Ulrich, Brockbank, and Yeung, "Beyond Belief: A Benchmark for Human Resources," 329.

84. Ulrich, Brockbank, and Yeung, "Beyond Belief: A Benchmark for Human Resources."

85. Tsui, "Defining the Activities and Effectiveness of the Human Resource Department: A Multiple Constituency Approach," 65.

86. Ulrich, Brockbank, and Yeung, "Beyond Belief: A Benchmark for Human Resources."

Case 8

ASSESSMENT OF HUMAN RESOURCE UTILIZATION

A bank has foreclosed on Core-Line Software, a software development company. Although Core-Line has a strong level of sales, its costs are far too high and it cannot repay its loans. The bank had hoped to line up a buyer before foreclosing; however, none was willing to pay the bank's price. As a result, the bank was forced to foreclose and operate the company until a buyer could be found. In order to recoup as much as possible of the value of its loans, the bank has decided to seek advice on how to improve the company's operating efficiency. With increased efficiency, the bank hopes to obtain a higher price. Because the bank's staff has no experience in the software business, it has retained a consulting firm to advise it on how to increase the efficiency of the company's operations. Since labor costs constitute the bulk of software firms' expenses, Core-Line's utilization of human resources is an obvious area in which to look for potential improvement. Like most software companies, Core-Line has a full array of specialists, including programmers, graphic artists, systems analysts, project managers, and systems architects. The consulting firm has decided to begin by assessing Core-Line's efficiency in the utilization of programmers by comparing its utilization level with that of other software developers.

In order to obtain data for its recommendations to the bank, the consulting company has conducted a survey of other software developers. The survey was designed to obtain information on several business practices including questions about staffing levels and human resource utilization. (The consulting firm has already determined that Core-Line's salaries are average for the industry.) Unfortunately, although the consulting firm has done some work with software developers and has a good reputation, many firms refused to supply data. Consequently, only 40 percent of the questionnaires were returned for a total of sixty-five responses. Nonetheless, the consulting firm has decided to proceed with the data that it has.

The analysis of the data will employ a comparative approach in which each responding company's staffing level of programmers (dependent variable) will be compared with potential explanatory variables (independent variables). In order to control the influence of each independent variable, the consulting firm has decided to use the statistical technique of multiple regression analysis. Each of the sixty-five responses will constitute a separate observation in the analysis. Thus, in the regression analysis the dependent variable (Y) is the number of programmers. The independent variables are the dollar volume of annual software sales (X_1), average number of hours worked each year by programmers including overtime (X_2), average years of experience of programmers (X_3), a rating of the quality of programming supervision (X_4), and a rating of the complexity of the software produced by each company (X_5). The rating of the quality of supervision is a five-interval scale ranging from 1 = poor ... 5 = good. Similarly, the software complexity rating scheme is a five-interval scale ranging from 1 = simple ... 5 = complex. The regression model is $Y = \alpha + \beta_1 X_1 + \beta_2 X_2 + \beta_3 X_3 + \beta_4 X_4 + \beta_5 X_5 + \varepsilon$ where α = the intercept or constant; β_1, β_2, β_3, β_4, and β_5 are the respective regression coefficients derived in the model; and ε = the error term.

In order to derive the values for α, β_1, β_2, β_3, β_4, and β_5, the consulting firm will run the regression analysis, with each observation being comprised of matched data from one of the sixty-five different software companies. (Under most conditions, the value for ε is assumed to be 0.) If the model is adequately specified, statistically significant, and a substantial amount of variance in the dependent variable is accounted for, the consulting firm will have confidence in the statistical justification for using its parameters. The adequacy of explanatory power is indicated by the R^2 and overall model's F values. (For the purposes of this case, assume that the model is statistically adequate on all of these indicators.)

To predict the number of programmers that Core-Line should be using, which is the value for $\hat{Y}$, the consulting firm will plug into the regression model Core-Line's X values for annual sales, average annual hours worked by programmers, average experience of programmers, rating of the quality of programmer supervision, and rating of software complexity. Using this model or equation, the consulting firm will then compute the predicted number of programmers ($\hat{Y}$ value). This predicted value or industry standard will then be compared with Core-Line's actual utilization of programmers in order to determine if it is overstaffed. Further, for each independent variable having a statistically significant relationship with the dependent variable, the positive or negative sign of the regression coefficient will provide direction for potential solutions to utilization problems.

Questions

1. What are the implications of using data from a survey of other companies in which only 40 percent responded? How could one determine whether there is any potential bias in the returned questionnaires?

2. What potential variables has the consulting firm left out of its model? How would any omitted variables affect the results?

3. The consulting firm has employed a cross-sectional approach, for its analysis. How might this be a problem?

4. What other methods should be used to determine whether Core-Line is efficiently utilizing its programmers?

5. How is the process of benchmarking similar to the process employed by the consulting firm?

AUTHOR INDEX

Aburdene, Patricia, 53, 63n, 193n, 209, 210, 221n
Adler, Nancy, 115, 133n
Agee, Bill, 212
Alexander, Ralph A., 251n
Alexander, Suzanne, 193n
Allen, Billie Morgan, 97n, 99n
Allen, Deborah, 63n, 67n
Allen, Robert E., 252n
Alpander, Guvenc, 145, 165n
Alvarez, Eden B., 62n
Annoni, Anthony J., 167n
Applegate, Lynda M., 27n, 61n
Armstrong, Daniel, 165n, 167n
Arvey, Richard, 11, 28n, 71, 97n
Atwater, D. M., 137n

Bacharach, Samuel, 250n
Bacher, Jeffery P., 221n
Baird, Lloyd, 135n
Baker, Douglas D., 98n
Baker, Stephen, 134n
Balkin, David B., 208, 220n, 221n, 252n
Ballard, Karen A., 65n
Bamberger, Peter, 250n
Barkman, Arnold L., 63n
Barnet, Tim, 99n, 100n
Barrier, Michael, 62n, 64n
Barsky, Neil, 64n
Bartholomew, Susan, 115, 133n
Basheer, Ahmed, 164n
Bass, Stuart L., 98n
Bassett, Joan, 191n
Bassman, Emily, 192n
Batt, Rosemary, 132n
Baytos, Lawrence M., 165n
Beatty, Richard W., 28n, 29n, 31n, 134n
Bechet, Thomas P., 165n, 166n
Beck, Istvan M., 61n

Becker, Brian, 5, 27n
Becker, Charles E., 90, 100n, 101n
Becker, Gary, 4, 9
Bedeian, Arthur G., 135n
Beechler, Schon, 132n
Beer, Michael, 26n, 28n, 132n, 133n
Belous, Richard S., 61n, 64n
Benton, Debra, 98n
Beoch, Dennis, 191n
Bergstrom, Robin P., 62n
Bhatt, Bhal, 132n
Bierman, Leonard, 100n
Blackburn, Richard, 62n, 63n
Blake, Stacy, 62n, 191n, 192n, 252n
Block, Richard N., 100n
Boettger, Richard D., 251
Bolt, James F., 26n, 28n, 29n, 222n
Booker, Ellis, 222n
Borg, Ingwer, 61n
Bortz, Jenny, 193n
Boss, R. Wayne, 30n
Boudreau, John W., 27n, 251n
Bowditch, James L., 31n
Bowe, Frank, 29n
Bowen, David E., 43, 62n, 237, 251n
Bowen, Donald D., 62n
Bowie-McCoy, Susan W., 221n
Bowles, Valerie B., 28n, 63n
Brady, Teresa, 82, 99n
Braham, James, 61n
Brandt, Richard, 222n
Breaugh, James, 191n
Brees, E. S. III, 137n
Bretz, Robert D. Jr., 62n
Bright, William E., 29n
Brimelow, Peter, 96, 101n
Brockbank, Wayne, 44, 62n, 232, 248, 250n, 252n
Brocker, Audrey, 193n

Brockner, Joel, 29n, 193n
Brown, Darrel R., 100n, 101n
Brown, William C., 221n
Bruckman, John C., 48, 63n
Bryant, Don R., 166n
Buller, Paul, 166n
Burack, Elmer H., 135n, 165n, 166n
Burjem, Steven, 192n
Burke, Michael J., 240, 251n
Burke, Steven, 252n
Butler, John E., 251n
Byrn, Judson, 167n

Caimes, Jackie, 65n
Campbell, Donald T., 241, 252n
Canner, Sharon, 63n
Cardy, Robert L., 220n
Carter, Carolyn, 193n
Carter, Norman, 165n
Cascio, Wayne F., 27n, 29n, 193n, 222n, 226, 238, 251n, 252n
Cash, James I., 27n, 61n
Castagnera, James O., 97n, 98n, 101n
Cavanagh, Gerald F., 222n
Cerruti, James L., 65n, 133n
Chang, Lei, 220n, 221
Cheng, Alex F., 221n
Cherrington, David, J., 221n
Chiang, Shih-Chen, 27n
Chiang, Shin-Hwan, 27n
Choa, Georgia T., 28n
Chope, Roger, 221n
Cibon, Patrick J., 97n, 98n, 101n
Clausing, Jeri, 100n
Coleman, Henry, 35, 61n, 123, 134n
Coleman, Sharon M., 137n
Collie, H. Cris, 193n
Collins, Eliza G. C., 98n
Colosi, Marco L., 61n
Conlin, Jessie, 65n
Conte, Christopher, 193n
Conway, Lynette R., 100n
Cook, Alice H., 99n
Cook, Deborah S., 132n, 180, 191n, 192, 222n
Coulson, Robert, 193n
Cox, Taylor H., 62n, 191n, 192n, 252n
Craft, James, 108, 133n, 135n
Crichton, Michael, 74, 98n
Cronshaw, Steven, 251n
Crown, Deborah F., 30n
Crystal, Graef, 223, 224n, 225n
Cunningham, Mary, 212

Darrow, Terri L., 64n
Davidson, Margaret, 29n, 64n
Davis, Bob, 65n
Davy, Jeanette, 193n
Day, Russell R., 239, 251n
Dean, James W. Jr., 46, 62n, 63n
de Bono, Edward, 209

De Meuse, Kenneth P., 42, 62n
Deming, W. Edwards, 43
Derr, C. Brooklyn, 27n, 28n
De Sousa, Bernardo, 45
Dessler, Gary, 193n, 221n
Devanna, Mary Anne, 132n
Devinney, Timothy M., 65n
Dewitt, Rocki Lee, 29n
Dobbins, Gregory H., 220n
Doeringer, Peter B., 27n
Doorley, Thomas L., 1, 26n, 27n, 132n
Driscoll, Lisa, 222n
Drucker, Peter F., 27n, 60n, 61n
Dube, Lawrence E. 98n
Dunbar, Edward, 222n
Dyer, Lee, 1, 26n, 27n, 28n, 64n, 132n, 133n, 166n, 250

Eichinger, Robert W., 164n
Elias, Jan, 192n
Elizur, Dov, 61n
Elsass, Priscilla M., 28n
Emerson, Sandra M., 220n, 252n
Epstein, Richard, 95, 101n
Evans, Paul A. L., 222n

Faley, Robert H., 71, 97n
Falkenberg, Loren E., 30n
Farrell, Christopher, 30n
Fay, Jon A., 29n
Feild, Hubert, 72, 97n
Feldman, Daniel D., 177, 192n, 193n
Fenton, James W., Jr., 100n
Ference, Thomas P., 28n
Fernandez, John P., 192n
Ferris, Gerald R., 132n, 180, 191n, 192n, 222n, 251
Ferry, Richard M., 222n
Fielding, Jane, 65n
Files, Jennifer, 99n
Fiorito, Jack, 62n, 147, 164n, 165n, 166n, 167n, 191n
Fisher, Cynthia D., 132n
Flamholtz, Eric G., 166n
Flint, Jerry, 65n, 67n, 135n
Flynn, Walter, 98n
Fombrun, Charles, 132n
Forest, Stephanie A., 60n
Forman, Craig, 63n
Forward, Gordan E., 61n, 172, 191n
Fossum, John A., 11, 28n
Frantzreb, Richard R., 166n
Fredrickson, James W., 222n
Freeman, Elizabeth B., 164n
Freeman, Richard B., 252n
Friedman, Sheldon, 65n
Frierson, James G., 99n
Fullerton, Howard, 63n, 192n
Fuquay, Jim, 195n
Futrell, David, 42, 62n

SUBJECT INDEX